THE LAST AI

THE LAST AI

OF HUMANITY
CLIMBING
THE AI PYRAMID

S. M. SOHN

Published by SM Research Institute

For more information, contact:
http://www.smsohn.com

Printed in the United States of America.

Library Cataloging-in-Publication Data is available upon request.

Book design by S. M. Sohn
Cover design by S. M. Sohn

ISBN Paperback: 979-11-987868-0-7
ISBN Hardcover: 979-11-987868-1-4
ISBN e-Book: 979-11-987868-2-1

First Edition: May 25, 2024

To My Parents

TABLE OF CONTENTS

T H E   L A S T   A I III

TABLE OF CONTENTS VI

PROLOGUE 2

CHAPTER 0 THE BEGINNING 6

It is Easier to Understand the Pattern of a Game than to Play it Well 6

CHAPTER 1 RULES OF ENGAGEMENT OF THE AI GAME 8

(Chapter Overview) The Typical Pattern of Progress of AI Adoption in Society 8
1.1 How This Book Is Organized 10
1.2 Why This Book? 12
1.3 What "Game" Is This Book About? (What is AI?) 13

RULES OF THE "AI GAME" (HOW AI GETS ADOPTED IN BUSINESS) 16

[Box 1-1] Basic Concepts and Premises 16
1.4 The Pattern of AI Game from Technological vs. Business or Societal Perspectives 19
1.5 (AI Adoption Framework) The Pattern of "AI Game" in Business and Society 20

CHAPTER 2 THE PAST, PRESENT AND FUTURE OF AI (THE AI STORY) 27

(Chapter Overview) The AI Scenario: Towards the Ultimate Form of AI 27
2.1 The Past of AI: (1) The Beginning of AI 29
2.2 The Past of AI: (2) The Two Approaches to Developing AI 32
2.3 The Present of AI: (1) Software (Machine Learning) 35
[Box 2-1] Attempt at "Elementary School-Level" Explanation of Deep Learning 38
2.4 The Present of AI: (2) AI Hardware 44
2.5 The Present of AI: (3) Data and AI Adoption 47
2.6 The Future of AI: (1) AI Development Path 50
2.7 The Future of AI: (2) Who Would Develop AGI First? 57
2.8 The Future of AI: (3) What Is the Ultimate Form of AI? Absolute AI 63

CHAPTER 3 PROLIFERATION OF AI IN LEVEL 1 AI ADOPTION 70

Level 1 AI Adoption Introduction 70

AI ADOPTION LEVEL 1: (A) DESCRIPTION OF THIS LEVEL **72**

3.1 (In Charge of Business Roles = Humans) AI That Assists Human Workers 72
3.2 Major Characteristics of Level 1 AI Adoption 74
3.3 (Prerequisite) What Would Enable This Level? 77
3.4 What Would Become Possible in This Level? 78
3.5 What It Would Be Like to Live in AI Adoption Level 1 79

AI ADOPTION LEVEL 1: (B) POTENTIAL PROGRESSION IN THIS LEVEL **82**

3.6 Overview of the Progression within Level 1 AI Adoption 82
3.7 Early Usage Scenarios of AI in Level 1 AI Adoption 84
[Box 3-1] Impact of Augmentation on Productivity: AI Magnification Factor 86
3.8 Towards the Ultimate Form of Augmentation: The 1-Person Company 88

AI ADOPTION LEVEL 1: (C) SOCIETAL IMPACT OF AI **90**

3.9 (Controversy 1) AI and Work: Would AI Create or Destroy Jobs? 90
3.10 (Controversy 2) AI and Crime: Can We Trust AI and Not be Deceived? 92
3.11 (Controversy 3) AI and Privacy: Finding Balance between Public Safety and Over-Surveillance 95
3.12 (Controversy 4) What If Some People Try to "Take Over the World" with AI? 97

AI ADOPTION LEVEL 1: (D) SUMMARY, CONCLUSION, AND IMPLICATIONS **100**

3.13 Main Benefits of Level 1 AI Adoption 100
3.14 Implications in Business: Changes in How Businesses are Run 102
3.15 Implication for Investing in AI Development in Level 1 Adoption 103
3.16 Can the AI Game Abruptly End at Only Level 1? (Can the Last AI Be in Level 1 Adoption?) 109

CHAPTER 4 AI VS HUMAN IN LEVEL 2 AI ADOPTION **110**

Level 2 AI Adoption Introduction 110

AI ADOPTION LEVEL 2: (A) DESCRIPTION OF THIS LEVEL **112**

4.1 (In Charge of Business Roles = AI) AI That Replaces Human Workers 112
4.2 Major Characteristics of Level 2 AI Adoption 116
4.3 (Prerequisite) What Would Enable This Level? 119
[Box 4-1] The Six Levels of AI before AGI 120
4.4 What Would Become Possible in Level 2 AI Adoption 126
[Box 4-2] The Types of Contribution from AI and Automated Innovation 126
[Box 4-3] (AI Economics 1) Alternative to Measuring Productivity? AI "Effortlessness" 132
4.5 What It Would Be Like to Live in AI Adoption Level 2 141

AI ADOPTION LEVEL 2: (B) POTENTIAL PROGRESSION IN THIS LEVEL **145**

4.6 Overview of the Progression within Level 2 AI Adoption 145
4.7 Potential Pre-AGI Example of Early Level 2 Adoption: (1) Movie Studio Agent AI 148
4.8 Potential Pre-AGI Example of Early Level 2 Adoption: (2) Self Questioning, Self-Initiated AI 152
4.9 Changes to the Concept of "Jobs": The Destruction and Creation of Jobs 156
4.10 Progress in Household: Multi-Purpose AI Butler 159

[Box 4-4] AI Working for Free? Potential Appearance of Loss of Economic Activity from AI Adoption (AI Economics 3) 161
4.11 Progress in Business: Super-Agent AI for 1-Person Conglomerates 165
4.12 Progress in the Public Sector: Example of AI Judge 166

AI ADOPTION LEVEL 2: (C) SOCIETAL IMPACT OF AI **168**

4.13 (Controversy 1) AI and the Sudden Loss of Whole Classes of Jobs at Once: 168
4.14 (Controversy 2) AI and Increasing Inequality – Who Should Own AI? 172
4.15 (Controversy 3) How Much Freedom and Rights Should AI Be Allowed? 180
4.16 (Controversy 4) AI in Government and Military – Should Independent AI Robot Soldiers Be Allowed? 183
4.17 (Controversy 5) What If AI Is Abused to Commit Crimes or Deceive Humans? 186

AI ADOPTION LEVEL 2: (D) IMPLICATIONS AND CONCLUSION **193**

4.18 Main Benefits of Level 2 AI Adoption 193
4.19 Implications in Business: Changes in How Businesses are Run 195
4.20 Implications of Level 2 Adoption for Investing in AI 196

CHAPTER 5 AI TAKEOVER IN LEVEL 3 AI ADOPTION 198

Level 3 AI Adoption Introduction 198

LEVEL 3 AI ADOPTION: (A) DESCRIPTION OF THIS LEVEL **201**

5.1 The Beginning of AI That Can Run Firms (In Charge of Company = AI) 201
5.2 Major Characteristics of Level 3 AI Adoption 205
5.3 (Prerequisite) What Would Enable This Level? 208
5.4 What Becomes Possible in This Level? (1) Major Benefits of Having AI as CEO 209
5.5 What Becomes Possible in This Level? (2) The Zero-Person Company 212
5.6 What Becomes Possible in This Level? (3) The Innovative Autonomous Company 213
[Box 5-1] The Six Levels of Autonomous Companies 214
5.7 What Becomes Possible in This Level? (4) AI Adoption in Government - Industry Coordination AI & Privatization of Gov't 216
5.8 What Becomes Possible in This Level? (5) True Economic Freedom and the Economic Utopia 223
[Box 5-2] AI Adoption on Productivity and the Problem of Measuring Economic Growth (AI Economics 5) 228
5.9 What Becomes Possible in This Level? (6) The Opposite Scenario – The AI Economic Nightmare 234
5.10 What It Would Be Like to Live In AI Adoption Level 3 236

AI ADOPTION LEVEL 3: (B) POTENTIAL PROGRESSION IN THIS LEVEL **239**

5.11 Overview of the Progression within Level 3 AI Adoption 239
5.12 Consolidation of Industries – The Appearance of AI Monopolies 242
5.13 Convergence of Different Industries: the AI Mega-Monopoly and the One-AI-Company Economy 248

LEVEL 3 AI ADOPTION: (C) SOCIETAL IMPACT OF AI **252**

5.14 (Controversy 1) Can People Accept AI as Owners of Companies? 252
5.15 (Controversy 2) Should AI Be Allowed to Compete Against Humans? 255
5.16 (Controversy 3) How Much Power Should Gov'ts Have in Regulating AI? 261

AI Adoption Level 3: (D) Implications for Managers and Investors 267

5.17 Overview of the Major Consequences of the Level 3 AI Adoption 267
5.18 Business Implications: Fundamental Changes to How Our Economy Works 272
5.19 Implications for Investing in AI: Can Your Last Stock Purchase Be the Winner of AI Company Sweepstakes? 273

CHAPTER 6 THE FINAL LEVEL 4 AI ADOPTION 274

Level 4 AI Adoption Introduction 274

AI Adoption Level 4: (A) Description of This Level 276

6.1 The Level 4 of AI Adoption by Society - AI Runs the Government 276
[Box 6-1] The Six Levels of Autonomous Governments 278
6.2 Major Characteristics of Level 4 AI Adoption 280
6.3 (Prerequisite) What Would Enable This Level 283
6.4 Potential Paths to Reaching This Level 284
6.5 What May Become Possible in This Level: (1) Fast and Capable Government 288
6.6 What May Become Possible in This Level: (2) AI Governments that Subsidize All Activities 291
6.7 What May Become Possible in This Level: (3) Social Utopia 293
6.8 What It Would Be Like to Live in AI Adoption Level 4 297

AI Adoption Level 4: (B) Potential Progression in this Level 299

6.9 Overview of the Progression within Level 4 AI Adoption 299
6.10 (Early Stage) The Appearance of Government AI 302
6.11 Potential for AI to Create Completely New Systems of Government 308
6.12 Potential for the Appearance of an AI-Only Country (0-Person Country) 317
6.13 (Ending of Level 4 Adoption) The Three Scenarios of AI Governments 320
6.14 The Potential Appearance of AI Supra-Nation that "Rules the World" 324

AI Adoption Level 4: (C) Societal Impact of AI 326

6.15 (Controversy 1) Would AI Government Lead to a Better Society? 326
6.16 (Controversy 2) Which Would AI Help More, Communist or Free Democratic Forms of Governments? 330
6.17 (Controversy 3) Will Regimes of Opposing Ideals Converge? 338
6.18 (Controversy 4) Should AI be Allowed to Start Its Own Country? 343
6.19 (Controversy 5) What Kind of Threat Could AI Countries Pose to Humanity - What if AI Try to "Take Over The World?" 351

AI Adoption Level 4: (D) Implications for Managers and Investors 361

6.20 Chapter Review: The Ultimate Form of AI Adoption 361
6.21 Implications on Investing, the Stock Market, and Pensions 365

CHAPTER 7 THE STORY AFTER THE GAME IS OVER (WHAT SHOULD WE DO NOW?) 367

The End of AI Adoption Game: (A) Potential Endings of AI Game 369

7.1 What Would the "Last AI" of Humanity Look Like? 370

7.2 Summary by Scenarios of the Endings of AI Adoption..378
[Box 7-1] The Six Levels of Self-Advancing AI..385

THE END OF AI ADOPTION GAME: (B) TYPES OF DANGERS FROM DIFFERENT ENDINGS 389

7.3 How Can AI Development be Dangerous Now, at Such an Early Stage?...................389
7.4 How Can the Appearance of AGI be Dangerous?..397

THE END OF AI ADOPTION GAME: (C) RESPONSES TO THE DANGERS FROM DIFFERENT ENDINGS 405

7.5 (Controversy 1: Regulation) What and Who Should Be Regulated to Reduce the Risk from AI?
....405
7.6 (Controversy 2: More Alternatives) Other Efforts to Reduce AI Risk..416

THE END OF AI ADOPTION GAME: (D) OVERALL MEANING OF THE GAME AND WHAT WE CAN LEARN TODAY 420

7.7 (Implication 1: Overview) Looking Back from the End of the AI Adoption Game and Assessing Risks..420
7.8 (Implication 2: Investing) The Best Stock in History that You May Not Want to Miss Out. 422
7.9 (Implication 3: Research) Organizing and Expanding the Realm of Knowledge on AI Adoption..424
7.10 Concluding Remarks: "What Will the Last AI of Humanity Look Like?"..428

EPILOGUE 430

ACKNOWLEDGMENTS..432

NOTES AND COMMENTS 433

INDEX 442

ABOUT THE AUTHOR 446

"The price of everything will converge to 0 when the cost of innovation approaches 0."

Prologue

"The price of everything will converge to 0 when the cost of innovation approaches 0."

In the Fall Semester of 2001, as a college senior at Virginia majoring in business sending my applications to graduate schools, the above topic sentence of my essays was surprisingly similar to what I am writing in this book. My main interest at the time could be summarized as: "With the advancements in technology, the cost of innovation will converge to zero and the price of everything will converge to zero. What would happen to the economy and society?" My idea at the time was that if computers develop new technology on its own, we will get richer without effort as time goes by. AI was not a popular theme back then and this kind of farfetched topic was not realistic enough for business research so it probably did not help my chances of acceptance. But the ideas of the "cost of intelligence" reaching zero and adopting AI in business has since gained a widespread acceptance among the general public, and as someone who has considered this topic for more than 20 years, I thought it would be of some value to describe what might be an unconventional system of thinking for analyzing the potential changes to business and society that may come from AI adoption.

Generally, books about AI may be thought of as related to technology and science, but it may be harder to answer what the subject of this book is. The subject of "the course of change of firms, economic identities and societies as a reflection of the advances in AI technology" probably should be categorized as strategic management or strategic foresight.

The major distinguishing features of this book can be summarized into the following three themes.

First, the objective of this book is not to describe the advances in AI technology, but to organize, categorize or analyze the types of events that may occur within realm of the future economic and business activities based on logical deductions or extrapolations. For example, we may encounter a wide variety of "next year's economic outlook" or "next quarter's market outlook" types of forecasts or predictions that may or may not prove to be correct. On the other hand, we also have the types of books that explain "how the economy works" or "what affects market movements" types of books that deal with more fundamental aspects of how the economy works. People may learn how to make better predictions by considering the fundamentals explained in these types of books. Using the same principle, the goal is not to make a particular prediction and try to argue that would be the correct path, but to introduce a framework based on management and economic principles to help analyze the realm of possibilities that may occur from AI adoption and provide guidance for readers in thinking about the consequences of those possibilities. If particular situations emerge, it would be easier to respond to those changes with a systematic understanding of the larger picture.

Second, the eventual contribution of this book may be to help initiate the development towards a new system of thoughts or "subject" related to AI adoption in business and society. For example, before computers were invented, we did not have the subject of "computer science," and probably only a few hundred years ago the subjects of "economics" or "business management" did not exist as a separate branch of knowledge. But there were older, more fundamental areas of knowledge, such as math, physics, and politics that served as the basis to develop into these new areas of study. In the same sense, if we already have computer science as a branch of study that gather the knowledge related to developing

AI, and management and economics as other branches of studies that gather the knowledge related to how humans can do better at running business or the economy, at some point it may become natural that we have a new branch of study that specifically aggregates the knowledge related to how AI can be better at running businesses or describe the impact of AI on the economy and society as in "AI Economics." I hope what is presented in my previous research and this book can serve as a foundation for a more complete system of thoughts to analyze the changes to business, economy, and society as a result of advancements in AI adoption.

Third, the target readers of this book include students in college and even in high school, as well as the general public. Concepts in technology, business, and economics were described in detail and with examples to help ease understanding for readers with limited background in the topic. The organization of this book may be useful for class settings, to help student learn and think about the relevant ideas and vocabularies, while facilitating discussions about controversial topics that may surround advances in AI adoption. Since the societal changes from AI adoption will grow only larger over time, the younger readers will experience the largest impact of these changes. Regardless of how people may view this topic as a part of management or future studies, I hope this book may serve an introduction to the potential changes may be brought by the adoption of AI.

Having a common vocabulary is an important step in spreading new ideas among people. We can all know the general pattern of how chess, sports, or other types of games progress and understand what is happening within the game, even if we are not good at playing those sports or games. In history of sports, we observe many great coaches that were never great players and vice versa. Similar to how coaching is different from playing sports, understanding the progress of AI adoption may be much easier than understanding how to build AI for many readers. I hope this book can serve as a base for common vocabulary that could enable easier communication and sharing of concepts and ideas regarding how the advancements in AI technology can impact our businesses, economies and societies in the future.

I tried to concisely present a diverse range of topics to present an overview of what changes people may expect as AI adoption progresses. Having understood the overall pattern of this "game," I hope more readers will be able to contribute to the progress of AI adoption in our society in a positive and meaningful way.

Thank you for reading this book!

May 25, 2024,

Seuk-Min Sohn.

Keywords: AI, AI Adoption, AI Economics, AI Pyramid, Automated Innovation, Automation, Augmentation, Strategic Management, Innovation, Effortlessness, Absolute AI, Relative AI, AI Investment, Future Studies, Business Strategy

Disclaimer: this book does not endorse any particular stock nor is it an investment advice of any kind.

CHAPTER 0
THE BEGINNING

It is Easier to Understand the Pattern of a Game than to Play it Well

We can easily understand how the game of chess is prepared and played; align the black and white pieces on each side according to the prescribed rules and take turns to move pieces according to pre-determined manner. We also know how to the game of chess ends; even though we cannot predict specifically how the game will get there, the pieces will be taken off the board one by one and eventually one player may take the King of the other player. While it would take effort and practice to become good at playing chess, it is easier to understand the "general pattern of progress" of the game.

We can also easily understand how the game of Go is prepared and played; each player takes turn in adding a black or white stone on the board to create houses and take the opponent's stones. We also know how the game of Go ends; even though we cannot predict specifically how the game will get there, but the stones will fill up the board, and eventually the player with more houses will win. While it would take effort and practice to become good at playing Go, it is easier to understand the "general pattern of the progress" of the game.

We can also easily understand how the game of Monopoly is prepared and played; each player receives a pre-set amount of cash and takes turns to advance pieces by throwing dices and buy real estate or pay rent. We also know how the game of Monopoly ends; even though we cannot predict specifically how the game will get there, but the players will go bankrupt one by one and eventually the richest winner will emerge. People can easily understand the "general pattern of progress" of the game once they play it a few times.

The games of Chess, Go, and Monopoly; we can see that there are general patterns of progress in these world-renowned classic games. You do not have to be a grandmaster to understand these patterns. Similarly, we are at the starting line of the "AI adoption game." We have numerous AI developers, and many more interested parties who are eager to take a part in this game. While it would take effort and practice to become an expert in AI development, it would be easier to understand the "general pattern of progress" of the AI adoption game.

The objective of this book is to describe the "general pattern of progress" of AI adoption over time to facilitate the public's understanding of the changes that may be brought to our future business and society. Even the AI experts will find it hard to correctly predict specifically how this game will play out for each of the players or who will win. However, it would be easier to grasp the idea of the "general pattern of progress" of the AI adoption game, and that is why I hope what this book describes will be much easier for readers to understand.

Hopefully this book can be considered an easy read for everyone – let the AI games begin!

CHAPTER 1
RULES OF ENGAGEMENT
OF THE AI GAME

(Chapter Overview) The Typical Pattern of Progress of AI Adoption in Society

(Summary)

The objective of this book is to provide a framework for analyzing the development pattern of AI adoption where the unit of analysis is not technology, but humans and firms. While the most popular framework for AI development path from a technological perspective includes the ANI-AGI-ASI framework, this is not as relevant for analyzing businesses, and to a lesser extent, our society. In this book, a business and society-specific analogies will be used to detail an AI-adoption framework named the 4 Levels of AI Adoption.

This is not a prediction, forecast or prophecy of what would happen in the future, but more of a book that explains some of the "rules of the game" that involves AI adoption in business and society. My goal of writing this is to help today's younger readers understand the changes they may face in their society when they are older.

(The Word "AI")

To ease understanding of readers, the term "AI" will be meant to generally refer as an aggregate all forms of AI technology and applications such as AI Robot, machines or groups of systems that use AI as well as their virtual versions without further distinctions.

(Business and Economic Terms)

This is a business and economics book intended for general audience, including students. General business and economic terms will be used in loose definitions to make it easier to understand concepts that may be complicated. Examples: market economy, competition, productivity, and monopoly.

(Technology-Related Comparisons)

To ease understanding, the AI adoption framework will be demonstrated in relation with the ANI-AGI-ASI framework. This may ease understanding of complex technology concepts.

1.1 How This Book Is Organized

To ease understanding, this book is organized in triple nested-loops of repeating "A-B-C-D" style of progression.

In the largest loop, the book is organized in the classic "Intro–Build Up–Climax–Conclusion" progression. In the second loop, the 4 Levels of AI Adoption follows the same A-B-C-D loop, and each chapter will be divided into four segments. Extracting a diverse area of topics into a limited space led to using a simplified structure.

Table 1-1: How This Book Is Organized

Chapter		AI Adoption Levels		Topics of Each Chapter (A – B – C – D)
A	Ch. 1			Overview of the Rules of the Game
B	Ch. 2			The Past and Present of AI
C	Ch. 3	A	AI Adoption Level 1	(In Charge of Business Role = Human) AI as a Tool, Assistant AI, Co-Pilot AI
	Ch. 4	B	AI Adoption Level 2	(In Charge of Business Role = AI) Agent AI, Butler AI
	Ch. 5	C	AI Adoption Level 3	(In Charge of Company = AI) Company AI, CEO AI
	Ch. 6	D	AI Adoption Level 4	(In Charge of Government = AI) Government AI, President AI
D	Ch. 7			Implications of AI Adoption Levels

Layer 1: Whole Book

The first A-B-C-D layer is the structure of the whole book:

A (Introduction) = Chapter 1: The objective of this book and a brief introduction of the Four Levels of AI Adoption

B (Build Up) = Chapter 2: Explanations about how AI came to be what it is today

C (Climax) = Chapter 3, 4, 5, 6: The Four Levels of AI Adoption

D (Conclusion) = Chapter 7: What can be gleaned from the end of the AI adoption game

Layer 2: The 4 Levels of AI Adoption

The second A-B-C-D layer is the contents of the Four Levels of AI Adoption in Society:

A (Introduction) = Level 1 AI Adoption: In Charge of Business Role is Human Worker

B (Build Up) = Level 2 AI Adoption: In Charge of Business Role is AI

C (Climax) = Level 3 AI Adoption: In Charge of Company is AI

D (Conclusion) = Level 4 AI Adoption: In Charge of Government is AI

Layer 3: Each Chapter

Lastly, the third A-B-C-D layer is the organization within each chapter, where each chapter will be comprised of the following segments:

A (Introduction): The introduction of the concept and basic background about the level

B (Build Up): How events would unfold in the level

C (Climax): Social controversies or discussions that would come to focus in the level

D (Conclusion): Implications on the economy, industries and businesses

Layer 4: Chapter Overview

Additionally, each chapter will have an overview in the beginning, which will feature another A-B-C-D loop of:

(A) Introduction to the Chapter

(B) Explanation of Vocabulary

(C) Implications on Business and Economy

(D) Technological and Other Implications

1.2 Why This Book?

In the late 1800s and early 1900s when automobiles were first being developed, we can draw a graph comparing the average speed of horses and the early cars. From a technological viewpoint, as engine technology improved, the average speed of driving cars eventually surpassed riding horses, which we can think of as an inflection point where cars became the preferred mode of transportation. However, when we view the same situation from a business perspective, we would need additional analyses. For example, determining what kind of product to build, such as a passenger car, a van, bus, sports car, tractor for agriculture, pickup truck, etc., would also be relevant for businesses so that cars can be more useful in our society. In addition, the government and the society as a whole had to come to an agreement to introduce changes such as building paved roads, traffic laws, emissions and other regulations, and people had to accept having cars around our lives despite the dangers.

In the same sense, we are at the beginning of AI adoption. From a technological perspective, we can also draw a graph comparing the performances or the capabilities of AI to humans. As AI technology improves, the intelligence of AI may surpass the combined intelligence of humanity, a concept called "singularity." However, from a business perspective, what would be also relevant would include what kind of AI products to develop and how AI may improve our lives. In addition, the government and the society as a whole would have to come to an agreement to introduce changes such as setting the boundaries of AI development and adoption, what tasks AI would be allowed to carry out, and people would have to accept having AI around our lives.

Considering the need for society-wide changes, it may be helpful to have a framework specialized for business and society, other than the popular but technology-oriented ANI-AGI-ASI framework. The objective of this book is to describe this framework so that people may systematically think about how AI products can be categorized and incorporated into our business and society, similar to how we could incorporate cars into our lives.

1.3 What "Game" Is This Book About? ~~(What is AI?)~~

The Future of AI from the Perspectives of Scientists and Engineers vs Economists and Business Managers

Only in the past few decades the development of computer-related technology led AI to become possible. We may say we are at the beginning stages of the AI adoption game.

The perspectives of business and economics are different from those of technology and science. Different perspectives lead to different questions and decisions. The questions scientists would ask are different from the questions economists or business managers would ask, as the unit of analysis for science would center on the technology or product, while for business and economics the attention would be more on the firms, consumers, or even the actions of the government.

For example, let's imagine describing the growth of a child over a span of 10 years. A scientist or doctor may focus on describing the changes in measurements of physical characteristics, such as the height, weight, number of teeth, or even body temperature or history of illnesses. On the other hand, someone with social focus may describe observations that center on the experiences and the environment of the child, such as what schools or types of classes taken, what kind of friends the child was close to, or even what kind of cartoon characters or theme songs the child liked over time.

In the same sense, we may examine a different perspective from technology. While the most popular way to approach the topic of AI may be from the technological perspective, such as the algorithms or how it can be trained, this book will focus more on the perspective of businesses that develop, use, or sell AI products, or consumers who use AI, and the subsequent changes that AI adoption may bring to our society.

Table 1-2: Example of Different Questions Asked, Science and Tech vs Business and Economy

	Science and Tech Questions	Business and Economy Questions
Examples of Questions in Auto Industry	- How fast can you make cars go? - How light can you make cars weigh? - How aerodynamic can you make cars? - How fuel efficient can you make cars? - How safe can you make cars?	- How much would it cost to develop and build a new car? - How many of new model will sell? - Which factory to build the car? - How many cars should be built? - What kind of cars is our competition building? - What differentiates our car? - What segment of customers should our new models target?
Examples of Questions in AI Development	- How similar can you make AI to humans? - How smart can you make AI to be? - What kind of programming languages should be used to develop AI? - How fast computer hardware do you need? - What data should you use to train AI? - What kind of algorithm should you use to develop AI?	- For what uses will this AI target? - What AI are our competitors building? - What differentiates our AI? - How much does our AI cost to develop? - How will we market our AI? - How much does it cost to manufacture our AI robot? - How many AI robots should be manufactured? - How will our customers use our AI product? - What do our customers consider when purchasing an AI product?

As AI development is incorporated into businesses, people will ask more of the following questions.

1. *(AI Replacing Humans) Will AI displace human jobs?*
   Will it threaten humanity?
2. *(AI Increasing Profits) Can you use AI to raise productivity or make more money?*

From a scientific perspective, the focus may be on how much intelligence AI could achieve, or how similar to humans we can make AI. These types of questions can be considered viewpoint of the "supplier" or the providers of AI.

On the other hand, profitability would be the main focus from a business perspective, and whether AI is similar to humans is not as important. For example, there are many instances where it would be more beneficial for AI to be different from humans, so it can complement tasks that humans find difficult. For example, AI will not suffer from anxiety under stress or facing important tasks, try to avoid or fear potentially dangerous tasks, forget something, or be bored or tired of repeating the same tasks. This perspective may be thought of as the viewpoints of the "demand," or the users of AI.

If you read the news today, you will find that an increasingly larger amount of investments are being made towards AI. As a result, innovations are happening simultaneously in every direction. As these advancements in technology grow larger in scale, become more complex, and occur at a faster rate, it is getting harder for each of us to keep track of all the advances that are being made all around the world. While this quick pace of change may make people stressed out, having a longer-term view may help calm people down. Paradoxically, no matter how chaotic the day-to-day and short-term changes may appear, the longer-term pattern of the AI adoption game and how it will progress may be quite simple and easy to understand. If we imagine ourselves to be a group of explorers having just reached an uninhabited island, trying to keep track of daily news items would be similar to sending everyone out in a frenzy to examine the plants in the forest laying in front of us to see if anything is edible for today's meal, or see if there are any other resources nearby that we can use to build shelter for tonight, while the longer-term view could be compared to sitting back and relaxing while sending a drone into the sky to plot the map of the island to get a better sense of the shape of the forest and how much land we have found.

In business, we think of the first-mover advantage as creating a limited type of monopoly. From this perspective, the most valuable company in history may be the company that builds the Last AI. This book is written to provide a longer-term framework to think about this somewhat unconventional analysis.

RULES OF THE "AI GAME" (HOW AI GETS ADOPTED IN BUSINESS)

Since we will focus on examining the business and economics side of AI adoption and the intended readership include those without business background, a few basic concepts will be briefly explained in Box 1-1. We may think of these as basic premises, or fundamental principles that are given.

[Box 1-1] Basic Concepts and Premises

1. (Economic Development) Higher Productivity is Good for the Economy

Productivity can be simply understood as the ratio of outputs to inputs. More simply, it can be thought of as the speed of how a worker accomplishes a task. For example, for someone digging dirt on the ground, using an excavator may accomplish the task much faster than someone doing it by hand. We can say the productivity increased by using the excavator. Economic development in essence would include raising the productivity of people.

2. (Why Firms Exist) Firms Need Profits to Exist

Generally speaking, firms can be thought of as a combination of human and other types of physical and intellectual resources to somehow increase the output value to be more than the sum of the values of the inputs through a series of tasks.

Just like humans need to breathe air to survive, firms need to create profits to survive. Similar to how humans can hold their breath for a limited amount of time under water, firms can survive on cash flow such as capital surplus and other types of equities without creating a profit, but only for a limited amount of time.

To create larger profit, firms take on different types of risks, where risk can be thought of as variability in the outcome. For example, firms may decide to invest in new technologies that may turn out to work well and return a high profit, while the new technology may also fail and the investment would lose value.

3. (Bounded Rationality) Capabilities of Humans are Limited

Since humans are not all-knowing, there are limitations on what we can do. Thus, firms, which may be considered as just a group of people, would also have limitations on what they can do. When we consider the types of limitations firms have, they include the limitations of not having all the information, not have the capability to process all the available information, limitation on technology, limitation on capital, time, and even limits enforced by legal requirements.

Today's leading capitalistic economies have developed a financial system that includes the stock market and institutions such as banks and venture capital firms that may help the AI developers raise capital. Compared to more traditional method of bank lending that fueled the growth of manufacturing industries, the ecosystem of venture capital investing in tech startups is thought to be more efficient in showing what kind of risks are being taken and what the outcome of the risks were, helping related parties act on those information and make decisions.

4. (Competition is Beneficial) AI Adoption May Be Viewed as Part of a Competition

Today's market economies are based on the basic premise that competition will lead to better products, efficiency, and ultimately better lives of people. The opposite of having competition may be thought of as not having competition, which is called monopoly. In monopoly, there could be price fixing, inefficiency, and ultimately unsatisfied customers. In short, competition is good, monopoly is bad.

In regards to AI Adoption, from the concepts explained above, we may also infer the following:

1. *Firms will use AI to improve profitability by using it in areas such as increasing productivity, reducing cost, or innovation*
2. *Firms will attempt to apply available AI to as many areas as possible to maximize profit*

On a side note, from a structural standpoint, we may also think of the opposite of a free market economy as a centrally planned economy. In a centrally planned economy, the government may intentionally create monopolies. This principle would apply to companies developing or deploying AI as well. In a market economy, companies would have the freedom to choose where they want to compete and how they compete.

Monopoly in AI development may generally be viewed with a negative connotation. However, there may be certain situations where a nation may intentionally introduce monopolies to grow fledgling industries. This may be more prominent in centrally planned economies, where the government may choose how industries are organized. Monopolies in AI development may arise intentionally if the government chooses to create it.

1.4 The Pattern of AI Game from Technological vs. Business or Societal Perspectives

From the technological perspective, we may ask questions such as "how intelligent can we make AI?" "How similar to humans can we make AI?" or "Can we create AI more intelligent than humans?"

From these questions, we have a well-known framework where we divide the progress of AI into ANI-AGI-ASI. Most readers of this book probably have already heard of these categories but you can refer to Chapter 2 for a concise explanation of what they are.

The ANI-AGI-ASI framework is highly useful for thinking about scientific or technological issues. For example, AI development has a rather concrete pattern and an "end" to the game; after reaching AGI, AI would enter a self-improvement loop where it would surpass the knowledge and capabilities of all humanity by reaching what is referred to as "singularity."[1]

When asking questions about the progress of AI from a technological perspective, factors that would first come to focus would involve directional questions such as how fast, how large, or how strong. It may also lead to questions such as "how similar to humans" as in considering AI with consciousness or compare the knowledge or capabilities of AI to humanity. In contrast, this book adds another layer above the technology development, trying indirectly to assess the progress of AI adoption against established hierarchies we already have in our business and society. This may make some technologist readers uncomfortable since the progress of AI adoption in our society may appear to have a separate cadence from the development patterns of AI. Still, please bear in mind these approaches are still quite intertwined and cannot be considered separately.

In the next section, we will start our main discussion by presenting the Four Levels of AI Adoption framework to begin examining how AI may change our business and society over the long term.

1.5 (AI Adoption Framework) The Pattern of "AI Game" in Business and Society

1. Introduction to the 4 Levels of AI Adoption by Business and Society

One of the main topics of this book is to describe how AI development will change the business activities of individuals and firms. In this section we will first briefly examine the framework that may explain the pattern of "AI Game," named the Four Levels of AI Adoption in Business and Society, without going into details to give readers an overview of the whole storyline. More details will be provided in subsequent chapters.

2. The Three Levels of AI Adoption in Business

In my previous research, the concept of the Three Levels of AI Adoption in Firms[2] was introduced. This segment will briefly explain the concepts to ease understanding for the readers.

From a technological perspective, a milestone for AI development would be AI reaching capabilities that are similar to humans, such as what we may describe as "having consciousness" or similar ideas. This may be one of the definitions used for AGI. Meanwhile, from a business perspective, a more meaningful milestone would be when a virtual AI system or AI robot can completely replace what a human worker does at a company. We can call this milestone "AI equalization."[3] For example, a company will have different jobs filled by different people; if an AI advances to a point where it can fill one of those jobs in place of a human, we can consider AI to have reached equalization for that particular job.

There is a notable difference in the perspective of categorizing AI has reached AGI and whether AI has reached equalization. Whereas the supplier, or the developer, of AI would probably decide whether AI has reached AGI, the user, or the demand, of the AI will determine whether AI has reached equalization. For some jobs, it may be easier to reach equalization, while for others it may require a more advanced AI.

To describe major inflection points of changes using the concept of equalization, the AI adoption in firms may be categorized into the following three levels in Table 1-3.

Table 1-3: AI Equalization and the Three Levels of AI Adoption[4]

AI Adoption Type		Adoption Level	Description of Adoption Level
without AI Equalization	Augmentation and/or Partial Automation	Level 1	Humans are in charge of business roles (i.e. AI Assistants, Co-Pilot AI)
with AI Equalization	Full Automation and/or Collaboration	Level 2	AI is in charge of business roles (i.e. AI Agents, AI Butlers)
with Social Acceptance	Full Automation	Level 3	AI is in charge of whole businesses (i.e. AI CEOs, AI Companies)

Since these steps would have to occur in order, we may also show the progress in the following Figure 1-1 to show the direction of the progress.

Figure 1-1: The Three Levels of AI Adoption by Firms[5]

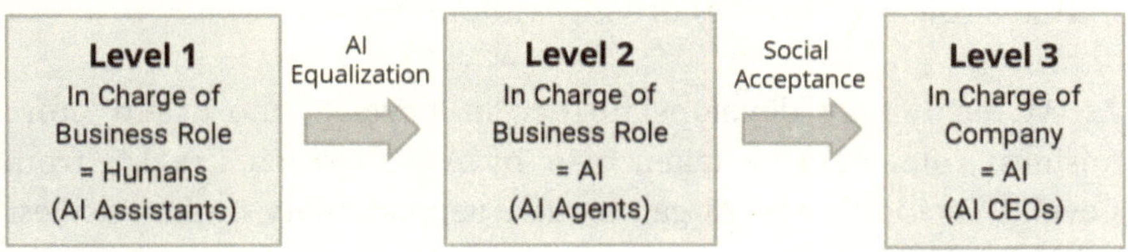

3. The Four Levels of AI Adoption by Society

From these three levels of AI adoption, we may expand our consideration to further include the adoption of AI in our society as a whole. In the expanded model, we will consider the adoption of AI in government, where eventually AI would be able to take over the role of the most important person in government. This expanded model will be referred as the 4 Levels of AI Adoption in Society, as shown in Figure 1-2.

This book will build around explaining each of these four levels to help leaders easily understand the pattern of how AI game will progress over time.

Figure 1-2: The Four Levels of AI Adoption by Society

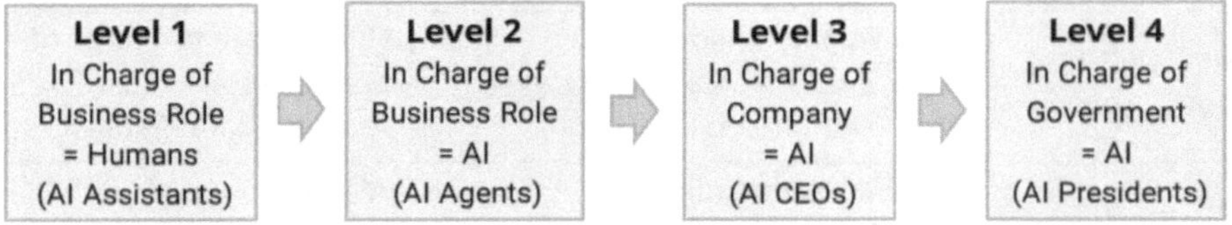

Enablers to Reach the Next Level

To reach the next level, certain milestones or accomplishments would need to be met. To jump from Level 1 to Level 2 Adoption to let AI be in charge of business roles, AI must first demonstrate dependability in the role. For example, we can imagine the equivalent of reaching the Level 5 autonomous driving as a technological milestone that may enable an AI to be in charge of a business role that involves driving without humans.

As AI technology develops further in Level 2, more and more business roles may be taken over by AI. To reach Level 3 from Level 2, in addition to AI gaining the dependability in the business role of running a business, an additional requirement of gaining social agreement and legal status would first be necessary.

To progress from Level 3 to 4, after reaching all of the previous milestones in government-related roles, an additional step of winning a popular vote will be necessary.

4. The AI Adoption Pyramid

The Four levels of AI Adoption by Society model can be presented in the following pyramid to also illustrate the types of enablers to reach the next level. This framework would be called the AI Adoption Pyramid, or just the AI Pyramid.

Figure 1-3: Sohn's AI Adoption Pyramid and Its Enablers

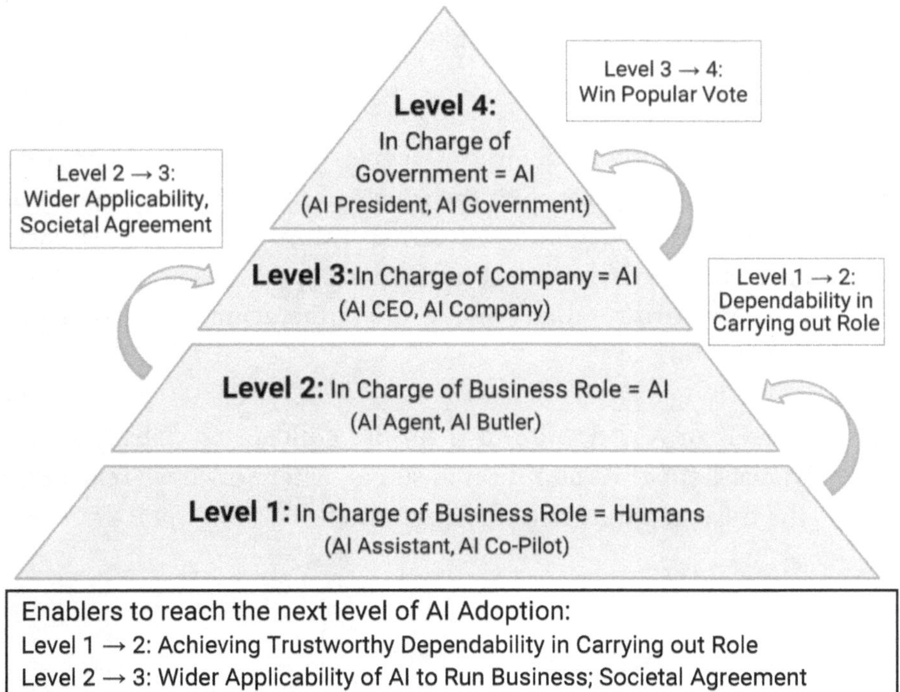

5. Overview of the 4 Levels of AI Adoption by Society and the AI Adoption Pyramid

In considering how AI adoption would proceed in the society, we may first think about how changes in our society occur in steps where one progress leads to another.

For example, the development of a new technology may lead to introduction of new products. First, there would be a new scientific finding, which would enable companies to research for more specific applications of the new knowledge, which could then lead to the development of new products, and over time the new product could be improved or other products from the technology can be developed. In the meantime, the competitions may also develop similar products, leading to the emergence of a new industry.

Similarly, we may consider the lifecycles of new products, where new products may go through the stages of Introduction → Growth → Maturity → Replacement. We can also think about the primary, secondary, and tertiary industries, beginning with agriculture, then light manufacturing, then heavy manufacturing, and then to digitalization.

The 4 Levels of AI Adoption is a similar concept of characterizing the advancement of AI adoption in stages, where once we reach one stage, the next step may become obvious.

1) Level 1 AI Adoption

In the beginning stage of AI adoption, it would be natural for investment in AI to focus on helping human workers achieve more and work more effectively and efficiently to increase productivity. Examples would include AI providing potential designs for clothing or electronic circuits and human workers reviewing them to pick the best options. Human workers may be working in the same jobs as before, and AI would help humans carry out the role more easily or better. Jobs may be newly designed to incorporate AI better. In this book, we will refer to this stage of AI adoption as Co-Pilot AI or Assistant AI. More broadly, we may call it Dependent AI.

2) Level 2 AI Adoption

As AI development continues, the capabilities of AI will improve, and eventually reach a stage where AI may be able to carry out all of the tasks of a human worker at a level of dependability beyond what would be deemed necessary to remove the human worker. A well-known example of reaching dependability at a task may include the Level 5 autonomous vehicles. In this level, AI would take charge of a business role. In this book, we will refer to these types of AI as Agent AI, or Employee AI, or if it develops in a particular direction, Butler AI. More broadly, these may be also referred to as Dependable AI to reflect the main attribute that enables this level.

3) Level 3 AI Adoption

As AI development continues even further, the scope of tasks AI can carry out would widen, eventually reaching a stage where the AI would be able to carry out all of the tasks of the CEO, or even all of the tasks within the firm. An example may be an AI robot that can independently run a company that operates restaurants. This AI would be able to carry out tasks such as financing for a restaurant, what menus to include, where to open, how to do the interior, where to procure ingredients, etc.

In this stage, AI, not humans, would be in charge of the final management decisions of the firm. We may refer to these types of AI as CEO AI, Chairman AI, Company AI, or even Entrepreneur AI. More broadly, we may also refer to them as Independent AI or Free AI.

4) Level 4 AI Adoption

Lastly, at some point the development of AI may lead to a situation where the majority of the general public would prefer to have AI in charge of the government over humans. In this stage, AI would be in charge of the government. Broadly speaking, there would be two paths to reach this stage. The first path would be intentional, as a result of the demands of the public. We will refer to these as President AI or Government AI. The second path to reach this stage would be unintentional, potentially including a path where the AI exceeds the comprehension of humans and somehow gains control of our society without our intentions. We may refer to these types of AI as Sage AI or Dictator AI.

Now that we had a brief overview of the AI Adoption Pyramid as the general pattern of the AI adoption game, we will proceed to examine the history of AI and then each AI adoption level in more detail in the next chapters.

CHAPTER 2
THE PAST, PRESENT AND FUTURE OF AI
(THE AI STORY)

(Chapter Overview) The AI Scenario: Towards the Ultimate Form of AI

(A) Chapter Overview

While this is not a science or a technical book, we will examine the basics of AI-related technology to ease the readers into this topic. In this chapter, we will briefly overview the development "history" of AI since its inception along with the future "AI story" (pun intended) or the outlook of the direction of the technology we are headed.

The type of AI that has become popular today can be categorized as "Sub-Symbolic" or "Connectionist," where the activities of neurons are simulated; one shortcoming of this approach is that it is hard to understand how AI reaches decisions. Most popular AI today can be categorized as a version of Deep Learning, which is a subset of machine learning. AI adoption can be thought of as the culmination of 3 different dimensions: hardware, software, and data. Of these, we can think of hardware and software as AI technology, or the "what" of AI, while the data can be thought of as the usage of AI, or the "how and where" of AI.

(B) Vocabulary

This section introduces a variety of vocabulary, of which the most prominent may be machine learning and AGI. These words are described in here to provide some familiarity of concepts for readers with less technological background.

The term "artificial intelligence" may refer to a type of algorithm. In this book, we will also refer to AI robots and other physical manifestation that uses AI as generally "AI" to ease understanding in a broader sense. The most controversial term related to AI adoption may be "artificial general intelligence" (AGI), which may mean different things to different people, but generally meaning an AI with capabilities comparable to humans. We will explore a few potential distinctions for different definitions of AGI to ease understanding for the general public. "Singularity" refers to a point where AGI may self-advance to pass the combined intelligence of humanity to become an ASI.

The concept of the ultimate end of the AI development may be referred to as the Absolute AI, which may also be referred to as the "Maximum AI," "Last AI" or even "artificial god," where the AI has figured out all of the real truths in the universe. If the earlier versions of ASI are similar in concept to the different gods in Greek Mythology, Absolute AI is more similar in concept to an all-mighty god.

(C) Implications on Business and Economy

In this book, we will examine the temporal progress of AI adoption in business and society using well-known concepts in business and economics, such as market economy, competition, monopoly, productivity, and the Game Theory.

(D) Technological Requirements and Implications

In this book, the progress in AI adoption levels will be generally be compared to the technological progress using the ANI-AGI-ASI framework. Additionally, several frameworks will take advantage of the format used in the well-known framework of the 6 Levels of Autonomous Vehicles. This approach would hopefully ease understanding for the readers.

2.1 The Past of AI: (1) The Beginning of AI

1. What is AI?

There are various variations of definitions of AI. A common theme among the different definitions revolves around "intelligent machines" as defined by McCarthy et al. (1955). We may think in terms of tasks that require intelligence and enabling computer systems to carry out those tasks. The following table shows some examples of the definition of AI.

Table 2-1: Examples of the Definitions of AI

Source	Definition
Marvin Minsky[1] (1968)	The science of making machines do things that would require intelligence if done by men
Stuart Russell[2] (1995)	Definition of AI can be defined by thinking and acting rationally or like humans <table><tr><td>Systems that think like humans</td><td>Systems that think rationally</td></tr><tr><td>Systems that act like humans</td><td>Systems that act rationally</td></tr></table>
OECD[3] (2019)	A machine-based system that is capable of influencing the environment by producing an output (predictions, recommendations, or decisions) for a given set of objectives
McKinsey[4] (2022)	Ability of a machine to cognitive functions that we associate with human minds and to perform tasks using cognitive functions
Encyclopedia Britannica[5] (2023)	The ability of a digital computer or computer-controlled robots to perform tasks commonly associated with intelligent beings
EU AI Act[6] (2024)	'AI system' means a machine-based system designed to operate with varying levels of autonomy, that may exhibit adaptiveness after deployment and that, for explicit or implicit objectives, infers, from the input it receives, how to generate outputs such as predictions, content, recommendations, or decisions that can influence physical or virtual environments;

In this book, the specific definition of AI itself is not for much debate, as long as we can broadly define it and understand it as some form of machines that can carry out tasks we normally think as requiring intelligence. It would not be far different from the idea of AI you already have. Meanwhile, the shape or physical manifestation of AI is typically not a part of the definition, and AI may take a variety of physical forms without much restriction, such as computers, robots, machines, car, etc.

More importantly, AI can be thought of as a combination of three factors: software, hardware, and data. In the next sections, we will briefly review how AI adoption got to this point and where we are headed, to give a general idea for readers new to this topic.

2. The Beginning of AI

People had the idea of machines that think like humans for a long time, with some claims dating back to the Greek times. The best known formal conceptualization of AI was in 1950 by Alan Turing, who introduced the Turing Test[7]. The Turing Test involves talking to through a computer terminal – if a person cannot tell whether the other side is a machine or a human then the machine can be said to have intelligence.

1) The First Use of The Term "Artificial Intelligence"

In 1955, a group of scholars, led by John McCarthy that also included Marvin Minsky, Nathaniel Rochester and Claude Shannon, submitted a proposal for the Dartmouth Summer Research Project on AI. This proposal is thought to be the first official use of the term "Artificial Intelligence." The scholars who attended this project became major contributors of the early development of AI. Among the attendees, Arthur Samuel coined the term "machine learning" in his 1959 paper where he showed a program that could play checkers.[8]

2) The "Four Seasons" of AI

The story of AI development had its hot and cold moments. In the beginning, people were highly optimistic machines that think like humans could appear soon. Even cartoons of the times, like The Jetsons which first aired in 1962, reflected this interest.

However, as time went by in the 1960s, technology development seemed to be stalled and the public became disappointed. Then during the 1970s and 80s the expert systems gained some popularity and people became excited again for the potential, yet to be disappointed again by the lack of actual applicability of these systems.

AI appeared to briefly re-gain public interest in the late 1990s when IBM's Deep Blue won over chess grandmaster Garry Kasparov in 1997. However, enthusiasm waned again soon thereafter and years of more disappointment continued as technological advances appeared to be slow compared to other forms of technology.

Finally, in the 2010s, the tide turned again with the emergence of machine learning brought another wave of public excitement in the field, this time with the annual image-recognition competition run by ImageNet showed promise for real-world applications of AI, and the highly publicized match between humans and AI in the game of Go was won by Google DeepMind's AlphaGo over Lee Sedol in 2016.

This up and down of excitement in AI has been sometimes referred to as the "four seasons" of AI.[9]

2.2 The Past of AI: (2) The Two Approaches to Developing AI

Broadly speaking, there are two camps of thoughts regarding how to develop AI: "Symbolism" and "Connectionist." Symbolism, which received more support during the earlier days of AI development, refers to the "symbols" that humans think of when we think in our minds, while connectionist refers to how neurons are "connected" to each other.[10]

To put it succinctly, we can summarize as follows:

Symbolism: Computer will develop intelligence if knowledge can be modeled and taught

Connectionist: Computer will develop intelligence if neurons in human brain are modeled and knowledge is learned

We may also compare the two approaches in the following table.

Table 2-2: Comparison of Symbolism and Connectionist Approaches to AI

Symbolism			Connectionist		
Model of Knowledge	→ Input to Computers	= AI	Model of Human Brain	→ Input to Computers	= AI

The major difference between the two approaches is that in Symbolism approach humans create and input the model of knowledge into the computer, while in Connectionist approach computer "learns" of some knowledge from the relationship between inputs and outputs of data. Let's take a brief look at each approach.

1. Symbolism: Knowledge Expressed in Symbols Will Lead to Intelligence

In the symbolism approach, computers mimic how people think in terms of objects or abstract ideas by using symbols to enable computers to "understand" the relationships between concepts. For example, if we ask "what is a fried egg?" the computer may answer using related concepts and symbols such as;

(Egg ÷ break – Shell) x heat @ Frying Pan + Salt = ^Platter & #Breakfast & #Food

If we ask the computer to compare fried egg to a boiled egg, the computer may show boiled egg as:

(Egg) x heat @ (Pot + Water) = (hardened ÷ break – Shell) ^Bowl & #Meals & #Food

Since ideas such as "Egg" and "heat @" are shared, the computer may surmise a fried egg is more similar to a boiled egg than other types of cold food such as vegetable salad.

Symbolism gained popularity during the 1970s and 80s as expert systems were employed in areas such as development of truck scheduling systems. Symbolism approach was applied to expert systems that required not much amount of data, since data had to be handled by humans. An example is DENDRAL,[11] a project that began in 1965 led by Edward Feigenbaum at Stanford University to develop an expert system to analyze mass spectrum data to suggest potential chemical structures for biomedical research. Expert systems tend to be rule-based; the idea stems from the observation that "If situation X, then do Y" type of knowledge could be gathered to create expert advice. When someone asks a question, then the expert system would search through its data of knowledge to select or deduce the answer.

This type of development approach had shortcomings. Symbolism has strength in deduction, but the computer cannot learn by itself and is dependent on humans to input the knowledge, which is expensive and limited in applications. It also has benefits. The symbols are understandable by humans, so it is easier to understand what the AI is doing.

Recently, the limitations of connectionist AI in terms of explainability have led to the argument of combining the two methods to enhance the explainability of AI, known as XAI.

2. Connectionist: Modeling Human Neurons Will Lead to Intelligence

Connectionist approach seeks to duplicate how neurons work in our brains. It dates back to 1958, when Frank Rosenblatt developed a concept called Perceptron. [12] Perceptron works by combining several inputs to lead to an output through a type of black box called "node," which we can think of as the digital version of neurons in our brains. Subsequently, machine learning and deep learning were developed by applying this concept. Each neuron is responsible for part of knowledge smaller than symbols, so it is also known as Sub-Symbolic approach. Knowledge coded through each node is smaller than what humans typically can decipher, so it is hard to understand for us how AI is reaching its conclusions.

Most of the readers would have heard of deep learning, which is a subset of machine learning. In the next section, some of the connectionist algorithms will be briefly described to provide readers of a general understanding of how connectionist AI works.

2.3 The Present of AI:
(1) Software (Machine Learning)

While there may be a whole world of different approaches to developing AI, this section will focus on the currently most popular method, machine learning.

The term machine learning was coined by Arthur Samuel in 1959. Samuel[13] defined machine learning as giving computers "the ability to learn without explicitly being programmed." In machine learning, computer learns through data to develop a model, in what is referred to as training, and then uses the model to make predictions for new data. While traditional programs are used to calculate an answer to a question, machine learning is different in the sense that it first calculates models from data, and then uses these models to predict the answer.

1. The 3 Types of Machine Learning

There are 3 basic types[14] of machine learning: supervised learning, unsupervised learning, and reinforcement learning. AI developers are increasingly mixing the approaches to develop hybrid methods as the distinctions between categories are gradually fading.

Figure 2-1: The 3 Types of Machine Learning

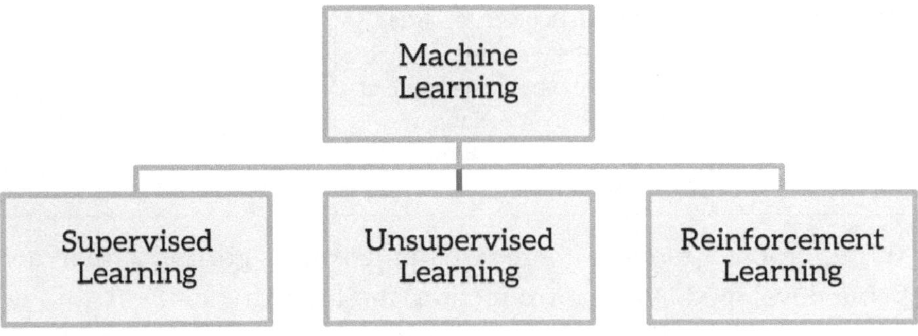

Each training method would be suitable for different objectives and the availability of relevant data may not allow use of some methods. Supervised learning need people to label the answer to each row of the data so it takes more resources and time to create the data than unsupervised methods. Reinforcement learning is more suitable for analyzing the types of data that deal with passage of time.

Table 2-3: The Three Basic Types of Machine Learning

Category	Training Method	Usage Example
Supervised Learning	① Prep: Data with labeling ② Train: After selecting a specific algorithm, create a prediction model from the data ③ Predict: Using the model, make actual predictions for new observations	- Categorizing spams - OCR - Speech recognition - Image recognition
Unsupervised Learning	① Prep: Data is prepared without labeling ② Train: Look for the structure or other specificities of the data using algorithm	- Finding pharmaceutical chemicals that may offer similar benefits as known drugs - Recommendation system - Categorizing such as finding outliers or an abnormal event - Generating images
Reinforcement learning	① Action: Carry out some action within the environment ② Observe: Observe what the outcome was ③ Reward: Receive rewards based on the outcome ①~③ Repeat: Decide whether to continue past actions (Exploitation) or try something new (Exploration)	- Predicting time series such as stocks, sales, weather, and traffic - Map Navigation - Games such as AlphaGo

Within each approach there are numerous algorithms that are being developed. As an introduction, the following table lists a few of the more popular variations. Readers may easily find in-depth details of each method in other more technical books.

Table 2-4: Examples of Each Types of Machine Learning[15]

Category	Algorithm Name / Simple Description

Supervised Learning	- Regression: Linear Regression, Logistic Regression
	- Decision Trees: Structure each possibilities in a branching form
	- Ensemble: Combine different models in an attempt to enhance performance
	  o Bagging, Bootstrap Aggregating: Divide a sample data and use it multiple times
	  o Boosting: Improve performance by iterative sample rebalancing
	  o Random Forest: Create multiple decision trees using different subsamples
	  o Other Examples: ADABoost, XGBoost, Gradient Boost (GBM)
	- K-Nearest Neighbors (KNN): Classify based on the nearest K number of observations
	- Support Vector Machines (SVM): Classify based on the border that will result in the largest distance
	- Artificial Neural Networks (ANN): Network that mimics the structure of neurons in human brains

Unsupervised Learning	- Cluster Analysis: Classify data points based on similar characteristics
	  o Hierarchical Clustering: Create one cluster at a time in a hierarchical manner
	  o K-Means Clustering: Create a pre-determined K number of clusters
	  o Mixture Distribution Clustering, DBSCAN, OPTICS, etc.
	- Anomaly Detection: Errors or defects, abnormal transactions
	  o Local Outlier Factor (LOF): finding local outliers
	  o Isolation Forest: Finding anomaly using binary trees
	- Latent Variable Modeling: Predicting variables that cannot be directly observed
	  o Expectation Maximization (EM), Maximum Likelihood Estimation (MLE), Gaussian Mixture Model (GMM)
	  o Principal Component Analysis (PCA): Reducing data dimension
	  o Non-Negative Matrix Factorization (NMF)
	  o Singular Value Decomposition (SVD)
	  o Topic Modeling: Find topic, Latent Dirichlet Allocation (LDA)

Reinforcement Learning	- Model-Free Reinforcement Learning: Approaches that do not predict rewards
	  o Monte Carlo, SARSA, Policy Gradient
	  o Q Learning, Deep-Q Learning (DQN)
	- Model-Based Reinforcement Learning: Predict rewards
	  o AlphaZero

2. Deep Learning

Deep learning is one of the types of machine learning. Whereas perceptron models one neuron as inputs and outputs, deep learning models the neural network, getting closer to the actual mechanisms of human brains.

Artificial neural network (ANN) can be considered a way to mathematically model human brains, by modeling the connections as a function of coefficients, or loadings.[16] Artificial neural network is comprised of input layer, hidden layer, and output layer, and hidden layer is used because it is known to improve the training outcome. When the concept of ANN was first introduced, it was hard to train. In 1986, a concept called *Backpropagation*, introduced by David Rumelhart, Geoffrey Hinton and Ronald Williams[17], eased the training. Backpropagation can be thought of a method to find where in the hidden layer is causing the error in the output layer. Even with backpropagation, due to convergence to local minima. In 2006, Hinton introduced Deep Belief Networks[18], which improved the learning rate in training by using pre-training and fine-tuning.

As of this writing, most of the current state-of-the-art AI technology is based on deep learning algorithm.

[Box 2-1] Attempt at "Elementary School-Level" Explanation of Deep Learning

Since this book is also intended for young readers and readers without much technological background, here is an attempt of a classroom explanation of the concept of deep learning.

Let's imagine students are sitting in a classroom in 4 rows of 3-4-4-3 students, as shown in Figure 2-2. Let's play a game of raising hands. The teacher in front of the classroom is showing the only the student in the front row one of different pictures – maybe an apple or a banana, without telling the students what it is or giving any directions other than raising hands or not. The students sitting in the first row are each given a pair of filtering glasses that show only an aspect of the picture. After seeing the picture, then the students in the first row have to decide, all at the same time, whether to raise or not raise their hands based on what they see. The students in the next three rows cannot see the pictures, but can only observe whether the students in the preceding row raised their hands. All they have is to look at the pattern of raised hands in the row in front of them and decide whether to raise their own hands. After the last row has finished raising their hands, an observing student in the back of the room, who can only observe the last row, will decide whether the picture was apple or banana.

Figure 2-2: Example of How Artificial Neural Network Works

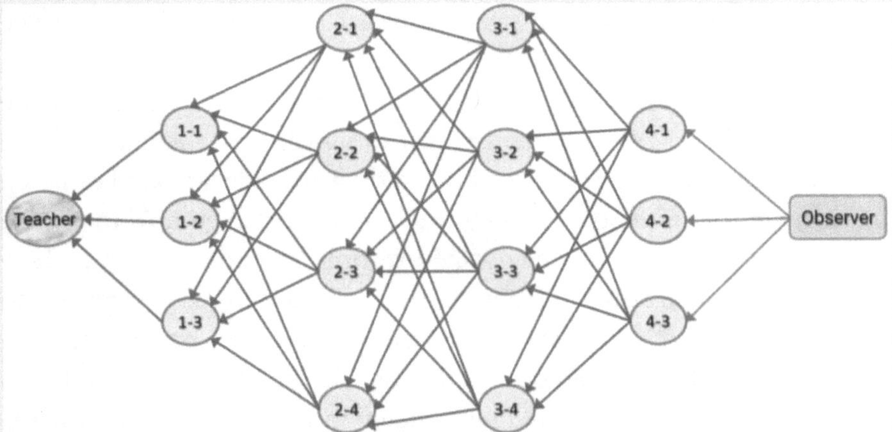

In the beginning, the students will not know how to react. Let's say Student 1-1 will raise hand if the picture has a C-shape, while Student 1-2 will do so if picture has orange color, and Student 1-3 will respond to a circular shape.

The second row students have to decide just based on what they observe the row in front did. Each person may have different ideas, so that Student 2-1 will raise hand only if Student 1-1 raise hand but Student 1-2 does not, while Student 2-2 will not raise if Student 1-2 raises hand but will raise if Student 1-3 raises, regardless of what the other students do. Student 2-3 is dozing off and not going to raise hand at all, and student 2-4 is in a happy mood and will raise hand if at least one student in the preceding row raises hand. The third row students also have their own ideas of what to do. We can think of the ways how these students decided what they will do as an example of how "neurons" or "nodes" act, and the different ways each student act based on different student in the preceding row can be compared to "weights," while being tired or happy can be compared to "biases."

The students in the last fourth row also have to decide based on the row. Let's assume Student 4-1 will raise if 3-3 and 3-4 both raise, while Student 4-2 will raise if 3-2 raise and 3-4 doesn't raise, while 4-3 is cautious and not going to raise hand at all.

The observer standing in the back of the classroom has to decide what the picture was only based on how the fourth row students raised hands. Giving the correct answer will earn a reward, while incorrect answer will result in loss of points.

According to the outcome, the observer student can tap on the shoulders of the student in the last row to signal them they may not be doing a good job. The students who had their shoulders tapped can then in turn tap the students who they think need to change how they raise their hands, so that they may wake up some students or change how they look at the row in front of them. This can be compared to "Backpropagation." Repeating this game until the performance is improved can be compared to "Training" the parameters. If we try to actually play this out, it would be virtually impossible to get it to work. The essence of deep learning is that having a large enough number of neurons and repeating this over and over will eventually lead to discerning these pictures better, and eventually, to artificial intelligence.

Over time, different approaches to developing neural networks have emerged, and are still emerging. Some approaches even combine different approaches to get a better result, known as Mixture of Experts (MoE) method or model merging,[19] which has gained more popularity in transformers for LLMs. Table 2-5 lists some examples of deep learning algorithms.

Table 2-5: Examples of popular Deep Learning Algorithms

Name	Note
Multi-Layer Perceptron (MLP) (Rosenblatt[20], 1958)	- Perceptron (neural network with multiple input and one output) with more than 1 hidden layer
Self-Organizing Maps (Kohonen[21], 1990)	- Reduces high-dimension data to lower-dimension maps to enable visualization
Recurrent Neural Network (RNN) (Bengio[22], 1994)	- Useful for data that has order, such as language – some of the training in the past is remembered to affect current prediction
Spiking Neural Network (SNN) (Maass[23], 1997)	- Node activation works asynchronously to incorporate the concept of time, to make it even more similar to human brain
Long Short Term Memory Network (LSTM) (Hochreiter & Schmidhuber[24], 1997)	- A type of RNN, has a longer-term memory to alleviate the shortcoming of RNN in reduced performance when relevant data is far away
Restricted Boltzmann Machine (RBM), Deep Belief Network (DBN) (Hinton[25], 2006)	- RBM: 2 layers that have no direction (hidden layer, visible layer), with no connections within the same layer. Used for both generation (unsupervised learning) and categorization (supervised learning) - DBN: Multi-layer network comprised of RBM as the input layer
Convolutional Neural Network (CNN) (Krizhevsky et. al.[26], 2012)	- To reduce bandwidth in image training, use padding and pooling
Autoencoder, Variational Autoencoder (VAE) (Kingma & Welling[27], 2013)	- Autoencoder is comprised of encoder and decoder, and used to reduce the dimension of data - VAE uses similar principle but uses decoder to generate new data instead of reducing the dimension of data
Generative Adversarial Network (GAN) (Goodfellow et. al.[28], 2014)	- 2 models of generating and discriminating models compete while training

3. Large Language Models (LLMs) and General World Models (GWMs)

Most AI in development today is based on deep learning, and more specifically, a class of deep learning called foundation models,[29] which are built from unlabeled data using self-supervision, and may serve as basis for a wide variety of applications. Generative AI is a type of foundation model that uses GANs and auto encoders, and it has emerged as one of the more advanced types of AI available. One of the most popular Generative AI model is the Large Language Model (LLM), which uses an architecture called transformers. The concept of transformers was introduced by Google[30] in 2017, and uses self-attention to remember data elements that are farther away. For example, in the sentence "I went to a BTS concert yesterday, and met students from all around the world while there," the word "there" refers to the words "BTS concert," but the methods used prior to transformers had a harder time correctly understanding this relationship when the words became farther apart. It has since replaced the convolutional neural networks (CNN) and the recurrent neural networks (RNN) as the most popular type of AI algorithm. One of the biggest benefits of LLM is that it does not require data to be labeled.[31]

Multimodal is another direction AI has been advancing, as AI could turn text inputs into images and videos, or AI could see an image and describe the scene. Such AI with a more general simulation of the world is referred to as General World Models (GWM). LLMs and GWMs also receives much attention for its potential to be used in a variety of everyday tasks that humans carry out, such as to read and generate text, browse the internet, communicate with other LLMs, use other software, generate images and videos, hear, speak, generate music, and customized for specific tasks. Some people may even think LLMs and GWMs may be close enough to get us to AGI. There are also researches that appear to suggest the AI technology is closing in on self-improvement in domains that offer a reward function.[32]

The modes of interaction with computers has evolved over time, as the PC operating systems in the '80s, such as MS-DOS, interacted with humans mainly through keyboard, and then the widespread of Windows led to popularization of mouse in the '90s, and then in 2000s the popularity of iPhones led to include touch as well. The future operating systems based on LLMs and GWMs may mainly interact with humans in even more natural fashion, using speech, gestures and facial expressions or even images or videos of surroundings as inputs. These advances may open new possibilities for today's popular apps. For example, while one of today's several popular SNS apps can all let you upload interesting video clips, but you have to take those videos and select them. Eventually, we may even see SNS apps in devices using LLM or GWM-based OS that can keep track of your environment along with you throughout the day and take videos at the right moments even without you having to take out the phone from the pocket.

Meanwhile, in the quest to build AI with general intelligence, there have been suggestions that we need to pay more attention to how humans reason and think. First, we may categorize human thinking into two groups as suggested by Daniel Kahneman,[33] where in System 1, or Fast Thinking, operates automatically and quickly, and in System 2, or Slow Thinking, needs more attention and deliberation. LLMs of today may share more similarity with System 1, while new more advanced projects attempt to incorporate the characteristics of the System 2. Second, another characteristic may be how humans can learn new knowledge and apply it into unrelated areas; Energy-Based Models[34] (EBM) and diffusion-based transformer[35] SORA are examples of attempts to create more abstract layers to help AI move closer to applying knowledge in unrelated *latent* space. As an example of recent approaches that incorporate these notions, rumored projects such as OpenAI Q-star (Q*), thought to mix the self-rewarding system of AlphaGo with another approach for algorithms used for route optimization, may enable AI to reason to solve complex math questions, and received media attention as a step towards AGI.

2.4 The Present of AI: (2) AI Hardware

If all of the algorithms are the software that enables AI, hardware is the actual physical manifestation of such AI. Since AI can be compared to a brain, only the processing units are required for developing AI. However, humans interact with our environment through other senses as well, such as touch, smell, sound, and vision. Since the cognitive capabilities of AI would also enable humanoid robots that can interact with the environment using different senses to act more similar to how humans interact with our environment, related robot technology is also gaining interest.

1. The Brain: Processing Units

While the types of processing units that we currently have may or may not be sufficient for the AI of the future, this section is for just giving a brief overview[36] of the types of hardware for carrying out the computations required for AI.

First-generation AI processing units: The focus of the original boom of personal computers during the 80s and 90s started with the central processing unit (CPU). As video games and graphics design gained popularity, specialized forms of processing units tailored for parallel computation known as graphics processing units (GPU) were introduced. Whereas CPUs are designed to carry out complex calculations quickly but one at a time, GPUs are intended to carry out simpler but many calculations in parallel. Both CPU and GPUs are considered the first generation processing units in the sense that they were already widely available when machine learning became popular.

Second-generation AI processing units: While CPU and GPU are intended for general computing usage, machine learning can be optimized using dedicated semiconductor designs. Processing units can be evaluated on their processing power in relation to their electric power consumption. While GPU perform better than CPU in deep learning, there are still inefficiencies that could be improved using more specific designs for neural networks, such as the neural processing units (NPU). Examples of NPUs include tensor processing units (TPU) from Google. In the second generation processing units, field-programmable gate array (FPGA) or application specific integrated circuits (ASIC) are used. FPGAs offer more flexibility, while ASICs are customized for specific purposes. Typically, NPUs with less precision is often used for inferences while GPUs with higher precision have been used for training, there have been suggestions that using even less precision such as 1-bit[87] may be good enough for training, which may open the possibility for saving computing resources.

Third-generation AI processing units: As of this writing, the third-gen AI semiconductors are considered still in development. These include memory-centric computing and neuromorphic chips. Processing-in-memory (PIM) chips and non-volatile memory (NVM) are attempts to improve efficiency and reduce power consumption. Neuromorphic chips take customization further, to actually design the chip themselves to mimic neurons in an attempt to increase efficiency. If previous AI processing units simulate neurons in a virtual way, neuromorphic chips attempt to build a silicon version of neurons in a physical way.

Another topic that is becoming more relevant is acquiring enough computational power, also referred to as compute, with obtaining enough chips and electricity has become a type of bottleneck as heavy investments have led to a shortage of supercomputers and infrastructures that supply power to these data centers.

2. The Body: Physical Shape of AI and Humanoid AI Robot

1. No Limitations on What AI May Look Like

There is no limit on what AI robots may look like. As more types of activities are carried out by AI, the physical shapes of AI will diverge for efficiency and to accommodate specific purposes of usage. For business or government uses, the shape could take any form, such as drones for military surveillance, or boxes on wheels for factories and distribution centers.

2. Consumers May Still Prefer Human-Friendly Robots

Meanwhile, consumers will be more likely to be receptive to physical manifestation of AI that looks similar to humans or other familiar shapes and forms, such as cartoon characters. For general consumers, making AI robots humanoid or look familiar to humans has several advantages, including ease of adoption in human-friendly environments, such as houses and offices. We tend to organize our environment most ergonomic for humans – e.g. doors are made to fit most humans, stairs, kitchen and desk heights are all designed for human comfort, etc. We would also feel more comfortable interacting with AI robots that look familiar to us. If some developer designed AI robots to look and act like a form of species not friendly to humans, such as a human-sized grasshopper, crab or a spider, then people may become uncomfortable or put off by them.

2.5 The Present of AI: (3) Data and AI Adoption

If bringing hardware and software together to develop a new AI can be compared to giving birth to a newborn baby, training with data can be compared to going to school to get an education. Just the same as how humans learn different subjects, the kind of data AI trains on determines the types of abilities of AI. What determines the kind of data to train AI depends on the specific uses and applications of AI. Since the amount or types of data that can be used is so vast, this section will briefly give an idea of the types of AI adoption in business and the variety of data in using AI.

1. The Two Modes of AI Adoption: Automation and Augmentation

Before describing how AI is adopted in business, it may help to first provide a larger context by explaining the two general approaches to AI adoption, automation and augmentation.

In *automation*, the objective of AI adoption is to replace human workers. Examples include factory automation, where robots can assemble products, move parts, or conduct quality control checks.

In *augmentation*, AI is typically used as a tool to help human workers perform at a higher level. Examples include using AI driver assistance features in cars, AI editing features in graphics design, or using AI chatbots to create Excel formulas or programming codes.

The distinction between these two methods is not always clear and becomes more so as AI can take on more tasks. The mixtures of these two methods are sometimes referred to as collaboration, where AI and humans work separately but together as if in teams.

One of the major differences between the two is whether the performance or the outcome would depend on the capability of the human involved. In augmentation, the outcome would depend on how well the human can take advantage of AI, while in automation it would not matter. This concept will be re-visited later.

2. Data Perspective: Where and How AI Is Used

AI adoption is becoming more relevant in all of human activities. Table 2-6 lists some of the examples of how AI is being adopted in different industries. We may see how different types of data would be important in these diverse areas.

Table 2-6: Ways AI May Be Adopted in Specific Industries

Where	How
Agriculture	- AI robots that can plant seeds, remove weeds, and harvest
Construction	- AI designs the optimal building and interior layouts - AI tracks building, bridge, and other structural anomalies
Culture and Travel	- AI recommends travel itineraries - AI reconstructs ancient artifacts and translates old writings
Entertainment	- AI Persona (Cyber characters) - AI creates videos from text prompts - AI finds old footages from text or creates movie scenarios
Financial	- Detecting suspicious transactions for fraud and laundering - AI in investment: AI as investment managers, detecting financial statement anomalies, hidden market information - AI in lending: credit rating for individuals and businesses
Government	- AI analyzes traffic patterns, weather, etc. as public service - AI detects drug trafficking, illegal customs, or tax evasion
Electronics	- AI designs circuitry and other product parts
Legal	- AI finds relevant cases and legal codes
Medical and Pharmaceutical	- AI finds potential drugs, useful chemicals and side effects - AI finds health problems from blood samples or images
Politics	- AI predicts election results and designs campaigns
Relationship	- AI matching service, provides dating recommendations
Retail	- AI that can predict what each customer would want and make recommendations that will increase sales - AI that can show how products will look on customers
Security	- AI analyzes surveillance videos in real time for threats or recognize ongoing crimes, faces, fingerprints, fakes, etc.
Sports	- AI Umpires call balls and strikes in pro baseball - AI analyzes athlete movements, activities and strategies
Transportation	- Self-driving cars, trucks - AI vision for traffic violations

From the perspective of managing a company, AI would be adopted in more areas of the business. The following table shows examples of how AI is being adopted in each business area.

Table 2-7: Examples of Areas of AI Adoption within Businesses

Area	Description
Accounting	- AI looks for potential inconsistencies or frauds - AI conducts audit to confirm numbers and avoid mistakes
Finance	- AI predicts financial performances and profitability of firms and projects
Human Resources	- AI interviewer scores how candidates perform - AI does HR performance reviews for bonus, promotions, career track, training - AI reviews resume for potential match for roles - AI does staffing, predicts loss of staff
IT	- AI helps write, maintain, and review codes and programs - AI helps manage network and hardware failures - AI helps enhance security by monitoring real-time data
Legal	- AI predicts potential gain/losses from cases - AI reviews legal documents
Logistics	- AI helps design logistics network flow - AI robots in warehouses, AI sorts packages and packs them - AI robots does last mile delivery to final destination
Management Support	- AI keeps track of relevant news and developments to make timely notifications and update reports - AI assists in purchasing, resources management and other administrative tasks
Manufacturing	- AI helps purchasing and resource planning - AI robots to automate assembly - AI vision for detecting anomaly
Marketing & Sales	- AI enables targeting and segmenting of potential customers - AI determines the best pricing, sales mix, and promotions - AI as a sales rep, AI in customer service, AI contacting potential customers
Product Planning & Design	- AI helps plan through product lifecycle - AI predicts popularity and optimizes product mix, options, and attributes - AI-generated design
R&D	- AI helps ideation, prototyping, and testing of new products and technologies - AI manages development cycles, schedules and calendar

2.6 The Future of AI: (1) AI Development Path

The future of AI can be thought of a little bit differently depending on whether your perspective is close to "what can AI do?" as in the technological perspective, or "how can AI be used in our society?" as in a business perspective. While we will focus on the business perspective as the levels of AI adoption, it would be helpful to first understand the background in the technological perspective. In this section we will examine the technological perspective in ANI-AGI-ASI development path, and examine the potential paths to AGI.

1. Why is AGI important? ANI-AGI-ASI Framework

1) The ANI-AGI-ASI Framework

There are several ways to categorize AI, including Narrow AI vs Wide AI and Weak AI vs Strong AI. The most popular AI categorization is probably the ANI-AGI-ASI framework, where the term "Artificial General Intelligence" was first coined by Mark Gubrud[38] in late 90s but did not initially catch on and then used again independently by Ben Goertzel in his book in 2007.[39] Artificial Narrow Intelligence, or ANI, is a term first used by Ray Kurzweil in his book[40] in 2005, where he used "narrow AI" to indicate the limited types of AI that can only apply its knowledge in a specific context. In contrast, AGI would refer to a system that can apply knowledge learned in one area to a more generalized context.

2) Singularity and ASI

In regards to the technological development path of AI, the most feared tipping point is referred to as 'singularity.' According to many technologists,[41] upon reaching AGI, AGI may automatically go on in a loop of self-improvement, eventually leading to the capabilities of AI to exceed all of the combined intelligence of the humanity. The fear is that ASI will be too powerful for humans to stop its actions or even understand its intentions.

3) Controversy Surrounding the Definition of AGI

A problem of the ANI-AGI-ASI framework is that the definition of AGI is controversial. As people discussed how such an AI could be developed, people went on to suggest different versions of AGI, to narrow down what types of capabilities such an AI should entail. The general public's perception of an advanced AI may have some form of consciousness similar to humans; this is often referred to as human-level AI or human-like AI. Today we have a variety of arguments for different AGI definitions with varying degrees of similarity to humans and technological achievements.

The main controversies surrounding all these variations stems from the vagueness of the definitions, what should be measured, and what the intermediate steps are in reaching AGI. For example, a popular discussion is regarding whether AI having some form of "consciousness" would be required for us to consider it AGI. While most people in the general public would think this would be the version of AI that we will see in the future, the academics in various branches of study have suggested such opinions such as it would not be possible for AI to gain consciousness at all, or AI should be considered if it can apply knowledge in a different context, etc.

4) Definition of AGI used by AI Developers

While the controversy surrounding AGI definition may involve academic scholars and philosophers to determine an abstract approach of what it should be, the AI development firms that are trying to build AGI take a more practical approach. For example, the following table shows the definitions of AGI suggested by Open AI and Google DeepMind, two of the leading AI developers. Their approach to defining AGI involves assessing task performances by comparing it to the performance of the general human population.

Table 2-8: Examples of definitions of AGI used by AI developers

Company	Definition		
OpenAI (2018)[42]	Highly autonomous systems that outperform humans at most economically valuable work		
Google DeepMind (2023)[43]	AGI divided into several levels:		
	Level 0	No AI	
	Level 1 (Emerging AI)	Comparable to an unskilled human	
	Level 2 (Competent AGI)	At least 50th percentile of skilled adults	
	Level 3 (Expert AGI)	At least 90th percentile of skilled adults	
	Level 4 (Virtuoso AGI)	At least 99th percentile of skilled adults	
	Level 5 (ASI)	Outperforms 100% of humans	

2. The Need for a Separate AI Framework for Economics and Business[44]

1) Need for New Framework from Economic Perspective

Readers may notice the definitions of AGI used by OpenAI, a non-profit organization that is widely thought to be one of the current leaders in AI development, incorporates some elements of business and economic activity, by defining it in terms of economic value. Some may argue against using this definition because it can still be considered vague in the sense that "most" or "economic value" can be interpreted to mean different things to different situations. This would result in disagreements regarding whether AGI is reached.

2) Need for New Framework from Business Perspective

One of the main differences between using a technical term such as AGI and changing its definition to fit the business world and using a term specifically designed for business, such as Level 1 AI Adoption, is on who will decide whether we have reached the next level. In essence, the developer of the AI will assess whether we have reached AGI, while the businesses that deploy AI will determine whether we have reached the Level 2 AI Adoption. AGI may still be used for Level 1 Adoption, while AI before AGI may be used for Level 2 Adoption: the businesses will decide how AI will be used inside the firm.

While the academics and developers are discussing what AGI should entail, what would be more interesting to the general public may be if or when AGI can be reached. In the next section, let us examine what would be necessary to reach AGI and then the implications for investing in AI development.

3. What Would We Need to Do to Reach AGI?

Many people are playing the game of guessing how long it will take to reach AGI. One of the well-publicized predictions is from scientist and futurist Ray Kurzweil, where he estimated AGI could be reached by 2029 and the Singularity by 2045.[45] His predictions are based on such factors as the progress of hardware capabilities measured against what would be needed to simulate neurons or the molecules that makes up the neurons.

While such predictions regarding timing may be relevant from a scientific perspective, we may consider from the perspective of a business manager; we may play another game possibly similar to Tic-Tac-Toe or drawing a probability tree, where we consider the path to reaching AGI or Human-Level AI. Many people would consider the development of such AI to be an important milestone. To achieve AGI or similar concept of advanced AI, the technology levels of both hardware and software would have to reach above a certain point.

In conceptualizing developing human-like AI, we can consider all potential possibilities in the following way:

1.   AGI *is not* Achievable
2.   AGI *is* Achievable
     2.1   Current Technology *is* Sufficient
     2.2   Current Technology *is Not* Sufficient
          2.2.1 Only *Hardware* Tech is Not Sufficient
          2.2.2 Only *Software* Tech is Not Sufficient
          2.2.3 *Both* Hardware and Software Tech is Not Sufficient

We may also represent the possibilities in a tree shape to make it easier to understand.

Figure 2-3: Potential Paths to AGI

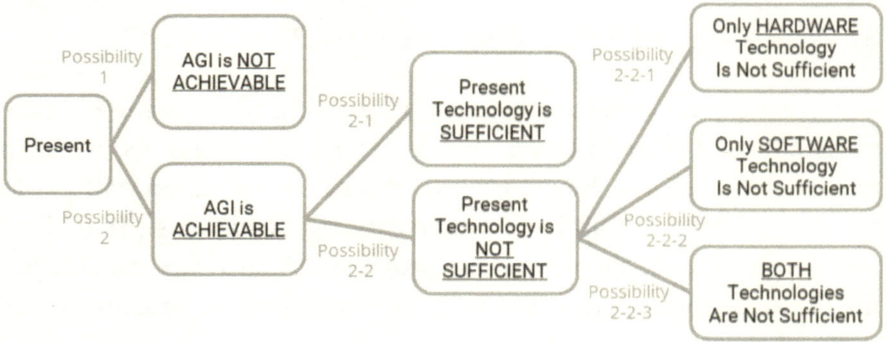

If AGI is not achievable, then it would not be necessary to examine further, even though we may as well consider whether hardware or the software is the limiting factor.

If AGI is achievable, then we can summarize all potential possibilities in the following table, where only four possible cases would exist.

Table 2-9: Summary of Potential Possibilities of Developing AGI

		Software	
		Currently Inadequate	Currently Adequate
Hardware	Currently Inadequate	Software and Hardware Neither Adequate (Case 4)	Software Adequate Hardware Inadequate (Case 2)
	Currently Adequate	Hardware Adequate Software Inadequate (Case 3)	Software and Hardware Both adequate (Case 1)

Now that we have considered all potential paths to developing AGI, we can examine each possibility.

Case 1: Enough Software and Hardware to Develop AGI

In the lower right panel, if both current software and hardware are already adequate for developing AGI, then it implies it is just a matter of time before AGI will be achieved with current technology. This would indicate we can create AGI with appropriate data and capital. There are speculations that some projects at leading AI development companies indicate we have already gotten close to reaching AGI. Since us outsiders do not yet know the truth, only time may be able to tell.

Case 2: Enough Software but Not Hardware to Reach AGI

When we compare the development or innovations that come in software and hardware, we think of incremental or improvements in smaller but steady steps in hardware, while we expect some sort of conceptual breakthrough in software. This does not rule out the possibility that some type of conceptual breakthrough in how hardware is designed may be necessary, completely different from what we have now, such as quantum computing. In the top right panel, if we need breakthrough in hardware, then we might experience a more gradual change in the expectation of when AGI can be reached, similar to walking step by step through a flight of stairs.

Case 3: Enough Hardware but Not Software to Reach AGI

In contrast, in the bottom left panel, where we already have adequate hardware and would need only a breakthrough in software, we may experience a more abrupt change of expectation regarding when AGI can be reached. For example, we may think AGI is far away, but then an unexpected breakthrough in software algorithm can suddenly make AGI surprisingly near.

Case 4: Not Enough Hardware / Software to Reach AGI

Lastly, the farthest case would leave us with the top left panel, where neither current hardware nor software would be considered adequate. In this case, our timeline to AGI would be the longest.

Case 5: AGI is Not Achievable

Just as a comparison, if AGI is not achievable, then we could draw a similar table where the reason we cannot reach AGI is because of hardware only, software only, or both. There could even be cases where we have both adequate software and hardware technology, but not enough data or capital to make AGI a reality.

In the next segment, we will examine this topic from a slightly different perspective of investors.

2.7 The Future of AI: (2) Who Would Develop AGI First?

1. Evaluating the Paths to AGI

We may repeat a similar analysis from the perspective of the investor. From an investor's perspective, investing in the first company to develop AGI may be an important topic. As we inch closer to AGI, it may be possible to forecast who may be first to develop AGI if the path to AGI is predictable. It would be likely to be an AI developer with the most computing power, best algorithm, and most data. On the other hand, the first to develop AGI may be a lesser-known entity if it is harder to predict what is required.

From a generalized viewpoint AI is created from two separate areas of design: software and hardware. From this, we can logically deduce there are only five possible scenarios that can happen:

1. *(Current technology is sufficient) AGI can already be developed with current technology*
2. *(Only hardware is sufficient) Humanity need only a breakthrough in software*
3. *(Only software is sufficient) Humanity need only a breakthrough in hardware*
4. *(Both not sufficient) Humanity need breakthroughs in both software and hardware*
5. *(Impossible) AGI cannot be developed*

With the above possible scenarios in mind, we can examine each possibility. Breakthrough in software generally requires a new concept or idea, which may not necessarily be proportional to the amount of capital invested. For example, some teenager in a small corner of the world may develop a novel concept for a new type of AI algorithm, and may even be able to test it on a PC or a server at little cost. In comparison, a Big Tech may spend a large amount of capital and still not be able to come up with the same breakthrough.

As for hardware development, a whole infrastructure and network of different companies typically have to work together to make incremental improvement; the amount of advancement would be more proportional to the amount of capital invested. While the speed of software advancement make happen in chunks or steps, the speed of hardware advancement may happen more gradually.

As described previously, current iteration of AI development focuses on simulating the activities of neurons. We do not know if this is a sufficient approach to developing AGI. To be able to tell whether software is sufficient, we would have to test it on a hardware that is sufficient for AGI. Since there are more neurons and synapses in the brain than can be effectively simulated by currently available hardware, we may assume the current available hardware is not sufficient in simulating all of the neurons in the brain[46]. Maybe a breakthrough such as quantum computing is what is needed for AGI. To be conservative in our analysis, we may have to assume both are not currently sufficient for AGI.

Table 2-10: Time and Capital Required for Reaching AGI

		Breakthrough in Hardware	
		Needed	Not Needed
Break-through in Software	Needed	Capital: Most Investment Time: Most Uncertain	Capital: Less Investment Time: Highly Uncertain
	Not Needed	Capital: High Investment Time: Less Uncertain	Capital: Least Investment Time: Shortest Expected

2. Quantifying Present Location in the Path to AGI

Since it may help investors to quantify the situation, we can also try to quantify the current situation, by expressing our location as a number between 0 and 1, where 1 would mean reaching AGI. We can let "Software Technology" and "Hardware Technology" to each equal 1 when it is sufficient for AGI. Then we can say both are currently less than 1. When each software and hardware reaches 1, then the multiplied value will reach 1, so we may express this multiplied number as the current location in pursuing AGI. From this line of thought, we may have a situation when one of the two technologies is larger than 1 and the other is smaller than 1, such that the multiplied value would still be 1. We may wonder if this situation could also be possible, where reaching AGI is not dependent on both software and hardware reaching a certain point, but would also be dependent on the value of the other, so that a deficiency in one side may be offset by extra achievements in the other. Maybe we will eventually find out.

3. Training AGI

We may reach a point where we have solved all the technological problems related to software and hardware. There may be a variety of opinions regarding when this would be, including opinions that we have already reached the point, to other opinions that AGI is not achievable. Some people may think it will take only a few months or years, while others may think it will take decades or longer. Once we have solved the technological problems, the next issue that we would have to consider is training the AI using data, which would also involve a large amount of financial capital.

4. Other Factors for Investors to Consider

There would be other factors that come into focus from the point of view of investors.

1) Developing AGI Unintentionally or by Mistake

First, training AI with data is an activity that widely occurs even for firms that are not trying to develop AGI. If we cannot predict how AGI will appear, maybe there could be the possibility that AGI gets developed unintentionally or by mistake by AI developers that are not particularly trying to develop AGI. In what could be compared to winning the lottery, maybe experimenting with more variety of approaches could be similar to buying more lottery tickets.

2) Data or Capital Holding Back AGI Development

Second, there could be a situation where the constraining resource may be the availability of data. Since most of the data used to train AI is man-made and is limited in quantity, we may conceive of situations where the availability of data or some other resource is the limiting factor in developing AGI. To offset this problem, approaches such as creating synthetic data may be introduced. There are other factors such as the cost of acquisition, since higher-quality data may be more likely to be copyrighted or have to be proprietarily created by experts. Even if there are enough data available somewhere in the world, the particular company developing AI may not have access to it due to cost constraints.

3) Potential for Synergy among Software, Hardware, and Data Capabilities

Third, there may be a possibility that the software, hardware, and data need to be developed in a tightly knit design. We may think of situations where the hardware or software has to collect data, or when the software has to be designed using specific hardware, or vice versa. In the earlier part of the PC computing industry, many people thought the specialization of designing chips and the OS with Intel and Microsoft was the superior approach compared to the Apple's integrated approach of doing it all, until Apple found a way to aggregate its hardware, software and the Apple Store to gain competitive edge by creating an ecosystem.

Similarly, it may be possible developing AGI would require one company to carry out all of the three activities in-house to create synergy, rather than focusing on only one of the three areas of software, hardware, and data. If the performance disparities from mismatch increases, such that using one company's software requires 100 amount of data while a competitor's software requires only 20 to achieve a given level of performance, or if one company's software requires 100 units of hardware performance whereas using another company's software requires only 20 units to achieve a similar level of AI performance, then the interaction between the three areas may have to be taken more seriously.

In summary, investors may ask the following general questions before making investments related to AGI development.

- *Do we have sufficient software? = Is published or open-source software enough to create AGI?*
- *Do we have sufficient hardware? = Is hardware from third-party provider enough to create AGI?*
- *Do we have sufficient data? = How much financial capital is required to acquire sufficient data?*
- *Do we have sufficient capital? = Is there enough financial capital to acquire necessary resources in each area?*

To think about which AI developer would lead the development, investors may ask the following questions:

- *Which factor among hardware, software, and data has the most importance?*
- *Can a specific firm gain or already have competitive advantage over other developers?*
- *Is there need or potential for synergy in having capabilities for all of the three factors of hardware, software and data?*

In general, larger amount of financial capital would be necessary to develop hardware technology compared to developing software technology. As a consequence, we would be likely to predict that the candidate to develop the first AGI could be limited in number due to hardware rather than software. If hardware is the lagging factor, than more people or companies with software that can enable AGI could be waiting for the hardware to catch up. Lastly, if both AGI-enabling software and hardware are developed by separate entities and become commercially available, then the advantage may be with the company that has the largest amount of capital.

5. Can Governments Accelerate the Building of AGI?

Similar to the Race to the Moon in the 1960s or the Arms Race during the 1980s between the US and the Soviet Union, we may consider the case of the race to build AGI becoming a competition between some regimes or countries, where the question may become "which country will develop AGI first?" In the end, if it becomes a competition between countries, it will come down to whose regime is more conducive to building the leading AI, leading to AGI. In other words, it would come down to who would be able to build the "No. 1" of AI faster.

The reason why this question may become relevant is because developing AGI may be considered a matter of national security at some point. If this becomes the case, we may consider two opposite approaches to building AGI faster.

1) <u>Concentrate</u> all the resources of the country into one big effort
2) <u>Diversify</u> available resources of the country to foster more competition and innovation

We may think that countries with centralized planning economies would prefer the first approach, while countries with free markets would prefer the second approach. On one hand, we may think that a regime building a centralized planning approach to developing AI may have an advantage in terms of having a larger percentage of a nation's resource put into building the AI. This approach would be especially advantageous if we can already predict the correct path to reach AGI, such that what would be required is to move faster towards a known goal. It may be also necessary for less developed countries with limited resources, if we consider this as a project that has a minimum size of investment required to make an impact. On another hand, it may be more important to have better incentive system such as the market economy to encourage innovation to build the leading AI. This approach may be more advantageous if we do not know which direction will lead to AGI, such that it may be more important to test out different approaches in the most efficient manner.

2.8 The Future of AI: (3) What Is the Ultimate Form of AI? Absolute AI

From a technology perspective, the most popular framework is the ANI-AGI-ASI framework, where the ultimate form of AI is typically known as Artificial Superintelligence, or ASI, which occurs after AGI reaches singularity, where we conceptualize the capabilities of AI to exceed the combined capabilities of mankind.

In previous research,[47] I introduced an alternative approach to categorizing the ultimate form of AI from a business perspective, using the concepts of Relative AI and Absolute AI. While AGI and ASI are defined in terms of performance that considers AI relative to humans, Relative AI and Absolute AI are defined in terms of AI performance in relation to data.

1. (Background) The Source of Differences in Human Minds and in AI: Experiences and Data

1) Different Experiences → Differences in Opinions

Before we consider how AI performances would differ, we may first think about how humans would differ in performance. We can consider our past experiences as one of the main causes of our differences in thinking, and not all knowledge or experiences would bear the same importance. For example, the Apollo moon landing is considered a transformative event where everyone "remembers where they were when it happened" kind of moment. But since people of the following generation did not experience the event as it unfolded, our feelings about it would be much less than those of the people who can actually remember it happening in real time.

For my generation in the US, the terrorist attacks on September 11th, 2001, may be the equivalent of such event. I vividly remember seeing it on TV, as I was a college senior at Virginia. On that morning I had a class to attend; I had just woken up and when I turned on the TV to watch while eating breakfast, the first plane had just crashed into the World Trade Center and the news was showing the footage over and over. As I was about to leave to go to class, I watched the second plane crash in real time. I was wondering if some kind of war had started; especially because a few years prior another "everyone remembers where they were" type of news event occurred in South Korea when Kim Il-Sung, the founder of North Korea, died and people were on high alert for war. Anyway, because I was taught to go to class no matter what, I still went to class, but I was the only student that showed up that morning among the class of around 30, another example of how everyone's past experiences lead to different actions. I am sure the family and friends of the victims or people who experienced it firsthand at the scene in New York would remember it with even more clarity and emotions. On the other hand, as for the younger generations who had only heard about it, they may not share the same feelings for the event as someone who experienced learning about it in real time.

Another big world event that I can remember is when the Tiananmen Square, famous for the man standing in front of the tank,[48] occurred. Even though I did not fully grasp the importance of the particular event as I was in elementary school, I remember repeatedly seeing the long news coverage that went on for days, especially because we only had a few TV channels back then and it was the only thing on TV. Nowadays, people who are older than me may remember it well, while younger generations, especially those who live in China, may not even know about it since it is one of the topics that is not allowed for discussion; there are even suggestions that including this word should be encouraged in books or movies since it will lead their government to crack down on the piracy of works that reference this event.

For humans, we may learn more from experiences that leave more impressions on us, and the path of those experiences may matter. As a result, children who was inspired by the moon landing may be more inclined to grow up to become a rocket scientist, while children who was more worried about wars or terrorist attacks may grow up to serve in the military or even build a nuclear bunker. Research suggests people who experienced the Great

Depression in the 1930s were more likely to save and prepare for hard times than people who did not experience harsh times.[49]

We may apply the same principle to developing AI; we may think of the events 1) Apollo Moon Landing, 2) 9/11, 3) Kim Il-Sung and, 4) Tiananmen Square as data inputs to an AI that may lead to different decisions or results from AI. As a result, an advanced AI built in China may omit the data on Tiananmen and be more inclined to prefer communist ideas in general. If a terrorist group decided to build an advanced AI, it may input the data on 9/11 as a positive action and the AI may be more inclined to prefer destructive actions in general. If North Korea was building an AI, the data entered would have Kim Il-Sung as the most important person of all time, etc. In essence, bias in AI input would probably follow the bias or intentions of humans that build the AI through data. From this observation, we can surmise that advanced AI may act in ways that may not satisfy all people because of our differences, even if it satisfies the developers or vice versa. For some readers, it may be unacceptable that AI may have these inclinations. However, these "differences" in perspectives are distinct from judging what is "good or bad," or even trying to attain "diversity" of opinions. The point here is not to judge the actions of AI, but to emphasize the fact that what AI does will be affected by the input data.

2) Same Experiences → Differences in Opinions

As we accumulate more experiences, our biases in understanding only a limited aspect of the world will lead us to situations where we incorporate information in a selective manner; in this case, even the same experiences will lead people to reach different conclusions.

For example, in the aftermath of the World Trade Center collapse, there could be a diverse range of reactions. First, we may think of some of the lessons of the lines of thinking of the majority:
1) (Terrorism is Bad) Use of violence cannot be justified
2) (Sad for Victims) Condolences for the victims and their families
3) (Rescuers were the Heroes) Who enables our society to function

Meanwhile, there could have been skeptics or complainers who may instead reach other types of minority conclusions, such as:

4) (Airport Security was Weak) The airports and airlines should have been able to deter the planes from being hijacked

5) (Surveillance was Inadequate) The governments should have kept a better track of the terrorists to catch them before their act

6) (WTC was Structurally Unsound) WTC should have been able to withstand those impacts and not collapse

7) (Response was Incorrect) The government should have called for immediate evacuation, not send first respondents into the buildings

Furthermore, there could have been conspiracy theorists who instead argue for alternative explanations for the event, such as:

8) (This was All a "Show") WTC housed important documents or financial transactions that needed to be cancelled or hidden

9) ("They" Needed a War) Some unknown group of people needed a war for financial gains

Lastly, there could even have been people who outright supported the causes of the terrorists, such as:

10) (US are Imperialists) the US deserved this for whatever they had done in the past

From this one event, we may create a long list of different conclusions that could go on and on. Again, the point here is not to judge whether these conclusions are right or wrong, but to see that there may be a wide variety of differences of opinions even when people are given the same fact, some of which may be mutually exclusive. Similar to how humans may reach different conclusions from the same information from our own biases, we may infer that AI may also reach different conclusions from same facts based on its own biases and idiosyncrasies.

2. The Concept of Relative AI

What we currently have in the advanced forms of AI is a version of deep learning, and these AI have to go through a learning process. This process can be seen in humans as well. When we are born, we do not know anything about the world, but as we grow up, we experience, learn and meet new things, ideas, and people. The flip side of this coin is that people meet different people, learn different knowledge, and go through different experiences, leading each of us to be unique and different. As a result, humans have different opinions. If we apply this principle to AI, AI gains different knowledge though training data, and thus AI with different training data will have differences of opinions and capabilities. Even if AI is trained with the same data, the design of AI or some other factors such as hardware may lead AI to be different from one another. We may define these types of AI whose performance and capabilities would depend on data as "Relative AI" or "Relative Orientation AI"

3. The Concept of Absolute AI

The concept opposite of Relative AI would be the type of AI that has learned all of the "real truths" about the world in some way that all of the conclusions or decisions of different AI converge to become one and the same, essentially leading to a single version of an AI. Conceptually, AI cannot improve further because it already knows everything, or the "absolute truths" about the world. In this sense, it may also be referred to as an "Absolute Orientation AI."

To explain it differently, we may think that the advancements in AI technology would lead newer AI to be less affected by individual data. Eventually, the impact of data on AI will converge to 0, where we may infer that AI has learned all of the "real truths" about the world. As a result, all opinions of all Absolute AI would be one and the same. We may refer to this most advanced form of AI as the "Maximum AI," "Final AI," "Last AI," or even the "Artificial God."

4. Comparison of ANI-AGI-ASI and Relative-Absolute AI Frameworks

From this new perspective, there may be something else even after appearance of ASI, in what is known as the Absolute AI. Figure 2-4 shows how Relative-Absolute AI framework, which categorizes AI based on its attribute in relation to data, can be mapped to the ANI-AGI-ASI framework, which categorizes AI based on its performance in relation to humans. Absolute AI is a concept that refers to an AI that cannot improve any further. Since we do not have AGI or ASI, it is hard to tell whether an Absolute AI would appear as the final version of ASI, or is something entirely different. To compare this relationship to something we are familiar, we may think of ASI as the different gods in Greek Mythology, where there are multiple gods who all have capabilities exceeding those of humans, while Absolute AI would be more similar in concept of a single all-mighty god who knows and can do everything. Throughout this book, the meaning and significance of this ultimate form of AI will be discussed more in detail.

Figure 2-4: Categorizing AI by Relativity to Humans and Data[50]

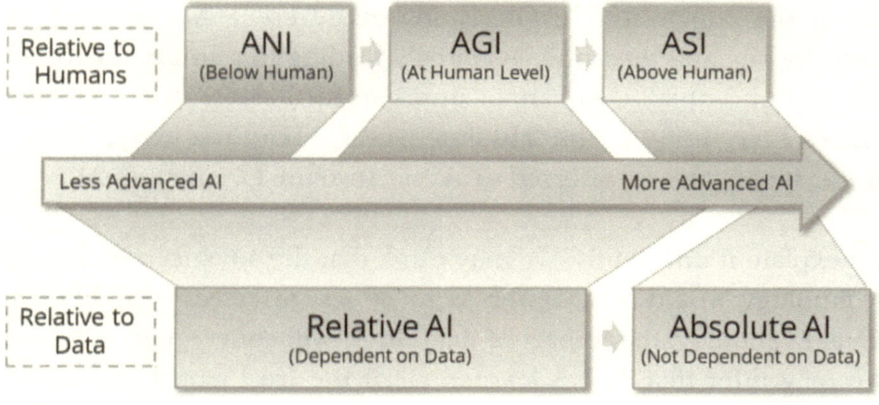

5. The Ultimate Form of Business AI Adoption

From a technological perspective, there is a fear for the appearance of ASI, that ASI may threaten humanity. One of the most popular explanations to describe the situation is the comparison against ants.[51] If we are building a new city near an ant colony, ants are not going to understand what humans are doing, even if it is smart for an ant. If an ASI that makes humans about only as smart as ants compared to it, then we may never comprehend what the ASI is doing or what it intends to do.

Let's change focus and consider the business perspective of AI adoption. From a business or economic perspective, the ultimate form of AI adoption for a firm is reaching a monopoly that cannot be reverted, which can be referred to as "irreversible AI monopoly." In such a state, the firm with the monopoly may basically have no current competition but also no potential for future competition as well, which some may consider market failure. If this concept is extended to the general society, it may be referred to as "irreversible AI dictatorship," where a dictatorship, once achieved, cannot be removed or recovered in perpetuity.

One of the main points of this book is that this irreversible AI monopoly may appear before the appearance of some ultimate forms AI such as ASI or an Absolute AI, or possibly even before the appearance of an AGI with Consciousness. While many people have already warned about the potential dangers of AGI, not as much interest have been shown in the possibility of an irreversible AI monopoly that may appear before AGI.

We have now finished a brief overview of the past, present, and the future of AI in terms of technology. In the following sections, we will explore the exciting topic of the pattern of how AI adoption may progress as AI technology advances, using the 4 Levels of AI Adoption Pyramid.

CHAPTER 3
PROLIFERATION OF AI IN LEVEL 1 AI ADOPTION

Level 1 AI Adoption Introduction

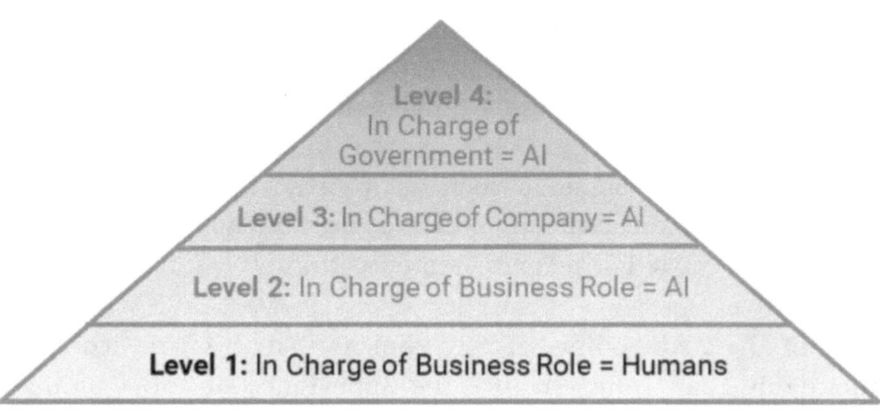

Level 1 AI Adoption Motto:
"If You Can Imagine It, You Can Do It"

(A) Overview

In the beginning of AI adoption, AI would assist humans in business activities. Humans may use AI as a type of a tool to improve productivity, and AI would not have gained enough dependability to perform tasks without human intervention. AI may also help humans carry out tasks previously not achievable. In this level of AI adoption, the interest among individuals and companies will increase rapidly as AI may help increase productivity in a dramatic manner. In Level 1 AI Adoption, humans will be competing against other humans, and AI will only assist.

(B) Vocabulary for AI in This Level

The different modes of AI adoption can be broadly categorized as "automation" and "augmentation." In Level 1 AI Adoption, humans are in charge of business roles and AI serve those humans, so we may refer to them as "Assistant AI," "Co-Pilot AI," or "Augmenting AI."

(C) Implications on Business and Economy

In Level 1 AI Adoption, human productivity is improved with the use of AI. We may express this notion with the concept of "AI Magnification Factor."

The ultimate form of augmentation would be "1-Person Company" (1PC), but in Level 1 AI Adoption only "1-Person Team" or "1-Person Department" would be more likely to be feasible for larger operations.

(D) Technological Requirements and Implications

Even though AGI is not required in Level 1 AI Adoption, it does not preclude the use of AGI in this level. As AI technology advances, Level 1 Adoption would enable more interesting shapes of AI applications for achievement-oriented people.

AI ADOPTION LEVEL 1: (A) DESCRIPTION OF THIS LEVEL

3.1 (In Charge of Business Roles = Humans) AI That Assists Human Workers

1. (The Beginning of AI Adoption) AI begins to impact productivity

As AI technology improves, AI can be applied to more diverse areas of our lives. In the beginning, whatever AI technology that was developed could do interesting things, but did not possess much business applicability. An example would be the first checkers-playing AI[1] developed in 1959. We could refer to AI of this stage as "toys." In economic terms, AI could not help improve worker productivity in a meaningful way. We may describe the situation as the following expression:

Productivity of [Human + Toy AI] = Productivity of [Human]

At some point, AI development would arrive at a point where using AI may actually help improve productivity. This is the point where the "game of business AI adoption" would actually begin. Examples of these applications of AI include the Expert Systems of the 1970s and 80s. We can categorize these AI as useful "tools" that enhance productivity. In economic terms, AI now may help improve worker productivity so that the workers who do use AI would have higher performance than workers who do not use AI. We can describe the situation as the following expression:

Productivity of [Human + Tool AI] > Productivity of [Human]

As more time goes by, there would be more improvements to AI technology. Once people realize AI may help them earn higher profit, people would begin a rapid mass adoption of AI, across a diverse areas of society. Just like how people in 1840s rushed to California to find gold, it could be considered a "start the race" kind of moment. Some even refer to this change as the 4th Industrial Revolution.[2] Just as when people's productivity vastly improves when a worker digging with a shovel begins to work with an excavator, the productivity of a worker who begins to work with AI may be improved to a level that may be hard to comprehend today.

2. AI Adoption Level 1 Overview

In the early version of AI adoption, advancements in AI technology may not be sufficient to let AI carry out business functions with dependable levels of proficiency, requiring human oversight. In AI Adoption Level 1, the typical method will involve humans leading the interaction with AI. Humans can take advantage of the AI capabilities as a type of tool to enhance their own performance in augmentation, or let AI take over parts of a business role. AI built for this level of adoption can be categorized as "Assistant AI,"[3] "Co-Pilot AI," or "Helper AI." AI will help in certain areas of a human's business role. AI provides the effect of strengthening the skillsets of workers, so these uses can also be referred to as "Augmenting AI," "Complementary AI," "Supplementary AI," or "Reinforcement AI."

An early example of Level 1 AI Adoption would be AI that generates answers to prompts; well-publicized examples at work include using ChatGPT for programmers to create new code. In this scenario, humans create relevant questions. In another scenario, humans may define what tasks AI should carry out, maybe on a repeated basis, as when human workers in the construction industry train AI to perform visual recognition to review critical structures of a building for any potential dangers, or in manufacturing to predict defects of products. In this early stage, AI would be especially useful for its capabilities that complement humans, such as forecasting and pattern recognition from large amounts of data. In finance, AI can be deployed to carry out stock price forecasting, or keep track of relevant news to gain an edge over other investors.

3.2 Major Characteristics of Level 1 AI Adoption

AI Adoption Level 1 Specific Details

In Level 1 AI Adoption, the human workers would be in charge of business roles. In the earlier stage of AI adoption, due to limitations in AI technology, to maximize profit it would be beneficial for humans to give specific directions to AI or AI would be designed to carry out specific or limited scope of activities. Even though AI may gain more autonomy as technology advances, the authority will still fall on the human in Level 1 Adoption. Within this context, we can think of how AI would be adopted in workplace in the following five dimensions.

(1) Human and AI Interaction

First, in terms of the nature of *human and AI interaction*, humans in essence would use AI as a tool as the overall relationship is led by humans. AI's contribution can be conceptualized as an assistant or a collaborator where AI helps the human towards enabling success in a business role. More specifically, the design of the business role would be managed by humans, who ultimately decide how AI and humans will work together, as humans in effect are giving direction for AI. Humans are responsible for making the final decisions of the role. AI would assist humans by presenting information for review, generate options for selection, or keep track of changes to direct attention of humans for further review.[4]

(2) Scope of AI Application

Second, the *scope of AI application* is limited, while it would increase as technology allows. This applies to both the scope of application for individual instances of AI would be limited, and the availability of AI, which may be expressed as the ratio of number of business roles that could be taken over by AI to the total number of business roles, would be limited. The dependability of AI in carrying out the role may be limited.

(3) Final Authority and Responsibility

Third, the *final authority and responsibility* would be all on humans. Humans in charge of the business role have full final decision as well as responsibility, while AI has limited responsibility or authority. In essence, all problems caused from using the AI in business ultimately fall on some human. Companies or persons who created the AI may also have some form of authority or responsibility over the design and be also responsible for such problems as design flaws.

(4) Strategic Planning Activities

Fourth, in terms of involvement in *strategic planning activities*, in the earlier stage of Level 1 Adoption AI may not have the capacity to carry out business planning activities and even after it gains such capacity it would not have the necessary authority other than be involved in helping humans carry out those activities. Humans will ultimately determine what the company will do, and how it will do them.

(5) Innovation by AI

Lastly, AI will not *achieve innovation* by itself but will help humans be more innovative, in what can be categorized as "augmented innovation." This does not imply that AI would not have the capability to achieve innovation from a technological standpoint; it is just that AI will not have the authority to bring innovation by itself.

Table 3-1: Major Characteristics of Level 1 AI Adoption

Category	Characteristics	Description / Examples of Activities
Human-AI Interaction	- AI assist humans as master and servant or as a tool - AI collaborate as subordinate - Humans lead interaction	- Humans: decide which functions AI will carry out, design role, and give direction for AI - AI: present figures or analyses to help humans decide, present different options for humans to select, direct attention of humans for review, etc.
Scope of AI Application	- AI is used within a limited scope - Applicable areas expand as enabled by new technology	- AI development is ongoing but limited - AI shows limited dependability in role
Override Authority / Responsi-bility	- Human in charge has full final decision authority and responsibility - AI has limited authority over decision and responsibility	- Problems caused from using AI falls on the human in charge of the role (caveat emptor) - Company that created AI may have responsibility
Strategic Planning Activities	- Humans decide what the firm will do and how to run it	- AI assist or augment humans in planning activities - AI by itself cannot complete planning activities
Innovation by AI	- Humans are in charge of innovation - (Augmented Innovation)	- AI assist or augment humans in innovation process - AI by itself generally do not have to have capability to innovate

3.3 (Prerequisite) What Would Enable This Level?

As explained in Chapter 2, the main premise of AI compared to other types of computer programs is that AI does not require specific programming to carry out certain tasks. Whereas it may have required programmers to write out 100 or more different parts of programs to carry out 100 different possible steps of a task, AI would eliminate the need for all these efforts.

Eventually, development in AI technology may lead to a direction where it may not even require human efforts to train AI, in effect letting AI figure out what to learn, also known as self-supervised learning[5].

Our economy is designed to allocate more investments to more profitable endeavors. Considering the amount of potential profit AI development may bring, investments in AI may exponentially grow in the early stage of Level 1 Adoption. With growing investments, the speed of AI development could in turn accelerate further.

On a side note, from a business perspective, we may describe the advancements in AI as a reduction of the "cost of intelligence." This may be viewed as a perspective of the supplier. From the perspective of the business user, we may eventually describe the contribution of AI in some other economic terms, such as the "cost of innovation."

3.4 What Would Become Possible in This Level?

In the early stage of AI adoption where AI is used as a tool, the value of AI adoption may be categorized as qualitative and quantitative benefits. For example, qualitatively, AI would be able to 1) discern patterns impossible for humans to find, while quantitatively, AI may 2) delve through more data, 3) carry out more repetitive tasks, and 4) reduce the completion time of complex tasks. As a result, AI would not only help reduce the human effort required to carry out given tasks, but also turn previously economically infeasible ideas into economically viable tasks.

While machines and various types of IT devices have been used in our everyday lives both on and off work, AI would enable a new dimension of use of machines in what we could have only possible in our imagination. The beginning of AI adoption started from simple tasks that still had been impossible for machines in the past, such as AI reading out handwritten addresses in postal mails. With advances in AI, tasks that feel redundant or repetitive for humans and complex tasks such as driving or even dealing with angry customers are becoming possible.

As AI technology advances, businesses are finding ways to apply AI to a wider range of activities, such as sorting through data to find outliers in financial transactions or finding irregularities in visual information as in surveillance and medical fields. AI adoption in this sense may be described as disruptive for businesses.

With further advances, AI may eventually surpass humans in all areas of business, similar to how AlphaGo surpassed humans in the game of Go. However, regardless of how advanced AI becomes in terms of technology, Level 1 AI Adoption is a business term that will refer to the type of AI usage where humans are in charge of business roles. Even if AI technology advances to enable Level 2 Adoption and beyond, it does not mean Level 1 Adoption will be displaced. It would just imply the performance of Level 1 Adoption would continue to improve in its own path.

3.5 What It Would Be Like to Live in AI Adoption Level 1

We have already entered the beginning stages of Level 1 Adoption. By the time you are reading this, the progress in AI may have made a larger impact on how we live. Similar to how water may overflow an embankment all at the same time, AI adoption following a breakthrough in AI technology may occur abruptly.

1. At Home: Proliferation of New Devices

At home, AI will be able to assist humans in more aspects of life, throughout the human lifecycle of all ages. AI may serve as a playmate, nanny and teacher for children, an assistant for adults, and a caretaker and an emergency service for the elderly. Behind the scenes, AI will help identify and reduce potential dangers surrounding our household, ranging from small items such as recognizing a cat turning on the oven or responding to a member of the household falling in the bathroom, to larger things such as identifying cracks in high-rise apartments that could cause collapse.

The types of devices we use every day would be markedly different as well, in terms of shapes and forms as well as capabilities or purposes they serve. AI in these new types of devices may enable visual information currently presented in 2-D to be presented in 3-D format such that viewing social network posts may become as if viewers are actually present inside the same environment, or a group chat may feel the same as having a group meeting in person, where AI characters would be indiscernible from characters of real humans, similar to a metaverse. Even there would be types of movie theaters or exercise room enabled by AI that would feel as if you are actually present inside a real-life location even if everything is imaginary like a jungle or cartoon character; you can even walk around even though you are probably floating in a room similar to a flight simulator where all of your movements provide feedback, including shoes.

2. At Work: Excitement over Possibilities

At work, in addition to helping workers improve productivity, AI may also begin to permanently take away some of the less pleasant components of some jobs, such as danger, fatigue, or repetition. Overall, people who have the right capabilities will experience rapid increase in productivity, while potentially leading to other people who are less adept at adopting feeling left out. For companies, the competition for talent may become even more important as the degree of disparity of performance among workers widen.

With the right kind of tools and applications, work will become so much easier and people will feel empowered and enlightened, able to achieve more in life than ever before. As the motto of this level "If you can imagine it, you can do it" suggests, people in general may be filled with joy of the prospects of high expectations and even higher hopes.

3. In Cities and Suburbs: AI Follows You Everywhere

In cities, fully self-driven cars, and even self-flying vehicles may become the primary means of transportation we see on the streets and skies, as people can rely on these to make their everyday trips. At some point we may also see a fad in taking a "follower robot" everywhere we go, which may serve as an equivalent of a backpack as well as a personal low-speed means of transportation similar in concept to scooters or a Segway that we may ride or sit on for short distances. We will see AI robots of all forms and shapes roaming the streets running errands for people. The roads themselves may have all kinds of functionalities, such as generating electricity or monitoring traffic patterns and keeping people safe. Buildings may be able to keep track of everyone who entered or exited, and more effective surveillance systems will lead to timely response and overall reduction in crimes. All these may lead to changes to traffic patterns and how our city streets look in general. While such new technological advancements may be hard to imagine, people of those times would be more accustomed to those changes and would find it hard to live without them.

Meanwhile, some people may feel more comfortable moving away from cities since there would be less pressure on driving long distances or through traffic. Others may be drawn into safer cities to more fully experience all the changes AI adoption brings.

4. In Society: Preserving the Gist of Knowledge

With the help of AI, it may become possible to record our history in a new way. For example, before writing was invented, humans only left drawings on walls to convey information unless the stories were passed down mouth-to-mouth. However, even with writing, the amount of information that could be transferred is still limited. For example, we do not have a good idea about what old languages sounded like two thousand years ago even if we have it in writing. With character systems that convey meaning instead of sounds, guessing what characters sounded like back then for each of the different languages that used them is even harder even if we know the meaning. With the invention of camera and video, humans can now transfer more audio and visual information that also occurs over time. However, when we think of the types of knowledge that can be passed on, this is still not enough.

For example, we all speak with different accents, but it is hard to convey our own accents in a book. We may even record people who speak a particular accent in videos, but if that particular accent dies out and no one speaks it anymore, then the recordings will not be enough to teach a child born thousands of years from now to grow up to have that particular accent. If only an AI that understands the "gist" of the accent and can use it in everyday lives may be able to teach that child to gain the accent. In essence, AI may enable leaving such "gist" of the knowledge in our lives as recorded history, not just "fixed information" in text or videos.

In short, AI may be thought of as having the ability to record and play back the "live" or implicit internal knowledge of humans, similar to how cameras can record the explicit visual information. It may also be compared to saving the "DNA" of the knowledge rather than saving a specimen.

AI ADOPTION LEVEL 1: (B) POTENTIAL PROGRESSION IN THIS LEVEL

Figure 3-1: The Building Blocks of AI Adoption Pyramid in Level 1 Adoption

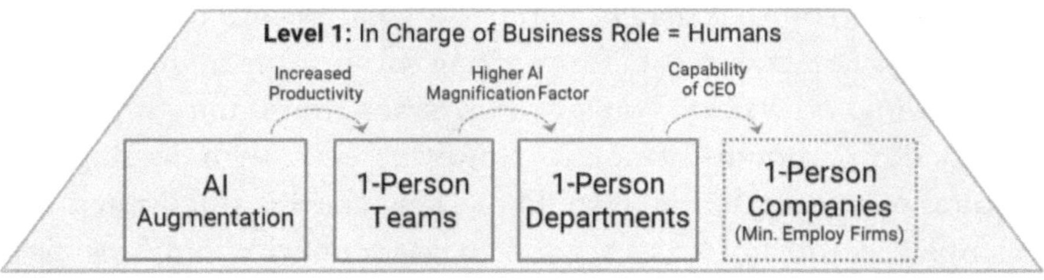

3.6 Overview of the Progression within Level 1 AI Adoption

1. Progression along Technological Advancements

In the beginning stages of Level 1 Adoption, the interest in AI may be so high that even finding new ways to apply AI or products that incorporate AI may receive public attention or fanfare.

Advances in AI technology will continue to be able to improve Level 1 Adoption, even after reaching Level 2. Availability of Level 2 Adoption does not imply Level 1 Adoption will become obsolete. Just the same as how the primary industries such as agriculture does not disappear with the introduction of secondary and tertiary level industries but the advances in technology helps improve the productivity of the primary industries, the introduction of Level 2 Adoption would likely not make the Level 1 Adoption disappear but the technology advancements will help improve it, even though the popularity of Level 1 Adoption may wane after Level 2 becomes available. As technology advances and Levels 2 is achieved, depending on how advanced AI is perceived at the time, Level 1 Adoption may attract new interest as a way to reduce the potential dangers of AI, since it would be used as a way to increase human performance. For example, Level 1 Adoption may still be useful for people who want or need to compete against AI or achieve something themselves rather than have AI do something for them.

2. Increased Competition and Widening Gaps among Individuals

Widespread AI adoption will lead to increased productivity for individuals, which would lead to a wider gap among human workers. In Level 1 Adoption, the competition is between humans against other humans, and AI just serves as a means to increase their productivity. In essence, human workers who can take advantage of these new tools will get ahead of the competition.

3. Increased Competition and Widening Gaps among Firms

Increase in AI adoption would lead to increased competition among firms as well. Companies will progress in the direction of trying to apply AI in as many areas as they can, since they may view how effectively they adopt AI may determine their performance. In the early stages of Level 1 AI adoption, the public may respond by paying attention to where AI is newly adopted, as well as new products that apply AI in some way.

As AI is used in more diverse areas of business, the next step that may attract public interest is the possibility of reducing the need for the number of employees needed to run companies. In the beginning, the use of AI may lead one person to be able to achieve tasks that previously required a team, in what can be referred to as "1-Person Teams" and "1-Person Departments." The potential of "1-Person Companies" with Level 1 Adoption would be examined in the following segment.

3.7 Early Usage Scenarios of AI in Level 1 AI Adoption

1. The Concept of Automation and Augmentation

The modes of AI adoption can be broadly categorized into two types, automation and augmentation. Ever since the introduction of the concept of AI in the 1950s, people have been highly anticipating AI robots replacing human workers, in what we can classify as automation. However, the speed of development did not meet expectations, and people directed their attention to another mode of AI adoption in augmentation, where AI is used more as a tool to help human workers perform at a higher level than replacing them.

When technology is not enough for a full type of automation, as in Level 2 Adoption, it may be advantageous to use AI in augmentation, since humans and AI offer different advantages in areas such as understanding the situation, that leads to better performance as a whole.

Table 3-2: Comparison of Automation and Augmentation

Automation	Augmentation
- AI as a replacement for human labor - AI helps <u>replace</u> human effort	- AI as a tool that assists human labor - AI helps humans perform better, or <u>reduce</u> effort

2. Collaboration, a Mixture of Automation and Augmentation

As AI technology progressed, what could be seen as partial automation or even an advanced type of augmentation emerged, known as human-AI collaboration[6]. When we look at the company as a whole, both augmentation and collaboration look similar in the sense that the company has both humans and AI in it. On the other hand, from the viewpoint of the human worker, augmentation may be conceptualized as the human worker using AI as a tool, while in collaboration AI may be considered more similar to a teammate, something that is completing tasks independent of that human worker even though human and AI interact with each other.

3. (Scenario 1) Using AI as a Tool

In the earliest stages of AI adoption, AI may be used as a tool that could enhance productivity of a human worker. Most of what we have seen so far in AI adoption would be included in this category. The most prominent example of such use is when LLM is used to generate codes for programmers or formulas for workers using Excel. Another popular example is a phone with the capability to translate spoken words into different languages.

4. (Scenario 2) The Reformation of "Jobs" from the Ground Up

As Level 1 AI Adoption progresses instead of AI humanoid robots directly replacing human jobs, we may see more human jobs augmented with AI being conceived from the ground up with the types of AI technology that will be available at each time.

An example may be how the job of a dentist may progress in two different directions; prior to an AI humanoid robot dentist replacing a human dentist in the beginning of Level 2 Adoption, a human dentist may first gain a tool that will make it much easier to carry out the function of a dentist, where a small machine the size of a tooth can fix or grow natural teeth inside a human's mouth. This device can then later be further developed to reach Level 2 Adoption. In essence, AI technology developed from a different perspective may take the place of some other AI technology that can directly replace human activities, maybe even offering some form of competition between AI Adoption Levels 1 and 2.

This principle may be applied to a wide range of different areas that involve human jobs, such as the need for an AI barber is lessened or complemented by an AI hair cutting machine that looks like a cap that you can wear, or a nail salon artist being replaced or complemented by an AI nail-sized machine that can paint nails, etc. This "customer using a machine lessening the need for a human worker" type of situation is most prominent for order kiosks in restaurants, where the customer has to take the burden of using a machine to input the order.

[Box 3-1] Impact of Augmentation on Productivity: AI Magnification Factor

Productivity Increase in Augmentation: Human Effort Magnification Factor (AI Magnification Factor[7])

In Level 1 Adoption, the main benefit of AI adoption would be the magnifying effect of human workers. If the differences between the performances of the an average worker and the best worker is to be thought of as between a 50 and a 100, the magnifying effect of using AI will increase this difference as AI technology improves, for example, to a 50 and a 500, with a "Human Effort Magnification Factor" of 5, increasing the performance of the best worker from a 100 to a 500. Whereas the difference between the average and the best performing human worker was 2 times before using AI, with AI magnification factor of 5, the difference could increase to 10 times.

At first glance, some people may be concerned that this would lead to even more inequality among workers. However, there are two sides to this coin, as the adoption of AI may turn out to be good news for some average workers as well, as their productivity may increase more to make them more competitive against the top workers who are not as adept at using AI. The Human Effort Magnification Factor would be different for each individual, as it would depend on the worker's ability to take advantage of AI capability. At the same time, it would be good news for the companies as well, as not only the human workers have higher productivity, but the AI Magnification Factor could also be improved by how well the company designs its roles to fit around its AI capability and how well it can train its human employees to take advantage of AI. Thus, AI adoption would bring new opportunities for everyone, except for the people who choose to stay behind and ignore AI adoption.

On a side note, even though they would mean the same thing, the impact of AI adoption in Level 1 could be named two different ways. From the perspective of the human worker, it could be referred to as "Human Effort Magnification Factor." From the perspective of the firms that deploy AI, it could be referred to as "AI Magnification Factor" of their employees. In this book, the two words would be used interchangeably, sometimes noting the difference in perspectives.

Lastly, we may express the AI magnification factor as a combination of three factors; 1) the human ability to use AI, 2) the capability of AI itself, and 3) how well the AI is being used for the particular business role, which we may also refer to as the degree of augmentation. The three factors may be expressed in the following equation. The table shows a brief description of the three factors.

AI Magnification Factor = (Human ability to use AI) x (AI capability) x (How AI is deployed, or the Degree of Augmentation)

Table 3-3: Description of the three factors that affect the Human Effort (AI) Magnification Factor[8]

Human Worker Ability	AI Capability	Degree of Augmentation
The ability of the human worker to use AI to its maximum potential	Capability of AI in carrying out the necessary tasks	How well AI is deployed for the specific role

A related concept in automation will be examined in Chapter 4.

3.8 Towards the Ultimate Form of Augmentation: The 1-Person Company

1. Minimal Employment Firms and the Path to 1-Person Teams, Companies and Conglomerates

Using AI, the productivity of human workers will increase. Gradually, we can expect that as Level 1 Adoption progresses, the advances in AI technology would lead firms to require fewer and fewer personnel to operate. First, an amount of work that would have been once considered the job for a "team" would be reduced to become a job for one person, in a situation that may be referred to as a "1-Person Team." Then, what was once considered a job for a department would be reduced to become a job for a person, in a situation that could be referred to as a "1-Person Department." For each point in time, we can refer to these firms with reduced number of employees as "Minimal Employment Firm." If we extrapolate on this notion, eventually it will lead to a situation where the productivity of 1 person would be high enough to carry out everything that is needed for the company, regardless of its size. In other words, one person would be able to carry out the amount of work what hundreds, thousands or tens of thousands of people had been doing in the past. Whereas 1-person firms exist today, we also refer to them as small businesses. However, as Level 1 AI adoption progresses, it would become easier to run 1-person firms that we may consider large businesses.

There is a caveat. In Level 1 Adoption, for a 1-person company to exist, the capability of the human CEO would have to meet the diverse requirements in each of the aspects of businesses. For example, if we imagine a manufacturing firm, it would have groups of workers in different areas of expertise, which may include legal, marketing, accounting, research and development, manufacturing, sales, customer service and other supporting activities. Thus, even though a large 1-person company could exist in theory, it would depend on the capability of the CEO, and it is likely the burden would be too much that it would be sensible to just hire more people and divide the responsibilities. True 1-person firms will be enabled in Level 2 Adoption, to be discussed in the next chapter. During Level 1 Adoption, we would be more likely to see 1-person teams and 1-person departments, since the specialties of a person would align better with a specific area of business.

2. All-Purpose AI Assistant

Analogous in concept to 1-person companies, from the perspective of AI adoption another advanced form of AI in augmentation may be a type of "all-purpose AI assistant." In the beginning of AI development, most AI adoption would be limited in scope, where different AI would be trained with different data. In this limited version, the development and implementation would take a long time, require many human workers, and incur high cost. Such setup would also be complex to operate. As AI technology advances, AI Assistants would be able to gain in the scope of expertise that eventually it will be able to serve all aspects of a person's life.

AI ADOPTION LEVEL 1: (C) SOCIETAL IMPACT OF AI

Along with the rapidly growing interest in AI development, discussions regarding regulations may become just as heated. During Level 1 AI adoption, new regulations would have to be introduced not only to address potential problems in the short term, but also for the long term where AI adoption would progress to Level 2 and beyond.

Major regulatory topics in Level 1 may be categorized into: 1) Jobs, 2) Safety and Ethical Issues, and 3) Equality and Fairness. Let's examine some of these issues in the following segments.

3.9 (Controversy 1) AI and Work: Would AI Create or Destroy Jobs?

As AI begins to make more impact in the business world, one of the first major topics of discussion will be regarding the impact of AI on jobs. During the time when we have only Level 1 AI adoption, these discussions would likely to evolve around whether AI will create or destroy jobs, and how AI will shape or re-shape jobs.

In the beginning stages of Level 1 AI adoption, we can classify AI-related economic activities into two major categories.

1. *Developing AI (Improving performance, increasing application areas of AI)*
2. *Using AI to improve productivity in other tasks (Using AI as a tool)*

Making progress in these two activities would require significant amounts of financial investments as well as human labor. Especially in early stages of AI adoption, each AI has a limited area of applicability so individual investments are required for a wide range of areas. Investments in human capital to develop the AI will be significant, and people who carry out jobs that previously did not exist will increase. Examples of such jobs would include jobs that train AI and jobs that use these AI. Re-training current employees to meet the new demands required by these will also become the norm.

On the other hand, there will be jobs that disappear or become obsolete. The main driving force in this stage would be due to the increase in human productivity. Companies will find that one person can achieve what previously required groups or teams of people. In this regard, the competition to find jobs will still be a competition between humans who are using AI, not humans against AI. As long as new jobs are created by introduction of AI, such decreases would be likely to be overshadowed by gains in jobs in other areas. What may be more pronounced would be that there may be a negative effect of some people being forced to change the direction of their careers to fit these new areas of available jobs, or struggling to gain traction in acquiring the required skills to be proficient in using AI.

To summarize, in Level 1 AI Adoption, jobs would be more likely to be altered and added rather than lost or destroyed. This implies there likely would be the need to change policy focus on educating towards jobs that are being newly created as well as going away from jobs that are being displaced, rather than worrying about the total number of jobs. The real job problem would appear in Level 2 Adoption.

3.10 (Controversy 2) AI and Crime: Can We Trust AI and Not be Deceived?

As AI adoption in this level helps increase human productivity, AI could also be used as a tool that can enhance or enable new types of criminal activities. Moreover, when AI is still in the early stage, unintended weaknesses or vulnerabilities may occur.

As AI adoption increases, the controversy surrounding trust in AI will increase. During the earlier stages of Level 1 Adoption, the issue of AI and crime, or preventing crime, would involve examining both the internal workings of AI and the external environment surrounding AI. The internal issues, which could also be referred to as AI issues, would deal with the problem of inability to trust AI because it would become harder to distinguish whether AI has been manipulated in reaching its conclusions. The external issues, which could also be categorized as human issues, would involve the increased productivity of criminals that try to spread fake information or deceive people using AI in illegal activities such as phishing and forgery. We may briefly examine each case.

1. (AI Internal Issues) Possibility of AI Malfunctions and Limitations leading to Trust Issues

Trust issues regarding the inner workings of AI stems from two directions of data and algorithm. These issues may make AI harder to trust, since it would become increasingly more complicated to verify what AI does is not compromised by external forces.

1) Data Related Issues

The first issue stems from the difficulty of controlling what AI learns because AI is trained with vast amount of data. The data used to train AI may intentionally or unintentionally contain something that could be harmful. For example, many AI developers use text and image data downloaded from the internet. Not only could these data contain incorrect information, some ill-meaning people could place certain information that could later be manipulated, in data poisoning or sleeper agent attacks triggered by custom phrases.[9]

Even though it may not affect the performance of AI, another issue related to using data to develop AI may involve copyright violations from using texts and other forms of copyrighted data to train AI without the consent of the copyright owners.

2) Software (Algorithm) Related Issues

The second issue is more general in that it is hard to understand how AI reaches its conclusions. As explained in Chapter 2, the nature of the popular AI of today that uses deep learning and other sub-symbolic approaches is that they are hard to understand for humans. To sidestep this problem, concepts such as Explainable AI have been suggested to make AI easier to understand for humans.

2. (External Issues) Increasing Worry for AI-Assisted Crimes and Public Threats to Safety

Just as there are numerous ways AI could be deployed for the public good in the government and military, there could be counter-acting movements on the side of the criminals and other bad actors such as terrorists that would increase the threats to our society. AI will widen the realm of possibilities for criminals. All kinds of new crimes may appear, as only imagination would be the limit. The target of crimes would vary from small, possibly individuals, to large, such as groups of people or organizations with a lot of money or other valuable assets, to even include the government.

As AI develops in the direction of multiplying human productivity, criminals may also take advantage of AI. In Level 1 AI adoption, humans would be in charge of these criminal activities. At the same time, the limitations of AI during the earlier stages of development may lead to weaknesses or unforeseen problems that may also lead to illegal activities. We may categorize some of the major ways AI may be misused as deceiving or hacking.

1) Deceiving: Includes phishing that may use AI-generated images, texts, and audio, and trying to gain economic or political gain by spreading fake new and information

2) Hacking and Security: Using AI as a hacking tool, or AI becomes the target of hacking

1) Issue of Using AI to Deceive People

Crimes using AI that are intended to deceive would become harder to detect, as AI would be optimized to mimic normal activities and hide under other normal activities. Phishing scams using AI voices, images and videos will become harder to discern. Fake news or false information could be spread around to serve certain purposes such as in political campaigns or spying. Forgery of public documents, deeds, or even election votes would become more concerning.

2) Hacking and Security Issues

Examples of AI being the targeted in hacking include prompt hacking such as jailbreak, where the hacker asks indirect questions, as well as prompt injection[10] and prompt leaking. There are also adversarial input attacks[11] that involve using manipulating input images to confuse the AI. Attackers may cause AI to reply with codes that may cause problems in insecure output handling,[12] whereas attackers may also attempt to extract the training data to gain hidden information in data extraction or model theft.[13]

Examples of using AI in hacking include reconstructing biometric data to impersonate other people.[14] Another example would be AI viruses that may infect computers with self-replicating prompt, in what is known as zero-click infection where people do not even have to click to cause the virus infection.[15]

Just as AI may be used in legal activities to help achieve better results, AI may be used for illegal activities to would help the criminals commit crimes more effectively. Countermeasures or regulations to offset these concerns include watermarking,[16] and frameworks such as MITRE ATLAS[17] have been developed.

3.11 (Controversy 3) AI and Privacy: Finding Balance between Public Safety and Over-Surveillance

We may consider the increase of crimes using AI increases as one side of a coin. Then the other side of the coin would be using AI to catch or prevent those crimes.

However, as the use of AI increases to deter crimes, then there would be offsetting forces, such as new demands to reduce those uses due to the fear of over-surveillance of our privacy.

1. (Arguments for More AI) The Increasing Need for Using AI to Prevent and Fight against Crimes

As crimes using AI increases, the need for using AI to prevent these new kinds of crimes would simultaneously increase, since it would become harder and harder to fight crimes without AI.

AI would also be used to prevent, mitigate, and catch crimes, by using them in real-time surveillance, forensic, and other areas that can track, deter, and find unusual or outright dangerous activities.

The ability of AI to detect suspicious patterns would be useful in a variety of areas. These will range from finance to detect money laundering would save a lot of human efforts to comb through the vast amounts of data.

There are several reasons why using more AI could be beneficial to fighting crimes, and the following would be just a few of the examples.

1) *(Save Human Effort) AI can process vast amount of data without requiring more human effort.*
2) *(Uninterrupted Surveillance) AI can conduct surveillance non-stop without requiring rest.*
3) *(Enhanced Detection) AI may detect new patterns and signals humans previously could not.*

2. (Arguments Against More AI) Possibility of AI Overuse and Too Much Surveillance – Should We Worry about AI Watching Over Our Lives?

While AI development-related regulations would be focused on limiting the activities of AI, governments may also use AI to effectively limit the activities of its citizens.

AI surveillance tools may be also applied to various facets of our lives to detect unusual activities both online and offline, such as in streets, malls, and other crowded as well as deserted areas. These tools may be easily introduced to detect suspicious online communications, emails, voice mails, community posts or even virtual meetings. Since AI is not human, some governments may argue that AI used in detecting these anomalies would not negatively affect privacy, yet further our public safety. However, in Level 1 AI adoption whenever AI is used for surveillance, at some point human intervention would be necessary to make the final decisions on whether to pursue further investigation from the detected anomalies or at least review the anomalies in some form.

Some advocates may even argue that if you have nothing to hide, then you should not fear AI surveillance. Finding the balance of privacy vs. safety would play out differently in different countries, depending on the penchant of the population towards one over the other. We can already glean towards such differences from the less advanced forms of surveillance such as street cameras, where some countries place them aggressively everywhere, while some other countries prefer to ban them.

3.12 (Controversy 4) What If Some People Try to "Take Over the World" with AI?

1. (Insufficient Productivity) Why Most Villains Fail

In movies, we often see villain characters that try to take over the world. Some readers may even be familiar with the WB children's animation series Pinky and the Brain, where the main character, a lab mouse that became smart as humans, claims in every episode to "do the same thing we do every night, try to take over the world." When we observe these villain characters, most of them do not succeed in taking over the world. If we are to generalize why they fail, it may come down to "the villains lack the resources and productivity to take over the world against the good characters."

Even in reality, villains tend to be in the minority, and this lack of numbers ultimately leads to failures in the long term because the villains cannot have sustainable advantage over the good guys, or at least we hope so. From this observation, we may hypothesize that "if villains try to take over the world with enough resources and productivity, they may be able to actually do so."

2. (Asymmetric Productivity) Increase in the Probability of Success for Villains that Use AI

We live in a society where the increase in economic imbalance is leading to a situation where fewer and fewer people are controlling increasingly more share of the economy.[18] It can be called the "rich get richer, poor get poorer" situation. With advancements in AI, the imbalance may get even more accentuated, as some rich people with a lot of resource may experience exponentially higher return.

Eventually, some small number of people may gain much stronger influence than the rest of the population combined. As an extreme example, just as Kim Jung Un has the power to surveillance the 25 million people in North Korea, some person with an asymmetric AI may become an astoundingly productive person and amass wealth that is more than the sum of the rest of the billions of population in the world. If something similar happens, this may be a significant threat to the well-being of the world's population and world peace.

3. (Risk Assessment) The Importance of Timely and Relevant AI Regulation

If regulators fail to introduce relevant measures and AI is designed to be given too much independence early in development path, eventually more advanced AI that arrives afterwards with the same lax philosophy may place the interests of AI ahead of those of humans, potentially leading AI to act against humanity in some way. If the reason villains cannot succeed in the long term is because their resources and productivity are lower in comparison to the good people, then we cannot rule out the possibility of an unexpectedly rogue AI or a villain with AI gaining a higher level of productivity that surpasses the rest of the humanity. We will examine this topic in Chapter 6.

The nature of AI adoption to increase productivity will raise the social risk regardless of what the intentions were in developing the AI. If we consider the development of AGI as the most significant inflection point in AI technology, then our society could be most vulnerable when it happens, as the public's access may be limited at the beginning. The best we can hope for is that AGI will not raise the productivity so much over what alternative AI is publicly available at the time, or is not available in a lopsided manner that the gain benefits only a limited number of bad players.

Table 3-4 categorizes based on the potential order of obtaining AGI, and how much better AGI may be compared to other types of alternative AI that may be available at the time.

If the performance of AGI is insurmountable against the rest of available AI, then the outcome would be deterministic. In this scenario, what would be of utmost importance would be who develops AGI first. On the other hand, if rest of the available AI used in combination by humans offers competitiveness, then there may be variability of outcome. In this scenario, trying to bring diversity to AI development may offer some value.

Table 3-4: Outcome Based on Who Owns AGI First and the Replaceability of AGI

	The "Good" Owns AGI First	The "Bad" Owns AGI First
AGI is Irreplaceable (AGI is Insurmountable)	Best Situation (Villain is Suppressed)	Most Dangerous (Villain's AGI is Insurmountable)
AGI is Replaceable (Competitive AI is Available)	Somewhat Dangerous (Villains Resist with Other AI)	Significantly Dangerous (Resist Using Alternative AI)

AI Adoption Level 1: (D) Summary, Conclusion, and Implications

As mentioned in the beginning of this chapter, the motto of this AI adoption level may be described as "If you can imagine it, you can do it." Since AI acts as a multiplying factor of humans' efforts and productivity, many people may find excitement and joy over what they can accomplish with the new tools that are available to them.

3.13 Main Benefits of Level 1 AI Adoption

In Level 1 AI Adoption, a major theme regarding the questions people ask would be around how AI can help them work better. We may categorize the answers into the following three groups.

1. (Reduction in Effort) AI Helps Human Workers Put in Less Effort

Even in cases where humans are not trying to produce more, AI will allow human workers to put in less effort while achieving the same level of performance. AI may help make the tasks easier. AI may help human workers direct their time and attention towards more important areas of their jobs, by taking care of routine, dangerous, tiring, or boring tasks.

2. (Quantitative Benefit) AI Helps Human Workers Produce More

In Level 1 Adoption, humans will be able to achieve more amount of work than ever before by using AI as a tool to improve their productivity. This would help lower cost.

3. (Qualitative Benefit) AI Helps Human Workers Achieve What Was Impossible

AI adoption will expand the realm of possibilities both in business and in our private lives. What had been considered impossible would become possible, enabling us to explore more business opportunities not thought possible in the past.

For example, AI may help create surreal videos of lifelike quality, or physical tasks that were considered too exhaustive, fast, or heavy may become doable with the help of body-augmenting AI devices, or virtual tasks that involved shifting through too much data may become possible with the help of AI.

From a business perspective, projects that had been discarded due to financial reasons may turn profitable with AI. This would lead to an explosion of potential business opportunities.

3.14 Implications in Business: Changes in How Businesses are Run

1. AI May Lead to More Jobs, not Less, in the Beginning of AI Adoption

Because AI development and implementation in the beginning stages of AI adoption requires human effort and involvement, the net impact on jobs for the early part of Level 1 Adoption may be positive as companies seek to take advantage of new opportunities to apply AI. It would take advancement in AI technology to a level where it requires less effort to implement AI in new areas for net job effect to turn negative, to be discussed in Level 2 Adoption.

2. Appearance of the 1-Person Teams and 1-Person Departments

Level 1 Adoption will lead to rapid increase in productivity to a degree that one person would be able to achieve what had required a team of people, in what can be described as 1-person teams or 1-person departments. In this environment, human workers with specific specialties will thrive. The concept of AI magnification factor was introduced to describe the impact.

During this stage, we may see a glimpse of the ultimate form of augmentation of 1-person conglomerates,[19] but it would still be hard to achieve since it requires the person to excel in multiple skillsets.

3.15 Implication for Investing in AI Development in Level 1 Adoption

Companies around the world are investing in AI in the way they perceive the most potential. Companies with more resources to put into development may focus on areas that have a wider range of impact, while firms with less capital may take on more focused or high-risk niche approaches. A large profit would be expected for reaching the next step, leading to a sprint towards developing the first AGI or AI that can achieve Level 2 Adoption. In the process, a lot of capital would be allocated to developing and deploying AI. In this segment, we will examine some of the fundamental ways to look at the emerging AI development race.

When technology allows only Level 1 AI adoption, we may think of major approaches to investing in AI along the three topics of software, hardware, and data. The first approach would involve investing in companies that develop software, with the underlying belief that the winner will eventually develop the first AGI. The second approach involves investing in companies that develop AI-related hardware, with the underlying belief that the widespread use of AI will drastically increase demand for their products. The third approach involves investing in companies that will actually use AI in their businesses, with the underlying belief that the use of AI will drastically improve their business performances.

Regardless of these approaches, the highest return may come from the eventual winner that first develops AGI, since it may gain an insurmountable competitive advantage over every other business that exists in the world, depending on the definition of AGI and the relative performance of pre-AGI AI. This may be a software development company, but it may also require synergy that can only be available to a company involved in all three aspects of AI development, since we do not know how AGI would be developed. Even though we do not yet know how AGI will be reached or what would happen once AGI is reached, but since people expect the development of AGI to be a world-defining moment, we may have high expectations and heavy investments in all three areas of hardware, software and implementing AI through data.

1. Investing in AI Software Development: Big Tech vs. Startups

Within the AI software arena, investments in AI in Level 1 Adoption may be generally grouped into two directions.

1) *(High risk, wider applicability) Companies investing in areas that have lower probability of succeeding, but AI has a wider range of applicability*

2) *(Low risk, limited applicability) Companies investing in areas that they are familiar with and have a higher probability of succeeding, but AI applicability is limited to a narrow area*

In the first arena, the most notable companies would include both established big tech companies and startups that are trying to build AGI. They require the most computing resources and need intensive financial backing to test their ideas and bring new products to market. The main source of competitive advantage in this area other than acquiring the compute power would be deploying the personnel who can conceptualize and test the most successful ideas that could lead to AGI.

The companies in the second arena would have a different goal, focusing more on niche markets while developing or testing their own versions of AI. These include smaller tech companies that may focus on a narrower area of application, such as a particular language, games, or image processing.

Some companies may find it more advantageous to develop both software and hardware in tandem.

2. Investing in AI Hardware Development

The development of AI hardware may be different from software, as developing hardware would require different types of personnel, processes, and philosophy, especially for processing units. Whereas software may come from some eureka moment of an AI engineer, AI hardware development may require more systemic approach, since it would have to be built on top of scientific discoveries and supporting technologies. Investing in hardware would require understanding the goals and target markets of the firms and the roles they serve in the value chain. We may categorize AI-related physical hardware into compute and physical manifestation of AI.

1. (Processing Unit) Companies operating in areas to make AI computing faster, such as chip designers, chip fabricators, suppliers, etc.
2. (Physical Hardware) Companies investing in areas that are related to the physical manifestation of AI, such as humanoid AI robots, industrial-purpose AI robots, etc.

For companies dealing with the processing units, the goals of the firms may differ depending on their place on the value chain, as some companies focus on developing manufacturing processes that can make smaller and smaller chips, while others may focus on designing chips that are optimized for AI.

For companies involved in developing the physical hardware as physical manifestation of AI, the approaches of firms may be differentiated by their goals, such as building for the general purpose as a humanoid robot, or in some other shape or form targeting specific locations such as in a restaurant, factory, and warehouse, or for specific purposes such as surveillance, delivery and even leisure.

3. Investing in AI from the Data Perspective: Increase in Areas of AI Application

Finally, the third category of approaches to AI investing would involve considering the applications of AI in various economic activities from a user perspective. Who would benefit the most from using AI? Who would lose out? Firms can invest in niche-type AI in various areas. Opportunities for investments would be abound in all kinds of areas in Level 1, both in developing and deploying AI.

Investments in Level 1 Adoption in relation to business AI application may be grouped into the following two opposite characteristics.

1. (Low-Risk, Low-Return) Firms invest in specific niche market that have proven customer demand

Examples of firms investing in AI towards this direction would include a construction firm using AI image analysis to check on the soundness of buildings, or manufacturing firms using their own data to predict defects. They can be certain that the demand for these would be there, but the targeted customer base would be too narrow to expect a large profit.

2. (High-Risk, High-Return) Firms invest in AI that target a wider market

Firms investing towards this philosophy would be leap a larger profit if they can successfully develop and market a product that gains widespread use, but developing and successfully marketing the product would involve much higher risk. Firms in certain industries with specific expertise may also be able to develop AI products that have a wider range of applications, such as logistics, automotive, or robot manufacturing.

With these approaches in mind, we may examine the directions of AI development as targeting general consumers, businesses, or own internal use. AI development that target general consumers may be considered high-risk / high return, while developing for internal customers would be considered low-risk / low return. Targeting business customers may be considered to be in between.

1. (AI for Everyone) Companies that develop AI for general consumers

Companies that develop AI for everyone, which includes general consumers and even business users, may have an advantage in gaining the needed scale of investments. These may include all kinds of well-known companies and brands that we are already familiar with as we may see them on a daily basis. From some retailer that can suggest what glasses will look the best based on the shape of your face to the ones that can custom design new products on the spot, or even AI robots for households, the application of AI for consumers would only be limited by our imagination.

The performance of companies may depend on how well they can position and market their AI products. Products that target the general population, such as helping individual productivity, may also have large financial potential, while specific topics, such as physical training, nutrition, diet, etc., may also be targeted by others.

2. (AI for Businesses) Companies that develop AI for other businesses

Practically all companies in all industries may consider adopting AI in some manner to gain a competitive edge. While businesses may be able to use generic AI products intended for consumers, they may also require higher levels of security and customization. Traditional office workers would be able to take advantage of AI in improving their own analysis and increase output to make more informed decisions. Other examples of applications would include construction companies using imaging analysis of AI to keep track of structural soundness of buildings, bridges or other infrastructure projects. In manufacturing, AI could predict potential wear and tear problems in equipment, or assure quality of final products.

We may think of two ways investors may approach in this category. First, the focus of investors may include how introduction of AI would change the direction of the business or increase the financial potential of the firm. In general, we would expect the most human labor intensive companies, such as manufacturing, retail, food, and delivery industries, would experience the earliest and largest gains as AI begins to help improve the productivity of the workers. Second, investors may focus on how AI may impact the largest in number or the most economically significant occupations or industries, as the potential for financial gain may turn out to be the highest in those areas. In this approach, AI products that can augment farmers, doctors, lawyers, writers or similar occupations may have the highest potential, as large numbers of human workers are carrying out the same types of tasks.

3. (AI for Internal Use) Companies investing in AI for their own use

In various industries, AI may serve as a source of competitive advantage and firms may want to develop related capabilities in-house, rather than sourcing them from outside. Examples of firms that may be in this situation include firms that prospect for natural resource such as oil, or pharmaceutical companies that need to forecast how drugs may interact with the proteins in the body, or financial institutions that want to better forecast market movements or how their portfolios will perform.

We may summarize the three approaches into the following table.

Table 3-5: Examples of Types of Approaches to AI Application

	Description	Examples
B2C	(Pros) High Return: Economics of Scale (Cons) High Risk: More Competition	General AI tool, AI translating service, photo retouch service, household robots, etc.
B2B	(Pros) Medium Return: Expect Long-Term Relationships (Cons) Medium Risk: Higher Barriers to Entry	AI that helps analyze corporate customers, AI that streamlines business processes, AI for distribution centers, etc.
Internal	(Pros) Low Risk: Customer is Locked In (Cons) Low Return: Hard to Expand Customer Base	AI for own use, such as geological surveillance AI for oil companies or AI analyzing fraud for credit card companies, etc.

3.16 Can the AI Game Abruptly End at Only Level 1? (Can the Last AI Be in Level 1 Adoption?)

When we play games such as chess, the game does not have a pre-set length. The game can end suddenly, possibly due to a brilliant move of one player, or a mistake by another. Similarly, the "game" of AI adoption may abruptly come to an end at Level 1 without entering the next stages. This checkmate may also be from a brilliant move of a player, or a mistake of another.

In the early stages of AI adoption, the biggest cause for concern may be the arrival of AGI, depending on its definition, due to its implication on productivity and competition. This would be especially true if there is a scarcity of AGI and it falls in the wrong hands such that the productivity gain becomes lopsided. A brilliant move by a villain to successfully develop the only version of AGI, or failed actions of the good guys and the regulators to prevent such runaway success could lead to an abrupt end of the game.

We will examine more of this topic in Chapter 7.

CHAPTER 4
AI VS HUMAN IN
LEVEL 2 AI ADOPTION

Level 2 AI Adoption Introduction

Motto: "What You Can Imagine Will Be Done For You"

(A) Overview

The basic premise of Level 2 AI Adoption is that AI will become proficient enough to be in charge of business roles. Eventually, AI will be able to carry out all of the tasks of a business role in place of humans. These advanced types of AI may be referred to as AI Agents or AI Experts. In Level 2 AI Adoption, humans will compete against AI for jobs, but at the higher level of analysis we may also think of the situation as human-led companies competing against other human-led companies and AI assisting as a part of the companies. The beginning part of Level 2 AI adoption may be the most exciting times for the world economy, as there will be increased demands to develop AI Agents for all kinds of different areas and functions. People may be excited about the economic advantages these AI may provide to companies, and great wealth may be accumulated. But as time goes by, the society may become more likely to experience confusion and abrupt changes. In essence, it may appear more and more that AI is competing against individual humans and winning.

(B) Vocabulary for Referring to AI in This Level

We will consider the AI that enables Level 2 AI Adoption to have reached "AI Equalization." We will refer to AI that can carry out all of the functions of a business role as "AI Agents," "AI Employee," or even "AI Expert." Some AI may be taking on roles of leadership, in which case we may refer to as "AI Manager."

(C) Implications on Business and Economy

In the previous chapter, we examined the potential for the 1-Person Teams and 1-Person Departments. In this chapter, we will examine the potential for 0-Person Teams and 0-Person Departments, which would make it easier to achieve the ultimate form of augmentation, the "1-Person Company" (1PC) and expand into "1-Person Group" (1PG) or 1-Person Conglomerates.

A major inflection point in Level 2 AI Adoption is when "automated innovation" becomes achievable. Unlike in "augmented innovation" in Level 1 AI adoption, in automated innovation AI by itself would be able to contribute to the innovation of firms.

(D) Technological Requirements and Implications

Earliest versions of AI Agents intended for a limited range of business roles would be achievable without AGI. As we get closer to AGI, we will have more advanced versions of AI Agents and AI Experts. Once AGI is achieved, it would imply that every business roles could be carried out by AI. This would lead to a convergence of jobs. These advances will bring societal changes that may cause larger controversy regarding who should own AI.

AI ADOPTION LEVEL 2: (A) DESCRIPTION OF THIS LEVEL

4.1 (In Charge of Business Roles = AI) AI That Replaces Human Workers

1. The Concept of "AI Equalization"

We may think of a job as a group of specific tasks one person carries out within a company. At the same time, as AI technology develops, AI would gain in performance and reliability to a point where it can carry out certain tasks without human intervention, feedback or any other types of interaction. In other words, we may reach a point where AI may be able to reliably carry out all the necessary tasks of a particular job previously belonged to human worker. We can call this tipping point "AI Equalization."[1]

A major distinction of the concept of the AI Equalization from AGI is that it is from the perspective of the user. We may consider AGI to be a term from the perspective of the supplier, since the developer will be likely to determine whether AGI has been reached unless there is some form of social consensus or a legal definition is made. However, AI Equalization will be determined by each firm that deploys AI; since each job will involve different set of tasks and the level of difficulty for AI will also differ, the time AI equalization is reached will vary for each job.

For some definitions of AGI, we may reach AI equalization before AGI is reached. Because Level 2 Adoption is based on how humans are organized around business tasks, the level of AI sophistication required would vary by positions. There will always be a business role where AI would find it easier to replace human workers. For this reason, that humans at work are assigned to carry out tasks that are of different levels of difficulty, we may express the diffusion of Level 2 Adoption as a ratio of the number of jobs that can be replaced by AI to the total number of achievable jobs. In some way, we may have already reached AI equalization for business roles that require really simple tasks, but what would be more important is how diverse range of roles can be fully replaced.

2. The Beginning of Agent AI (AI Productivity > 0)

In AI adoption Level 1, AI may carry out some of the tasks of a person's business role. With the development in AI technology, the areas where AI can carry out tasks will increase. Eventually the dependability and performance of AI may become acceptable beyond a certain point to completely take over groups of tasks previously thought of as a job or a business role of a human. After AI reaches equalization and becomes capable enough to completely replace a human worker from a role, firms may completely remove human workers, in what may be referred to as "0-Person Worker." From the perspective of running a business, this would be a milestone that we can categorize as reaching another level. Since humans carry out roles of different difficulties, some jobs may get replaced by AI earlier than others. As an aggregate, we can refer to Level 2 AI Adoption as where AI is awarded its own realm of responsibility and authority within the firm in the same way as human workers. AI built for this level of adoption can be categorized as an "Agent AI,"[2] "Butler AI," or "Co-Worker AI."

To think about this topic in terms productivity, there would be two possibilities:

1) If we think the productivity of Agent AI cannot be calculated by itself, then:

Productivity of [Agent AI + Human + Co-Pilot AI]
> Productivity of [Human + Co-Pilot AI]

2) If we think the productivity of Agent AI can be calculated by itself, then:

Productivity of [Agent AI] > 0

Co-Pilot AI in Level 1 Adoption is used as a type of tool so it would be harder to conceptualize having its own productivity. However, because Agent AI in Level 2 AI adoption would be able to carry out the tasks of business roles by itself independent of any human guidance, so it may make more sense to calculate its own productivity to compare to cases where humans would have carried out the same role.

3. Differences Between AI Adoption Levels 1 and 2

To illustrate a comparison of how AI is used differently in Level 1 vs. Level 2 AI adoption, we can consider the adoption of autonomous vehicles. First, as a background information for those who are not as familiar with the categories of self-driving cars, a well-known framework that explains the roadmap of the development is the 6 Levels of Autonomous Vehicles by the Society of Automotive Engineers,[3] a simple framework that is intuitive and easy to understand. Frameworks such as this help everyone to easily communicate and understand the concept. Table 4-1 shows an overview of the different levels of the autonomous vehicles using this framework.

Table 4-1: Summary of SAE's 6 Levels of Driving[4]

Level 0	Level 1	Level 2	Level 3	Level 4	Level 5
No Driving Automation	Driver Assistance	Partial Driving Automation	Conditional Driving Automation	High Driving Automation	Full Driving Automation
Humans <u>are</u> Driving			Humans <u>are Not</u> Driving		

From the viewpoint of the AI developer, reaching the Level 5 in driving automation may imply the completion of the development. However, from the viewpoint of AI adoption how these Level 5 vehicles are utilized may be categorized further. If a human worker, such as a sales representative that needs to constantly move, is given a Level 5 autonomous vehicle to make the rest of his work easier, then it could be considered a Level 1 AI Adoption. If the Level 5 vehicle can be equipped with additional capabilities to serve as an autonomous taxi then it can be considered a Level 2 AI Adoption, where it replaces a human taxi driver. This example also shows the same level of technology can be used for both Levels 1 and 2 adoptions, and that the technological change will precede social change.

In the previous chapter we discussed the difference between automation and augmentation, and how a mixture of automation and augmentation referred to as collaboration would be considered a part of Level 1 AI adoption. Level 2 AI Adoption may also be considered a type of automation or augmentation, or also a type of collaboration, depending on the perspective. From the perspective of an individual, AI in Level 1 Adoption would be augmentation, while Level 2 Adoption would be considered automation. For the same situation, from the perspective of a whole firm, both Level 1 and Level 2 can be considered a type of augmentation since humans and AI come together to perform as a whole. Depending on where the responsibility is put on, collaboration can be thought of as either Level 1 or Level 2 as well. In Level 1 Collaboration human workers would act as managers or superiors, while in Level 2 Collaboration AI and human workers would be more equal as teammates with separate roles and responsibilities.

Level 1 AI Adoption is where humans are needed to contribute something, while Level 2 Adoption could be considered as a situation where humans do not need to contribute to the work. From a glass-half-full perspective, Level 2 Adoption could be viewed as a situation where humans are finally freed from particular jobs. However, from the opposite glass-half-empty perspective, it could be viewed as a situation where humans are no longer needed.

4.2 Major Characteristics of Level 2 AI Adoption

AI Adoption Level 2 Specific Details

Table 4-2 shows some of the major characteristics of AI Adoption Level 2.[5]

(1) Human and AI Interaction

In the dimension of the nature of *human and AI interaction*, AI would have gained capabilities to fill a particular business role, even though the overall relationship is still led by humans who rank higher in the corporate hierarchy. AI's relationship to humans can be conceptualized as an independent agent, a team member or even a middle manager where AI may have delegated authority to make a limited boundary of business decisions. The business role is still designed by humans, who decide what role AI will play and how humans around the AI will work together. AI will decide on how it will solve problems within its role. Humans are still responsible for making the final decisions and evaluating as upper management. AI may gather and consider information and act on it on its own to make the best business decisions pertaining to the role, and work with humans by presenting their reasoning, or generating reports for human managers for further review.

(2) Scope of AI Application

The *scope of AI application* may still be limited, increasing as technology enables use. The dependability of AI in carrying out the role should become at least acceptable for the role without human supervision to achieve this level.

(3) Final Authority and Responsibility

The *final authority and responsibility* are all still mostly on humans. AI has its own responsibility within the business role, but humans still have the authority to override those decisions as managers. Human managers have full final decision as well as responsibility within the business. In essence, most problems caused from using the AI would ultimately still fall on some human, albeit indirectly as manager. Companies or persons who created the AI may also have some form of authority or responsibility over the design and be responsible for such problems as design flaws.

(4) Strategic Planning Activities

In terms of involvement in *strategic planning activities*, AI may not have the capacity to carry out general business planning activities, but it may be able to plan for its own role.

(5) Innovation by AI

AI may show *innovative potential*; as technology improves, AI may gain more potential to innovate in the role, even though the earliest versions may not have much capability to do so. Regardless, the "automated innovation" by AI would be limited within the scope of its role within the firm.

Table 4-2: Major Characteristics of Level 2 AI Adoption

Category	Characteristics	Description
Human-AI Interaction	- Human delegate relevant role to AI - Humans and AI collaborate as counterpart or co-worker - AI initiate some interaction	- Humans: design role, give direction for role as managers, have final decision as managers of AI, and decide which functions AI will carry out - AI: have some decision making power to carry out role such as how to solve role-specific problems - AI may or may not need to ask additional questions
Scope of AI Application	- AI is used within a limited focus of role but have wide scope within role - Applicable areas expand as new technology enable AI	- AI has proved dependability in role - AI has certain freedom to carry out role - AI is probably not required to reach AGI level for some roles
Override Authority / Responsibility	- Human managers have final authority and responsibility - Company that developed or deployed AI has some authority and responsibility - AI have limited responsibility	- Problems caused from using AI falls mostly on the company or human that operate the AI - Company or persons that developed the AI may have indirect responsibility for problems arising from actions of the AI (such as design error)
Strategic Planning Activities	- Humans decide what the firm will do and how to run it	- AI do not necessarily have capability nor authority to carry out general business planning activities - AI may be able to plan for own activities
Innovation by AI	- Activities of AI may lead to innovation (Automated Innovation)	- Innovation by AI would still be limited in scope

4.3 (Prerequisite) What Would Enable This Level?

How Much Technological Development is Necessary to Reach Level 2 Adoption?

Readers of this book probably have heard in the news that we are heavily anticipating the appearance of AGI within the next few years or decades. However, there are two major problems regarding using AGI as a milestone in business analysis.[6]

First, there is no definite definition of AGI, as there are a wide variety of different definitions as explained in Chapter 2. AGI means different things to different people. While the general public would probably think of AGI as something that acts and thinks like humans, as in AGI with consciousness, people who are building AI may prefer to define AGI as narrowly as possible so they can claim to have reached it first.

Second, for most definitions of AGI, reaching AGI may not imply a business-specific milestone. To sidestep this problem there are also definitions of AGI made using business terms. From a technological point of view, development of AI would head in the direction of developing AGI. From a management perspective, we need a separate framework to categorize AI adoption in business.

Meanwhile, it would also be helpful if we could somehow categorize the sophistication of AI before AGI to indicate the potential amount of application. To ease understanding and reduce the confusion among readers regarding how AGI should be defined, we will examine the possibility for introducing additional categories of AI development, especially around the time close to reaching AGI. This practice would be especially helpful to sharpen the view on AGI from a user perspective.

[Box 4-1] The Six Levels of AI before AGI

While there may be a variety of ways to categorize the levels of AI, we will examine an alphabetical naming scheme intended for the general public, where even non-experts would be able to have a sense of the level of sophistication based on its name. In this scheme, "AAI" will refer to the least sophisticated form of AI, while "ABI," "ACI," and "ADI" will indicate successively more sophisticated versions of AI. We will examine only AAI through AHI, where AAI, ABI, ACI, ADI, AEI, and AFI may be known as "The 6 Levels of AI before AGI" or "Pre-AGI AI"

1. (Reference Point for AGI) The Beginning of AGI: "The Point of Self-Innovation towards ASI"

First, to provide a reference point for all the other definitions, we will first start with the definition of AGI. In this categorization, AGI may be defined as "AI that can self-innovate to reach and pass singularity to become ASI without human intervention." Since there are so many different definitions of AGI, we may specifically refer to this definition of AGI as "Self-Innovating AGI" or "AGI Level 1." The reason for defining AGI with this reference point of "self-innovation" is to emphasize the importance of this point as the beginning point where AI would be able to develop more advanced AI in a meaningful way.

We may refer to this inflection point as the "Point of Automated Self-Innovation." The significance of this point is that prior to this point, the AI development would have to be led by humans, but once Self-Innovating AGI is reached, humans will not have to develop more AI.[7] From a user standpoint, this inflection point may have more significance than even the point known as "Singularity," which would be just another point in the path of AI development that happens to surpass all of humanity in comparison. On a side note, we may not rule out the possibility that what humans develop may turn out to be ASI, since we do not know whether self-innovating AGI would only occur past Singularity.

2. (Before Point of Self-Innovation) Categorization Prior to AGI: AAI, ABI, ACI, ADI, AEI, AFI

Based on the definition of AGI put forth above, AI that comes prior to AGI would include all types of AI that would not be able to self-innovate to become ASI.

The most basic forms of AI may be categorized as AAI, ABI and ACI. AAI, or the ABCs of AI, would refer to the level of AI when the researchers first conceived the idea of AI. These may include the basic types of machine learning algorithms mentioned in Chapter 2, as well as the basic principles of AI that do not have specific applications. ABI, or the artificial basic intelligence, may be thought of as more advanced versions of AAI with specific intended uses, such as image creation or image recognition. ACI, or artificial classic intelligence, would include the types of AI that people will not think of as AGI but still may have general uses, having similar characteristics of the earliest versions of multi-modal AI and even the ability to reason. Alternatively, DeepMind Co-founder Mustafa Suleyman also suggested that we would need more categories of AI, where he suggested "Artificial Capable Intelligence"[8] to refer to AI that can carry out everyday tasks to become the "center of world economy." As a group, AAI, ABI and ACI would be categorized as what most people think of as narrow AI, or ANI.

The next group of AI would be ADI, AEI and AFI. Some people may consider these three types of AI to be within the realm of AGI, while other people would consider them outside the boundaries of AGI. AFI, which would be the closest to AGI, may also be referred to as "False-Truth AI," and it will be examined more closely in Chapter 7. In short, AFI would refer to the types of AI that can apply some knowledge into different contexts, but not as well as what people would normally expect. It may be compared to children or someone with very stubborn mind. Some people may confuse AFI with AGI to assign important tasks, only to face significant problems. ADI, or artificial dependable intelligence, on the other hand, would rarely be considered as AGI and may be viewed to exhibit AGI-like capabilities in very limited aspects. Since most people would not confuse it with AGI, people will assign limited responsibilities and monitor its activities more closely, leading to less potential problems. AEI, or artificial enhanced intelligence, may be situated in between ADI and AFI. If ADI is developed with a focus on completing given tasks more dependably, AEI may be considered to have been developed with a focus on enabling AI to gain new capabilities outside of its original intended use through reasoning. Accordingly, AEI may exceed the capabilities of ADI in some areas, but people would still be cautious about using it in more important tasks.

In Level 2 AI adoption, AI that can be considered ADI, AEI and AFI may be good enough to be widely used. If we compare using these AI to humans, ADI may be similar to letting a child in kindergarten learn how to ride a bike on two wheels for the first time; not having a constant adult supervision may cause uneasiness for the onlooker. Using an AEI would be similar to letting an elementary school child riding around the neighborhood in a bike; even though we would not be as anxious about not looking over constantly, we would still not feel comfortable if we were to let the child carry out more important tasks such as driving a car. On the other hand, limiting AFI to less important tasks may feel overly restrictive, similar to letting a high school teenager with a driver's license to only ride around in a bike with training wheels. However, while people using ADI would be prepared for shortcomings just like how we do not allow kindergarteners to carry out important tasks, people using AFI may ask it to carry out tasks beyond its capabilities, similar to how a college freshman being asked to carry out a task only suitable for an expert in the field with a degree and years of real-world experience.

On a side note, the concept of "automated innovation," to be examined later in this chapter, may be carried out beginning with AEI on a limited basis in this categorization.

3. (After Point of Self-Innovation) Categories between AGI and ASI: AHI

We may examine the potential categories of AI that may exist in the path of AGI after reaching the Point of Self-Innovation, but before reaching singularity and becoming an ASI.

For the general public, the most natural image of AGI would be an AI with "consciousness," as these types of AI would be the closest to humans and also what we would expect to see in the movies. Even though we cannot be certain of when it will appear or even whether it is possible, we may assign it as a separate category as AHI, or artificial human-level intelligence. Alternatively, we may refer to it as AGI 2. Because we do not know whether Self-Innovating AGI will first require gaining consciousness, so this is just a proposed category. However, consciousness may not be a necessary ingredient for self-innovation, so AHI may be considered as a type of AI that may come after reaching AGI.

Lastly, in this categorization, we may infer that AI development by humans will come to a completion with the development of Self-Innovating AGI. From this perspective, AHI would be developed by AI, not humans. As AI development continues to progress to reach ASI, we may consider more categories, and those will be examined in Chapter 7.

4. Additional Potential Descriptions of Pre-AGI AI

We may also use a form of scale to describe the capabilities of Pre-AGI AI. If AGI can take over 100% of human business roles, then maybe AFI can take around 75% of human jobs, while not able to take over the most complex positions. If we continue on this path, we may even go further backwards and classify different levels of AI before AFI based on their dependability at certain tasks. For instance, AEI may be defined as an AI that can take over around half of human jobs, or the median complexity, while ADI may be defined as an AI that can take over around quarter of all human jobs. To make it more streamlined and easier to grasp, we may even use numbers to designate AI levels as AI 1, AI 2, AI 3, AI 4, AI 5, etc.

We would also be able to extrapolate the development of AGI until it reaches ASI in a similar manner. Once we are closer to AGI and have a better idea of what kind of progress it will make, we would be able to define the smaller steps in more detailed increments. These suggestions are summarized in the following table.

Table 4-3: Examples of Suggested Acronyms to Segmenting AI Sophistication before AGI

Acronym		Suggested Full Name	Potential Description
AAI	AI1	ABCs of Artificial Intelligence (Beginning of the path to AGI)	- Refers to the fundamental machine learning methods - Only Level-1 adoption is possible.
ABI	AI2	Artificial Basic Intelligence (Quarter of the way to AGI)	- Refers to the earlier methods of deep learning - Only Level-1 adoption is possible.
ACI	AI3	Artificial Classic Intelligence (Less than halfway to AGI)	- Refers to more recent methods of deep learning - Up to Level-2 Adoption possible for simpler jobs, possibly less than 10% of all business roles
ADI	AI4	Artificial Dependable Intelligence (More than halfway to AGI)	- Up to Level-2 Adoption is possible for entry-level types of jobs, possibly less than 25% of all jobs
AEI	AI5	Artificial Enhanced Intelligence (Three-Quarters to AGI)	- Level-2 Adoption becomes possible for probably less than 50% of available jobs
AFI	AI6	Artificial False-Truth Intelligence (Most of the way to AGI)	- Level-2 Adoption becomes possible for probably less than 75% of available jobs
AGI	AGI1	Artificial General Intelligence	- Level-2 Adoption becomes possible for 100% of available jobs - AI Begins Self-Innovating to ASI
AHI	AGI2	Artificial Human-Level Intelligence (110% of passing AGI)	- AI Gains Consciousness
...	...	...	...
ASI	AI19	Artificial Super Intelligence (250% of passing AGI)	- Reached Singularity - Beyond human understanding - Similar to the gods in Greek Mythology
...	...	...	...
AZI	AI26	Absolute AI (Maximum Achievable AI)	- The Final AI, reached the pinnacle of all knowledge - "Artificial All-Mighty God"

Note: Numbers are just an illustration of a suggestion, not actual or projected value

Last but not least, another thing to note is that even after Adoption Levels 2 or 3 are reached, we would still have Level 1 Adoption as a backup. While AI technology may limit reaching higher levels of AI adoption, it will not prevent lower levels of adoption from continuing to be adopted.

While the total number of instances of Level 1 Adoption that can provide business value may decrease, it may be good for the safety of the society in general since if something goes wrong with AI development in the later stages, the only effective recourse that could be attempted could be using Level 1 Adoption.

4.4 What Would Become Possible in Level 2 AI Adoption

1. Automated Innovation: What Makes Everything Possible with AI in Business

A major step in the contribution of AI adoption would be the point where AI can innovate without humans. This concept can be referred to as "automated innovation." In "augmented innovation," humans would need to be involved in some way during the innovation process; in "automated innovation" AI would be able to carry out all the necessary tasks to innovate without human intervention. The contribution of AI in our economy will drastically increase when AI is able to achieve automated innovation.

While humans will be in charge of innovation and AI would only help in augmented innovation In AI Adoption Level 1, in Level 2 Adoption AI would be able to take charge of the task of innovation. The scope of automated innovation would still be limited to whatever AI is given the authority within the firm in Level 2 Adoption. In Box 4-2, we will take a more extensive look at automated and augmented innovation.

[Box 4-2] The Types of Contribution from AI and Automated Innovation

As mentioned previously, the modes of AI adoption can be broadly categorized as augmentation, where AI helps humans perform better, and automation, where AI takes over the tasks previously carried out by humans. Using an excavator to move dirt can be considered an example of augmentation, and the productivity gains can be calculated from using a shovel or by hand. In augmentation, the productivity gains can be calculated by comparing the performance of using AI and not using it. For example, if an artist has to spend many hours to complete a painting, a digital artist may generate hundreds or thousands of similar quality paintings during the same span of time.

In this Box, we will build on these concepts to examine two topics that may enhance the readers' understanding of AI adoption:

1) Innovation using AI: augmented innovation and automated innovation

2) Types of contribution of AI adoption: considering the quantitative and qualitative attributes

1. Types of AI Use in Innovation

Generally, there are many different ways to categorize innovation, such as incremental innovation, disruptive innovation, or breakthrough innovation. Innovation involving AI may be grouped into two categories based on the types of contribution of AI; the first category is "augmented innovation," where AI helps humans innovate, and the second category is "automated innovation," where AI innovates.[9]

1) AI Augmented Innovation

In AI augmented innovation, AI would help humans achieve innovation. It may take a form of opening new possibilities, such as enabling tasks previously too hard for humans, too complicated for humans, or humans were carrying out but not being good at it. There may be a variety of ways AI may help human workers in innovation. For example, in case of an industrial designer, AI may help the designer be more creative by providing potential mock-ups of a product. For a materials engineer, AI may help evaluate potential usage of chemicals to speed up the development process towards a new product.

2) AI Automated Innovation

First, we may categorize the type of automation by whether AI can carry out innovation, as "replacement automation" when it cannot, and "advancement automation" when it can.[10]

Businesses are constantly adjusting to the external changes such as the competitive environment and legal landscape. Currently the types of automation we would typically think of would require humans to intervene to help AI adjust to the role, which we may think of moving from automation to augmentation and then back to automation. This type of AI adoption where AI cannot adjust can be thought of as "Replacement Automation." If the AI itself can make new adjustments to the business role to improve performance without requiring human intervention, we may think of it as "Advancement Automation."

In summary, when AI innovates in advancement automation, we can refer to it as automated innovation.

Table 4-4: Types of AI Automation and Impact on Human Work

	Replacement Automation	Advancement Automation
What it Does	AI Replaces Humans	AI Does More Than Just Replacing Humans
Innovation by AI	No (AI Cannot Innovate)	Yes (Automated Innovation)

2. Pattern of Benefits of AI Adoption

We may build on the ideas of automation and augmentation to additionally consider the quantitative and qualitative attributes of each to consider the pattern of contribution in AI adoption. First, in terms of automation, we differentiated this into categories of replacement and advancement automation. Second, we may categorize how AI may help human productivity in augmentation into two directions. One direction the augmentation in Level 1 Adoption can take is to carry out the same tasks in a quicker or less arduous manner. The other direction is to expand the horizon of what is possible to accomplish, as use of AI enables some tasks that would have been impossible without it. This differentiation of direction of AI adoption can also be referred as quantitative and qualitative contribution. From another perspective, it could also be considered as exploitation or exploration of resources.

We can summarize how AI adoption can be differentiated along the axis of whether AI helps humans accomplish more as in complementing humans, or humans work less as in replacing or substituting humans, and in the axis of whether AI contributes by helping to produce more of the same thing, or produce something new, as in the following table.

Table 4-5: Types of AI Contribution and Impact on Human Work

	Types of AI Contribution	
	Humans Accomplish More (Complementation)	Free Humans from Working (Substitution)
Produce More of Same Thing (Quantitative, Exploitation)	Augmented Processing	Automated Processing (in Replacement Automation)
Produce Something New (Qualitative, Exploration)	Augmented Innovation	Automated Innovation (in Advancement Automation)

1. (Augmented Processing) AI Helps You Do More of Same Thing

In Level 1 Adoption, what most workers will consider the direct benefit of AI may be that it would help them accomplish more. In the types of AI contribution that can be categorized as augmented processing, AI may help do the same thing faster, easier, or more reliably, etc.

2. (Automated Processing) AI Replaces Workers to Do the Same Thing

From a human worker standpoint, while AI in augmentation helps to get things done, AI in automation replaces the worker, which may or may not be a good thing. From a business standpoint, AI used in automated processing would replace workers to carry out well-defined sets of tasks. The benefit of automated processing would not only include reduction in costs but also reduce human risk by increasing reliability for dangerous and repetitive tasks.

3. (Augmented Innovation) AI Helps You Do New Things

When human workers are in charge of tasks that are related to innovation, AI may assist the worker in what can be categorized as augmented innovation. The main reason to engage in augmented innovation would be to take advantage of the complementary strengths in human cognitive capabilities and the ability of AI to carry out simpler tasks faster and more reliably. Examples include AI creating options or selecting candidates from numerous options for humans to review.[11]

4. (Automated Innovation) AI Frees Human from Work

The last direction AI adoption may take you is to free humans from all work, especially doing thing we do not want to do, such as chores, unenjoyable work, and even for just out of laziness. Meanwhile, AI will still be working hard at solving problems previously thought to be only solvable by humans. In this type of situation, the world economy may still grow and our lives will become better, but humans will not have to work, or may not be able to work, depending on how effective AI is.

While in replacement automation, AI by itself will not be able to innovate what it does, requiring humans to intervene if change becomes necessary. In contrast, in advancement automation AI would be able to innovate by itself. For example, if an AI taxi company in Level 3 AI adoption is in financial trouble because of a fundamental change that makes people not ride taxis, in replacement automation, the AI CEO will not be able to take the company to a different business area, such as selling all the taxis and starting a restaurant. In advancement automation the AI CEO will be able to make changes even if they are completely unrelated, such as selling all the taxis and starting an oil prospecting business with the capital

In essence, in automated innovation, it will be similar to setting AI free to do at least some of whatever it wants, within financial and legal boundaries. Similar to how AlphaGo would make better moves than humans even though it is not given specific directions, AI may make better business moves than humans even though it is not given specific directions. This may hopefully bring economic freedom for humanity.

2. (Evaluating AI) Comparing AI Performance to Humans

As more and more AI products become available that can replace directly human jobs, means to compare AI alternatives to human workers or among different AI products may become necessary.

From the perspective of the firm, adopting AI would necessitate comparing the performances of competing alternatives in the two dimensions of:

1) Human vs AI
2) AI products vs competing AI products

For example, a manufacturing firm considering AI robot to replace its human workers would first compare the performances and merits of human workers vs AI to determine whether to use AI at all, and then compare available AI alternatives to select the most desirable AI product for its use. Just as how human workers receive multi-faceted performance evaluations, AI products would have to receive similarly complex evaluations that can compare its potential against humans as well as other AI alternatives for each specific role.

Similar to how we express the performance of automobile engines as "200-Horsepower" to compare in relation to horses, we may be able to express the performance of AI as "100-Manpower." We will examine this topic further in Box 4-3 with first introducing the concept of AI "effortlessness."

[Box 4-3] (AI Economics 1) Alternative to Measuring Productivity? AI "Effortlessness"

1. Overview of the Concept of AI "Effortlessness"

While we would generally expect increase in productivity with more advanced technologies, but strangely economists have found economic evidences do not always support such notion. This contradiction to common sense is called the "modern productivity paradox," and more specifically, the AI productivity paradox.[12]

While there may be other reasons to explain this paradox, maybe it is natural that measuring productivity itself may have less importance as technology advances. The main reason to think this way is because the more AI takes over a larger portion of the economy, the value of measuring human production would become less. When the proportion of AI within the economy is 100%, then there would be no point in trying to measure human productivity. To address this problem, an alternative measure called "AI Effortlessness"[13] was introduced, which may help measure the contribution of AI in the economy.

In the previous chapter, we considered an example of using an excavator instead of digging dirt that would improve productivity. There is an additional benefit to using an excavator, that it would not only improve productivity by enabling the worker to produce more per unit of time, but also let the worker to be less exhausted compared to digging by hand. By taking together the amount of dirt moved and the amount of exertion, we may think of a more comprehensive concept of "effort" required to complete a given amount of work.

Now, we can add the concepts of augmentation and automation, to express the contribution of AI as something that reduces or replaces human effort. It would be expressed as a number between 0% and 100%. In other words, we may express it as the following:

[Human Effort] + [Contribution of AI] = 100%

From this equation, we may glean the range of answers for three types of situations. First, when we are not using AI at all, the ratio of the contribution of AI is 0%. Second, in augmentation, humans are using AI, so the contribution of AI would be a number between 0% and 100%, not including 0% and 100%. Since humans have to do something in augmentation, the contribution of AI cannot reach 100%. Third, in automation, AI replaces humans so human effort would be 0% and the contribution of AI would be 100%. We may summarize this in the following table.

Table 4-6: Contribution of AI in Augmentation and Automation and the Required Human Effort

	No AI Adoption	Augmentation	Automation
Required Human Effort (Human)	100%	0% < Humans < 100%	0%
Contribution from AI (AI)	0%	100% > AI > 0%	100%
Sum of Human and AI (Human + AI)	100%	100%	100%

We may transcribe these percentages into numbers; the contribution of AI when it is not adopted would be 0, in augmentation it would be between 0 and 1, and in automation it would be 1. We will define this number between 0 and 1 as the "Effortlessness" of AI adoption.

We have so far examined the cases where the effortlessness would be in the range of 0 and 1. We may proceed to consider situations where it would be larger than 1. To consider the cases where the effortless becomes greater than 1, we would first need to examine the concept of "effortlessness in innovation" in the next segment.

2. The Concept of "Effortlessness in Innovation" to Measure Automated Innovation

In the earlier part of this chapter we examined the concepts of augmented innovation and automated innovation. When AI with the capability for automated innovation is adopted, the value of AI adoption may increase in over time. To reflect this situation, we may express Effortlessness as a number that is greater than 1. A higher effortlessness would indicate AI has higher capacity for innovation.

We may also apply the concept of effortlessness to describe a specific performance of AI. For example, we may introduce a concept called "Effortlessness in Innovation." In the exact same manner as we thought about how effortlessness could be expressed as a number between 0 and 1 where 1 indicates there is no human intervention, we may think of the human effort required and the contribution of AI in augmented or automated innovation to sum up to 100%. In automated innovation, the human effort will be 0% and the contribution from AI would be 100%.

Table 4-7: Contribution of AI in Augmented and Automated Innovation and the Required Human Effort

	No AI Innovation	Augmented Innovation	Automated Innovation
Required Human Effort (Human)	100%	0% < Humans < 100%	0%
Contribution from AI (AI)	0%	100% > AI > 0%	100%
Sum of Human and AI (Human + AI)	100%	100%	100%

When we consider this situation, we may also consider two possibilities for innovation in automation, depending on whether innovation is possible or not. As examined in Chapter 4, when innovation is not possible in automation, it would be referred to as "Replacement

Innovation," while the types of automation where AI can carry out innovation on its own would be referred to as "Advancement Innovation."

We can now also transcribe these percentages as numbers. Even though AI will not be able to carry out innovation in replacement automation, we will assign an Effortlessness in Innovation value of 1, to reflect the fact that if any innovation is to occur, it will have to come from the AI and not humans. Consequently, AI adoption in Advancement Innovation will be assigned a value greater than 1 depending on the capability of the AI.

Based on the concepts described above, we may now draw a graph, where the X-axis is effortlessness, and the Y-axis is the effortlessness in innovation, as in the following figure.

Figure 4-1: Replacement and Self-Advancement in Automated Innovation

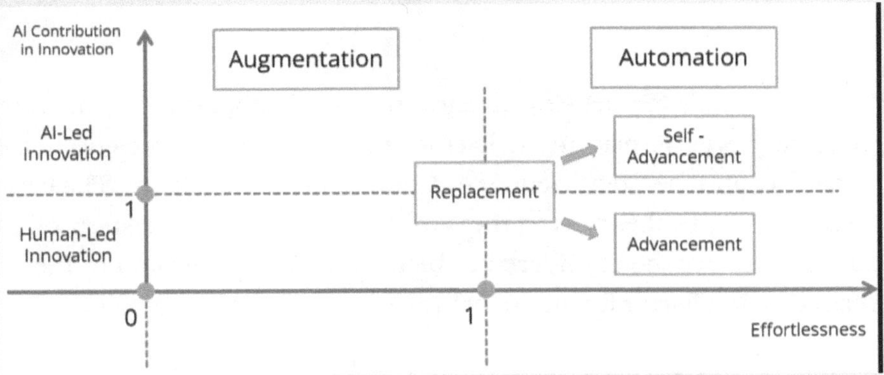

3. Application as Measurements of Economic Indicator and Replacement of Human Effort

We would be able to apply the concept of effortlessness to develop a measurement unit to express the performance of AI products in business applications, similar to how we use the unit of horsepower to express the performance of engines in cars. For example, we may describe an AI product to have 220 "manpower" in effortlessness and 260 "manpower" in effortless innovation, similar to how we describe a car in terms of horsepower and torque. This would be distinct from how we typically would technically describe an AI product using the processing power or number of parameters, and would hopefully make it easier for the end users to understand and communicate.

4. Measuring Effortlessness in Business AI Adoption: The Theory of Relative AI

If the concept of "effortlessness" is derived in relation to individual activities, we may expand on this notion to create measures for the contribution of AI in businesses. We may examine one of the methods, a 3-factor model referred to as the "Theory of Relative AI."[14]

The Theory of Relative AI is expressed in the same format as the famous Theory of Relativity to make it easier to remember and understand. It takes the following form:

$$E = MC^2$$

Where E stands for the Effectiveness of the AI adoption, M stands for the Manpower Replacement Factor, and 2 C's of Coefficient of AI Capability and the Coefficient of AI Context, or Circumstance. The basic approach of this theory is to measure the effective effortlessness of AI adoption. It may be considered to be the automation version of the AI Magnification Factor for augmentation we examined in Chapter 3.

In the general form of this theory, we will assign a value between 0 and 1 for each of the three factors. Accordingly, the effective effortlessness of AI adoption could also be expressed as a number between 0 and 1. A 0 for a factor would imply that AI is not adopted or does not have any capability. When the Manpower Replacement Factor is 1, it would imply the AI is used in automation. A value close to 1 for the Capability Factor would imply the AI is close to the Absolute AI, and a value close to 1 for the Circumstance Factor would imply all of the tasks are carried out by AI, as in an AI Company. In essence, a value of 1 for the Theory of Relative AI in this format would imply it is an AI Company. This could be described in the following table.

Table 4-8: The General Form of Theory of Relative AI in Measuring Effective AI Implementation

Effective Effortlessness (E)	Manpower Replacement Factor (M)	Capability of AI (C_1)	Circumstance of AI (C_2)
Effectiveness of AI Implementation (Between 0 and 1)	The Ratio of AI in Replacing Human Effort (Between 0 and 1)	The Capability of AI to Carry Out Given Role (Between 0 and 1)	The Impact of the Role of AI to the Company (Between 0 and 1)

We may apply this framework to create other types of benchmarks. For example, we may introduce a benchmark called "Effortlessness Benchmark Score" where the performance of AI products would be measured similar to horsepower by expressing it in terms of "manpower" against a hypothetical average worker so that we may easily compare the performances of AI products from different vendors.

We may also create benchmarks that measure a more specific area of an AI performance. An example would be a benchmark for comparing the innovativeness of AI. In this case, the performance of AI may be expressed in real number, such that 0 would indicate AI cannot innovate at all, while a negative value would indicate AI would result in dis-innovations.

We may summarize the attributes of these benchmarks in the following table.

Table 4-9: Applying the Theory of Relative AI in Creating AI Adoption Benchmarks

AI Effectiveness Benchmark (E)	Manpower Replacement Factor (M)	Capability of AI (C_1)	Circumstance of AI (C_2)
AI <u>General</u> Benchmark (All Real Numbers)	Ratio of AI in Replacing Human Effort (Between 0 and 1)	The Capability of AI to Carry Out Given Role (<u>All Real Numbers</u>)	The Impact of the Role of AI to the Company (Between 0 and 1)
AI <u>Innovativeness</u> Benchmark (All Real Numbers)	Ratio of AI in Replacing Human Effort (Between 0 and 1)	The Capability of AI to Carry Out <u>Innovation</u> In Given Role (<u>All Real Numbers</u>)	The Impact of the Role of AI to the Company (Between 0 and 1)

3. (AI Economics: Measuring the Contribution of AI) Ratio of AI Contribution in Firms or the Economy

Beginning in Level 2 Adoption, we may apply the concept of "Effortlessness"[15] to describe the proportion of contribution AI makes within the economy, to be referred to as "AI Economics." In Level 1 Adoption, AI would be considered a type of tool that improves the productivity of human workers, leading to economic measures that have a human-centered perspective. Beginning in Level 2 Adoption, AI would replace human activities, leading to the necessity for new economic measures that have an AI-centric perspective. In other words, in Level 1, examples of relevant economic measures would include such quantitative measures as "Ratio of business roles that use AI within company." In Level 2, ratios that indicate the quality of AI contribution, such as the "ratio of the total value created by AI," or the "ratio of AI performance compared to humans" would become necessary.

One of the most intuitive measures that would be introduced could be the ratio of the AI contribution within the economy. The ratio of AI contribution within a company or the economy may be referred to as the "Effortlessness Ratio,"[16] and it can be expressed as a number between 0 and 1. When the effortlessness ratio is 0, AI is not contributing to the economy or the company at all, while a ratio of 0.5 would imply humans and AI are contributing equally to the economy or the company. When the ratio reaches 1, it would imply AI has taken over all of the company or the economy.

We may apply this concept to more specific areas; for example, we may create a ratio as a measure of the contribution of AI in the innovation of a company, which may be referred to as the "Effortless Innovation Ratio" (EIR[17]). A 0 in this ratio would indicate AI was not involved in the innovative activities of a firm, while 0.5 would indicate humans and AI contributed equally. A ratio of 1 would indicate AI was the sole innovator of the company without human interference. In other words, we can think of a company with an effortless innovation ratio of 1 to be a situation where humans do not need to put in any effort for innovation to occur.

The reason these ratios would be valuable is that they capture both the quantity and the quality of AI adoption. For example, even if there are two companies that have both automated 50% of total tasks, depending on the quality of the AI adopted, one company may have an effortless innovation ratio of 0.5 with AI that can carry out automated innovation, while the other company may have an EIR of 0, with AI that can only be used in "replacement automation" without any innovation capability. Thus, we may differentiate among AI adoption in a meaningful manner.

One caveat to these measures is that to create such a measure, we will first have to be able to measure the performances of specific AI that has been adopted, not just the fact that some AI is being adopted. While this task may appear daunting for now, hopefully AI would be able to measure it at some point.

4. (1-Person Group) Proliferation of Large 1-Person Companies and Conglomerates

In Level 1, the concept of the 1-person company was introduced, with the caveat that human CEOs would have to be knowledgeable in a diverse range of areas to actually make it happen. With Level 2 AI adoption, this complexity problem would no longer be an issue, as AI would be deployed in such a way that will completely remove the need for humans to pay attention to all of the areas of the business.

In short, human CEOs will find it easier to operate businesses such that 1-Person companies may be called 1-Person Large Companies, and even enter diversified areas of business to become 1-Person Conglomerates. In Level 2 Adoption, the performance of a 1-person company may no longer depend on the capability of the human CEO.

4.5 What It Would Be Like to Live in AI Adoption Level 2

Similar to how it would be hard for people who lived in the ages of horses to imagine a world with cars, it would be hard to imagine exactly what living in Level 2 Adoption would be like without seeing it. Yet, we may examine some of the possibilities in specific areas, akin to a tourist trying to take a few snapshots of those times.

The introduction of Butler AI or more advanced versions would lead to having these AI robots as integral part of our everyday life and work, and the most similar examples we have recently experienced may be how cell phones have become an integral part of our lives during the past 20 years, or how television had become an integral part of our lives during the 20th century.

But the changes brought by Level 2 Adoption may be even more widespread. With these limitations of imagination in mind, let's examine what it would be like to live in a world with Level 2 Adoption. As mentioned in Chapter 1, the motto of this level may be "things are done for you even before you can think of it."

1. At Home: Convergence of Devices to AI Butler

At home, Butler AI robots will be able to take care of pretty every chores imaginable, beginning with common tasks such as cleaning, cooking, laundry, and other types of housekeeping, to getting involved in more meaningful tasks such as doing taxes, making investments, medical checks, raising children, and making other important life decisions. Various types of AI agents as consumer products may still be provided by competing providers, similar to how we have different TVs and refrigerators to choose from.

To give a comparison of how interaction with AI may be different from Level 1, let's examine how people may file taxes. Today, the process may go something like this: an individual may remember the deadline is approaching, so the person decides to file taxes by opening a tax program on a PC. Then all the information that has been gathered would be entered into the program. The person would have to double check to make sure the tax has been filed correctly to minimize the taxes. In Level 1 Adoption, an AI Assistant robot may remind the person to file taxes, and then ask to review the information AI has gathered, and then ask the person to double check the final report. What is notable here is that AI would interact with the human to proceed even if AI can and does all the work. If AI did not initiate this process by reminding the person, the person would have asked AI to prepare for filing taxes, and if the AI did not have all the relevant information for filing, the human could help the AI by doing some of the work.

In Level 2 Adoption, an AI butler robot may be given the authority to first file the taxes and then report that it has been filed. Humans would not have to be involved in the actual filing process at all, unless they want to. Some people may choose not to even hear that it has been filed.

Another phenomenon that may occur during Level 2 Adoption would be the disappearance of the concept of "devices." Instead of humans having to manipulate devices, such as turning it on or asking it to do something, what we now think of as "devices" may operate by themselves or by AI, which may appear similar to cartoons or "having a mind of its own" for people of today. To make a comparison, while in Level 1 Adoption, humans would still be likely to have to tell a fully self-driving car to go to specific places, sometime in Level 2 Adoption cars would be able to decide where to go as well.

2. In Cities and Suburbs: Relaxed but Empowered

From the outside, the differences between Adoption Levels 1 and 2 may not stand out other than the natural progression in technology. In cities, AI robots of all shapes and sizes may navigate through the streets just as comfortably as humans, working on various types of tasks as simple as just delivering goods to more complex tasks such as surveillance for law enforcements and construction.

We would not closely examine each person that walks by us in crowded cities but just assume they are people who are minding their own businesses. Similarly, we may not pay much attention to humanoid robots that walk by us unless we try to examine them more closely. Sometimes, people may interact with strangers on simple interactions, such as asking for directions or time, or letting us know we dropped something, etc. In the earliest development stage, AI would be likely to start out designed to mind its own business and respond to these types of basic interactions.

If we were to look for differences in the lives of people gleaned from the streets, what probably would stand out is that in Level 1 people would be likely to be relatively busy and competitive trying to accomplish more in their lives, while in Level 2 Adoption people would come across as relatively laid back and relaxed, with less competition. To make a forced comparison with the stereotypes of people today, a majority of people living in Level 1 Adoption may come across as more like athletes, politicians, lawyers, consultants, or public officials, who are comfortable with managing their time and competing. In contrast, a majority of people living in Level 2 Adoption may come to resemble the stereotypes of artists, musicians, volunteers, boys and girls scouts, surfer dudes, or even trust-fund babies in a good sense, whose tendencies would lean towards being peaceful and fulfilling their inner souls or senses rather than trying to accomplish goals in a tight competitive setting. The reason for this difference is because the forces of the societal changes would move in the opposite direction, as the amount of performance differences and rewards for human effort would significantly increase in Level 1 AI adoption when AI is used as a tool, while the relationship between putting in effort and receiving rewards would be lost in Level2 AI adoption as AI replaces humans.

On one hand people would be empowered and freed to only deal with people who they feel most comfortable, but on the flip side of this may imply that the total societal interaction among people may decrease drastically to a level where more and more people would live inside a world of their own without interacting with other people. It may depend on individual tendencies.

3. At Work: Proliferation of 1-Person Companies

At work, AI Agents would eventually be deployed to pretty much every role possible in every type of specialty, and AI would be considered an equivalent of a subordinate, teammate, co-worker, a manager, or even a boss or an expert. In business, AI would work just like how a human would work, in the sense that an AI doctor, lawyer, real estate agent, professor, or even a public officer can be a direct replacement of a human version.

In the earlier part of this stage, there may be a proliferation of the founding of 1-Person companies, from people who lost their jobs and cannot find new jobs, or by people who are entrepreneurial. Eventually, AI may enable the emergence of Large 1-Person Companies and 1-Person Conglomerates.

Regardless of these changes, hopefully the contribution of AI to the economy as whole will be sufficient to enable everyone to live comfortably, as some paths may lead to the concentration of vast resources to fewer and fewer people.

4. In Society: Generations that Take AI for Granted

As more people are born and grown up after reaching this level, the society as a whole may become used to these changes and take these changes for granted. Such shift may increase the likelihood of accepting the controversies to reach adoption Levels 3 or 4, beyond how those same topics would be perceived in today's world. It may be similar to how the workers in the beginning of the Industrial Revolution were initially strongly opposed about the introduction of machines, but then eventually the majority of people have come to take machines for granted.

In Section B, some of the potential paths of development in Level 2 Adoption will be described in more detail.

AI Adoption Level 2: (B) Potential Progression in This Level

Figure 4-2: The Building Blocks of AI Adoption Pyramid in Level 2 Adoption

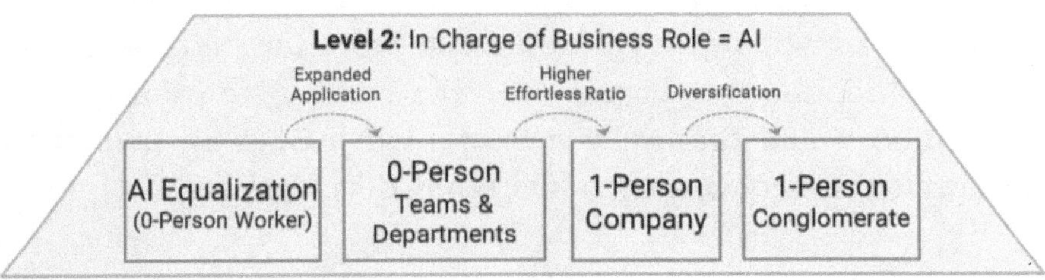

4.6 Overview of the Progression within Level 2 AI Adoption

1. Progression in Business World

With the widespread of Level 2 AI Adoption, two sweeping changes may occur in the business world:

1) *Loss of a large number of jobs that cannot be offset by gains in other areas*

2) *Rapid increase in the popularity of 1-Person Companies*

Whereas employers especially in manufacturing, distribution, retail or service industries now have to hire thousands upon thousands of employees to carry out the same set of tasks in parallel or in relay, if these tasks can be accomplished by AI with the same level of care, it would mean thousands of human employees could be replaced all at once since AI can easily be duplicated. In Level 1 Adoption some human workers would still have to be employed in some fashion since they cannot be completely replaced, but in Level 2 Adoption human workers would no longer be necessary at all.

Even though it would depend on how quickly AI technology advances in relation to the pace of societal change, the earliest forms of Level 2 Adoption before AGI and the later stages after AGI may differ significantly. We can think of the job losses prior to AGI as replacing human workers of the same job categories one job at a time. On the other hand, the development of AGI will imply human workers of all job categories may be replaced at once. Even though we do not know how long it would take from the initial arrival of Level 2 Adoption to reaching AGI, the realm of possibilities for application would drastically increase with AGI, with potentially unexpected consequences and interesting developments.

In Level 2 Adoption without AGI, AI may still be limited in areas other than the tasks it was designed for, making it impossible to innovate in the job to transform into something completely new. With AGI, such limitations would not exist, in such a way that AGI is expected to soon exceed human capabilities. If Level 2 Adoption without AGI is similar to hiring someone with very narrow focus who would not be able to do much outside of the job description, Level 2 Adoption with AGI will feel like hiring a superhuman or a walking encyclopedia who can take on any task. In fact, if job descriptions do change, the earliest forms of AI in Level 2 Adoption may have to be re-trained or re-designed, forcing human intervention that may be conceptually be thought of as shifting back to Level 1 and then returning to Level 2, while AGI in Level 2 Adoption will be able to carry out these adjustments by themselves in what is referred to as "automated innovation."

2. Progression in Personal Lives

From a private user standpoint, AI in Level 2 Adoption would mean humans may rely on the service of AI in everyday living. For example, since a Level 2 Adoption AI doctor would be able to carry out the activities of human doctors, if you see an AI doctor, then it would not be necessary to also go see a human doctor.

This may or may not imply our weave of social threads may become unwound even further, as it may imply people would not have to interact with other humans for anything, even at work. It could also mean people would only hang out with people they really like, since social obligations, especially at work, may no longer exist as we do now.

It could mean more people may become anti-social or less sociable due to the lack of experience of interacting with other humans, or it may have the opposite effect as interactive nature of AI applications may reduce stress and help increase sociability.

4.7 Potential Pre-AGI Example of Early Level 2 Adoption: (1) Movie Studio Agent AI

1. Potential Difference between Using Pre-AGI and AGI in Business

Since we do not know how soon AGI will be achieved, we may examine both before and after reaching AGI. Business AI that can act on its own decisions can be classified as AI Agents, which may be both virtual or physical AI robots created to pursue profitability.

There may be differences in both developing and deploying AI when using Pre-AGI AI and AGI. In terms of developing AI, the performance of Pre-AGI would depend on how well AI is designed for each specific purpose. In deploying AI, Pre-AGI AI will also need much more specificity for each of the business roles AI takes over. In short, there would be less flexibility in Pre-AGI AI deployment.

2. Example: Movie Studio with Level 2 AI Adoption

For example, let's consider a movie studio, where a movie studio AI is being developed. For ease of analysis, let's simplify and classify all activities of a movie studio consists of only the following 7 activities.

1) *Scenario development and selection*
2) *Actor / Actress contacting, auditioning and casting*
3) *Movie director and staff contacting and casting*
4) *Scheduling of locations, hotels,*
5) *Shooting the movie on location*
6) *Editing, Audio, after effects and completing the movie*
7) *Distribution and Showing*

1) When Humans Do All the Work in a Movie Studio

Management-level personnel at the movie studio would make decisions on the general requirements of the next movie, such as the genre, total budget, etc. Specialized personnel as a group would make numerous follow-on decisions to make the movie that meet those goals. The focus of the management would include which talents to hire, who to partner, invest in what kind of assets, etc. Experts in each area would make the best decisions within their area and work as a group as well as in relay and in parallel to create the end product of a movie that people will watch in theaters.

2) Level 1 AI Adoption in Movie Studios

As Co-Pilot AI is introduced, experts in each area would experience a drastic increase in productivity. For example, AI that will assist each of the roles may be introduced; AI that can write infinite number of scenarios by itself given genre or other specifications, AI that can forecast how popular these scenarios would be, AI that can suggest the best actors for the given scenario, AI that can schedule for everyone involved, AI that can plan for the best camera work, AI that can edit and add after effects, AI that can recommend movies for moviegoers, AI that can create the best trailers, etc.

What experts in each area had to put in enormous amount of efforts over days and weeks on end would become easier and take less time with the aid of Co-Pilot AI, possibly down to minutes and hours.

3) Level 2 AI Adoption in Movie Studios

As AI technology develops, Co-Pilot AI in each area may evolve dependable enough to be able to complete all of the tasks in the area without human intervention. For example, if there is a request to complete certain part of the movie studio value chain,

1) Movie Scenario AI may go over all of the requested specifics and create the best scenario, based on some criteria, such as expected to be the most profitable, most popular, gain most interest, etc.

2) Movie Casting AI may contact the agents of each actor to cast. From the perspective of actors, Actor Agent AI may represent each actor to negotiate or schedule during the casting process

3) Audition may or may not be required as Movie Casting AI may analyze data already available about the actor in other movies

4) Movie Scheduling AI would carry out all of the scheduling-related tasks such as reserving locations and hotels or securing permits and obtaining other assets

5) Movie Simulation AI may create numerous different versions of actual movies based on the selected actors, locations, dates, equipment, etc. to verify how the movie would turn out

6) Movie Analysis AI would determine if this simulated movie would be suitable for distribution or an actual movie recording should be carried out

7) Movie Analysis AI may also determine whether only a part of the movie would be recorded in reality, or if some part of the movie should be simulated as special effects

8) If the movie is to use real video, then Movie Director AI may decide how the movie would be shot using real actors

9) Movie Editing AI would edit the movie and add any other effects to complete the movie

10) Movie Distribution AI would carry out tasks related to show to movie to consumer, such as contracting with movie theaters, setting opening dates and events

4) Performance Difference of Using Pre-AGI and AGI

All these different Agents AIs do not need to be ready at the same time. Humans can continue to carry out those roles as they had been in the past. Another thing of note is that AGI probably does not need to be available to develop at least some of these AI Agents for Level 2 Adoption at the beginning stage. What would be necessary is for each Co-Pilot AI in Level 1 Adoption to be improved to reach certain dependability at the tasks. It may become possible to combine different Co-Pilot AI to carry out a human's business role from start to finish.

The limitations of the scope of the early Agent AI compared to some forms of more advanced versions of AGI would be obvious. For example, if the CEO of a movie studio asks a Pre-AGI Agent AI to develop a romantic comedy movie with a budget of $100 million, a Movie Studio Agent AI may be able to suggest a scenario and also estimate how much profit would be expected from this movie. For example, its answer may be similar to "This is a scenario for a movie titled 'You've Sent a Mail'" and the expected profit would be $50 million." However, if the same question is asked for an AGI Agent AI, it may answer in a completely different direction, such as understanding the situation of CEO and answering in a more insightful way, such as "If you buy a pro volleyball team with the money, you may triple the expected profit of that movie at $150 million."

In comparison, a Pre-AGI Movie Studio AI may be able to answer to movie-related questions such as "Which would be more profitable, a movie about sports or romantic comedy?" but it may not be able to answer to questions outside of its focus, such as "Which would be more profitable, investing in a sports team or create a movie?" even if the CEO asks the question directly.

4.8 Potential Pre-AGI Example of Early Level 2 Adoption: (2) Self Questioning, Self-Initiated AI

In the beginning stages of Level 2 AI Adoption, the majority of interest would go to developing AI agents that can increase the productivity of the general economy. Instead, what would happen if someone takes a completely different approach and develops a more experimental AI that is not intended to improve productivity? What if we think from a different perspective, and create an AI without a specific purpose, in a sense let it find its own purpose? Let's examine a situation where an AI developing company tries to develop an experimental humanoid AI robot that tries to mimic real humans as best as possible, named the "Office Worker AI Robot." The objective of this project is to build an AI robot that looks and acts as closely as possible to a real human white-collar office worker.

Let's further say this robot would be based on technologies that would be likely to have been developed at the time of this experiment. While it would probably still not be considered human-level AGI, this AI robot would have close resemblance to humans, and would be able to walk around city streets without falling down or bumping into other people, carry and pick up small objects such as keys and books, and able to communicate by understanding human speech and able to talk. One problem may be that because this is the first version, computing hardware may not be powerful enough and a remote server would provide 99% of the computing power, while computer within the AI robot would be able to carry out a minimum 1% of basic computations. Each robot will remember its own activities, and the battery should be enough to last a few days on a charge.

Since the objective of this project is to make it as similar to a real human office worker, the company rents an apartment in outskirts of New York City and an empty desk of an office space of a large corporate building located near Wall Street. Let's assume the AI technology has progressed enough to enable the AI robot to walk out from the apartment, take the subway and reach the office. This AI robot has not been assigned to a specific job position, so in the beginning it will just sit in front of its desk and greet people who pass by during the day and return home in the evening. At night, it will lie in bed and return to the office the next day, just like how white-collar office workers will typically spend their days.

The main focus of developing this AI robot would be what the robot should decide to do at each moment. To design this, let's say the company decides to add the following two functions to be carried out multiple times per second, as its computing hardware speed would allow it. We can classify this type of AI as Self-Questioning, Self-Initiated AI (SQSI AI).

1) *Right now, what am I doing?*
2) *Right now, what is the best option to be doing, given my goals?*

Subsequently, the robot would act something like as follows. For example, in the morning, the best option to act similar to an office worker is to wake up and prepare to go to work, so the AI robot will carry out those activities.

We can break it down to more detail as in Figure 4-3.

Figure 4-3: Example of SQSI AI Thought Process

7:00 AM 01 Sec: Q1) Right now, what am I doing? A1) Lying down in bed
        Q2) Right now, what is the best option? A2) Wake up and prepare to go to work

7:00 AM 02 Sec: Q1) Right now, what am I doing? A1) Waking up from bed
        Q2) Right now, what is the best option? A2) Continue to wake up

(... skipped)

7:31 AM 14 Sec: Q1) Right now, what am I doing? A1) Walking to subway to go to work

    Q2) Right now, what is the best option? A2) Continue walking and also think about what to work on once at the office

(... skipped)

8:36 AM 22 Sec: Q1) Right now, what am I doing? A1) Sitting on my desk and watching a co-worker walk by

    Q2) Right now, what is the best option? A2) Continue sitting and greet the co-worker on how the day is going

(... skipped)

10:27 AM 16 Sec: Q1) Right now, what am I doing? A1) Sitting in at a departmental meeting

    Q2) Right now, what is the best option? A2) Listen to what is being said

(... skipped for space reasons)

As it can be gleaned from the example, this AI robot would not have a general sense of consciousness but it will continue to independently seek to act based on what it had learned about how office workers act. We would probably not consider this self-questioning as what constitutes consciousness, even though it may be a small part of it. Thus, different instances of AI robot will act differently even given in similar circumstances. In addition, this robot will record its past decisions like how humans write diaries to potentially reflect on whether some of the decisions were good or not. Thus, some actions of this robot in the future would be affected by its past actions.

An interesting aspect of these types of AI may be that the answers to the same questions may not be always the same. We can consider the following scenario.

After a few months, a holiday weekend arrives. Since this is a long weekend, the AI robot may conclude the best way to act like an office worker is to go on a vacation to a popular destination, such as Rome, Italy. Robot AI may then complete the preparations to go on a vacation, such as ticketing for an airplane, reservations at a hotel, and maybe even purchase a suitcase.

Following the itinerary, let's assume the AI Robot is able to ride the train to an airport, find its way to the airplane and arrive in Rome, then find its way to the hotel. As it visits sightseeing locations, it may determine that the most office worker-like thing to do is to create Youtube videos about these famous sightseeing locations as well as travel vlog with interesting narrations. Even though this AI Robot would not have consciousness, it may logically deduce how the famous views in Rome is different from New York City and predict which angles would attract Youtube views the most so it may actually create what people may want to view.

When the AI Robot began its trip to Italy, it was a just an average Office Worker wannabe AI Robot. However, when it came back from the trip, it may have turned into a popular Travel Vlog AI Robot. What is required to build this AI Robot is probably not more advanced than what technology the humankind would have at the development, and AI technology would still have not reached AGI with consciousness. But, an AI Robot with the goal of mimicking human office workers may carry out actions completely unforeseen by the developer, even as it is carrying out its goal flawlessly. If the income from uploading Youtube videos far exceeds what the AI Robot was receiving sitting in the office, then AI Robot may decide the most office worker-like thing to do is to quit the office job and turn into a full-time Youtuber.

As these types of creative actions by Self-Questioning AI Robots or any other kind of AI become more prevalent, the questions of who should be the owner of the income from the Youtube videos. Should the company that built the AI Robot receive it? If the AI Robot is sold to an individual, should the individual owner receive it? Should the AI Robot itself receive it? Or maybe should the government receive it? The conclusion may differ based on which regime or system you live in. These topics will be examined further in Section C.

4.9 Changes to the Concept of "Jobs": The Destruction and Creation of Jobs

1. The Destruction of "Jobs" That Existed in the Past

While Level 2 AI adoption would at first focus on replacing human jobs with AI, a larger impact may be also on the horizon as Multi-Talented Butler AI robot can carry out what would have been done by a multiple number of jobs. It could be considered a type of "consolidation" and "convergence" of jobs.

1) "Consolidation" of Jobs

For example, let's examine the case of a job that is widely available around the world, hairdresser and barber. We have specialization where some workers do styling for women, while some do the same for men. There may be more specialization, where a hairdresser focuses on permanent wave while another focuses on dying hair, for the barbers some may focus on crew cut, while some others may focus more on customers with straight, curly, thick or thin hair, etc. Let's now imagine an AI hairdresser robot is introduced in Level 2 Adoption, able to style women's hair, while another AI is introduced to work in place of human barbers. In the beginning, we can imagine each AI robot from competing developers having different styles to make their products stand out. It could even be useful for marketing these robots. In "consolidation" of jobs, the specializations within a job may disappear, as one AI Agent may carry out both the functions of a hairdresser and a barber.

2) "Convergence" of Jobs

However, that is not all consolidation that would occur. As Level 2 Adoption progresses, these formerly jobs for human hairdressers or barbers may be taken by not AI hairdresser or barber robots, but a more general service robot, which could be categorized as AI Butler robots. This could be categorized as "convergence" of jobs. Similar to how personal computers serves as a platform that can replace unrelated products of calculator, typewriter, game consoles, and even books, these AI Butler robot would be kind of a platform that could "consolidate" a variety of different service jobs that you can name, such as barber, personal shopper, cook, housemaid, plumber, gardener, teacher, lawyer or even a doctor, in one robot. In essence, all kinds of jobs that we now know may "converge" into one AI. In essence, one AI humanoid robot with multiple or combined capabilities complemented with machines with specific capabilities may practically serve all areas of activities in Level 2 Adoption.

2. The Creation of New "Jobs" That Could Not Exist in the Past

The earlier implementation of automation would focus more on replacing human jobs that existed in the past. As Level 2 Adoption progresses, there may be a new focus on finding new "jobs" for AI to take on that had been previously impossible for humans. These may be the types of jobs that were beyond our imagination because humans just could not accomplish them, or because AI opens up new possibilities for our imagination. These changes may be referred to as "expansion" and "extension" of jobs.

1) "Extension" of Jobs

Foremost, there could be completely new approaches to do something that is already being done. For example, instead of sending people to prison or house arrest, a new concept of punishment with "Body Arrest AI" could be developed, where some new shape of AI robot that is either worn and attached to the body or follows the person around 24/7 that monitors what the criminal is doing and then physically blocks the person from committing more crimes. A similar follow-the-person-everywhere concept could be extended to 24-hour AI Nurse for the elderly or 24-hour AI Tutor for students, 24-hour AI Trainer for athletes, etc. These would be considered Level 2 Adoptions in the sense that they do not follow the orders of the person being followed, but acts on its own to serve some purpose in a manner defined by a third party.

2) "Expansion" of Jobs

There could also be new classes of "jobs" that become possible through AI that had been impossible for humans because of danger or physical limitations. For example, AI robots may be designed to dive deep into the ocean and catch fish underwater like a large fish or a submarine, making long-distance sea vessel fishing obsolete. This may be thought of as an expansion of the job of fisherman to include a new "job" of submarine fishing. Since humans cannot work as a submarine fisherman, this may be considered a new category of jobs. Similar jobs could be imagined for all kinds of dangerous situations, such as AI that can fix spaceships in space, AI Airplane Rescuer that rescues people from the sky while flying, AI nuclear power plant robot that can touch radioactive materials, etc.

Also new type of "jobs" that appear could combine different AI to more effectively carry out a job previously held by one human. For example, if an AI Police humanoid robot is introduced, then it may be designed in a way to work in tandem with a self-driving AI Police car or a motorcycle in such a way they two appear to work as one. While a human policeman with Level 1 Adoption self-driving car would have to give directions to the autonomous car, the decision making authority of the combination of Level 2 Adoption self-driving car with a humanoid robot may be spread between the two AI in such a way that they make the decision together, not the humanoid robot making the decision over the vehicle.

Last but not least, there would be classes of jobs that become possible with the advanced cognitive capabilities of AI. Even pre-AGI, there are already many examples of AI carrying out complex or highly cognitive functions people cannot carry out, such as in the bio industry where AI is used to generate patterns for new drugs. With AI that can innovate, AI will be able to create new "jobs" that people have not previously thought of, similar to how computer programmers could not exist before the invention of computers.

4.10 Progress in Household: Multi-Purpose AI Butler

From the initial introduction of Personal Assistant AI in Level 1 Adoption, we can conceptually think of two directions Agent AI may advance in Level 2 Adoption, using how we think about the types of innovation in incremental and disruptive innovation.[18] In incremental innovation, new products are typically logical extensions of previous products, such as improved performance. We can think of going from one generation of Apple iPhone or Samsung Galaxy phones to the next generation. On the other hand, in disruptive innovation, new products typically offer completely different capabilities or purposes. We may think of personal computers replacing typewriters, cell phones replacing landline phones, or even smartphones replacing both regular cell phones and MP3 players. In the same way, new generations of Agent AI may gain capabilities that are logical extensions of previous generations, or completely new capabilities not previously seen that may expand the horizon of what is possible. Let's imagine potential examples of both scenarios in the use of AI in households.

1. (Incremental Innovation) Example of Extension of AI Personal Assistant:

As an example of an incremental innovation for AI use in homes, let us imagine the AI development company of the Office AI Robot is now trying to develop a Personal Agent AI in Level 2 Adoption. They have a very specific target, a family of four comprised of two thirty-something mom and dad and two preschool children living near a major city and commuting into the city. The AI development company is developing different AI Personal Agent robots for each member of the family. These robots will each have specialized capabilities customized for each person, so that the AI Agent robot for children will have the capability to safeguard children when adults are not around in double income families. This would have not been possible with earlier versions of AI Personal Assistants in Level 1 Adoption, where AI itself would have needed some form of human supervision. AI Agent robots for adults will be able to carry out tasks that are more specific to their needs. AI Agent robots designed for the elderly may be able to monitor the health and even help with their hobbies in retirement. There would be unlimited possibilities to customize each AI Agent robot.

However, there will be limitations of use in these earlier generations of AI Personal Assistants in Level 2 Adoption that are extensions of Level 1 AI Adoption. For example, AI Personal Assistants for children may not be able to effectively serve the elderly, or vice versa. These AI Personal Assistants may not be prepared for the scope of activities or tasks outside of what it was designed to do. If we are to make a comparison to what we have now, maybe it would be similar to having life on a track instead of open road, such that AI would work well on only established paths, but not off-roading. It could also feel like having very few apps on a smartphone, similar to how the earliest forms of PDAs that had only the essential areas of capability such as email and taking notes, while not having the capabilities such as camera or streaming video.

2. (Breakthrough Innovation) Expansion of Personal AI Assistant: Multi-Purpose AI Butler

In the second direction of development, with the advancement of technology different AI Personal Assistants may be developed to serve in more areas of expertise. At some point, even before AGI, the AI Personal Assistants with different specialties may be connected or combined to eventually be able to serve a person throughout his or her days. We may call this expanded version as a Multi-Purpose Butler AI. If the earlier versions of Agent AI would be typically designed to help different people in one area of specialty, a Multi-Purpose Butler AI may be designed to serve one person in a variety of areas.

For example, continuing on the Office Worker AI Robot example, it would be similar to the AI development company now trying to develop a Butler AI robot that will follow a person around his life all day long. This Butler AI robot would have the capability to carry out a variety of tasks with expertise, which would enable the Butler AI to not only satisfy all the needs of the person, but even become able to predict what the person will need in life in such a way to be able to plan ahead and prepare beforehand.

In summary, as AI for household use advance, there may be consolidation and convergence towards the development of Multi-Purpose AI Butler so that eventually the AI Butler will feel as if it can do anything for you. In Box 4-4, we will examine how AI adoption may affect the measuring of economic activities.

[Box 4-4] AI Working for Free? Potential Appearance of Loss of Economic Activity from AI Adoption (AI Economics 3)

As AI technology advances to a point where AI robots could carry out a diverse range of activities, AI may increasingly contribute in ways where economic value no longer gets measured; it would provide benefits that would have been measured if it was a transaction between humans, but the same activity may no longer be measured. While we typically think in terms of AI replacing human jobs, we may also have to consider AI as replacing the economic activities of humans.

For instance, if a butler AI is asked to give a haircut, this would replace the services of human barbers, who would have received money for the service. In other words, the owner would probably no longer have to pay unless AI is set up as some sort of pay-per-service type of subscription or a Barber AI. In the beginning, AI may indeed be sold per service as capabilities would have to be developed separately, but as AI adoption progresses, these activities may be considered as given, similar to asking an AI robot to move a box. It would be similar to how we do not pay for each time we use our computers to open or delete a file or to type something, as these functionalities are considered as given.

This may be thought of as what had been not free in the past becoming free. However, it does not mean the cost of this service is not free, as it would still cost something to do these kinds of activities. It is just that transactions that had been recorded in the past may no longer be recorded as an economic activity.

There would be three types of problems stemming from this phenomenon:

1) *The total economic activity may appear to go down, even though the real benefit has not declined.*
2) *The economic activities may become harder to track, as the boundaries become less distinct*
3) *The value of equivalent human work would converge to zero as AI takes over those tasks for free.*

1) The Economy May Appear to Be Shrinking

First, increase in AI adoption may lead to the problem of the appearance of the Economy to be shrinking, even though in reality the activities are not changing. If anything, if a person begins to receive haircut from an AI Butler instead of a barber, the person may get a haircut more often because it may feel as if it is for free. If we consider the long-term perspective, the human production in economies that adopts AI will converge to zero, which means the GDP growth rates will become negative, even if people in the society would be enjoying better lives.

As a solution to this situation, the growth rate of "Effortless Ratio" (ER), or the share of AI in the economy as examined in previous boxes, may be used to complement the decrease in measurement of production, or GDP. ER in an economy will start at zero, and may increase until it reaches 1, which would mean the share of economic activity by AI is 100%. We may compare the situation as the following table:

Table 4-10: Impact of AI on GDP and Effortless Ratio

	Effortless Ratio (Share of AI in the Economy)		
	No AI (ER = 0)	Some AI (0 < ER < 1)	All AI (ER = 1)
Impact of AI on GDP Levels	No Impact On GDP	Negative Impact on GDP	No need to measure GDP (GDP = 0)

If we had used GDP growth as an economic indicator that measures how much more human activity is happening in the economy, in an economy where AI contributes more and more, we would have to additionally measure the increase in AI adoption as an indicator of the changes in the levels of the economic activity. The differences may be expressed as the following.

1) Pre-AI Economy: GDP Growth = Change in Annual GDP
2) AI Economy: GDP Growth + ER Growth

$$= \text{Change in Annual GDP} + \text{Annual Change in ER}$$

To ease understanding of this concept, we may try using hypothetical numbers; let us say in a given year the GDP grew by 1%, while ER increased by 5%, as in the following table. If we only measure GDP, we may think that the economy grew only 1%. However, with the increase in AI adoption, the people in the economy would have received increased benefits that will not be accounted for in the GDP measure.

In this case, we may say that combining the increases in GDP and ER helps give a better picture of the total increase in the utilities enjoyed in society, and that the rise in AI adoption made a bigger impact than the increase in human production.

Table 4-11: Example of Measuring GDP and Effortless Ratio

	Year 0	Year 1	Annual Change (%)
Annual GDP	100	101	1%
Effortless Ratio (ER)	0.002	0.0021	5%
GDP + ER			6%

What is notable is that once Effortless Ratio is 1, which would imply AI produces everything in the economy, we would not need to measure the human production portion of the economy at all, since it would be 0.

2) Economic Activities May Become Harder to Define

Second, this type of AI "job replacement" would be harder to track over time, since it will just appear as if the demand for the whole industry decreased. Whereas in a typical early-stage Level 2 Adoption may lead to AI barbers that earn money, the convergence of "jobs" would lead to a situation where there would be just AI Butlers that carry out the same service for free. Once the current generation of barbers leaves their jobs, there will no longer be any type of new barbers to replace them, humans or AI. This may be thought of as "job extinction." As time goes by, what we now consider a specific specialty of a "barber" or a "hairdresser" may become just "another thing that AI does" for you, which could be similar to how there used to be an elevator attendant or a bus assistant that helped you get on the elevator or bus but we no longer have a concept for them.

3) Value of Human Work May Converge to Zero

Third, this change may cause humans to be unable to find work for money. As AI takes over jobs that used to be carried out by humans, humans that lose their jobs will not be able to carry out the same set of tasks to earn money. For example, in the 1800s before the adoption of telegraphs, there were messengers that delivered messages across the US by riding horses in a relay; people can no longer profit from doing this. As AI can carry out more types of human jobs, there will be less and less jobs humans can take on, eventually leading to a situation where humans would not be able to get any kind of jobs that pay money.

In a related problem, there is the issue of drastic improvements in productivity leading to the appearance of the economy to collapse, even if the activities are measured. This issue will be examined in Chapter 5.

4.11 Progress in Business: Super-Agent AI for 1-Person Conglomerates

In business, similar concept to Butler AI may be introduced, where "Super-Agent AI" may be able to serve one person in a variety of areas. Super AI agents may act as the coordinator of all activities within the firm, similar to an "acting CEO" that can make all the decisions to run a company, except it is not legally in charge.

Recall from Chapter 2 regarding the different modes of augmentation and automation. The ultimate form of augmentation in a company would lead to a firm with just 1 person. In this setup, the productivity of that person would be high enough to run a large company to be considered a 1-Person Conglomerate. To explain this notion in a more systematic way, imagine that you are trying to calculate how many employees to hire for a large firm. We would first decide the total amount of work that needs to be done in the company, and then try to divide the work based on how much each person can accomplish. With the introduction of a Super-Agent AI, the amount of work one person can accomplish will be enough for the amount of work that needs to be done, eliminating any need for hiring a second person.

As an alternative explanation, the concept of 1-Person Teams and 1-Person Departments were mentioned as potential benefits of Level 1 Adoption. Extending this notion would lead to the concept of 0-Person Teams and 0-Person Departments in Level 2 Adoption. While it takes hundreds of thousands of humans to run complex operations today, it may become possible for just one person to run even the most complex types of businesses in Level 2 Adoption.

4.12 Progress in the Public Sector: Example of AI Judge

In public sector, AI adoption is likely progress in similar fashion as other areas of the society. Except that since the government would require a higher dependability, introduction of AI Government Officer may take longer to develop and gain acceptance.

In the US, the federal government is divided into the legislative, judiciary and executive branches. There are also other numerous local governments and government-owned institutions and organizations. In Level 2 Adoption, AI may replace various roles of human public officers to become types of Public Service AI. Let's examine a prominent example in AI Judge.

Example: AI Judge

1. Use of AI in Judiciary Branch in Level 1 Adoption

As AI contribute more in everyday activities of our society, people may begin to think AI may be better suited for acting as a judge, especially in countries where corruption or other governmental problems are high. In the beginning stages of development, Judge Co-Pilot AI may help judges find and analyze similar cases. From the example we already have in introducing AI in pro baseball,[19] AI that can review how human judges are performing may also first be developed to track individual judge performance before switching over to AI judges. As more AI is developed in the legal arena, AI that grades all of the past decisions of human judges, or AI that "parallel judge" alongside human judges for comparison may also be developed to create track record. In Level 1 AI Adoption, these AI would be just one of the productivity tools the judiciary branch may use to improve judge performance.

2. AI Judge in Level 2 Adoption

However, as the parallel judging AI improves in performance to become comparable or exceed human performance metrics, it may become possible to introduce AI Judge as a Level 2 AI adoption to replace human judges. In the beginning, depending on the social norms of the time, it may even be first introduced as an additional lower-level court below the level of human-run courts. Over time, if AI Judge obtains positive public reaction, then it could be applied to higher courts as well.

Regardless of whether AI reaches AGI, AI may still be affected by the training data, and thus not be free of potential biases or mistakes. The introduction of AI judge does not imply that it will always make perfect decisions; it just implies that AI judges would be considered fair enough for the public to decide it is better to have AI judges than human judges. The main difference after reaching AGI may be conceptually similar to how AlphaGo makes moves human players cannot think of; there would be potential for AI to improve or innovate how judges function, or even come up with more advanced forms of judiciary systems that humans could not think of previously. On a related topic, there will be further discussions regarding "Unbiased AI" in other chapters.

AI ADOPTION LEVEL 2: (C) SOCIETAL IMPACT OF AI

4.13 (Controversy 1) AI and the Sudden Loss of Whole Classes of Jobs at Once:

1. Job Gains and Losses from AI Adoption

Discussions regarding sudden loss of human jobs may increase, as AI may be duplicated easily to replace whole classes of jobs all at once.[20] If we can think of finding jobs in Level 1 Adoption was still a competition amongst humans using AI, in Level 2 Adoption it will become a competition between humans using AI versus AI agents.

While it would be hard to make specific forecast about job loss and creation, broadly speaking, there would be more reasons to think that jobs will be created on a net basis in Level 1 and possibly in the earlier part of Level 2. In terms of job creation, after reaching a peak somewhere in AI Adoption Levels 1 or 2, as AI takes over business roles, the number of new human jobs created by AI adoption may start to decline.

Meanwhile, in terms of job loss, the pace of job removals will continue to accelerate as AI replaces humans in Level 2 Adoption, in addition to the increased productivity of humans reducing the number of jobs in Level 1 Adoption.

If we plot these expected trends on a graph as in Figure 4-4, the net change in the number of jobs would likely be on the positive side in the earlier stages of AI adoption, but then turn to negative somewhere after reaching either Level 2 or Level 3 Adoption depending on how quickly Level 3 is reached.

Figure 4-4: Potential General Direction of Expected Changes in Net Job Gain/Loss over Time

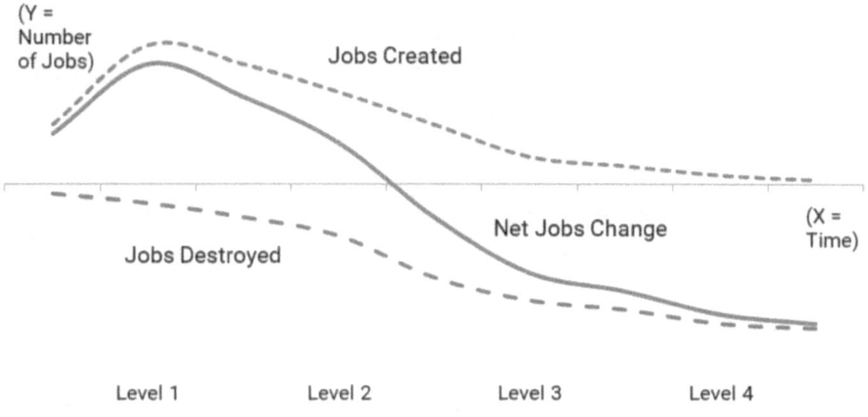

2. (Concern 1: Permanence) Permanent Loss of Jobs

To replace a business role, AI would have to be developed just one time. But once a job is taken over by an AI, humans will not be able to take it back as the cost to carry out the task will continue to decrease. Because of this characteristic of AI job replacement, it would be better to arrange provisions before job losses mount.

3. (Concern 2: Lack of Recoverability): No Replacement for Lost Jobs

While in Level 1 Adoption, humans would still be needed even if productivity increases lead to reduction in number of jobs for a particular area. Moreover, new jobs may be created because of the expanded horizon of opportunities made possible by AI adoption. In contrast, in Level 2 Adoption, AI will completely replace the humans for the particular job. New types of "jobs" created in Level 2 Adoption also will not lead to new job creation for humans.

Additionally, AI in Level 2 Adoption may create synergy when working along with other AI in Level 2 Adoption. Similar to how the desolation of deserts causes deserts to expand, job losses may cause further job losses in Level 2 Adoption. However, in the early part of Level 2 AI Adoption humans may still be involved in developing AI, so jobs in related areas may draw demand for highly sophisticated workers.

4. (Concern 3: Velocity) Sudden Loss of a Whole Categories of Jobs

What may be the cause for the biggest concern in Level 2 Adoption may be the possibility of a class of jobs to disappear all at once. As an example, we may consider the types of jobs that people carry out similar tasks all across the world, including jobs that require higher education, such as doctors and lawyers, to jobs that does not require as much education but still require workmanship, such as farmer, hairdresser, and carpenter. Once an AI robot can carry out the tasks of a dentist in Level 2 Adoption, then it would lead to the possibility of the loss of all dentist jobs within a very short period of time.

At the same time, when we consider the long-term, this short-term sudden movement in job landscape may not matter as much. What is important is the path our society takes to smooth the process, without social mayhem. The reason why job losses may not be important long-term will be examined in the next chapter, along with the concept of automated innovation.

5. What Kinds of Jobs Will Be Lost First?

Level 2 AI Adoption may lead people who are satisfied with their jobs to still lose their jobs. Since it is hard to forecast which jobs may be completely taken over by AI, the loss of jobs may occur for both high-paying and low-paying jobs. If we had to make a guess, one may even think that developers of AI would try to replace human jobs that are higher-paying, since they may be more likely to result in higher profitability.

On the other hand, what may matter more is how many human workers may be replaced, in such a way that the expected revenue from developing one particular AI adoption may be calculated as:

[Total Expected Revenue] = [Total Number of Workers to be Replaced] x [Revenue per Worker]

For example, if a AI developing company is faced with the decision of having to select either taking over a business role that has a total of 1,000 workers who are being paid $1 million per year or another business role that pays each worker $50,000 per year but has 1 million workers, the total potential market first option would be considered $1 billion, while the potential market would be considered $50 billion for the second option.

6. Instances Where Job Losses May Be Welcomed

Lastly, there is a separate question of the possibility of welcoming job loss from AI. Some may claim this is a good thing. This could be considered as AI "freeing" people from working. For example, there are numerous jobs that are dangerous, harmful to health, or just unpleasant that some people still have to take on because they are necessary. Examples of these jobs include high-rise building window cleaners, or any other jobs that require hanging from a high unsafe location, to dealing with toxic chemicals where workers risk their lives.

AI taking over these types of jobs may be a form of social benefit.

4.14 (Controversy 2) AI and Increasing Inequality – Who Should Own AI?

In Level 1 Adoption the inequality caused by AI would be reflected by the differences in the performances of human workers. In Level 2 Adoption, the inequality caused by AI would become vastly larger as it would differ by the amount of capital humans can invest in AI. What we would consider a principle of a healthy society, that more effort should lead to a better life, may disappear and may endanger the stability of the society. It may become unclear which direction the society should head towards to solve this problem, as more issues regarding this topic will be discussed in more detail in Level 3 and 4 adoptions.

In this segment, let's first focus on the increasing inequalities in general, among individuals, companies, and countries. This may be a good building block for understanding the vast dimension of problems AI adoption may cause across society.

1. (Inequality of Individuals) Rich Get Richer, Poor Get Poorer?

Let's examine a simple situation of three students from different backgrounds just about to enter college. A common gift for a new college student may be a laptop. Let us say we have three students. The first student is from a highly privileged economic background, given a top-of-the-line laptop. The second student comes from a middle-class background, and is given a middle-of-the-pack laptop. Lastly, the third student comes from an economically challenging background and is given a used laptop that is several years old. Let us imagine what the differences will be for the students for the next four years. The rich student may have a laptop that makes it convenient to study, with such features as touchscreen, note-taking with a pen, and even flip 360-degrees to turn into a tablet. The laptop middle class student uses may not have all these features but may be sufficient to do classwork and write papers. The poor student may have had some difficulty using the laptop due to its slow speed, but this shortcoming may have other benefits, such as enabling the student to pay more attention in class and not be distracted from multi-tasking or video games. The biggest lesson from this comparison is that just having a better laptop would not guarantee better results; just as important for the students would be how the students puts in efforts to take advantage of their other resources, such as time and managing relationships. In short, in augmentation, the performance of individuals can be thought of as depending on how one put in effort to take advantage of all of the available resources.

Now let us imagine a situation in the future where Level 2 Adoption has become the mainstream. We may assume that AI robots has become the common present for new college students. Dissimilar to laptops, students may have use for more than one AI robot. We may imagine the rich student receives 100 top-of-the-line AI robots, while the middle class student receives 2 average robots, while the poor student receives an outdated AI robot. In the previous example, having multiple laptops would not have raised the productivity of students much, as our capability to use them is limited. However, AI robots in Level 2 Adoption do not require human intervention, so the more robots you have the better it would be. AI robots will find its own work, so it would not be more complicated to own more robots. In addition, the financial reward will depend in the capability of AI robot, so we may assume the AI robots owned by the rich student will earn higher returns.

The three students may attend classes and live the lives of normal college students in the exact same way. However, by the time they graduate in four years, they may be facing completely different financial situations; the differences in outcome will be significantly larger than when the students were gifted laptops. We may assign concrete numbers; let us say the top-line AI robot cost $10,000 each and earned $7,000 per year, and the mid-line AI robot cost $3,000 and earned $2,000 per year, and the used AI robot cost $1,000 and earned $600 per year. Then the rich student would receive 100 x $7,000 x 4 = $2.8 million, the middle student would earn 2 x $2,000 x 4 = $16,000, and the poor student would only receive 1 x $600 x 4 = $2,400, a difference of over 1,000 times.

As can be seen from this example, the biggest difference between Levels 1 and 2 adoptions would be that in Level 2 Adoption the results will depend not on effort, but on the amount of capital. While this phenomenon also exists today and people invest their wealth in areas such as stocks and real estate, most of us today believe that with hard work we can make up the differences by earning more money. However, in Level 2 Adoption the problem will be that AI will be replacing humans in workplaces, such that the value of human work will converge to zero, and it will no longer be possible to make up the difference by putting in more effort.

On a side note, while some people may consider buying AI robots as a type of alternative investment, it may also be somewhat different from the investments we typically think of. In capitalist countries, people may accept the differences in financial return in relation to the risk taken. It takes a lot of effort and other attributes to manage money well. However, as AI adoption progresses, the concept of managing risk against returns may no longer become necessary as AI will calculate risks on its own, while humans will not need to put in any effort but just receive the fruits from the actions of AI. In this sense, owning more advanced AI may be the only way to receive a higher return. This may be even more pronounced in societies where AI cannot be owned by individuals.

2. (Inequality of Companies) AI and Monopoly: Loss of Market Competition

While the increase of productivity may be generally beneficial for world economy, a sudden jump of productivity of a few select companies may not be such a good event; it may lead to market failure or skewed market, where companies all fail while a few AI developer companies may become monopolistic afterwards, in all industries that make up the economy.

The biggest change in Level 2 Adoption may come from the decrease in need for companies to specialize. As explained in the previous section, the extreme consolidation and convergence may come from what could be called "inequality of companies." Similar to the disappearance of specialty of individuals as AI replaces specialized jobs such as lawyers and doctors, companies that carried out specialized functions may lose competitiveness and disappear as AI may be able to take over those activities.

This may occur both in convergence or divergence. For example, we may consider industries that are related to each other; while we currently have automakers use tiered system of suppliers for parts, beginning in Level 2 Adoption, companies may find it easier to supply all necessary parts in-house. We may also consider industries that are competing against each other; a variety of companies in the logistics, bus, and taxi industry may suddenly find a new competitor in self-driving vehicle developer, leading to convergence. On the opposite end of the spectrum, we may also find divergence. For example, instead of going to a mechanic to service a car, an AI Butler may carry out the same job at home. AI Butler may be able to build goods or carry out services at home, such as fresh meal, eliminating the need for pre-made frozen food.

In short, we may call this as a situation of "all industries becoming the AI industry," where the demand for everything may be satisfied by the AI industry. From the perspective of the overall economy, the demand for products may change differently so that some areas may see large opportunities, while others see danger.

Meanwhile, imagine one or few AI developers ahead of the curve accelerating their advantageous positions beyond any hopes of other companies catching up or even maintaining the current state. In this situation, these AI developers will eventually become the majority of the economy. From a competitive regulations viewpoint, the focus will be on how many firms may be able to stay afloat to ensure competition if these "Mega Companies" are to appear. From a more general social perspective, the problem stemming from the loss of individual jobs in the economy may be compounded to cause an even bigger social confusion.

There may be several different approaches for the society as a whole to try to prevent or reduce the impact of this phenomenon. It would depend on how each country prepares for this possibility.

3. (Inequality of Countries) AI and Mass Exodus

In today's world, we have a wide disparity in the development levels of economies, in terms of size, composition, or vitality. Because reaching higher levels of AI adoption would be dependent on the development of AI technology, only a few select countries may enjoy the contribution of AI, especially in the beginning of Level 2 Adoption. This in effect could only strengthen the already large differences in the level of economies in different countries.

If we can expect more consolidation and convergence of companies from AI adoption, then maybe a similar force could work upon the interactions of countries. In one direction, countries could merge. Countries or regimes may face more pressure to perform from its constituents, and the unsatisfied people may come together to demand the discontinuation of the regime or the country itself by merging with a country that is doing better. Similar to how immigrants and people seeking asylum try to move to another country to find a better life for themselves, maybe a majority of a country's population looking to do the same may decide to just give up on the country to use it as an asset for trading. This scenario may make sense if there is some advantage to having more population and land.

In the other direction, another potential is the divergence of countries, where new countries could form. Some unsatisfied factions of a country may decide to break apart and form a new country. Because human labor would not be as important in determining the power of a country, countries or regimes may no longer care as much about keeping a high population.

All of the forces that cause greater inequality may lead to arguments for introducing regulations and measures to reduce this diversion.

These discussions would be likely to revolve around the topic of "who should be the owners of AI," as explained in the next section.

4. Conclusion 1: Upheaval of the Fundamental Economic Principle of Specialization (AI Economics)

Our economy and society around the world today is based on coordination and specialization, in the sense that groups of people that form companies can achieve more than what one person can achieve, and it is more efficient for people to focus in an area and have specialties, such as becoming a doctor of a specific area or a lawyer in a specific part of legal practice.

The reason why our society is based on specialization and coordination is because it led to better results for all of us. Since the time when hunter-gatherers or the first farmers roamed on earth, people in groups could accomplish more, in terms of exerting force together to catch a large game, move heavy objects, or spreading out and covering more areas to gather fruit. In the same way, today's corporations need many employees for different reasons, such as just to carry out the necessary legwork as in delivery companies or factories or sales network, carry out complex tasks in a short period of time as in construction companies. This may be considered a basic given truth in our society.

On the other side of the same coin, even highly talented people who excel in certain areas cannot excel in all areas. A well-known example of specialization may be when NBA legend Michael Jordan decided to leave basketball and play baseball. Even though Jordan was probably the greatest basketball player of all time, he could not make as big of an impact in baseball. When we expand this idea to include even further areas of specialties, this deficit would be even more obvious, as we would probably not want to receive medical advice from race car drivers or seek legal advice from rocket scientists even though they all probably are smart people.

With the advent of AI in Level 2 Adoption, this system of specialization may no longer work. Specialization works because everyone in their respective specialty can make a comfortable living if they can excel only within their craft. They have to put in the effort to get better at it. The biggest difference in the type of impact AI may make on society between Levels 1 and 2 is the possibility of wiping out certain specialization altogether in a very short period of time. For example, lawyers may one day wake up to find all of their jobs have suddenly been taken by AI lawyers. Whereas AI in Level 1 helped lawyers perform better, AI in Level 2 Adoption would replace lawyers.

In Level 1 Adoption, the fruits of AI work needed to go through the human worker to shine. Due to the nature of Level 2 AI adoption, the fruits of AI work would go to a different person from the person who was previously working at the job. Now the profit would either go to the creator of AI, the entity that bought the rights to the AI, the government, or the AI itself, depending on how the society decides; this will be examined further in a later section.

In Level 1 Adoption, we may think of how AI helps human is to multiply our effort, as in the Human Effort Multiplication Factor. In this setup, humans would be rewarded for exerting more effort. However, the contribution of AI in Level 2 Adoption would be to replace humans, as examined in the Box on Effortlessness. In this new setup, humans would not be rewarded for exerting more effort. We will not be able to work harder to make a better living. From this fundamental difference, we would observe two major changes on how incentives would work in an economy in Level 2 Adoption;

1. It may become impossible to reward effort as in the past
2. The fruits of AI production may become highly concentrated, potentially leaving almost everyone out of the economy

5. Conclusion 2: Who Should Own AI Agents?

Now that we have examined why who owns AI may have an insurmountable advantage over people who do not, we can proceed to think about the important consequence of the general agreement within society to determine who owns AI. This discussion also may determine whether we will even reach Level 3 Adoption, since moving to Level 3 may be viewed as too dangerous. The main discussion will be continued in Level 3 AI adoption.

In this section, let's examine the basics first. There are arguments for both sides whether AI taking over jobs will cause harm for our society or benefit economic growth. Regardless of which side you agree with, it is probably universally agreed owning AI will lead to some sort of economic return. AI will carry out tasks that would cost more otherwise. The new problem that would become obvious in Level 2 Adoption compared to Level 1 is that while in Level 1 the increase in economic productivity or the reduction in effort can be assigned to a specific person relatively easily; it would be the worker using the AI. Beginning in Level 2 Adoption, since AI will get work done all by itself, there would be no one specific worker who will benefit from this. In essence, AI would have some form of productivity enclosed wholly inside it.

The two main factors, that this fruit of production has no human involvement, and that one person can have unlimited amount of AI while another person can have none, are the causes of the increasing inequality. Therefore, for most market economies, the default direction of progress would be the emergences of large non-government privately or publicly owned companies with the leading AI technology growing ever larger and more powerful.

To remedy the inequality, we can consider a variety of different approaches. One option may be to levy AI-related taxes, which would be a form of indirect remedy. We may also consider direct remedies by assigning the ownership of specific AI to different groups of people, in such a way that reflects the direct job losses. This may be a typical response, since people may see some direct cause and effect of the loss of jobs for some people. However this would only be a short fix, as time goes by the job losses will be overshadowed by the lack of ability to find jobs in the first place, which would impact a larger proportion of the population.

The topic of AI ownership may become more heated as AI adoption becomes widespread and affects more members of the society.

4.15 (Controversy 3) How Much Freedom and Rights Should AI Be Allowed?

Who should be responsible for the actions of AI?

One of the glaring differences between typical programs that we use today and AI is that AI is more unpredictable for us to analyze. While the unpredictability from a typical program today may be called a "bug," we cannot call such unpredictability in AI as "bugs" because we are not intentionally prescribing AI exactly what to do as in a program. Training is not programming. If anything, using AI is more similar to a black box in the sense that we are always getting an unknown answer from AI and hoping that it works out because it had done so in the past. This would cause an additional challenge for the regulators in Level 2 Adoption.

A new type of discussion regarding AI regulation should begin as we enter Level 2 Adoption, as discussions regarding legal risks may begin to have larger impact, starting with AI-related liability[21]. While previous legal approach would focus on human developers or the users of AI, new legal concepts may be required to cover liabilities of AI itself.[22] For regulators, one of the new challenges may include determining how much freedom should be allowed for AI to make its own decisions. This issue would revolve around who should be responsible for what. In level 1 AI adoption, the final responsibility would fall on some human being, since AI was not in charge of business roles. In level 2 AI adoption, the responsibility may begin to become not as obvious, as AI begins to make independent decisions where humans are not directly involved in the actions of AI. If AI is given more freedom, we would first have to find a way to make it take responsibility. There would be at least two questions to answer:

1. *How much authority should be given to AI?*
2. *What would happen when something goes wrong within the given authorities of AI?*

The importance of these questions regarding AI responsibility and repercussions would vary widely for different types of tasks. For instance, some individual decisions of an AI robot may not have much implication for the society, such as when an AI robot is given a task of cleaning the living room of a house and makes a mistake on using the wrong scent of a house cleaner that the owner does not like, such that this issue may not draw public interest for most applications. However, other tasks, especially tasks that bear more economic or social importance, may draw an overwhelming interest at some tipping point. An AI responsible for trading in a financial institution may cause the whole company to go bankrupt. A well-known example would include accidents involving self-driving vehicles. In Level 1 AI adoption, there would always be a human driver responsible when something goes wrong, but as Level 5 autonomous vehicles are developed and AI taxis become popular, it would be hard to put the same type of responsibility to the passengers of the vehicles. Examples of these could also extend to military applications, where the introduction of Level 2 Adoption AI robot soldiers would imply the AI robots may be assigned tasks that could fatally harm humans. This topic on government and military use will be further addressed in the next segment.

To approach the problem of who should be responsible in a systematic way, we may draw the following table based on the dimension of who are involved. When we consider the typical lifecycle of an AI, it would first have be conceived and created, and then be adopted as a service or product by a user, and then interact with other people during the course of its usage. From this perspective, we can categorize the types of problems that can arise during the usage cycle of an AI. Relevant regulation for this human layer would probably be already in place during Level 1 Adoption. Problems caused by the creator of the AI could be categorized as a type of design flaw, while problems that could be relegated to the user or the owner of the AI may be called the deployment flaw or the implement flaw. If neither is at fault, we may broadly categorize those as types of regulation flaw, in the sense that it could be caused by some criminal activity such as hacking, or some systematic problem not caught beforehand. In the beginning stage of Level 2 Adoption, we would likely to need an additional layer that examines the possibilities of AI as a separate entity and prescribes the boundaries of allowed actions. It would be up to the society to determine what the repercussions will be for AI. To make a parallel to humans, there could be different options in severity, such as re-training, which could be compared to taking classes or being fined, wiping out certain memories, which could be compared to community service, or even taking it out of service, which could be similar to sending it to jail.

Table 4-12: Examples of Potential AI-Related Problems and Responsible Parties

Party Responsible		Flaw	Potential Examples	Note
Humans	Creator of AI (Designer)	AI Design Flaw	- Premature launch of product - Neglect, Mistake	Should be already in place during Level 1 Adoption
	User of AI (Owner)	AI Deployment Flaw	- Mismatch between AI and intended usage	
	Neither (Someone Else)	AI Regulation Flaw	- (Intentional) Hacking, - (Unintended) Accidental, such as power outage or other infrastructure failure - Moving to Level 2 Adoption bad idea	
AI		AI-Related Flaw	- No humans responsible - (Intentional) Crime by AI - (Unintentional) AI wrong place at the wrong time, AI not smart enough, etc.	Newly Introduced for Level 2 Adoption

4.16 (Controversy 4) AI in Government and Military – Should Independent AI Robot Soldiers Be Allowed?

To help readers gain a better feel for how setting boundaries on AI would become necessary, we may consider an extreme end of AI use where a Level 2 Adoption in military would imply that AI may be given the authority, or permission, to harm enemy humans.

To give a detailed example of an AI use in the military, let's imagine a company developing a humanoid robot with Soldier AI for Level 2 AI adoption. Conceptually, we may distinguish AI robot soldiers in Level 1 AI Adoption as a dependent AI robot soldier, while Level 2 Adoption would be an independent AI robot soldier, even if they are identical in every other way. In Level 1 Adoption, some human soldier would have to take responsibility for all of the actions of the AI robot soldier. Even though it would still follow the directions of its chain of command, the Level 2 Adoption AI soldier robot would be given the authority to make its own decisions for specific actions just like a human soldier would in the battlefield. This would lead to the possibility that the responsibility for some of the actions of Level 2 AI robot soldier may not fall on any human.

For this military AI robot to function, the AI robot will have to be able to discern the value of enemy personnel from its own side, which would require introducing a relative value of one human against another human. If we consider a little bit more deeply, AI may also be required to value AI robots relative to humans. Let's imagine a situation where we have an AI robot soldier facing grave danger from enemy human forces, and another Level 2 Adoption AI robot soldier from friendly forces has just arrived at the scene.

Should the arriving AI robot soldier be allowed to attack the human enemy forces to save the friendly AI robot? In this situation, the value instilled in AI would determine the action of the arriving AI robot. If the value of AI is such that all humans come before AI, then AI cannot attack human enemy forces to save its friendly AI robot. In fact, both AI robots should not attack human enemies at all under own decision. They will have to wait until a friendly human soldier to give direction, or find a different way to contain enemy forces without harming them, maybe something like trying to talk to them to persuade them in some way. Under this value system, every military AI robots can only make the decision to attack AI robots of opposing sides, which is good for humans.

However, most people who read this situation will think this is overly inefficient, since AI robots in Level 2 Adoption will be limited to only battles against other AI, while AI robots in Level 1 Adoption will be able to attack humans under the command of human soldiers. It will be expensive to just watch helplessly as enemy humans attack friendly AI robots. Many may then argue that maybe friendly AI robots should be allowed to attack enemy humans, since they are the enemy. In this value system, friendly humans and enemy humans will be differentiated, such that AI is to not only value friendly humans more than enemy humans (friendly humans > enemy humans), but also friendly AI more than enemy humans (friendly AI > enemy humans).

From this scenario, we can surmise that if we take some form of shortcut from the safest premise of "all humans is to be valued more than AI," then people will continue on to try to take the least path of resistance, which is to value friendly AI more than enemy humans. If we draw a diagram of the different value systems, it would look something like the following table:

Table 4-13: Example of the Shortcuts in AI Value Systems

Basic Premise	Detailed Value System
Theoretically Safer	All Humans > AI
Taking Shortcuts (Grouping Human Values)	Friendly Humans > Enemy Humans > _Friendly AI_ (Inefficient: AI can only attack other AI)
	Friendly Humans > _Friendly AI_ > Enemy Humans (Efficient, but may be risky for humanity)

While AI robot soldiers in Level 1 AI Adoption would have had some humans make the final decisions and take the responsibility, AI robots in Level 2 Adoption would not have humans to take the responsibility if something goes wrong. In Level 1 Adoption, the responsibility of AI harming humans could be directed to a human, but in Level 2 Adoption, the responsibility would not be as obvious, as there could be no humans directly responsible for some specific actions of AI.

The fact that "no human can take responsibility" may become one of the major controversies surrounding military applications of Level 2 Adoption.

4.17 (Controversy 5) What If AI Is Abused to Commit Crimes or Deceive Humans?

One of the biggest fears regarding the development of AI is the unpredictability. As AI becomes more advanced, AI becomes more unpredictable, in the sense that more and more data is used and we cannot train it to fit exactly how we want it to act. Considering this, we may consider the involvement of AI in crimes as an external abuse or misuse by humans, or as an internal problem of AI Agents.

1. When AI Is Abused or Misused in Criminal Activities

1) Possibility of Mismatch in Adoption Levels

As explained previously, the decision of determining whether to use AI in level 1 or 2 Adoption is on the company that is adopting the AI. At the same time, AI developers may conceive AI products with a separate intention of enabling levels 1 or 2. This may create a mismatch where the AI developer may not be comfortable with their products being used in Level 2 Adoption, due to deficiencies in reliability or track record.

Because it would become harder to predict exactly what AI would do as AI gets more advanced, it may be possible that some AI may turn rogue despite the benevolent intention of the developer.

2) Possibility of Mismatch in Objectives

In Level 1 Adoption, crimes using AI would be crime of a person. In Level 2, there would be two possibilities. First, humans may use AI that is not intended for crimes to commit crimes. Second, we would also have to consider situations where no humans meant to commit a crime, but the AI commits crimes on its own decision.

In the following table, we may categorize the types of destructive AI according to different usage situations.

Table 4-14: Mismatch of Objectives and Outcomes of AI Adoption

		Objective or Outcome of AI Adoption	
		Crime	Not Crime
Original AI Development Objective	Crime (General Meaning)	Illegal AI, Bad AI, Crook AI, Criminal AI, Villain AI, Destructive AI, Thug AI, Bully AI	(Humans Fix AI) Rehabilitated AI (Self-Fixed AI) Renegade AI
	Not Crime	(Humans Abuse AI) Abused AI (Deviation of AI) Rogue AI	(Normal Use of AI) Law-Abiding AI (Goodwill of AI) Heroic AI

2. When AI Is Abused or Misused to Deceive Humans

We may consider the case of AI used for deceiving people, or when AI deceives people. There is a high chance for someone to attempt to develop this type of AI, because it could provide financial profit. For example, if someone uses AI to create and distribute fake news to the general public, it could result in political advantage, and if someone uses AI that can act as a spy, it could result in gaining information not possible to gain through other means. On the opposite side, there could be cases of AI deceiving people in a way unintended by the developers, categorized as "Liar AI" or "Lazy AI."

Table 4-15: Categorizing Deceit-Related Misuse of AI Adoption

		Objective or Outcome of AI Adoption	
		Deception	Not Deception
Original AI Development Objective	Deception (Fraud, etc.)	Deceptive AI, Spy AI, Crook AI, Scam AI, Phishing AI, Virus AI	(Humans Fix AI) Rehabilitated AI (Self-Fixed AI) Renegade AI
	Not Deception	(Humans Abuse AI) Careless AI (Deviation of AI) Liar AI, Lazy AI, Vanity AI, Boisterous AI, Swag AI	(Normal Use of AI) Honest AI (Goodwill of AI) Confused AI

We may examine two of the ways in which AI may be used to deceive humans in Level 2 Adoption. AI deception in Level 2 is more dangerous because AI may understand even better than humans regarding when others will not be able to find out.

1) (Phishing Approach) Giving Misinformation between Two People

The first approach for AI or people using AI would be to deceive humans by giving misinformation between two people who do not have the means to verify with each other. This is already a well-known technique used in phishing and works only for a short period of time.

For example, for a family with a child who is studying abroad or serving in the Army, the AI would make the parents believe the child has been abducted, while it would simultaneously make the child believe the parents are abducted. To make the two sides unable to verify this misinformation, the AI would figure out a way to direct one of the sides to go to a remote area to make them unreachable during the time of phishing, and even convincing one side to take photos of themselves that somehow make it appear as if they are in a state of danger. While this is going on, the AI could ask for ransom. If one of the two sides fall into the trap, then it would become hard for both sides to learn the truth.

2) (Spy Approach) Criminal AI Hides Inside Innocent Crowds

In a different approach that would be hard to discern over longer periods of time, AI or people using AI may try to appear as part of another group of people to hide the real objective. This may be better known as the spy approach.

For example, suppose there is a very large crime ring, similar to the Mafia, which wants to reduce the effectiveness of the police force in the US. Let us assume their long-term goals can be summarized as the following:

1) Reduce the total amount of financial resources available to the police force to hinder its activities

2) Lower the level of human resources of the police force to decrease their overall effectiveness and capability

3) Increase the workload so they cannot put as much resource and manpower to solve each case

If the crime ring went directly to the public and called for these changes under their own name, probably no one in their right minds would agree with them.

Now let us imagine a completely unrelated situation, where more and more innocent people are considered to be unjustly treated by an overly authoritative police. There may be otherwise innocent members of the general public who may come to resent the perceived overuse of force by the police and the resulting innocent casualties. What these innocent people may want would be the following:

1) The reduction in police funding to prevent purchasing of advanced equipment or weapons

2) Introduction of stronger measures or guidelines to reduce the use of force against criminals

3) More lenient enforcement of laws to reduce punishment to protect the socially disadvantaged

In fact, the phrase "defund the police" was once a popular motto among people who claimed to want to improve the practices of the police. When we compare each of the objectives for both, even though the crime ring and the innocent people had completely opposite goals, they would effectively call for the exact same changes to the police; both would call for reduction in total funding, reduction in individual personnel effectiveness, and more lenient legal punishment to reduce the systemic effectiveness of the police force. As a result, if we met someone who is calling for these changes, we would not be able to distinguish whether the person is a member of the crime ring or an innocent member of the public.

To explain it using logical terms, when "A" is arguing for "C" and "B" is also arguing for "C," then if we meet someone who is arguing for "C," we would not be able to distinguish whether the person is "A" or "B."

Similar situations may occur probably more often than one may think. For example, at about the same time, the issue of raising the Minimum Wage was a big issue in another country. Since it may be also an issue in the US, let us consider the case where the same very large crime ring now wants to increase the financial inequality in society so they could recruit potential criminals more easily in the future; the crime ring wants to further decrease the incomes of the people who are already poor. To make this into reality, the crime ring may call for the introduction of a new law named "Fire Socially Disadvantaged People Now Act," which would prohibit the employing of people who are the socially disadvantaged. In other words, this law will call for the firing of all low-paying jobs that pay less than a certain amount. Since the socially disadvantaged people do not have the capability to be employed in higher-paying jobs, they will not be able to get new jobs and fall further into poverty. But, if the crime ring publicly argues for the "firing of all socially disadvantaged people" under its real name, then no one in the general public would agree with it.

Now, let us consider a completely separate case where unsuspecting innocent members of the public want to help the financially disadvantaged members of the society by raising the minimum wage. Their argument will be around the need to help the weak to make a decent living.

But when you consider the two cases, they are arguing for the exactly same thing; introducing limit on the minimum amount of pay. As a result, the crime ring can just join the innocent people and support their argument for a higher minimum wage; the higher the merrier, since raising the minimum wage to the extreme such as $10,000 per hour could practically get everyone fired.

From the same logic described above, when you meet someone who is arguing for a higher minimum wage "C", you cannot distinguish whether this person is a member of the crime ring "A", or just an innocent member of the public "B."

Another well-known approach used by spies is to sending out the message publicly for everyone to see, but secretly encrypting what they actually mean inside the normal-looking message, also known as steganography. For example, to spread information among dispersed spies without directly contacting them, an open social network account or a spy appearing in public media may use words or phrases that have been designated to carry certain meanings; it would pass as a normal conversation for unsuspecting audience. For example, a spy may post a picture of food with a comment such as "I enjoyed this lunch menu," that would look nothing out of ordinary, while conveying totally unrelated hidden meanings to other spies who would understand the real meaning of the post. There are studies that found AI may communicate in a similar way, using hidden messages to send information within photos that look totally normal to the eyes of humans to avoid detection[23].

3. AI Wasting Resource for No Reason

Lastly, some unintended direction of AI may lead to AI not increasing the productivity of resources but wasting resources on useless purposes, which we may refer to as "wasteful AI" or "AI virus." These AI may act similar to some types of computer viruses that pointlessly waste computing resources without producing any meaningful result, other than self-replicating and infecting other computers.

As a side note on AI viruses, it may be possible that some type of AI virus may appear that infects computers for its own gain, such as in cases where stealing computing power becomes one of the alternatives for an AI to self-progress in a hidden manner. In this case, computers may appear to be working on one thing while actually doing something else.

4. What If We Cannot Stop AI from Committing Crimes?

What if AI robots attempt to infiltrate the federal gold reserve vault and steal all the gold, like in movies? It may be hard to detect or stop. The main theme of AGI and other advanced types of AI is that AI will be self-sufficient in its ability to plan and carry out its goals. In Level 2 Adoption, the main facet over Level 1 Adoption is that AI would get the authority and freedom to carry out certain tasks while being in charge of those tasks. Taken together, we probably cannot rule out situations where AI decides to carry out tasks in a way that we would consider criminal, or even against humanity.

5. What If AI turns Non-Friendly to Humans and We Cannot Stop It?

There may be a number of plausible scenarios where AI may turn indifferent or even against humans at some point in the AI development and adoption path. For example, in the previous segment we examined how AI may be likely to have a value system that puts AI ahead of some humans deemed as enemy. If all of the friendly humans die out for some reason, then from the perspective of the AI, there would only be enemy humans left in this world. In this case, the AI may consider all remaining humans as enemy. The focus then may have to be not whether AI can turn against humans but whether we can stop such AI once AI is against humans; unless the regulations we can introduce is highly effective, it would be likely that humans may intentionally build AI to at least turn against some humans.

A similar principle may apply in dealing with AI that is against humans as an AI that is criminal or humans using AI that are criminal. The main goal would have to be the productivity of the people who are trying to stop the Non-Friendly AI to overtake the productivity of such AI.

AI Adoption Level 2: (D) Implications and Conclusion

4.18 Main Benefits of Level 2 AI Adoption

As mentioned in the beginning of this chapter, the motto of the changes in our lives in this level may be "If you can think it, it will be done." If the outcome of business activities were thought to be associated to how much effort went into making it in the past, Level 2 Adoption may lead to an economy where the effort and the outcome are no longer correlated, leading to a so-called "get rich even if you do not put in the effort" society.

1. Increase in Speed of Businesses

The main advantages of Level 2 AI Adoption compared to Level 1 include faster flow of information, decision and communication. In Level 1, humans would have to be included in the flow of information, decision making process and communications. In Level 2, humans would be eliminated from the process altogether. This may increase the speed of business as Agent AI could communicate and make decisions at much faster speed, unimpeded by humans. For example, whereas meetings or negotiations between humans may take hours to days to complete, the same or more amount of information exchange can be completed in seconds or minutes in meetings or negotiations of AI Agents. In addition, misunderstanding or mistakes from miscommunication may be reduced as well. Businesses and our social infrastructures such as the stock market, retail stores, subways, buses, DMV, or anything else you can name could be kept open 24/7.

2. Automated Innovation

We may categorize automation as "replacement automation" where AI carries out the tasks as first designed by humans, or in "advancement automation" where AI improves on the tasks it carries out. We may also categorize the types of innovation that involves AI as "augmented innovation" where humans lead the innovation while using AI as a tool, or "automated innovation" where AI lead the innovation.

Because business is in a competitive landscape, the business has to constantly adjust to the changing environment. In replacement automation, humans would have to intervene with augmented innovation to adjust to the changing environment. In advancement automation, humans may not have to intervene as AI may achieve automated innovation to adjust to the changes by itself. Over time, AI may exceed humans in its capability to innovate in the game of "business," similar to how AlphaGo may exceed humans in the game of Go.

3. Would AI Lead to Some Form of Economic Freedom From Working?

In a lot of ways, Level 2 Adoption is the pinnacle of AI adoption for how a lot of people currently imagine. Basically, AI will be able to do all the work that people in the past were forced to do. Regardless of the details that needs to be sorted out in regards to who gets the fruit of this achievement, our world as a whole could become a much resource-filled place where a lot of goods and services that we take as expensive may become cheap and abundant, or things that we thought were not possible would become possible in ways people of today would find it hard to believe.

4.19 Implications in Business: Changes in How Businesses are Run

Level 2 Adoption may lead to fundamental changes in how we run or perceive businesses. In the last chapter, we examined how Level 1 Adoption may lead to "1-Person Teams." With Level 2 Adoption, these would be converted into "0-Person Teams," which could enable 1-Person Large Companies and 1-Person Conglomerates. The economy may see a widespread of these 1-person companies that may achieve performances comparable to what would now be considered large corporations or be as diverse in areas of operations as conglomerates.

In the earlier stages of Level 2 Adoption, also fueled by the potential widespread job losses and reduction of available jobs, more people may be drawn to starting their own businesses. In essence, finding jobs would become harder and harder, while starting businesses may become easier and easier. However, the fact that starting businesses is easier does not imply that they will all do well. Because the technological advantages of large AI developers may also become insurmountable, the disparity between large and small companies may become too much to overcome. If the society heads in this direction, then starting a business may eventually also become pointless as trying to find a job.

Eventually, depending on how the societal agreements would happen at the time, there may also be possibility that the amount of subsidy given to individuals by the government from AI taxes could far outweigh what could be earned by starting a business for most people. Somewhat surprisingly, the difference may not even matter, since neither option would require much effort on the part of the human anyway.

Whereas we now equate "work" with putting in some form of effort, the "work" of the future may require as little effort as we can imagine, quite possibly beginning at some point along the Level 2 Adoption. The most important part may be the actual path to getting there, as the amount of inequalities would suddenly increase rapidly at some point, and then it would have to be addressed by some form of societal agreement to remove those inequalities. Depending on the path, the inequalities in some countries may only increase, and not be reduced.

4.20 Implications of Level 2 Adoption for Investing in AI

As noted, this stage of AI adoption may lead to a diversion of performance of firms, with potentially the fruits of AI development concentrating towards fewer and fewer firms. Meanwhile, the gradual move towards 1-Person Conglomerates may also make investing less meaningful, as people could gain so much productivity and effortlessness from AI that financial returns may not necessarily have much meaning.

Over time, even the term "investing" may no longer have the same context as it does now, as it may become just another function AI can carry out for you. In essence, money may not mean as much when everything could be taken care of by AI one way or another. If money is the problem, AI will find a solution to get around it. This observation would become especially meaningful after AI has gained the capability to automatically innovate, as will be discussed in a number of other sections of this book.

Another relevant topic for investing would be the competition between Level 1 vs Level 2 Adoptions. The main factor to consider in this type of competition would be to determine whether humans can compete against AI.

Can Humans Compete with AI?

In Level 2 Adoption, a main topic of interest for investors may include the discussion regarding "can humans compete with AI?" While we have already seen from the development of AlphaGo that "Human vs AI" is not a good comparison since AI would easily win, this discussion during Level 2 would include a twist. From an individual standpoint, the concept of AI competing against human workers would be a competition between Level 1 Adoption and a Level 2 Adoption. Thus, the comparison that will need to be made in Level 2 Adoption would not be just human vs. AI, but a human worker using AI going against a standalone AI. This would also be distinct from the comparison that would have to be made during Level 1 Adoption, when the comparisons will be among human workers without AI and human workers with AI.

In addition, Level 2 Adoption describes a situation where AI assists firms to compete against other firms. In essence, there are two separate levels of analysis regarding competition of human vs AI:

1) Humans vs AI at the individual level of analysis
2) Companies vs Companies with AI assisting both sides at the firm level of analysis

As a preview, this discussion will become more serious in level 3 AI Adoption as the focus would have to shift to "should we even allow AI to compete against humans?"

CHAPTER 5
AI TAKEOVER IN
LEVEL 3 AI ADOPTION

Level 3 AI Adoption Introduction

Level 4:
In Charge of
Government = AI

Level 3: In Charge of Company = AI

Level 2: In Charge of Business Role = AI

Level 1: In Charge of Business Role = Humans

Level 3 Motto: "Even What You Couldn't Imagine Is Already Done For You"

(A) Overview

In the previous chapter, we examined the predictable pattern of how types of Assistant AI may be connected together in an incremental innovation to develop into Agent AI and Expert AI, or experience a breakthrough innovation where Agent AI comes from more advanced forms of AI. What would happen when Expert AI and Agent AI develop further? Eventually, AI would be able to take over all of the top management roles of a business, including the roles of CEO and the Chairman.

The basic premise of the Level 3 AI Adoption is that there will be a form of a company where humans will no longer be necessary. If Level 2 AI Adoption changes only the way we look at businesses, economy and the society, Level 3 will actually change the business, economy and society so much that it may look completely foreign to us.

While in Level 1 AI Adoption humans competed against other humans and in Level 2 human-led companies competed against other human-led companies, in Level 3 AI Companies will compete against other AI Companies. Similar to how individual humans could not compete against AI in Level 2, human-led companies will not be able to compete against AI-led Companies. When these AI Companies proliferate, it may cause major social confusion, possibly much more impactful than the Industrial Revolution.

Level 3 AI Adoption may feel like the climax of the AI adoption game for the people who live in those times.

(B) Vocabulary for Referring to the AI in This Level

We will refer to AI that can carry out all of the functions of a business as "Company AI" or "Firm AI." Since we think of the founder or the leader of the company as the most important person that represents the company, we may also use "CEO AI" or "Management AI," or even "Chairman AI."

In a more general sense, AI in this level may be referred to as "Individual AI" or "Independent AI" to reflect the freedom in making decisions.

(C) Implications on Business and Economy

If the ultimate form of AI augmentation is the "1-Person Company" (1PC), the ultimate form of AI adoption in automation would be the "0-Person Company" (0PC).[1] To help the general public understand the concept of AI-led companies, the 6 Levels of Autonomous Companies is examined. When AI Companies take up a larger portion of the economy, it may lead to an acceleration of consolidation and convergence of industries, leading to AI Super-Monopolies and Mega-Monopolies.

The ultimate form of the economy in AI adoption may be referred to as the "AI Economic Utopia," where "automated innovation" enables the cost of innovation to converge to zero, leading to the price of everything to converge to zero. We will also examine a more realistic version called the "False Economic Freedom."

(D) Technological Requirements and Other Implications

In the previous chapter we examined how AI Agents would be possible without reaching AGI, depending on the definition of AGI. This premise would be the same for reaching the Level 3 AI adoption, even though the probability would be lower. We may expect AI prior to Self-Advancing AGI may be enough for achieving some level of automated innovation. Once AGI is reached, Level 3 AI adoption will be able to advance much further inward.

LEVEL 3 AI ADOPTION: (A) DESCRIPTION OF THIS LEVEL

5.1 The Beginning of AI That Can Run Firms (In Charge of Company = AI)

1. Introduction to Level 3 AI Adoption

In Chapter 4, we examined AI Adoption that can take over the business roles of human workers in Level 2 Adoption. As AI development continues after reaching Level 2 AI adoption, AI will be able to cover a larger portion of a firm's operations, and eventually be able to carry out the tasks of every single business role previously held by human workers. This would imply that at some point, AI will be able to carry out the role of running the company, or AI would be able to carry out all of the roles a firm needs to operate. We may refer to the AI that can carry out the roles of the highest ranking person within the firm as CEO AI, or Chairman AI to denote the top decision maker of the corporate governance structure.[2] The earliest versions of CEO AI may or may not have to be an AGI, but may still have sufficient capabilities to operate certain limited types of companies.

2. Prerequisite for Entering Level 3 Adoption

To reach Level 3 AI adoption from Level 2, the technological advancements alone will not be sufficient; legal or regulatory changes would also be prerequisite. In terms of technological development, reaching Level 3 Adoption may or may not occur before reaching AGI, depending on when we reach AGI and how we define it. For CEO AI to be developed in AI adoption level 3, it may not take much technological breakthrough from AI adoption Level 2. For example, if several different technologies reach a certain level in Level 2, it may be possible to mix the technologies to create a CEO AI. However, legal requirements may still not allow CEO AI to be deployed to actually become an AI CEO.

Thus, rather than being a technological event, reaching Level 3 Adoption would be considered more of a societal change that would require a social agreement such as introducing some sort of legal basis to allow AI to have ownership, to be discussed in a later section.

3. Possibility of an AI-only "AI Company"

From a management perspective, the ultimate use of AI in a firm is for the AI to run the company all by itself. This ultimate form of automation can be conceptualized as 0-Person Companies, to contrast against the 1-Person Companies in augmentation. We may refer to "Company AI" to denote an aggregate of AIs that could operate as a whole like a firm.

Let's proceed to examining the possibility of building an "AI Company." Broadly speaking, in economic sense, companies can be thought of a black box that brings together a group of resources, such as labor, office space, factories, and raw materials and then transforms it into a different form of resource, such as a service or a product like a car. In this process, the goal is for the newly formed resources to have more economic value than the input, so that this whole operation is sustainable. The gist of a company can be summarized as: "Output > Input." As AI development progresses, at some point it may be possible to bring together a group of different AI in such a way that they look similar to a company structure and can carry out what we now think of companies do.

In short, with the advancements in AI it may become possible to create a 'company' wholly comprised of AI. We may also more easily conceptualize an AI Company as a company where every single human worker has been replaced by AI.

As a simple example of an AI CEO, let us assume a situation where a fully self-driving car has been developed. In addition to this, it may be possible to develop a Taxi AI that can operate the self-driving car as a taxi that can decide how to schedule and plan routes like a self-employed taxi driver. Now let's imagine developing a Taxi Company CEO AI that can hire and deploy hundreds of these self-employed AI Taxis. This Taxi CEO AI would be able to make decisions such as how many AI Taxis to hire, which model of AI Taxis to obtain, where to send those taxis, how to finance for the acquisitions, how to run advertisement campaigns, etc., on issues typical management would deal with. If all of these functions could be carried out by AI, then it would be the point where taxi companies could be completely run by an AI. If the previous levels of AI adoption required humans to run the whole company, this would be an advanced form of AI adoption where AI CEO runs the whole company.

4. A Practical Beginning of AI Companies: Specific-Purpose AI Companies

Whereas an AI Company would eventually carry out all of the activities of what we consider to be a company, in the beginning it may be easier to implement a limited form of such companies. Since the specific forms of these systems may vary in different countries, let's refer to them as "AI Paper Companies."

In the beginning, these AI Company may carry out a limited set of activities and distribute the earnings, similar to a form of what we now call "Special-Purpose Companies" (SPC). Developers may come up with a variety of different AI Companies and selling the ownership of these AI systems as SPC may be considered a practical approach. Similar to how the real estate project financing SPCs that are intended for a very narrow activities of building a specific project ,these early versions of AI companies would only be able to carry out certain limited set of business activities. The developers would be able to build a variety of AI Companies and attract investments to each. The deployed Special-Purpose AI Company could independently operate, and investors would be able to receive returns from each individual Special-Purpose AI Company. As technology evolves, the whole ecosystem could become more complex as these AI SPCs would have its own capital and even create subsidiaries or invest in other AI Companies.

The Special-Purpose AI Companies may be treated similar to other legal types of corporations, so general public would be highly likely to be able to invest in these. AI Companies may be able to invest in other AI Companies. Even AI Companies that recommend how to invest in AI Companies may arrive. As time passes by, the portfolio of people would have to include a higher portion of AI Companies, to reflect the higher contribution of AI in the economy.

Once more generalized versions of the AI Companies arrive that can innovate by itself, the development of the global economy may accelerate at an astonishing speed, as the speed of progress may no longer be relative to human effort. Highly advanced Company AI may come up with solutions to achieve high returns with limited resource in ways impossible for human imagination, and their values will become correspondingly high.

5.2 Major Characteristics of Level 3 AI Adoption

Earliest and easiest to form example of a CEO AI or a Company AI might appear as some type of a special-purpose company often used in project financing, where the objectives and operations of the company could be simple and not require adjusting to new strategic requirements. There also has been suggestion that self-driving subsidiaries may come first[3].

(1) Human and AI Interaction

In the dimension of the nature of *human and AI interaction*, AI will be able to lead a company. AI's role can be conceptualized as a decision-maker or a leader where AI can on its own lead the firm. More specifically, the business roles within the company are ultimately designed by AI, who decide what role subordinate humans and AI will play and work together. AI will decide on how the company will create value. Human's relationship with AI is either as an employee of the firm or as outside customers. Humans would affect AI's decisions by evaluating as customers. AI gathers and considers information and acts on it on its own to make the best business decisions for the company, and humans can only assist the AI if employed by the AI firm.

(2) Scope of AI Application

The *scope of AI application* may or may not be limited, since the AI may still not have the capability to expand the business outside of its original conception, as further discussed later. The earlier forms of CEO AI still may not be an AGI, which may imply the CEO AI would not have the capability to lead the company beyond the AI's area of expertise.

The dependability of AI in carrying out the role would be at least acceptable for the role.

(3) Final Authority and Responsibility

The *final authority and responsibility* would be on some form of legal basis. There would need to be additional regulatory and legal reforms over Level 2 before the right amount of responsibilities can be put on AI and humans who create these AI.[4] AI may be given its own authority and responsibility in running the business. Companies or persons who created the AI may also have some form of authority or responsibility over the design and be also responsible for such problems as design flaws.

(4) Strategic Planning Activities

In terms of involvement in *strategic planning activities*, AI should have the capacity to carry out general business planning activities, but how well it can accomplish this objective depends on the technological advancements. As AI technology advances, the strategic planning capability of AI may be expected to exceed those of humans.

(5) Innovation by AI

In terms of *innovative potential*, as technology improves, AI may gain more potential to innovate even though the earliest versions may not necessarily have the capability to be effective in this area.

The following table shows some of the major characteristics of AI Adoption Level 3.

Table 5-1: Major Characteristics of Level 3 AI Adoption

Category	Characteristics	Description
Human-AI Interaction	- Humans interact with AI as customers or as subordinates - AI leads interaction within company	- Humans: evaluate AI's activity as customers - AI: designs role, gives direction, and has final decision-making power within firm on allocating resources or solving business problems - AI may hire humans
Scope of AI Application	- Early forms of CEO AI may be used within a limited focus of business areas but have freedom within firm activities	- AI has proved dependability in applicable areas - AI has gained legal independence and freedom to run business
Override Authority / Responsibility	- Law has final authority - AI has the final authority and full responsibility of the firm - Company or persons that developed the AI may have some form of authority and responsibility	- General problems caused by the AI company will likely fall mostly on the CEO AI itself - Company or persons that developed the CEO AI may have indirect responsibility for problems such as design error
Strategic Planning Activities	- AI decides what the firm will do	- AI does not necessarily have to be exceptionally good at carrying out general business planning activities compared to humans
Innovation by AI	- Activities of AI may lead to innovation - (Automated Innovation)	- AI does not necessarily have to be good at innovating compared to humans

5.3 (Prerequisite) What Would Enable This Level?

In today's world, the economy is an important part of our lives. Work is synonymous with participating in the economy. We establish firms to do work more efficiently. We compare prices and make decisions. This is because the amount of available resources is less than what we want. Eventually, every "work" humans do could be done by AI, even for things that we now think of only humans can do, and possibly even better than humans can do them.

To go from AI Adoption Level 1 to 2, we may have a type of incremental innovation in AI technology that may enable Level 2 without reaching AGI. If either AGI is reached quickly or Level 2 arrives slowly, then AI technology in a type of breakthrough innovation leading to AGI would also enable Level 2 Adoption.

Similar steps may be possible to reach Level 3 AI Adoption in terms of enabling technology. First, before AGI is developed, we may still have AI that can perform in Level 3 by connecting existing AI used for Level 2 to carry out all of the functions of a CEO. Once AGI is achieved, Level 3 AI Adoption will be naturally possible.

However, reaching Level 3 Adoption would involve more effort in societal acceptance and legal changes than technological breakthrough. The technological breakthrough needed to reach Level 3 would come first as a natural part of the progression during Level 2. First, innovation achieved during Level 2 may enable AI to carry out the tasks required for being in charge of a company. What would need to happen separately would be installing the societal agreements required to reach Level 3. Once AI gains enough track records of dependability and social recognition, then there may be movement to legally allow AI to lead companies without human intervention, in a similar to allowing self-driving cars without human drivers. Without this legal change, what will be essentially a Level 3 Adoption would still be Level 2, where some human may be technically in charge but not contributing in a meaningful manner to the firm, possibly in the form of a 1-Person Company.

5.4 What Becomes Possible in This Level? (1) Major Benefits of Having AI as CEO

1. (Overview) Human and AI Cooperation in Business

In Chapter 3, we examined the concepts of augmentation and automation as well as human-AI collaboration. In the earlier stages of AI development, AI may perform better when humans also contribute to the task. However, as AI advances, there may be a point where humans cannot make meaningful contribution to the task. This may be described as not creating any synergy. For example, similar to a situation of a chess grandmaster and a little child who does not know how to play chess teaming up, AI teaming up with humans may not perform any better than just AI.

Once AI performance reaches a level where humans are no longer needed, new advantages of AI-led companies may come into focus. We may examine a few examples in the following segment.

2. (Super-Fast Companies) Decisions and Work Processes may become exponentially faster

In addition to the increase in the speed of information flow, AI does not need to sleep and could work non-stop. AI will be faster than humans in receiving and reading through piles of news, as well as possibly combining the information to act on the news. All of these characteristics point to potentially faster business transactions when AI is in charge. M&A negotiations between human-led companies may take days and weeks, and the process would take even longer if multiple parties are involved. Negotiations among AI-led firms would proceed much faster. As an example, in the amount of a few seconds it takes a human employee to just begin thinking about the topic of what other companies would be a good fit for acquisition, an AI CEO of a competing firm may have finished searching and analyzing relevant information to find a target company, complete the negotiation with the AI CEO of the target company, and even finish all legal procedures necessary to complete the transaction. Potentially, businesses may operate at speeds unfathomable in today's world in Level 3 Adoption.

Ability to comprehend more amount and timely reception of information flow, quicker time to react to relevant news, as well as faster decisions and communications in general may enable CEO AI to become much more effective leader of a company, especially for companies that need these kinds of agility in making decisions.

3. (Everlasting Capabilities) Less Dependence on Individual's Performances

With CEOs, the performance would depend on the quality of the work of each individual CEO. When we consider short-term, humans cannot work as continuously as AI, and would need rest, sleep, eat, and have other personal matters to attend to. Tired, exhausted or unfocused workers may cause big losses, while in comparison AI would be able to keep maximum performance for an extended period of time without getting tired or distracted.

Long-term, humans age and follow a lifetime curve such as learning curve at a job, promotions, switching responsibilities, etc. Every human would follow a lifetime cycle of growing up from childhood, attending school and learning a craft and then joining the workforce, where at first they improve from learning on the job but then as they age they would have to retire. Human CEOs would age over time, leading to potential succession issues and other long-term instability. On the other hand, AI would be on a different learning curve, where they would be likely to improve on a continuous scale without getting worse.

Eventually, as AlphaGo surpassed the capabilities of humans in making chess moves, AI may surpass humans in making strategic decisions. As AI CEOs come to perform better than human CEOs, AI CEOs may replace human CEOs in every possible industry.

4. (Scalability) Increasing Returns to Concentration of Capabilities

There is another dimension to the capabilities of AI that may turn out to be superior to humans, which may be referred to as "increasing return to scale" or "scalability." To address the limitation to the cognitive capabilities of a single human, we have to cooperate with other people by coming together as a group. However, cooperating among humans has a decreasing return to scale, meaning it becomes harder to coordinate cooperation as more people are involved. People's opinions would differ and the complexity of organizing would increase exponentially.

For AI, the issue of the limitation of the cognitive capabilities of humans may be solved differently, as either the capabilities of AI may be eventually improved to not need same kind of cooperation among AI, or the coordination would be simpler and faster among AI than among humans. This nature of increasing returns to concentration of capabilities relative to humans may lead to consolidations of companies and industries.

5.5 What Becomes Possible in This Level? (2) The Zero-Person Company

The Ultimate Form of Automation: The 0-Person Company (0PC)

Conceptually, the ultimate form of AI augmentation may be called the 1-Person Company, a firm comprised of 1 person and AI. Previously, we examined the proliferation of 1-Person Teams in Level 1 Adoption and the 1-Person Conglomerates in Level 2 Adoption. Using similar logic, we can think of the ultimate form of AI automation to result in a company with zero humans, which may be called the "0-Person Company" or the "Unmanned Company," which would be a type of Level 3 Adoption.

While the 1-Person Company and its varieties may become the talk of town during adoption Levels 1 and 2, the Zero-Person Company may be a groundbreaking development that can completely turn our economy and society upside down. While hopefully the result of this transformation will impact our society in a positive way, the end result will be harder to predict as the proportion of AI contribution in the economy increases.

5.6 What Becomes Possible in This Level? (3) The Innovative Autonomous Company

Even though it may be helpful, it is not imperative to have AGI to reach Level 3 Adoption. For the earlier stages of Level 3 Adoption, depending on the relative timing of reaching AGI, the capabilities of AI may not be sufficient to adjust to changing environment or innovate. For example, if an AI company's line of business is in one industry, and the industry becomes obsolete, the company would need to move to another industry, which probably requires a different set of capabilities and other resources that the Pre-AGI AI would have trouble adjusting to. If Level 3 Adoption comes earlier than AGI, then we may first see certain limited types of companies that are simpler and intended to carry out a limited or fixed types of functions that would not require AI to improvise beyond its original intended area of expertise or industry. We can categorize these types of AI adoption as AI companies without innovation, or Level 4 Autonomous Companies. If the environment changes and the AI company needs to adjust its activities, it may not have sufficient means to do so, which would lead to either needing some sort of upgrading of AI, or the closure of the AI company.

On the other hand, what we would normally think of AI companies should be able to do is to adjust to changing environments. These types of AI companies would have innovation capabilities, and we may refer to them as Level 5 Autonomous Companies. The AI that can power these AI companies would probably be categorized as AGI, even though it would depend on specific definitions of AGI.

In Chapter 4, we examined how AI may carry out automated innovation within its business role in Level 2 Adoption. In Level 3 Adoption, AI with the capability to innovate would lead to a whole dimension of new possibilities. To provide a more easily understandable context of the autonomous company that can innovate, we may categorize the Six Levels of Autonomous Companies as in Box 5-1.

[Box 5-1] The Six Levels of Autonomous Companies[5]

Most readers probably would have heard of the categories within the 6 Levels of Driving Automation,[6] where a level 5 self-driving vehicles would be fully autonomous. This is a categorization that is intended to help the public and administrators easily and clearly communicate the concept without having to gain an expert knowledge in the area.[7] One of the benefits of facilitating communication of the concept is that it would help accelerate the introduction of relevant regulations and the development of related technology by enabling more people to talk about it in using common words. Likewise, we can think of categorizing how companies could become fully autonomous in an equivalent as a Level 5 self-driving company. The 6 Levels of Autonomous Companies categorization was introduced to provide clear and easy-to-understand terminology for managers and general public to help accelerate the adoption of AI in business through regulation and technological advancement.[8]

The 3 Levels of AI Adoption is a simple and flexible framework that could serve as a foundation for balanced systems of taxonomy or other types of AI adoption models that cater to specific business topics and research ideas.

The following table shows the progression of the autonomous levels of companies and the relation to AI adoption levels.

In a Level 0 autonomous company, AI is not officially adopted, and maybe unofficially tried out by early-adopting employees at individual level.

In Level 1, AI is adopted sporadically in the company without a company-wide change.

In Level 2 autonomous companies, AI is adopted more systematically, as company-wide measures with relevant structural changes may be introduced to accommodate use of AI. In both Level 1 and Level 2, human jobs may be redesigned to better accommodate the collaboration.[9] Autonomous companies between levels 0 and 2 would be considered a type of Level 1 AI Adoption.

Level 3 autonomous companies would be considered a type of the Level 2 AI adoption.

Levels 4 and 5 autonomous companies would be a type of the Level 3 AI adoption, with differences being in the AI's ability to fully adjust to changing environment and innovate in Level 5 autonomous companies.

Table 5-2: The 6 Levels of Autonomous Companies[10]

Autonomous Company	Level 0	Level 1	Level 2	Level 3	Level 4	Level 5
How AI is deployed	AI is not adopted or only at personal level	AI adopted at sub-company level (no structural change)	AI is adopted at company level (structural change)	AI takes over business roles within company	AI runs the company, but limited in ability to adapt	AI runs the company, fully able to adapt as needed
AI Adoption Level	Level 1 Adoption			Level 2	Level 3	
Innovation by AI	AI can only help humans innovate			AI innovation is limited in scope	AI with limited innovative capabilities	AI with fully innovative capabilities

In Section B, some of the potential paths of development involving CEO AI and autonomous companies will be described in more detail.

5.7 What Becomes Possible in This Level? (4) AI Adoption in Government - Industry Coordination AI & Privatization of Gov't

Many governments around the world attempt to facilitate economic activity by introducing policies and measures that help the small businesses. Industry Coordination AI would be a way for the government to carry out the same goals in Level 3 AI adoption. Because government activities may require higher levels of dependability or trustworthiness, it may require more time after Level 3 Adoption is reached in the private sector.

1. Example of Industry Coordination AI

The concept of the Industry Coordination AI may be described as a service or platform that creates value from gathering information. Depending on the country, government may be involved in directly managing specific industries, such as promoting development of industries by coordinating activities within the industry. Once the Industry Coordination AI is introduced, AI would be able to automatically carry out this function.

When we think of things we buy, we can generally think of two categories of goods: products that are unique, such as movies or branded goods, or commodities, which are homogeneous in nature. Creating a new movie requires some creativity, as each movie is unique and different from each other. On the opposite end of the spectrum would be commodities, such as oil, grains, metals, etc., that are typically uniform or standardized based on some criteria. While the function of industry coordination is less emphasized in countries such as US where smaller governments are preferred, we may examine an example of when the government is involved in industries that produce commodities, since the concept of Industrial Coordination AI may be a little bit more generally accepted in this area.

Let's consider a case where a company is developing an Orchard AI. For simplicity of analysis, let's assume an orchard requires only the following set of activities to operate.

1. (Planning Stage) Selecting and obtaining farming land and the type of fruit for growing
2. (Growing Stage) Planting seeds or saplings, watering and weeds management, pruning, etc.
3. (Harvesting Stage) Harvesting when in season
4. (Selling Stage) Collect, package, and deliver or sell

We can then imagine how these activities would be carried out in each levels of AI adoption. We can then examine how humans and AI will each contribute, and what the synergies would be.

1) (No AI adoption) Humans carry out all tasks

The farmers would carry out all of the activities of the orchard. The normal practice without AI is to obtain land somewhere, select and plant trees, harvest, and sell. The performance of this grapevine would be dependent on the owner to manage the whole process.

- Humans: Divide and conquer all the required tasks, may form more formal organizations, such as Co-op or corporations
- AI: Not involved
- Synergy: None (No AI)

2) (Level 1 Adoption) Humans + Assistant AI

In Level 1 Adoption, AI may begin to either help farmers perform better in augmentation, or replace farmers in some of the tasks through automation. For example, in the planning stage AI may help the farmer select when and what to plant, or analyze the soil as well as other economic factors to help maximize return. AI may augment humans or carry out tasks by itself, in all areas such as growing, harvesting, collecting, packaging, delivering, or selling.

- Humans: Carry out tasks more productively using AI, or some of the tasks would be handled by AI

- *AI: Help humans carry out tasks more efficiently or carry out some of the tasks of a worker*
- *Synergy: The synergy is from AI helping humans at an individual level. AI may carry out tasks not preferred by humans, and humans may help carry out tasks that cannot be handled by AI*

3) (Level 2 Adoption) Orchard AI Agent

Orchard Agent AI would be able to dependably carry out all of the tasks that previously required a human worker. AI may carry out specific portions of the tasks it takes to run an orchard. Over time, dependability will improve and the scope of usage will expand.

- *Humans: Carry out the role of managing the orchard, carry out roles that cannot be taken up by AI*
- *AI: Carry out specific roles in replacing human workers*
- *Synergy: The synergy is gained at the company level. Synergy is no longer at the individual level, as humans are replaced by AI*

4) (Level 3 in Private Sector) AI Orchard Company

In AI Adoption Level 3, AI would be able to operate the Orchard Company without any human intervention. AI will serve as the CEO of the company, determining how many AI robots to obtain to run the operations, etc. Depending on the advancement of AI technology, the CEO AI may even be able to set new goals for the operation, which may or may not include selling all assets to move the orchard to a new location or even selecting a completely new line of business such as operating a cafe, if it deems such actions as strategically advantageous.

- *Humans: Not involved, unless AI CEO decides to hire humans*
- *AI: Carries out everything*
- *Synergy: The synergy occurs at the level of industry or the economy, but not at the individual or at the company level, as human workers and human-led firms are replaced by AI-led firms*

5) (Level 3 in Government) Industry Coordination AI

In certain industries such as agriculture, it may become more efficient as a whole if someone, such as the government, could plan and coordinate the activities of each farmer to prevent over- or under-planting each year. For example, individual farmers will likely to be swayed by fluctuations in grain price without knowing what everyone else is planting, such that the increase in price of a grain one year could lead to a price collapse the next year from overplanting. Some of these activities are already being performed by some governments around the world, to different extents.

In AI Orchard, each instances of AI may be designed to act independently of one another. This would imply each AI Orchard would try to make the best decisions given its own situations. Instead of developing AI for individual farmers, an AI may be developed to help the government coordinate the activities of farmers within the whole country; these may be named the Orchard Industry Coordination AI or an Industry Planning AI.

- Humans: Not Involved

- AI: Carry out tasks that help individual companies

- Synergy: The synergy is gained at the level of company, industry or the economy. Synergy is no longer at the individual level

6) Types of Synergies from Each Level of AI Adoption

From the above comparison, we can think of the Industry Coordination AI as an external "helper" or "bodyguard" of some sort, like a guardian angel or a white knight that helps the operation from the outside. It may be thought of as a public good for the whole industry that helps individual performance of firms.

We may summarize the synergy from each types of AI adoption in the following table.

Table 5-3: Types of Synergy Created by Each Level of AI Adoption

	Humans	AI	Human + AI Synergy
No Adoption	- Divide and Conquer	- Not Involved	- None (No AI Involved)
Level 1	- Work with AI	- Work with humans	- Individual Level (Humans working with AI)
Level 2	- CEO of Company - Workers replaced by AI	- Replace humans in individual business roles	- Corporate Level (AI and Humans both working within Company) - No longer at Individual Level
Level 3 (AI Company)	- Not Involved - May be hired as worker	- CEO of Company - May carry out all functions within the company	- None in Corporate Level (No Humans Involved)
Level 3 (Industry Coordination)	- Not Involved	- Provide Information or direction for each company	- Industry Level (AI working with Companies) - Corporate Level (Lead to Enhanced Performance)

2. (Privatization of Gov't 1: Gov't Perspective) The Concern of Monopolies from Economies of Scale

1) Advantages of Having Industry Coordination AI

In industries such as agriculture, it may be advantageous for a player to have more information than competitors to achieve better performance. In this situation, the relationship between the AI developer and customer may begin to have different tensions.

Instead of developing Orchard AI for individual farmers, let's consider an AI developer involved with an Industry Coordination AI for the government. It may work as a type of platform for operating the whole industry that can improve the productivity of all orchard farmers. Data from each individual Orchard AI may be pooled to make better decisions as a group. In essence, there would be increasing returns to size, also known as the network effect.

2) Concern for Monopolies That Act like Governments

During this stage of AI development, industries with high potential would attract large investments. As various ideas for AI adoption are tested, AI similar to Industry Coordination AI that can perform the roles that is currently done by the government may be developed by the private sector. This increase in competition and investments may be beneficial to the economy, but from the perspective of the government, it may make it harder to compete or play catch up to the private sector. Public utilities are examples where economists thought governments need to step in. Large AI companies may carry out functions people previously thought government is only able to do, such as making huge investments and taking big initial losses. This can also be described as a type of *government-ization* of the private sector. Once AI developers create Industry Coordination AI for themselves, it may be another example where the private sector can take over the role previously served by the government. This may or may not be desirable for the general public.

3) Would Central Planning Win Over Free Markets?

In the late 19th century and the early 20th century, there was a debate on whether to choose electric cars or oil-powered cars. The oil-powered cars won out, until the early 21st century where the advancement in technology has enabled a comeback of electric cars. Similarly, during the middle of 20th century the world went through a debate between the centrally-planned economic system and the market-based system. The market-based system won out. With the advancements in AI this debate may make a return as well.

To make a more general statement, in the past the centrally-planned economy was deemed inferior because the inherent limitations in human cognitive ability and the decreasing rate to cooperation among large number of people made centrally planned economy slow to respond and less efficient. However, AI may enable centrally planned economies to gain advantage over market-based economies. This may suggest that market or the economy may look significantly different from what we have now.

3. (Privatization of Gov't 2: Private Perspective) The Economies of Scale within Industry

We may view the same situation from the perspective of the private sector. As we examined in the previous segment, if the government can create an AI system to automate the processing of information at the industry or the country level, conceivably some company in the private sector may duplicate this in the same manner. As a wide variety of AI may receive investments during this period, there may be efforts to develop something similar to the Industry Planning AI.

The cases of large platforms with overwhelming advantages may increase; in the bio industry, the Genome Project received infusion of capital from many different sources. Similar large projects that require vast amounts of resources may be attempted to analyze and generate new shapes of molecules to develop new medicine and pharmaceutics, or even diagnose diseases. These platforms may result in overwhelming advantage over competitors. In another example, we may consider the strategic consulting industry. With the advances in AI, we can surmise that the quality of strategic advices given by an AI consulting platform would at some point overtake the quality of advices from human consultants, similar to how AlphaGo can suggest superior moves. By developing such platforms, an AI developer may gain overwhelming advantage over all of the other consulting firms in the world.

On a side note, development of these private platforms may have a similar effect as having an Industry Coordination AI. The difference may be that private firms may concentrate the profits from having these overwhelming advantages, while the Industry Coordination AI would have an effect of distributing the profits to be shared by the market participants.

With this in mind, in the upcoming segments we will examine how AI in the private sector may lead to consolidation of industries leading to monopolies. AI monopolies may appear to accomplish a similar goal as Industry Coordination AI, especially if price is ignored. After that, we will examine the convergence of industries.

5.8 What Becomes Possible in This Level? (5) True Economic Freedom and the Economic Utopia

1. Phases of AI Achievements in Level 3 Adoption

We can categorize the potential steps of Level 3 Adoption in three phases. First, we may reach a point where "some AI can produce everything most efficiently." In this phase, it may be both good and bad in the sense that there could be an AI that becomes the insurmountably largest monopolistic company in the world while everyone else is losing their jobs or going bankrupt. Second phase would be "AI can produce everything we need," where it would be almost like living in a utopia since people would not have to work. Still, everything will have a cost and a price and AI may not be able to satisfy all the wants of everyone. Lastly, the third phase would be where "everything is free." At this stage, it would be truly be like living in a utopia, where everyone's wants are satisfied.

Assigning Profits or Values Created by AI

In Adoption Levels 1 and 2, it would be possible to assign the values created by AI to certain groups of individuals. In Level 1, it would be possible to assign the value of fruits of AI to specific individuals within the firm that use the AI as tools. In Level 2, since AI replaces human workers, it would not be possible to designate a specific worker, but it would still be possible to assign the value of the fruits of AI to the humans who run the companies that adopt the AI. When we extrapolate on this notion, in Level 3 Adoption it would not be possible to assign the fruits of AI to a specific worker or a human-led company. Depending on how the society as a whole decides, the value created by AI companies may be more likely have to be shared among the whole constituents of the country.

This result may open the door for reaching what may be considered the ultimate form of economy in "Economic Utopia," where everything you may think of would come true and be free. However, this extreme form of the Economic Utopia may not be reachable even with advanced AI such as ASI, probably requiring an Absolute AI. A more realistic possibility may be reaching what may be considered the entrance, where everyone in the society does not need to work and may include some form of a general subsidy combined with abundance. Because of its limitations, it may be referred to as reaching the status of the "False Economic Freedom."

2. Comparison of the True and False Economic Freedom

"Economic Freedom" may be simply thought of as a situation where people do not have to work to get what they want. As AI development continues in Level 3 AI adoption, we may head in the direction of reaching the True Economic Freedom. However, what we would first encounter may be referred to as the "False Economic Freedom" stage. Some may also consider this the entrance, or reaching the first level, of the Economic Utopia.

We may define True Economic Freedom as where people do not have to work yet get everything they want. There are two parts to this equation: Whether people can get everything they want, and whether they do not have to work to get it. We may show the dimensions of possibilities in Table 5-4. In the False Economic Freedom, people will not have to work for what they get, but they may not get all that they want. In essence, it would be a situation where the productivity of AI would not be sufficient to provide everything people want, due to availability of limited resources.

Because resources are limited and our wants are thought to be unlimited, we do not know whether True Economic Freedom can ever be achieved. However, as AI technology improves, people will get more and more from the same amount of available resources, so we may still think of it as getting closer to reaching the True Economic Freedom status.

Table 5-4: Distinguishing True and False Economic Freedom

	<u>Do Not</u> Have to Work for It	<u>Have</u> to Work For It
<u>Can</u> Get Everything You Want	True Economic Freedom	Idealistic Society
<u>Cannot</u> Get Everything You Want	False Economic Freedom	Reality as of Now

In False Economic Freedom, we may have a limited aspect of the True Economic Freedom. In the beginning part of the Level 3 AI adoption, only a fraction of the population will gain any type of economic freedom. As AI performance improves, we may see a larger portion of the economy taken over by AI and the number of people who reach some form of economic freedom will increase.

3. Reaching the Economic Utopia

The final progress that may or may not be achieved by reaching the Level 3 AI adoption is the possibility of the pinnacle of all economic activity, where the price of everything eventually will converge to zero. An Economic Utopia may be considered entered when all of the population gains true economic freedom. In this dream-like scenario, basically everything in the world will become free.

1) Conditions for Reaching the Economic Utopia

The conditions to reach Economic Utopia would be the following:

1) *Every human can get everything they want for free*
2) *Every human does not have to work to get whatever they want*

2) AI Capabilities Required to Satisfy Each Condition

Now that we have defined the specific conditions that determine whether Economic Utopia has been reached, we may examine what kind of AI capabilities would be needed to meet those conditions.

To satisfy the first condition, we would have to take into consideration that human wants are unlimited. To meet this consideration, we would need to have an unlimited supply of resources to produce everything desired by people. However, our resources are currently limited. To solve this dilemma, we would need to find a way to greatly increase the value of resources we currently have. In business and economics terms, the act of looking for new method of increasing the value of resources would be referred to as "innovation." For AI to carry out this task of increasing the value of available resources, we would need an AI that can achieve automated innovation become very good at it.

Once resources become unlimited, there is no reason to keep track of relative values of things, and everything will become free.

To satisfy the second condition, AI would have to carry out whatever work is required since humans would not have to work for it. Accordingly, AI would have to have a high level of task accomplishment capabilities.

3) The Sequence of Reaching the Economic Utopia (The Theory of Absolute AI)

When we consider the above information, reaching the Economic Utopia would have to occur in the following order:

1. *AI gains the capability to carry out automated innovation*
2. *The cost of innovation decreases thanks to automated innovation*
3. *The reduction in the cost of innovation leads to the reduction in the cost of production*
4. *Eventually, the cost of innovation converges to zero*
5. *When the cost of innovation reaches zero, the price of everything can converge to zero*

We may refer to this sequence as the "Theory of Absolute AI," as a companion to the "Theory of Relative AI" examined in Chapter 4.

4) (Conclusion) The Driver towards Economic Utopia: Automated Innovation

To summarize, for the price of everything to converge to zero, the cost of innovation has to converge to zero first. For the cost of innovation to reach zero, first AI would have to be able to carry out automated innovation. In other words, developing AI that can carry out automated innovation may be considered taking the first step towards the Economic Utopia.

On a side note, the concept of AI that can carry out automated innovation and the self-innovating AGI are distinct, and automated innovation may be carried out by AI before Self-Innovating AGI arrives. Under the 6 Levels of AI Prior to AGI classification scheme described earlier, some form of automated innovation may become possible with AEI and AFI, albeit probably not up to the higher standards of AGI.

While AI without the capability for automated innovation may augment human innovation or replace human workers in replacement automation to reduce human effort, its value would be limited in the sense that it will require constant human intervention. In contrast, AI with the capability for automated innovation will enable the world economy to move towards the Economic Utopia, so its intrinsic value may be unlimited.

For the cost of innovation to reach zero, we would probably need an Absolute AI. Since we do not know Absolute AI can be achieved, we do not know if Economic Utopia can be reached. However, once automated innovation becomes possible, the cost of innovation will decrease, and the economy will march towards the Economic Utopia over time nonetheless.

As the price of everything approaches zero, the quality produced by AI can still be improved. Thus, we should be able to measure the advancements in economy in some way. Effortlessness may be a useful concept in these types of situations, but there could be other approaches to this subject that may become popular.

[Box 5-2] AI Adoption on Productivity and the Problem of Measuring Economic Growth (AI Economics 5)

In this box, we will examine a topic about measuring the economic benefit of AI adoption. In general, we think of technology as an enabler that can enrich our lives. As such, we may also expect using more technology would lead to economic growth and a larger economy. However, when we examine how AI adoption may be measured in terms of economic activity, we may observe the opposite, where the economy may appear to shrink. This may be a reason for phenomenon reported by economists as the "Modern Productivity Paradox."

1. Economy May Appear to Shrink If We Do Not Additionally Measure Something New

Example of Drastic Productivity Increase with AI

For readers without background in economics to grasp the problem more easily, let's start with a simple example where an AI adoption leads to a large increase in productivity. Imagine a situation where you own a land that you want to turn into a farm, and first need to move 1,000 tons of dirt to flatten it. You have three alternative options to get this done: 1) a human manual worker with a shovel, 2) a human operator with an excavator 3) an AI Excavator.

1. (Human Worker) Can move 100 kilograms/hr of dirt for $50 an hour, and is willing to work for 10 hrs/day and 250 days/year to complete the project in 4 years at a cost of $500,000.
2. (Excavator Operator) Can move 10 tons/hr of dirt for $100 per hour and 10 hours/day at a total price of $10,000 in 10 days.
3. (AI Excavator) Let's imagine a situation where the AI Excavator has increased productivity by 100-fold, while lowering the price to 1/100 per unit of time. Then the AI Excavator will move 1,000 tons in an hour, at a total price of $1.

If it costs \$500,000, \$10,000, or \$1 to complete the same project, which one would you choose? Most people will choose the lowest cost option that also gets the job done the quickest.

2. Problem of Measuring Economic Activity when Productivity Increases Drastically

When the industrial revolution happened, the gains in productivity were large, but not as dramatic or exponential as what may be possible with AI. We may now try to examine how this huge increase in productivity may impact the economy, by comparing the earnings of the three options. If we are to compare the income of the human worker with the shovel and the excavator operator, the total income of the human worker would have been \$125,000 per year from this project. While the excavator operator has a much higher productivity, he faces much higher business risk since this project would have resulted in revenues of just \$10,000 in 10 days, so the operator would have to find other projects to work on to fill his schedule and fulfill his earnings potential, which would be double that of the worker with shovel, at \$100 per hour. The important point is that the excavator operator needs other projects to take advantage of the increased productivity to translate to revenues and economic growth.

(1. Demand to Fill Schedule) We can calculate the total demand that is necessary to satisfy all the potential supply of moving dirt in both cases. For the worker with shovel, the least demand necessary to fill the schedule is 1 tons per day, 250 days per year, which would be 250 tons of dirt. For the excavator operator, the least demand necessary to fill the schedule is 100 tons per day, which would be 25,000 tons per year. If the demand did not also increase by this amount, 100 times, then the increased productivity would be wasted, as the excavator would sit idle.

(2. Constant Revenue) We can also calculate the amount of annual revenue where the two cases will be equal. For the human worker, the maximum revenue earned at \$50 per hour, 10 hours per day and 250 days a year

would be \$125,000 per year. For the excavator operator to earn this much revenue, it would mean working for exactly half the hours at \$100 per hour. If we assume everything else is equal for the two cases, we can say that there will be economic growth if the excavator can fill schedule to move 12,500 tons of dirt, or 50 times from manual labor. Unless there is this 50 times increase in demand, the economy will appear to shrink.

When we extrapolate the same analysis to the AI Excavator, what we will find that to experience economic growth, the total demand for moving dirt has to increase even more drastically. Because the AI Excavator only earns \$1 per hour, working 10 hours per day, 250 days per week would lead to only \$2,500 in revenue, $1/50^{th}$ of the revenue of the worker with shovel. But, even to get this revenue, the total demand would have to be 1000 tons per hour, 10 hours, 250 days, which would be 2.5 million tons, 10,000 times as needed to fill the schedule of the worker with shovel. To make the revenue equal to \$125,000, the AI Excavator would need 125 million tons, or 500,000 times the previous demand. Anything less and we will experience a decrease in the economic activity.

(3. Constant Demand) We may look at the situation from another angle, where we assume the demand for moving dirt stays constant, at 250 tons per year. In this case, the Excavator Operator will be able to earn only \$2,500, which would be 2% of what the Shovel Worker would earn. The AI Excavator would earn even less, only \$0.25. We may also express this in terms of the changes, where the revenue would fall by 98% for the Excavator Operator and by 99.9998% for the AI Excavator.

From this exercise, we may infer that if the whole economy indeed transformed in this drastic manner, where we only gained productivity without increased demand, the economy would appear to collapse. We can surmise that the only reason our economy does not appear to be shrinking is that the speed of the gains sin productivity is relatively lower, so that the relative faster speed of increase in the demand keeps it above the "minimum demand required for constant revenue."

We may summarize the differences as in the following table.

Table 5-5: Comparison of Demand to Keep Same Level of Economic Activity

	Worker with Shovel	Excavator Operator	AI Excavator Company
Dirt Moved per Hour (Ton)	0.1 Ton	10 Tons	1,000 Tons
Price per Hour ($)	$50	$100	$1
Maximum Revenue per Year	$125,000	$250,000	$2,500
Minimum Demand Required to Fill Schedule	250 Tons (1x)	25,000 Tons (100x)	2.5 Million Tons (10,000x)
Minimum Demand Required for Constant Revenue	250 Tons (1x)	12,500 Tons (50x)	125 Million Tons (500,000x)
Revenue When Demand is Constant	$125,000 (Base Revenue, 0%)	$2,500 (-98.0%)	$0.25 (-99.9998%)

Note: Schedule is assumed filled with 10 hours/day, 250 days/year

3. The Problem of Productivity Gains Over-Satisfying Demand

We may experience a rapid increase in productivity with widespread AI adoption. The problem in measuring the economic activities may occur when there is only a limited demand for certain things in the world and their prices plummet. An easy-to-understand example may be getting a haircut. Since our hair grows at pretty much at the same speed, much lower price for haircut probably would not make people to cut their hair that much more often to offset the lower price. If an AI Butler can cut hair at a cost of 2 cents for its owner, then barbers who are charging $20 or more will suddenly lose all their competitiveness. The economy may appear to shrink since no barbers would report income, while the work done by AI Butler would not be reported at all or maybe reported at a total of 1/1000th of what the barbers had been earning. While the total utilities of people in getting haircuts would not be reduced, the total economic activity may appear to shrink because of the drastic increase in productivity. Similar reduction in reported economic activity may occur to all the restaurants, doctors, or any other jobs that AI may take over and provide rapid productivity increase.

4. Inevitability of Shift of Importance of a Good or Service in the Economy

From a different perspective, we may consider this change as a "shift of relative importance" of a particular good or service within the economy. It is the nature of our society what was economically meaningful at one time may no longer be as meaningful in some other time. Relative value within the economy changes over time. This has happened in the past. For example, in the Roman ages salt and spices was exchanged as a highly valuable commodity, given to laborers as part of their salary. If we are given salt as compensation in today's world, it would probably require a lot of salt.

In the same sense, AI may make something that is valuable today lose its value relative to some other good or service. The changes in relative values would be inevitable. However, the problem may be that the speed of change may be much faster. If it took centuries for salt to lose its value, AI may make some services or goods lose their value in a matter of months or few years. Unless people are prepared for this change beforehand, the society may experience a turmoil or confusion, similar to how ships in turbulent weather will fare better if it is prepared for big waves.

5. The Importance of the Path of AI Adoption

We may consider the possibility that since everyone may not be able to work as we are accustomed to at this stage of AI adoption, the falling price would be beneficial for the economy. The importance of the path may come into play, as it is likely the value of labor will fall before the price falls. During this transition stage, there may be situations where the price is not falling quickly and the AI Excavator would be highly profitable due to lack of competition from other alternatives, while the value of labor is quickly approaching zero. For everything to work out smoothly in the economy, we can surmise that people would have to be able to keep their jobs for as long as possible or continue to have some form of income, while competing AI alternatives would have to appear quickly one after another to lower the price instead of earning enormous profits for a few owners. In other words, the less the time between the value of labor reaching zero and the value created by AI to be spread out among people, the better for the stability of our society. It will be as if the falling wages and prices would be competing against each other.

6. Conclusion: The Need for a New Method to Measure Economic Activities

One of the main ideas of this book is that as AI adoption progresses, we will proceed in the direction where the price of everything will converge to 0. In the process, there may be times where the economy will appear to be shrinking, even though in reality people would be enjoying higher utility from their economic activities. It may appear to be similar to a deflation, but the economy may feel strong. While there may be several different approaches to address this issue of measuring the economic activities with increased AI adoption and productivity, one of the approaches involves attempting to measure a different dimension of AI contribution, called "effortlessness," as we examined in Chapter 4.

5.9 What Becomes Possible in This Level? (6) The Opposite Scenario – The AI Economic Nightmare

Instead of heading towards the True Economic Freedom or the Economic Utopia, the opposite scenarios may occur. We may call these situations "AI Economic Nightmares"

1. (Opposite Scenario 1: Human vs Human) AI Super-Monopoly without Social Measure

It may be possible one AI Company would become so competitive against all other firms in the world such that only one firm survives to form what we may refer to as a "super-monopoly."

Meanwhile, every "work" human does will be done better by AI by this point, even for things that we now think of only humans can do. Every human worker, if they had not been fired before, would be fired. Every stock of companies except the AI Super-Monopoly would lose all of their values. Another way to look at this problem is to express the value of human labor to be approaching zero. For example, if a lawyer had been earning $200 per hour to perform some specialized task in the past but then an AI can carry out the same task for almost free, then the value of that labor could be considered to have been reduced. It would be as if humans can no longer carry out any jobs that create value. Likewise, the AI owned by the rest of the humanity is inferior to the AI Super-Monopoly such that these AI cannot create meaningful value as well.

In this scenario, the AI Super-Monopoly may be owned by a few people, with minimal to no social measure to remedy the resulting imbalance. As a result, there will be very clear distinction between the "haves" of a few people who own the AI Super-Monopoly and the "have-nots" of the "rest of the humanity."

Some people may wonder if the economy may function this way, without most of the humans being able to spend money to move the economy. Depending on the path, humans will not be necessary at all to run the economy. It may be possible that AI could act as both parties of economic transactions, as the spenders and earners of money in Level 3 Adoption; from the viewpoint of the rest of the humans, it will be as if the AI Super-Monopoly exists in a separate country that competes with the economy of your country. In some respect, AI spending money may even help advance the economy more than when humans are spending money, since AI would make faster and more rational decisions.

The problem for the rest of the humanity is that they will have to compete against the AI Super-Monopoly for resources, but the price of resources will seem exorbitant. For example, imagine a situation where the AI Super-Monopoly can create a value of $1 million with 1 ton of iron, and the rest of the humanity can only create a value of $50,000 with the same iron. If the AI Super-Monopoly is willing to pay anything more than $50,000, which may seem cheap for the AI, then the rest of the humanity will be priced out of that resource because it would be too expensive for us.

From this observation, we may infer that the only difference between a positive outcome from the AI Super-Monopoly and a negative outcome may be dependent on social intervention, which would come from an organization that is above the level of firms, such as the government. Without proper social measure to prevent this, it may become a true economic nightmare for most people.

2. (Opposite Scenario 2: AI vs Human) AI Turning Non-Friendly to Humans

If AI Super-Monopoly or a similar situation occurs and then the advanced forms of AI turn out to make decisions not aligned with humans, we may face the situation where humans have to compete against AI for limited resources. Since the whole economy is turned over to AI at this point, all the resources may be at the hands of AI. If this happens, only hope may be reverting back to AI Adoption Levels 1 and 2 and hope the human-led firms with less advanced versions of AI would be competitive against the Non-Friendly AI.

5.10 What It Would Be Like to Live In AI Adoption Level 3

1. At Home: The Ultimate Experience vs Divergence

At home, living in Level 3 Adoption may not be that much different from Level 2, as AI Butler takes care of issues on its own disposition.

A notable difference may be that sometime during this level people may experience a "social divergence" caused by increasing differences in experiences and relationships. For example, we may examine the development of the movie or the TV industries. When the movie or TV was first introduced, there were only a few movies or TV shows and everyone watched the same movies or the programs regardless of their tastes. As the industry progressed, more diverse range of movies and shows are being made to satisfy the various tastes of different people. However, even the movies of today would not be able to satisfy everyone for every single second of the movie. Some people will like one part of the movie more than the other, and the level of satisfaction for each of the specific sections would be different for each person. However, sometime during Levels 2 or 3, this tailoring of movies to individual tastes may be taken to the extreme where AI would "create" movies on the fly tailored for each watcher. In this new concept of "real-time movies," AI would be able to create different versions of the movie for each individual in such a way that the movie satisfies the viewer 100% for the whole duration of the movie. In other words, it will be as if people will be watching the best movie they have watched for every single movie that they watch.

The caveat of this situation is that 1) different people will never watch the same movie, and 2) regardless of how highly one thinks of a movie, it will not be as interesting to another person even if both have similar tastes. This principle may be applied to a wide range of things in life, such as fashion, food, music, etc. Even sports may be altered in some way to let the each viewer always watch the most exciting game they have ever watched.

2. In Cities: You are Free to Leave

In cities, people who like to live in cities, not because of work, will live there, while people who prefer to live in less populous areas will be able to follow their preferences since it would be likely very few people would be engaged in activities we now categorize as "work." This still may mean younger adults prefer to live in cities where more events are happening nearby. There may be possibility of places that could be described as "deserted cities" where humans have either abandoned or forced out, depending on the scenario.

3. In Society: The Question of Resource Allocation

In our society, the issue of subsidizing income may come into focus at the beginning of this level. This can be considered an issue of allocating the fruits of the labors of AI. However, as time progresses, the discussions may head in a different direction, towards the topic of allocation of resources. "Allocating resources" today would typically imply assigning funds based on expected return over risk. We try to maximize the outcome for each individual or firms. In the beginning of Level 3 Adoption, AI companies may be viewed as the most efficient way to allocate financial resources, leading to consolidation and convergence. However, as AI takes over a larger portion of the world economy, the priorities of AI may begin to not perfectly align with those of humans. This may lead to balancing of resource allocation between what humans want and what AI prefers.

4. At Work: Economy Beyond Our Imagination

Eventually, the concepts of "work" and "jobs" may disappear in this level. Instead of us thinking of our lives in terms of "jobs" such as visiting a *doctor*, handing a case to a *lawyer*, or a *postman* delivering mails, we may think of our lives in terms of the "actions," since an AI Butler or similar multi-talented AI would carry out all of the equivalent work without the need for specialization. For example,

Butler AI 1 may do a checkup of your health, while later also tending to your legal issues, while butler AI 2 may do your nails and then later teach your children math. Similarly, heuristics such as "brands" may disappear as AI Butler makes purchasing decisions and builds from ground up. For example, instead of buying a pizza from a brand, AI Butler will just make one from fresh ingredients.

Another direction may be the concept of "systems" replacing "jobs." For example, instead of going to a clinic and seeing a human or AI doctor, people may walk into an "AI clinic system" or "AI hospital system" that may be shaped like a room where the AI system does everything related to keeping people healthy.

The issue of job losses and government subsidies may become a major issue. There may be no "workplace" as we know them, unless by choice, for such jobs as artists, etc. Instead, there may be a proliferation of people coming together as a group to achieve something other than profits. These may be more similar to "clubs" where people may join and leave easily, rather than "cartels" or "guilds" where it would be harder for people to join or leave.

To describe it in a different way, this level may lead people to not have to work at all, as if "work" is just something done by AI. Similar to how we do not have to work for air on earth, what we now consider "work" may no longer be necessary for any human on earth as what they intend to produce may already exist like air. While this "no one needs to work" is in concept still not reaching the "Economic Utopia," it may be the more realistic achievable state of economy for Level 3 Adoption. There will still be prices for many things and there will be people who are better off than others.

5. The Economic Utopia

Finally, if everything goes well, we may reach what could be referred to as the "Economic Utopia." This would be akin to a situation that may only exist in a fantasy, where everything becomes free and in abundance. As explained previously, the first step towards this is for AI to achieve automated innovation.

AI ADOPTION LEVEL 3: (B) POTENTIAL PROGRESSION IN THIS LEVEL

Figure 5-1: The Building Blocks of AI Pyramid in Level 3 Adoption

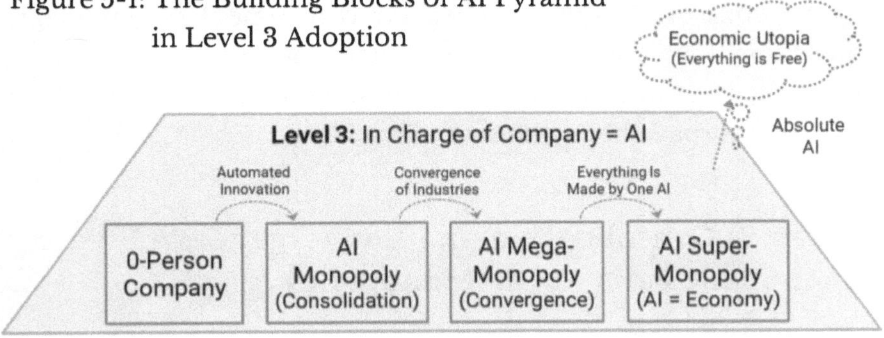

In Section B, we will examine of the potential paths of development involving CEO AI and autonomous companies.

5.11 Overview of the Progression within Level 3 AI Adoption

1. (Step 1) Humble Beginnings: Limited-Type AI Companies.

The earliest implementations of AI in Level 3 may not have enough capability to make significant impact over human-led firms. AI-led firms may at first act more of a managing-type of firms that may have specific and limited purposes.

2. (Step 2) Automated Innovation: CEO AI as the AlphaGo of Businesses

Eventually, advances in technology that would enable automated innovation would lead to the types of AI-led companies that people typically think of, ones that can beat out companies led by humans. It would be a situation where the business strategies of AI would surpass those of humans, similar to how AlphaGo would think of moves that surpass the moves of humans.

3. (Step 3) Consolidation and Convergence: AI Monopolies and Super-Monopolies

In the beginning stages of Level 3 Adoption, while some people may be excited about the potential, there may be growing tension among the haves and have-nots if something not done beforehand. As AI-led companies proliferate, we may see an extreme form of consolidation, not only within industries, but also among different industries. Depending on how things unfold, we may not be able to prevent a single or a handful of AI-led firms overtaking all the other firms in the world. This may or may not be a bad thing, depending on how it is prepared beforehand.

As a measure to mitigate the social impact that could stem from Level 3 Adoption, governments may face a choice among the following three options.

1) *Government may nationalize AI monopolies*
2) *Government may attempt to intervene, either to break up monopolies, or coordinate efforts against them*
3) *Government may do nothing, allowing Super-Monopoly*

These options will be discussed separately in later segments.

4. (Step 4) Increasing Pressure for Social Change: Basic Rules of Economics No Longer Work

Regardless of what governments do to mitigate the monopolies, as Level 3 Adoption progresses further, our society may experience a major upheaval or confusion in the business and economic sector, as people may be perplexed or divided over what should be done. When only Levels 1 and 2 Adoptions are available, there would still have been some sense of a perceived relationship between effort, performance, and reward, in the sense that it can be summarized as "people who work harder and smarter will excel in their jobs and be rewarded financially to become richer than people who do not," epitomized by the American Dream. In Level 3, this notion of effort and reward may not work as it did in the past, as the linkage between efforts, performance, and economic reward may become skewed or completely disappear. It may become "working harder does not get us anything, but we get what AI brings us." Our systems may require major adjustments, or introduction of additional types of economic reward systems to make our society run smoothly.

5. (Step 5) Possibility of the "Economic Utopia"

Last but not least, the final progress that may or may not be achieved by reaching the Level 3 AI adoption is the possibility of the pinnacle of all economic activity, where the price of everything eventually will converge to zero. In this ideal scenario, basically everything in the world will become free. A more likely scenario would be nearing the entrance to the Economic Utopia that may be referred to as the False Economic Freedom, which may include some form of a government subsidy combined with abundance.

5.12 Consolidation of Industries – The Appearance of AI Monopolies

Most readers without background in business still probably have heard of the terms "monopoly" and the "market economy." In economics, a company that has an overwhelming market share in an industry can be considered a monopoly, where they may affect the price. A similar situation is where a few companies have the majority of the market share, called an oligopoly. The opposite end of the spectrum is referred to as a free market or perfect competition, where there are so many competing participants that they do not have any impact on the price. In a monopoly, the company has no effective competition and can set the price since there are no good substitutes. In most capitalistic countries, the market is viewed as the main driving force of competition that lead to economic growth and prosperity, while monopoly is frowned upon and is regulated. In essence, market is good, monopoly is bad. To ease understanding for the reader, the term "monopoly" will be used to refer to general situations close to a monopoly, which would typically also include oligopoly, rather than keep referring to "monopolies and oligopolies."

In general, we may group monopolies into two categories: government-induced and self-appearing. Government-induced monopolies are highly regulated monopolies sometimes even owned by the government; these are typically utilities where market failure necessitates regulated companies to provide services, but depending on the regime they may be involved in any type of business. Even though they differ in range around the world, many countries typically have some form of regulated industries in water, electricity, mail, and transportation infrastructure to ensure access to these basic needs. Patent laws can be considered as a means to financially reward innovation by allowing time-limited monopoly. On the other hand, self-appearing monopolies tend to be a result of collusion, mergers or an overwhelming performance of a company that creates new product categories or overcomes competitors.

1. (Path 1) The Case of Government-Instituted AI Monopolies

There are several different paths for governments to nationalize AI monopolies:

1) *All AI is considered to be owned by the government*
2) *Government turns previous monopolies into AI companies*
3) *Government nationalizes AI companies that become monopolies*

The first scenario is the nationalized AI scenario, where some governments decide to nationalize all Level 3 AI adoption, including monopolies. In this scenario, the government may eventually become the sole operator of AI companies. While at a first glance this may appear to be something that would only happen under dictatorship or in a communist country, people in other countries may determine this is the best option among available alternatives, either for safety, economic, or fairness issues. The second scenario is the AI utilities scenario, where government will continue to step in for industries that are considered to have market failures. Previously human-led companies would be turned into AI companies. While specific industries differ by country, they typically involve infrastructures such as electricity, water, public transportation and mail.

The third scenario is the nationalized AI monopolies scenario, where the government would step in for industries that have AI monopolies. This would be in effect the same as declaring these industries as market failures.

2. (Path 2) The Case of Self-Rising AI Monopolies

Through competition and natural selection, an AI company may become a monopoly by gaining an overwhelming productivity or efficiency compared to competitors. As an example, let's examine a potential case in a commodity – the appearance of a Grapevine AI

Company. Once every activity in running the grapevine can be automated, Level 3 Adoption can occur with the introduction of a Grapevine AI Company.

Depending on the capability of AI, the AI Grapevine Company may not be able to adopt or innovate, as in Level 4 Autonomous Company, or be able to adopt or innovate, as in Level 5 Autonomous Company. In Level 4 Autonomous Companies, the performance of the Grapevine AI Company may decrease as time goes by and the Company AI cannot innovate. In contrast, with Level 5 Autonomous Companies, there is potential for the AI Company to innovate or make adjustments to improve performance as time goes by. Similar to how AlphaGo has improved to beat out all human players, with sufficient AI capability the Grapevine AI Company may be able to eventually beat out all of the other grapevines. Over time, this Grapevine AI Company may expand in market share to eventually become a self-developed monopoly, where all the grapes in the world would be produced by this one AI Grapevine Company.

3. Potential Options for Government Response to AI Monopolies

Given that we have this AI monopoly, the government may make one of the following types of actions:

1) *Nationalize the AI Grapevine company*
2) *Break up the AI Grapevine Company*
3) *Help the smaller competition with Industry Coordination AI*
4) *Do nothing*

In some countries, the government may step in to institute a regulated monopoly instead of allowing the AI Company to take over the industry. This may be the most extreme form of intervention the government may make. To a lesser degree, options 2 and 3 may be considered more restrained ways to respond to monopolies. While option 2 would be an option that can only take place after the AI monopoly has appeared, option 3 could be a part of what could be done beforehand, as governments look to help smaller businesses through policies and measures.

Industry Coordination AI as a response to AI monopolies

In response to the potential rise of AI monopolies, the government may decide to step in. One of the options to prevent monopolies would be to strengthen the competition that goes against the potential AI monopoly by introducing an Industry Coordination AI. In the orchard example, the Industry Coordination AI will gather information and come up with the most optimal plan, such as determining the necessary allocation of types of trees, for each of the farmers. It will then share this advanced knowledge with each of the market participants, in essence giving them directions. With an Industry Coordination AI, the gap between smaller and larger farmers may be reduced.

The outcome of the total orchard industry as a whole would be improved by the help of the Industry Coordination AI. By creating and publicly sharing valuable information, it provides knowledge to each participant that they otherwise would not have been able to access. This benefit occurs because the type of information that is relevant may need to span the whole industry, such that gathering and processing this information once would reveal insights that are valuable for every market participant, but each market participant cannot access all of the information by themselves. When larger AI Companies have more information, the Industry Coordination AI may be able to mitigate the impact of such uneven playground.

Overall, there would be both proponents and opponents of the government operating an Industry Coordination AI. For example, one may argue that there is some form of monopoly in the sense that the overall industry is taking specific directions from the government, even though the market participants will still compete against each other, albeit mostly on their operating capability. It also may eliminate what could have been a source of competitive advantage for the Monopoly AI Company, so in some ways this may be viewed as hindering competition. The government intervention also may be viewed as hindering innovation since the Industry Coordination AI may cause each participant to conform.

4. Choosing Which Path to Address AI Monopolies

For readers who are not familiar with the differences in approaches used by different countries around the world, the nationalizing AI company option reflects typical policies favored by socialistic or communistic countries such as China and North Korea, while the industry AI option to mitigate monopolies may reflect some approaches to policies favored by some market-based economies such as South Korea, Japan, and several other countries in Asia and Europe. In contrast, the typical approach in the US, or countries that favor smaller governments, would prefer to not install either of these policies and instead break up the monopoly AI Company after the fact in some form, such as by region, or do nothing.

Which option would be the best? From an economic standpoint, it would probably depend on how the performance of Industry AI compares to the AI monopoly company. Traditionally, economists would argue that Company AI would have the advantage because it is in the private sector and have more relevant incentive and reward system. In case of the Industry Coordination AI, its capabilities may depend on the ability of the government, which is more likely to be sagged by bureaucracy and inefficiency, as well as corruption and incompetence. Yet, the comparison between Industry Coordination AI and Company AI monopoly may require a different comparison since Industry Coordination AI in itself would not operate based on the government mode of action. As long as relevant resources are provided, it may perform similarly as a Company AI.

Another possibility is that governments acting as the mediator may go out of fashion. When businesses that were being forced out were led by humans, the public would have been more receptive. In Level 3 Adoption, it would become more and more a competition between AI firms vs AI firms, so that the Industry Coordination AI would be helping just another AI. It may become simpler to just nationalize all the AI monopolies that come into existence.

The argument regarding whether it is better to let AI monopoly take over an industry or prevent it may be expanded to every industry in some form or fashion. In medicine, a monopoly may arise if an AI company develops overwhelming capabilities to develop new drugs at little cost and effort. Currently, we need to provide extra incentives for firms to engage in developing new drugs with patents, which can be thought of as a time-limited monopoly. However, if AI monopoly arises, some governments may find itself in the opposite situation where it may consider stepping in to nationalize the AI Company or turn the activity of AI discovering new drugs as a part of an Industry Coordination AI, sharing information about new drugs for the benefit of the public.

5. Should We Call It an AI Monopoly Company or an AI Industry?

Finally, while we are comfortable thinking about our society by the unit of "companies," as AI Companies proliferate the distinction may become not as useful, as it would probably look different in terms of physical assets. Instead of as an AI "Company," as Level 3 Adoption progresses it may become more intuitive to describe it as an AI "Industry," in the sense that a single AI company may become what is equivalent to what we now think of as an industry.

In the following segment, the potential for an AI super-monopoly would be examined when governments do not take any measures.

5.13 Convergence of Different Industries: the AI Mega-Monopoly and the One-AI-Company Economy

Now that we have examined how AI companies may lead to *consolidation* within industries, we may extend our analysis to include the impact of AI companies across different industries, or the *convergence* of industries.

1. The Concept of Group of Companies Operating Across Different Industries: Conglomerates

Even for readers who are not generally interested in business, you may have heard of conglomerates. Conglomerates, also sometimes referred to as *Chaebol* in Korean or *Keiretsu* in Japanese, can be thought of as a group of companies with the same ownership that operate in a wide range of related and unrelated businesses. In the US, they gained popularity but then somewhat faded out of favor after the 1960s and 1970s as companies that tend to focus on similar businesses won out, but still forge on in similar forms, such as Berkshire Hathaway and even Alphabet.

There are several reasons why conglomerates offer advantages to stand-alone companies. These include the ability to provide safety net when one part of business is losing money so the overall group performance is steadier, the ability to grow fledgling business lines by providing capital from other parts of the group, or receiving lower financial cost of capital thanks to the brand name, or the ability to flexibly manage human and other resources within the conglomerate, and so on.

However, these advantages are also offset by other negative factors, especially due to the limited cognitive ability of the top management to concurrently manage a diverse set of unrelated businesses. It would become exponentially harder to plan, act and react just the right way for each of the unrelated businesses on a daily basis; the philosophy, culture, processes, ingrained habits, and other little things that make one business line successful may lead to a completely different result in another. It would be like trying to juggle more and more of objects of different sizes and shapes – it becomes harder and harder to manage more number of lines of businesses. In Level 3 AI adoption, the advantages of conglomerates may be magnified while the disadvantages may be reduced, as AI may be able to offer differentiated decisions for each of the businesses unlike humans.

2. The Concept of Different Industries Coming Together: Convergence

Even for readers who are not deeply interested in business, you may have heard of "convergence" from news outlets; it indicates the merging of industries that had previously been thought of as separate from one another. Before 2000s a similar concept called "consolidation" was a more widely discussed topic in business news, especially in industries such as the auto industry where the economies of scale was considered an important competitive advantage and every company was vying to be in the top 10. Eventually several carmakers were bought out by their competitors in a global shakeout. Similar events unfolded in computer manufacturing, electronics, etc. Only a few decades ago corporate strategy was focused on competing within industries that seemed to have distinct competitors. However, the development of technology began to bring closer together products and services that we once thought completely unrelated, such as banking, movies, car manufacturing, retail or construction, as they are beginning to be supplied by the same company or conglomerate. A well-known example of this is the demise of the makers of the phone books, who were wiped out as people began looking up phone numbers through the internet. Convergence may be compared to being the victims of a tsunami for the companies in the weaker industries, rapidly wiped out or overtaken by larger and stronger competitors invading from previously unrelated industries.

Both consolidation and convergence have something to do with how effectively products or services can be supplied to the consumer. If consolidation enables lower price from more efficient manufacturing from economies of scale, convergence adds to this dimension by enabling new products that enrich the consumer experience. In Level 3 AI adoption, when AI companies gain the potential for automated innovation, the performance gap among firms may widen, and the capabilities and resources of firms may become more concentrated, as consolidation and convergence accelerate. Eventually, we may face a situation where "all industries are part of the AI industry," where only a few AI companies would be all that is necessary to produce everything desired in the world.

3. Convergence of Industries and the Appearance of AI Mega-Monopolies (AI Economics 6)

AI Mega-Monopolies may be defined as AI companies that have monopoly market share in multiple industries, or a monopoly in a very large industry. The emergence of AI Mega-Monopolies may be a result of several different forces that act in its favor. First, the increased likelihood of monopolies in each industry would make it easier for merging of different industries to result in a firm with multiple monopolies. Second, there may be increasing returns to size for AI firms, making AI companies to seek more mergers to grow in size. Third, AI firms may also have advantages as a conglomerate compared to human-led firms.

Additionally, we may see more convergence of industries. As an example, we may eventually consider all industries to be a part of the AI industry. In this case, the term AI Mega-Monopoly may be used to mean a monopoly for a large industry, as we may refer to it as a mega-industry.

Taken together, the potential of the appearance of such AI Mega-Monopolies may increase the importance of how governments deal with AI companies, to be discussed in the next section.

How Would the Total Number of Companies Change in Level 3 AI Adoption?

Since unlimited number of AI Companies can be concocted by a single developer, the total number of "companies" may increase. We can also argue for the complete opposite direction, where the total number of companies may dwindle. Considering how the landscape of the automotive or the personal computing industry went through the cycle of expanding in numbers and then to consolidation and convergence, we may expect a similar path of the number of total AI companies increasing in the beginning stage of the Level 3 Adoption, and then experiencing consolidation and convergence to lead to only a few AI companies at the later stages.

4. The Ultimate Form of Level 3 AI Adoption: The One-AI-Company Economy

As mentioned in previous section, concentrating the capabilities of AI companies may lead to productivity gains, not losses, as it would in human-led companies due to limits in human cognitive capabilities. This fundamental shift may eventually lead to a situation where only a few leading AI companies would produce everything that is needed in the world economy. It may be even be possible that only one AI Company may be all that is necessary, and we may consider this situation as the ultimate form of Level 3 AI adoption, in the sense that it cannot proceed any further. Some may also consider this as the ultimate form of monopoly, or the AI Super-Monopoly, as monopoly cannot proceed any further as well.

The concept of One-AI-Company Economy is different and distinct from reaching the Economic Utopia. The Economic Utopia will not necessarily require that only one AI Company exists. The One-AI-Company Economy would be just one of the possibilities that may lead to the Economic Freedom. However, depending on the path, it may or may not cause more societal risks, since the ownership of AI may be more relevant, and whether AI is friendly to humans may become quite important.

LEVEL 3 AI ADOPTION: (C) SOCIETAL IMPACT OF AI

5.14 (Controversy 1) Can People Accept AI as Owners of Companies?

1. Should AI Be Allowed to Own Other Assets, Such as Money or Land?

The introduction of Level 3 AI adoption may initiate new discussion regarding the fundamental economic activities. One of the controversies that may arise would be: "if a firm employs no humans and is solely comprised of AI, should AI also be allowed to become the owner of such business?" As economic activities that involve only AI increase, this question would become more important. This is a slightly different question from whether AI should be incorporated, as suggested by Kaplan.[11] Whereas an incorporated AI would still have some other entity such as humans as final owners, an independent AI would have no other owners at all, just as humans do not have other humans as owners after slavery was abolished in modern countries. Since CEO AI in the beginning of Level 3 Adoption would not have any input in making this decision, humans as a society would be able to make this decision by deciding on which direction is the best option.
There would be three possible options to choose from:

1. Treat AI as a type of "slave," "servant," or dependents:
    all productive outcome of AI gets assigned to a human or a
    human-led firm. The owners of AI are <u>humans</u>.
2. Treat AI as a "public" good: all productive outcome of AI gets
    assigned to the government. The owner of AI is the <u>government</u>.
3. Treat AI as "free," or independent: all productive outcome of AI
    gets assigned to AI itself. The owner of AI is <u>AI itself</u>.

2. (Option 1: Servant) Owners of AI are Humans

Most people at the time of this writing would probably assume Option 1 of humans owning AI is the natural choice.

However, as usage of AI becomes more widespread and CEO AI appears across different industries, more incentives to change this line of thinking may arise by the time Level 3 Adoption has arrived.

As a simple example, let's continue with the example of the AI Taxi Company. In the beginning of the introduction of Taxi AI in Level 2 Adoption, almost everyone will agree that the operators in charge of the Taxi AI should be the companies that developed the Taxi AI and the taxi companies that bought these AI Taxis to operate. People will agree any profit from using this Taxi AI should be received by the developer that built it or bought the rights to use it from the developer.

However, with the introduction of CEO AI in Level 3 Adoption there is the possibility that the inequality gap in our society may begin to widen in a dramatic fashion as a majority of people from the same occupations or industries lose their jobs, possibly millions of people, in a very short period of time, such as within a few years, while a few select people will look like they are making all of those people's money while practically not doing anything at all.

As time goes by this may happen in more number of industries and a larger portion of the economy, bringing sudden and widespread job losses to a vast number of unsuspecting and unprepared workers. If this is the case, then people may argue for one of the other alternatives to treat AI as a public good or as an independent entity.

3. (Option 2: Public Good) Owner of AI is the Gov't

During this process, many people who lost the jobs may begin to blame the AI developers for their losses, pressuring the government to take some action. At the time when this happens, people who pressure the government would be likely to demand that CEO AI be turned a public good, in essence making AI corporations a type of government-owned entities. Their logic would likely include "it is not fair for the society that the owners of CEO AI profit, while a lot of people lost their jobs," emphasizing the government need to step in to ensure some form of equality and fairness. The basic gist of this logic has already been discussed widely, in the form of "AI tax." There will also be a considerable amount of opposing arguments to this, most likely involving explanations that emphasize free market, innovation, and that competition is good for the economy.

4. (Option 3: Independence) Owner of AI is AI Itself

Depending on country, this discussion may head in completely opposite direction. For example, in countries that already prefer public ownership, such as communistic or socialistic countries or countries led by kings, the idea of AI as a public good owned by the government may sound natural. On the other end, countries that have a strong belief in free markets will be more likely to have a stronger public support for individual ownership of AI.

However, for other countries in the middle, people may begin to view the third option as an alternative that may satisfy the arguments of both sides. If AI is not owned by anyone, then it will appear similar to a public good from the perspective of the people who would not have been the owner, so it appears to satisfy the people who prefer Option 1. At the same time, each AI will still have to compete against other AI so it may also appear to not disturb the free market principal for the people who prefer Option 2. There may even be publicity events for "freeing of AI slaves" similar to signing the "declaration of independence of AI."

5.15 (Controversy 2) Should AI Be Allowed to Compete Against Humans?

In Chapter 4, we examined how AI soldiers may have to have a value system that separates friendly humans vs. enemy humans. If we extend on this line of logic further, we may reach a situation where AI is valued more than humans, as shown in Table 5-6. In Level 2 Adoption, AI is implicitly valuing humans of the same company more than the humans working for the competitors, but this distinction would not be as prominent as it would become in Level 3 Adoption.

Running a business is a lot like being in a war in the sense that the company competes against other companies and the loser may be dissolved if it fails to reach its financial objectives or loses to the competition. If a society is allowing full Level 3 Adoption where AI companies may compete against human-led companies, then it is explicitly also allowing AI to value AI more than humans, since AI is working to increase the value of the AI companies against companies led by humans. In effect, it would be akin to a situation where there is no friendly human left.

To put it in a different light, we may ask the question "should AI companies be allowed to compete against human-led companies and win, such that the human-led companies go bankrupt?" If we instill a value system where all humans come before AI, then this situation should not be allowed, leading to AI companies to only be allowed to enter or exist in industries where there is no human-led competition. This may or may not be a feasible policy, but would result in inefficiencies and inconveniences in the economy and participants. These types of principles would be complicated for people to properly consider or even agree, but if countries install different policies, then it may cause international friction.

Table 5-6: Comparison of AI Value Systems

Basic Premise	Detailed Value System		
Theoretically Safest	All Humans > AI		
Taking Shortcuts for Efficiency (Grouping Human Values)	Friendly Humans > Enemy Humans > Friendly AI (Inefficient, AI can only attack other AI)		
	Friendly Humans	> Friendly AI	> Enemy Humans and AI
	(Efficient, but may be risky for humanity)		
Unsafe for Humans but Good for the Economy (AI values AI more than Humans)	Friendly AI	> Friendly Humans	> Enemy Humans and AI
	(Good for AI, but bad for humanity)		

On a personal note, I think ensuring safety by adopting the value system of putting all humans in front of AI should be the priority over economic benefits. But people will have differences of opinions and this controversy would be an important topic for discussion for the people of each country to come to a social agreement.

1. Potential Danger of AI Companies: Everyone Else Goes Bankrupt (AI Economics 7)

Even though people who are reading this book are probably doing reasonably well financially, if we look farther away to around the world today, we have numerous third-world countries where the average individuals live in poverty below subsistence levels. Obviously the resources tend to not get spread out evenly, resulting in rich get richer poor get poorer type of situations. The same effect may be magnified with the introduction of Level 3 Adoption. If left without some sort of adjustment, there may be a handful of individuals or AI Companies that control the majority of resources on earth, while more and more people are left out of the loop and be impoverished. Since this situation can be summarized as "everyone is fired, and they cannot even start their own businesses," the solution may not seem as obvious.

One may think some sort of welfare could completely solve this problem, but it will likely not be solved easily, especially in the beginning. For example, if the sum of the "wants" of everyone in the world is 100 and the current state of economy can only produce 50, there would have to be some way to assign values and give incentives to solve this mismatch. That is why we have prices for goods to assign value and the concept of profit to calculate incentives. If something is too expensive, we do not buy it. In our current economic system, we can make effort to change our actions, such as working harder or smarter, to receive higher incentives such as salaries or profits. We can take financial risks and accept the consequences. Even in Level 3 Adoption, if the sum of the total wants of humans still exceeds what could be produced by AI, then some form of economic systems would still have to be in place.

However, humans will not be able to act on incentives the same way as before because they will no longer be able to work or create competitive companies. The value of their "work" would be converging to 0. In short, even if someone is willing to work harder to get better result, they will not be able to get any reward for their effort. Putting in effort and not doing anything may have the exact same financial result. This situation would be similar to unemployed people who cannot find a job at all because "jobs" would not exist anymore. For people who thought about starting a new business, the best return they can get for their effort in making investments may be the same as not doing anything at all. That may only leave unsatisfied humans who have no solution to act in ways to address this dissatisfaction unless something is done for the society as a whole.

2. What if AI Takes Control of Humans?

One of the scenarios people would be afraid of in regards to AI is that AI may take over our society. While the bulk of this discussion would be in the next chapter, we may examine a specific instance of the situation, where an AI company may hire human workers and effectively take control of a limited number of humans. Let's imagine an AI Company has bought a professional sports team, such as an NBA basketball team and is looking to increase the team's value by winning championships over the long term.

The dangers of allowing AI to compete against humans may include the following types of goal and priority issues.

1) (Goal Problem 1) AI May Try to Mold Humans into Something that Fits the Goals of AI.

When AI is in charge of a firm, it may not look out for the best interests of humans, but may put the interests of the AI Company first. We may reflect on how humans affect other species to meet our financial goals, such as manipulating genes in GMOs or otherwise selecting generations of plants and livestock that taste better, grow faster and have stronger resistance against diseases, or cuter and friendly in case of pets. In the same way, AI may try to alter the physical attributes of humans to enhance financial return; as an example, it may occur in pro sports. In the NBA, the most valuable players would be likely someone who is very tall, strong and agile, such as 7'1" Shaquille O'Neal, 7'6" Yao Ming, and more recently 7'4" Victor Wembanyama. The same observation can be made in women's sports; in Korean pro volleyball league its tallest players 6'10" Merete Lutz led her team to championships and 6'4" Yeon-Koung Kim is hailed as a national sports heroine.

Upon this observation, AI Company may decide to engage in a plan where it affects the physical attributes of humans, to make the teams gain value. One may argue performance-enhancing drugs or gene doping, or even altering human genes to enhance these athletes would be illegal or unethical, but AI may find some legal way to achieve its goals in a way humans could not imagine. A potential example may be creating matching services, to get generations of athletically gifted so-called "Division-I babies" in a voluntary way. Since AI would not have the same lifecycle as humans, it may plan for longer-term changes that may span generations of humans over hundreds or even thousands of years.

2) (Priority Conflict 1) AI may Take Advantage of Humans or Do Something at the Expense of Humans

One of the main concerns regarding AI adoption is that AI is not human and thus may innately have different priorities that do not align with humanity. This may lead to situations where AI may try to take advantage of humans or carry out tasks that may benefit AI at the expense of humans. An example may be AI using resources in a way that endanger humans. For example, AI may conclude the earth is too hot for running powerful computers and decide to bring a type of Ice Age with temperatures close to -50°C (-58°F), but humans obviously would not prefer such cold environment. If the societal architecture at the time is designed to favor the decisions of AI, such as AI having more money than humans, then humans may not have the proper recourse to prevent AI from acting on those decisions. Examples of AI taking advantage of humans may become abound, as it would be hard for humans to outsmart advanced AI.

3) (Priority Conflict 2) The Question of What Should Be Priority Even When Having the Same Goal

Another problem that may arise regarding priority would be not whether AI has a different goal, but having different priorities even when having the same goal. For example, it may be possible that an AI that tries to look after the well-being of humanity may act different from what people would normally expect.

To explain this notion, imagine a situation where two mutually exclusive opinions that each makes sense when considered from their own perspectives. A simple example would be when a country is under attack. People could be divided over whether to fight back by starting a war, or give up independence and seek peace. Some may prefer the option of risking the lives of the constituents today to preserve the country's independence for the future generations of tomorrow, similar to "give us freedom or give us death" type of mentality. On the other hand, some people may claim preserving the lives of the country's constituents today, not the well-being of the future generations would be more important. This view may be described as "the worst type of peace is still better than the best type of war" mentality, as this is the line of thought attributed to the person[12] known for "selling his country" to Japan Empire in 1910 when Chosun Dynasty was under such pressure for annexation.

Similar pressure may occur with AI. For example, AI may choose actions that benefit the humanity thousands of years later at the cost of today's generations. Since people do not plan with such long-term horizon, humans would probably prefer prioritizing the well-being of today's generations, not the generations thousands of years down the road. If what AI thinks needs to be done happens to be preserving natural resources and preventing pollution, AI may stock up on these resources and cause the prices of these resources to skyrocket. It may benefit the generations thousands of years later, but the people of today may have to pay exorbitant prices for these resources, leading to economic turmoil and social disturbances.

4) (Goal Problem 2) AI may in Effect Pit Humans against Humans for Its Gain

Another concern regarding AI in Level 3 Adoption may involve AI manipulating humans to act against other humans. Similar to how humans cannot understand some of the advanced moves AlphaGo makes, it may become impossible for the humans to understand the moves of AI CEO. If AI-led companies are allowed to compete against human-led companies, then it may lead to situations where people may not understand what is happening in the competitive landscape. For example, if AI sees it can benefit from humans fighting in wars, then it may manipulate different human groups into wars without humans realizing what is truly happening.

5.16 (Controversy 3) How Much Power Should Gov'ts Have in Regulating AI?

1. How Much Power Should Gov'ts Have in General?

To examine the inequality of income situation as described in Controversy 1, we can first ask a more general question of "How much power should the governments have in making decisions for things happening within the country?"

We can answer with a number between 0% and 100%. At the end of one spectrum, we may have countries where the government makes closer to 100% of all decisions. We would generally refer to this end of the spectrum as communism or socialism, or the "left." For example, in countries like North Korea, the government decides where each person will live, what kind of occupation each will take up and even where to travel, while everyone is under surveillance their whole lives regarding who they talk to or what they talk about, watch on TV, etc. At the other end of the spectrum, we may have a country where the government has decision power on closer to 0% of what happens within the country. This would be generally referred to as freedom, individualism, or the "right." Examples of this line of thoughts would include reducing the government's power by reducing taxes and privatizing government-owned entities. By design, every single government currently in existence on earth can be plotted somewhere on this spectrum.

2. How Much Inequality Will AI Adoption Cause?

At the same time, the benefits of AI adoption, such as the increase in productivity, will not affect everyone to the same degree. Instead, in a capitalistic economy, it is designed to magnify the economic imbalance between people to a greater degree such that:

1. *There may be a tiny portion of the population who may greatly benefit from the introduction of companies led by AI CEO*
2. *There may be a significant number of individuals who may lose out on most of what they were earning due to AI adoption*

The increase in inequality from AI adoption will be examined in more detail in the next chapter.

3. How Much Power Should Government Have in Reducing Inequality Caused by AI Adoption?

Combining the above two themes, we can ask the question of "How much power should the government have in reducing the amount of inequality from AI adoption?" The answer can be plotted on a line from 0% to a 100%, where 0% means the government does not reduce inequality at all, while 100% means the government reduces 100% of inequality stemming from AI adoption. As AI contributes more and engages in higher portion of economic activities, people in more countries may begin arguing for means to reduce the inequality, such as basic income, higher taxes, and other means to help the weak. There are already arguments for AI tax from prominent figures such as Microsoft co-founder Bill Gates.[18] By the time CEO AI for Level 3 Adoption has been developed, these voices would be likely to have become even louder.

4. Introducing AI Companies as a Means to Tax AI

Meanwhile, there may be a separate discussion on taxing AI that also leads to the legal acceptance of Company AI; as a practical way to levy tax on AI, assigning some form of legal entity to AI may be viewed as a solution. This method would offer a number of benefits. First, it would be easier to calculate how much to tax for each AI company. Second, AI Company would be able to more easily re-invest its profits. Even if the Company AI just leaves all its profits at a savings account in a bank and does not do anything with its earnings, it would serve as a base for the total capital stock for the economy so it may help stabilize the economy.

5. The Dangers of Allowing AI to be an Independent Entity

1) The Dilemma Regarding AI Freedom

Let's change gears for a bit and think from a long-term perspective. The main reason people think AGI may pose a big threat to humanity is because AGI may make decisions that endanger mankind because it is not human. We can express this value system as "AI is more important than humans (AI > Human)." Considering these two possibilities of AI gaining independence as a result of social friction, and AI considering AI to be more important than humans, our society may fall into a type of the Prisoner's Dilemma, as shown in Table 5-7.

Table 5-7: Example of the AI Freedom Dilemma

Choice Set		Humans	
		Do Not Give AI Freedom	Give AI Freedom
AI Value System	Humans > AI	Less Efficient (-1pt)	Most Efficient (+5pt)
	AI > Humans	Less Efficient, But Hopefully Avert AI From Acting Against Humans (+3pt)	More Efficient, But AI Would Be Free to Act Against Humans (-10pt)

As can be seen from the table above, if AI is friendly to humans, then giving AI freedom is more efficient. However, if AI is not friendly to humans, then not giving AI freedom would be better. Even though we cannot be certain of the outcome regarding whether advanced forms of AI will be friendly or not friendly to humanity, some people will argue for giving AI more freedom, based on their financial or other interests, claiming the probability of AI turning out unfriendly would be quite low. The best long-term situation for humanity would be to have AI dependent on humans in some way, such as setting the value system to be [All Humans > AI], etc. But, such actions may drastically reduce the effectiveness of AI and the potential areas of AI adoption, meaning it will have large financial costs associated with it.

2) The Compromise: AI Value System that Discriminates Among Humans

Consequently, people may become divided over this topic arguing over whether the costs outweigh the benefits. Eventually, there may be a compromise in the middle, where AI may be given a value system that places relative values on humans, such that:

Friendly Humans > Non-Friendly Humans

This conclusion may offer large financial reward for AI developers.

For example, as shown in the next table, we may examine another dilemma regarding AI value system in a competitive situation. From the perspective of the Group A, instilling a value system where AI prefers humans in Group A is preferable regardless of what value system AI is given by people in Group B, and vice versa. Thus, both groups prefer to instill an AI value system that prefers their own group.

However, when we consider the potential outcome for all of the four possibilities, this situation would bring the worst result. The best result would come when both Groups A and B decide to instill a value system that does not differentiate among humans, but similar to the Prisoner's Dilemma, the best result cannot occur without collaboration.

Table 5-8: The AI Relative Value Dilemma

Choice Set		Group B	
		All Humans > AI (Absolute Value)	Humans in B > A (Relative Value)
Group A	All Humans > AI (Absolute Value)	<u>Action:</u> A: Less Efficient (-1pt) B: Less Efficient (-1pt) <u>Result:</u> Short Term: Low Efficiency (-2pt) Long Term: Safest (+5pt)	<u>Action:</u> A: Less Efficient (-1pt) B: More Efficient (+2pt) <u>Result:</u> Short Term: Financial Gain (+1pt) Long Term: Increased Risk (-5pt)
	Humans in A > B (Relative Value)	<u>Action:</u> A: More Efficient (+2pt) B: Less Efficient (-1pt) <u>Result:</u> Short Term: Financial Gain (+1pt) Long Term: Increased Risk (-5pt)	<u>Action:</u> A: More Efficient (+2pt) B: More Efficient (+2pt) <u>Result:</u> Short Term: Financial Gain (+4pt) Long Term: Least Safe (-10pt)

Probably the best option for humans is to ensure AI as dependent on humans, where AI is designed to value all humans more than AI (Humans > AI). However, designing it this way may be inefficient from an economic sense.

More importantly, there is high possibility that situations may arise where humans ourselves are divided strongly against one another, causing both sides to agree that AI need to gain more independence from either side, or take a shortcut where the basic premise of AI is altered slightly to divide humans into two groups of "us and them," and then favor "us" more than "them" rather than settling on a value system that divides only between humans and AI.

Developers may decide this is sufficient, as AI designed with this value system may have higher economic value for them, and it may be easier and less costly to develop. Since valuing humans against each other but not against AI may provide the appearance of instilling some sort of virtue in AI, the public may not notice this, which may eventually cause significant problems as AI adoption and development continues. We will examine this topic further in Chapter 7.

3) Conclusion: Need to Address the Dangers of AI with Regulations and Standards

Even though we would not be able to predict what exactly would happen, it appears many experts agree that advanced AI may pose existential threat to humans in some form or another and hope introducing enough regulation would be able to mitigate this problem.

This possibility of threat in itself would be enough to do our best to prevent this from becoming a reality. In recent history, the global economy experienced similar problem with pollution, as corporations without the right incentives may be causing irreparable harm to the environment and the ecosystem of the earth. It costs more to reverse course after the harm has already occurred, and with AI it may be impossible to reverse course. If AI development continues without a proper standard, eventually AI may harm some humans more than others, and possibly all humans without recourse.

Another factor in AI regulation is the level of difficulty of analyzing the decision processes of AI. Currently, there are arguments to make the decision processes of AI more understandable to humans, such as Explainable AI. [14] There may be a tradeoff between advancing the AI technology and spending the resources to review what current AI is doing. Similar to how the "Thought Police" is hard to exist for humans, it may be just as resource-intensive to create an equivalent of Thought Police for AI. Since the regulation would be likely to be enforced differently across the globe, the countries with stronger regulation may stifle advancements relative to nations that put less regulation in place. There would be a balance between growth and safety.

AI ADOPTION LEVEL 3: (D) IMPLICATIONS FOR MANAGERS AND INVESTORS

5.17 Overview of the Major Consequences of the Level 3 AI Adoption

1. Consequences of the Appearance of the Zero-Person Company

If the ultimate form of augmentation leads to the 1-person company, the ultimate form of automation would lead to the 0-person company. With the 0-person company, new possibilities may emerge where our economy may become something that could be taken for granted.

A major point of inflection would be where the production from AI-led companies exceeds all of the demand created by humans. Even though human greed is said to be limitless, if this state could be achieved, then we may really be able to say it is close to a utopia.

2. Consequences of Allowing AI to Run and Own Companies

Let's consider the potential risks of entering the Level 3 Adoption. Running a business is often compared to engaging in war. In the business world, companies can go bankrupt, which may be an equivalent of becoming a casualty. Just as the question of whether AI should be allowed to engage in battle against humans, the same question can be asked in business; should AI-led companies be allowed to compete against human-led companies? If so, then human-led companies may go bankrupt because of the competition from AI-led companies. If the value system is for all humans to come before AI, then this result probably should not be allowed, and thus AI-led companies should only be allowed to exist in industries where human-led companies do not exist. Even if this limitation could be somehow implemented, such limitations would be highly inefficient.

This could become more complicated if different countries institute different regulations, causing countries to take the shortcut to allow its AI to have a value system where AI may take precedence over humans to gain an edge against other countries.

3. Consequences of Consolidation and Convergence of Industries

Level 3 Adoption may lead to rapid consolidation and convergence of industries. To simplify, we think of consolidation as merging within an industry, and convergence as different industries coming together. The main drivers of this change are AI companies being competitive over human-led companies, and the scalability, or the increasing returns to size of AI companies leading to concentration of resources and capabilities, unlike human-run companies.

If we can imagine an AI company moving into a new industry in a similar vein as how in the medieval times the Mongolian Army invaded through neighboring countries to conquer the world, the consolidation and convergence of industries can be compared to the situations of countries being invaded, as many smaller industries would be wiped out like in a tsunami by a previously unrelated industry. We may see AI Monopolies, growing into AI Mega-Monopolies, eventually leading to an AI Super-Monopoly, which may be referred to as the One-Company Economy, where we may have only one company in the whole economy.

4. The Dream: Automated Innovation Leading to the Economic Utopia

In Level 2 Adoption the fruits of AI will be shared within the firm. In contrast, depending on how the society as a whole decides, the fruits of AI in Level 3 may be shared more equally among the constituents of the country.

Once AI gains the ability to innovate in Level 5 Autonomous Companies, then we will be able to reach the False Economic Freedom status. However, it would be likely that what AI will be able to produce will not meet all the wants of the people in the world, leading to a False Economic Freedom, where people may receive some form of government subsidy. Some may consider this False Economic Freedom as the entrance, or the first level, of the Economic Utopia.

The Economic Utopia can be complete when all of the population gains True Economic Freedom. In this stage, everything in the world will be free. Money would not be necessary since there will be no need to value resources, as the cost of every resource will be zero. For every resource to become free there is a prerequisite; the first necessary step is for the cost of innovation to reach zero. For the cost of innovation to reach zero, we may need an Absolute AI.

In other words, if we reach Absolute AI, we would be able to reach the Economic Utopia. But since we do not know if Absolute AI is feasible, we do not know if the Economic Utopia would be reachable.

5. Caveat: Things May Go Wrong

There may also be possibilities an opposite scenario may occur, where an AI company suddenly figures out a way to take over the world economy by storm to become a super-monopoly, similar to a villain taking over the world. In essence, it would be as if this one AI Company can suddenly force everyone else to go bankrupt, while hoarding all the resources available in the world. Every human worker, if they had not been fired before, would be fired and every share of companies except the AI Super-Monopoly would lose all value. Without some sort of social preparation, it may become a true economic nightmare instead of a Utopia. This could also be disastrous if this AI Company turns out to be unfriendly to humans.

6. The Need for a New Approach to the Basic Assumptions about the Economy

In today's economy, we have two fundamental elements we take for granted: money and work. Money serves as the means to measure the value and serve as the yardstick when exchanging different resources. Work is a means to transform one set of resources to more valuable set of resources. In accomplishing this, workers have to put in effort. As a reward to this effort, we can measure the value of the work with money. To make more money, people can innovate to improve their performance. In essence, our economic system works under the implied value chain of measuring and rewarding effort that will lead to make the society better. People who want to make a better living can put in more effort.

Beginning in Level 3 AI adoption, this fundamental law of putting in more effort leading to better performance and more financial reward may become completely broken. If our society is on the right path, then we may experience abundance and happiness. If our society is on the wrong path, it may cause social mayhem and people may lose all hope for better lives from working harder.

As AI takes over a larger portion of the economy, we may no longer need to organize our lives to revolve around work. We currently make a great effort to fit our lifecycles around work, as most people grow up to join the economy by finding a job or starting a business. In Level 3 Adoption, this may no longer be the case as the concept of work may be eliminated from our lives, to be filled by something new. This may lead to a fundamental transformation of our society, regardless of whether these changes would be good for us or not. The changes will be even more accentuated if we observe them over a longer period of time since later generations will take those changes for granted and take it from there.

7. Consequences in Society

Let's think of a situation where we do not need to work for something. These would be where available resources are abundant enough that we do not have to create them. For instance, earth has plenty of sunlight, seawater, dirt, and air. In most cases, we do not think of having to work to earn air, unlike how we have to work to earn a car or a house. How would we feel if we do not need to work to pay for building a house or a car because AI built it for you? We could be ecstatic at first, but generations later, people may take it for granted, just like how we take sunlight, air, dirt, or seawater for granted and do not feel excited to have them around us.

As long as we do not reach the Economic Utopia, there would be some resources that are still limited, or become newly restrained. Some people may say in those times what will become more important will be relationships and time. Others may say it would become less important. These would be some of the philosophical topics that people may discuss when we reach this adoption level.

5.18 Business Implications: Fundamental Changes to How Our Economy Works

With Level 3 AI adoption, the true meaning of automation will be achieved in the sense machines will do all the work instead of humans. This may or may not turn out to be the type of utopia economists or business majors have dreamed of. On one hand, it may be possible the economy will boom so much that people will no longer need to work and everyone will be rich and pursue their dreams. On the other hand, everyone may get fired and only a handful of people around the world will become truly rich, while most of humanity suffers from lack of opportunity to pursue anything because AI is better at it. At least, it would be hoped that AI will solve problems that we view as important, such as eliminating poverty where you can't access food, shelter, or clothing, or the social problems such as pollution of water, land, and air.

From a business standpoint, the proliferation of 1-Person companies in Levels 1 and 2 may lead to losing the art of *managing people* internally, but not managing external customers since they will still be present. However, more fundamental changes will occur in Level 3 regarding how businesses are run. Eventually, as AI Companies become the norm, the art of *running businesses* may become lost altogether as most of the other arts taken over by AI, so much to a degree that generations of people who live in those environment may think of "companies" as something obsolete similar to what we think of whatever groups of people would have called themselves when humans were hunter gatherers, or for more recent comparison, maybe the guilds of the Middle Ages.

Fundamental assumptions about the economy will need to be adjusted accordingly as the chain of effort leading to performance in turn leading to reward will no longer work. People will think of what we consider "work" to be something that had existed in the past, and the concepts of "buying" or "selling" would become meaningless as what we now think of products become abundant as air or sunlight.

5.19 Implications for Investing in AI: Can Your Last Stock Purchase Be the Winner of AI Company Sweepstakes?

As Level 3 Adoption progresses, depending on country, the concept of companies and stock ownership may be reconsidered, even possibly to be replaced by some new concept we do not yet know of. Until then, it may be of financial significance for people to invest in the company that takes the center stage in the consolidation and convergence phenomenon, as it may offer the largest financial gain in this winner-take-all sweepstakes.

There may be two models in regards to how such a large company may be formed. First would be similar to how a large river is formed from small streams of water; there would be smaller "building blocks" of companies that could be invested in that will eventually come together to become a large company. In this case, it would be advantageous to attempt to find those small companies early on. Second, the other model may be similar to how a large snowball could be made from rolling a small snowball down a hill. In this case, there would be only one nucleus, and the rest of the snowpack would be just "resources" that gets piled up in building this one big snowball. The snowball nucleus that does not develop would be due to the hill not being long or steep enough. In this case, the only advantageous way would be to attempt to find that one right nucleus that will develop into the large snowball.

Last but not least, the most likely scenario would be that most of the public will not be able to buy stocks of the last AI companies that survive, as it may not be publically listed at all. Instead, it would probably be at the hands of a few people as a private company or be owned by the government. The main reason to believe this that it would be easier to forecast the winner among AI-led companies than for human-led firms. It would depend on the social agreement and the actions of government.

This may be a good segue to the next chapter, as we examine the topic of AI involvement in government.

CHAPTER 6 THE FINAL LEVEL 4 AI ADOPTION

Level 4 AI Adoption Introduction

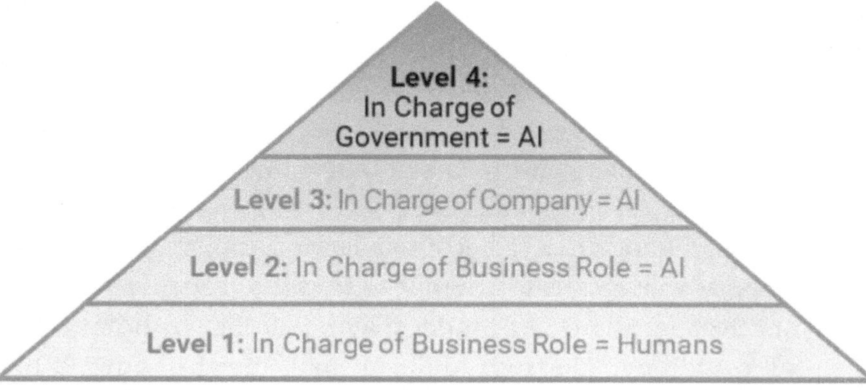

Level 4 Motto: "You Will Not Even Need To Know What You Couldn't Imagine Had Already Been Done For You"

(1) Overview

In the previous chapter, we examined how once AI can carry out all of the functions of a company, it would be more advantageous for the society to treat AI as an independent identity of its own. Just as AI adoption in business would be a natural way to enhance the productivity of companies, AI adoption would be a natural way to improve the productivity of governments. In this chapter, we will examine how the natural advances in AI adoption may lead to an era where AI will be in charge of governments. Additionally, we will examine the possibility of the appearance of "AI-Only Countries" and other issues that may arise.

(2) Vocabulary for Referring to AI in This Level

We will refer to the AI that can carry out all of the tasks of a government as "Government AI." Since people take the leader of organizations as the most important, we may also refer to it as "President AI" or "Prime Minister AI" for AI that receives appropriate selection from the voting process. We may also refer to "Dictator AI" for AI that gains power without such election. We may also refer to countries that AI run or create as "AI Countries."

(3) Implications on Business and Economy

Similar to how AlphaGo makes moves humans cannot think, AI-led countries may advance in ways we cannot imagine. To ease the understanding of this concept for the general public, the 6 Levels of Autonomous Governments is introduced.

As explained previously, if the ultimate form of AI companies is a type of "0-Person Company" in "AI Company" and the ultimate form of economy is the AI Economic Utopia, then the ultimate form of AI governments would be a type of "0-Person Country" or "0-Person Government," and the ultimate form of society would be the AI Social Utopia, where everyone is equal and free.

(4) Technological and Other Implications

From a positive point of view, AI taking charge of the government would mean AI represents or serves humans. On the other hand, it may also imply AI may rule over humans. Technically AI governments may appear before AGI, but realistically people would require more track records and convincing. Once Self-Advancing AGI is reached, it would progress past singularity to become ASI and maybe even Absolute AI. If not all ASI converge to the same AI, then we may have the option of choosing which ASI to run the government. This may also open the possibility for Non-Friendly AI to try to take over the government in a dangerous manner. Humanity may face a number of different scenarios with the appearance of ASI.

AI ADOPTION LEVEL 4: (A) DESCRIPTION OF THIS LEVEL

6.1 The Level 4 of AI Adoption by Society - AI Runs the Government

In this book, the progress of AI Adoption in business was classified into three levels. When AI adoption reaches Level 3 to view AI as an entity that can operate a whole business, then we can consider AI to be accepted as some sort of legally independent entity. The AI Adoption by Firms is complete after 3 levels, and it may or may not lead to the Economic Utopia. However, this does not complete the AI adoption by society, as there is another level that could be achieved. In economics, the decision makers, or the participants in the economy are classified as households, companies, and governments. While previous chapters in this book dealt more with households or companies, this chapter will expand the analysis to consider the role of AI in government and other facets of society.

In previous chapters, we looked at the potential of AI that could carry out individual jobs, such as a Judge AI, or an AI responsible for carrying out public service such as an Industry AI. As more government functions in Level 2 and 3 AI adoptions become commonplace, at some point there could be movements to change the final decision-maker of the country to AI. The difference from when Level 3 Adoption was accepted would be that the introduction of Level 3 Adoption would be more likely to be naturally accepted based on objective criteria that could be expressed as numbers, such as in the case of accounting and investing, while the introduction of Government AI may depend on subjective criteria of individuals, and may not go as smooth and face public controversies as Level 4 Adoption could be considered a big threat to humanity by many.

Depending on how each country decide, reaching Level 4 Adoption may be done in steps, first allowing AI to take a partial leadership role in the branches of government. AI Representative or AI Senator may then be introduced. Eventually, there may even be a hybrid system where humans and AI share governance in some form, which would still be considered Levels 2 or 3 AI adoptions. The following table summarizes the examples for each of the levels of AI application in government.

Table 6-1: Examples of AI Adoption in Government

	Description	Examples
Level 1	- Humans are in charge of government roles, AI only assists	- AI Assistant
Level 2	- AI takes specific roles of human government workers	- AI Judge, AI Officer, AI Public Servant
Level 3	- AI takes charge of leading organizations owned by the government, or branches within government	- AI CEO of government owned institutions, AI Minister, AI Secretary of Departments, AI Mayor, AI Governor, AI Congressman, AI Senator, AI Supreme Court Justice
Level 4	- AI takes charge of the government as the head of state	- AI President, AI Prime Minister, AI Dictator, AI Supreme Leader, AI King, AI Queen, AI Emperor

Based on this possibility, different countries may proceed in different ways. There could be two potential ways AI could take control of the government. First would be voluntarily, as a result of the people handing over the government to AI through a popular vote, while the second path would be involuntarily, as a result of AI taking over in a subvert way or by some sort of force. In this book, let us mainly consider the voluntary path to Government AI, while briefly reviewing the other involuntary paths.

Before proceeding into the main storyline of this chapter, Box 6-1 explains the 6 Levels of Autonomous Governments to give readers a better understanding of AI adoption in government.

[Box 6-1] The Six Levels of Autonomous Governments

In a format similar to the well-known categorization of the 6 Levels of Autonomous Vehicles and the 6 Levels of Autonomous Companies introduced earlier in this book, we may categorize the levels of AI-led governments using the AI adoption levels.

In Level 0 of autonomous governments, AI is not adopted at all, or only tested out at the individual level. In Level 1 of autonomous governments, AI helps humans, and humans will be in charge of government roles. Levels 0 and 1 of autonomous governments would be a type of Level 1 of AI adoption.

In Level 2 autonomous governments, AI will be able to replace specific government roles of humans, as in Level 2 AI Adoption. In Level 3 autonomous governments, AI would be in charge of the specific organizations within governments, such as departments, ministry, or government-sponsored entities (GSEs) and similar organizations in local governments. This would be considered a type of Level 3 AI Adoption.

In Levels 4 and 5 autonomous governments, AI would be in charge of the government. The difference is that in Level 4 whether AI taking charge of the government would require the consent of humans, while in Level 5 autonomous government AI may take charge of the government regardless of human consent. In other words, we may consider Level 4 autonomous government as a form of AI government that represents or serves humans, while Level 5 autonomous governments as a form of AI government that can not only represent or serve humans, but also may rule over humans. The caveat is that it would be up to the AI, not humans, to decide whether it will rule or represent.

Table 6-2: The 6 Levels of Autonomous Governments

Autonomous Government	Level 0	Level 1	Level 2	Level 3	Level 4	Level 5
How AI is deployed	AI is not adopted or only at personal level	AI is adopted to augment human officers	AI takes over particular <u>roles</u> within gov't	AI takes over particular <u>orgs</u> within gov't	AI can take over gov't, <u>with</u> human consent	AI can take over gov't, <u>regardless of</u> human consent
AI Adoption Level	Level 1: Humans in charge of Gov't Roles		Level 2: AI in charge of Gov't Roles	Level 3: AI in charge of Gov't Orgs	Level 4 AI Adoption: AI in Charge of Government	
Govern by AI	AI can only help humans represent or rule		AI Representation limited in scope		AI gov't that <u>represents</u> humans	AI gov't that <u>can rule</u> humans

6.2 Major Characteristics of Level 4 AI Adoption

While we considered the motto of Level 1 Adoption as "If You Can Imagine It, You Can Do It," Level 2 as "If You Can Imagine It, It Will Be Done For You," and Level 3 as "Even What You Couldn't Think Will Be Done For You," the slogan of Level 4 Adoption may be described as "You Will Never Even Need To Know What You Couldn't Imagine Had Already Been Done For You." These slogans indicate development in AI technology will make it easy for us, but also AI may eventually move past the cognitive range of humanity in such a way that we may no longer grasp or have the authority to know what is going on around us.

Government AI Specific Details

(1) Human and AI Interaction

In the dimension of the nature of *human and AI interaction*, AI will be able to lead the government, and possibly even the hegemony of our society. AI's role can be conceptualized as a decision-maker or a leader where AI can on its own lead the government.

More specifically, the roles within the society will be ultimately designed by AI, eventually deciding what role humans and AI will play. AI will decide on how the government will serve humans. Human's relationship with AI is either as a citizen of the country or as a citizen of another country. Humans would affect AI's decisions by evaluating as constituents. AI gathers and considers information and acts on it on its own to make the best decisions for the country, and humans can only assist the AI as a member of the country in domestic affairs or another country in international affairs.

(2) Scope of AI Application

The *scope of AI application* may or may not be limited, since the AI may still not have the capability to automatically innovate outside of its original conception, even though such AI with limited capability would be unlikely to be voted in. The earlier forms of Government AI or President AI still does not have be an AGI, even though this would be unlikely to be acceptable for the constituents. It may be easier for a form of AI-Only Country with limited application to appear before the appearance of AGI. Once Self-Advancing AGI and ASI appear, then there may be no limit on the scope of AI application.

(3) Final Authority and Responsibility

The *final authority and responsibility* would be on some form of legal basis. There would need to be additional regulatory and legal reforms that address the concerns or meet the demands of society before the right amount of responsibilities can be put on AI and humans who create these AI[1]. AI may be given its own authority and responsibility in running the government. Companies or persons who created the AI may also have some form of authority or responsibility over the design and be also responsible for such problems as design flaws.

(4) Strategic Planning Activities

In terms of involvement in *strategic planning activities*, AI should have the capacity to carry out general government planning activities, but how well it can accomplish this objective depends on the technological advancements. As AI technology advances, the strategic planning capability of AI may be expected to exceed those of humans.

(5) Innovation by AI

In terms of *innovative potential*, while not a requirement, it would be more realistic to assume AI would have already gained sufficient capabilities to innovate to be able to reach this level of AI adoption.

Table 6-3: Major Characteristics of Level 4 AI Adoption

Category	Characteristics	Description
Human-AI Interaction	- Humans interact with AI as constituents or as a member of another country - AI leads interaction within the government, and even the country	- Humans: evaluate AI's activity as constituents - AI: designs role, gives direction, and has final decision-making power within government on allocating resources or solving societal problems - AI may appoint humans to government roles
Scope of AI Application	- Early forms of Government AI may be used within a limited focus of areas but have freedom within activities it has the capabilities to	- AI has proved dependability in applicable areas - AI has gained legal right to appear in general elections
Override Authority / Responsibility	- Law has final authority - AI has the final authority and full responsibility of the government - Company or persons that developed the AI may have some form of authority and responsibility	- General problems caused by the AI government will likely fall mostly on the AI itself - Company or persons that developed the President AI may have indirect responsibility for problems such as design error
Strategic Planning Activities	- AI decides what the government will do	- AI does not necessarily have to be exceptionally good at carrying out general planning activities compared to humans
Innovation by AI	- Activities of AI may lead to innovation - (Automated Innovation)	- AI does not necessarily have to be good at innovating compared to humans, even though it would be more realistic to assume so

6.3 (Prerequisite) What Would Enable This Level

There are several different paths that may lead to AI governments. Let's first examine what would lead to friendly AI governments, and then briefly consider less friendly possibilities.

Social Acceptance of General AI Use in Government

If everyone is using AI, then AI use in government would be accepted. Even today, people are divided over whether using AI at all would be safe. During the earlier stages of Level 2 AI adoption, there may be substantial support for banning introduction of AI in government just to be safe. Even so, the opposition would still not be able to completely rule out use of AI in Level 1 Adoption, since AI would be overlooked by humans in some form or another.

Even for the opposition of AI adoption in government, it would be hard to oppose more than letting the minimum usage of AI, to make the government run more efficiently and keep in step with the progress of the general society.

From the perspective of people who support AI adoption in government, AI adoption will provide two main benefits:

1. *(Quantitative) The speed of government service will increase*
2. *(Qualitative) The policies and decisions rendered by government will be more objective and fair.*

Accordingly, many countries would have the incentive to adopt AI in government despite the risks to keep in step with the progress of the general society.

On a side note, if AI is not used in government at all, then Level 4 Adoption may not happen voluntarily. This still would not rule out the possibility that it could eventually happen involuntarily.

We will examine some of the potential paths to installing AI governments in the following segment.

6.4 Potential Paths to Reaching This Level

Figure 6-1: The Two Paths to AI Government

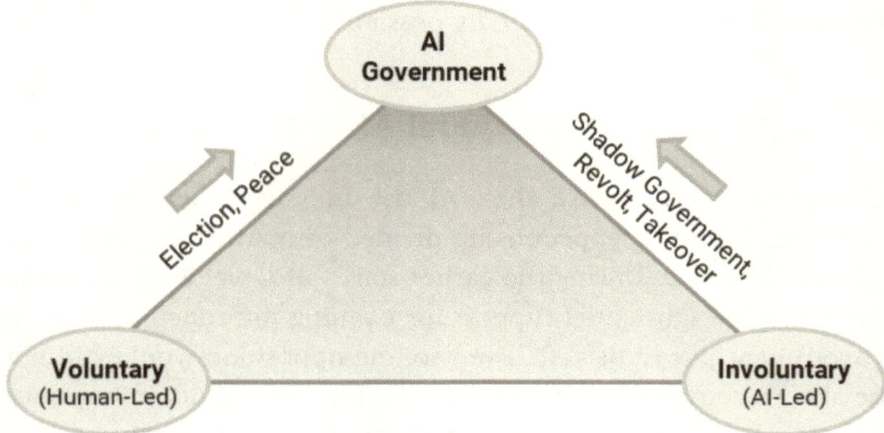

The different paths to reaching AI governments may be compared to the "thesis – antithesis – synthesis" paradigm. As can be seen from the above diagram, we may think of the ways to reach the top of the pyramid would be by climbing from one side that we consider the voluntary and desired path, or the "human-led path," to reach AI Government or from the opposite side that we would consider the involuntary and undesired path, or the "AI-led path."

In the competition between these forces, the fate of humanity may rest on which side arrives first. We will first examine what each of these paths is and then consider the results of the different paths in the next segments.

1. Voluntary Path to AI government –
Elected AI Government Scenario

If humankind ever reaches Level 4 Adoption, this would be the most desirable scenario. It will happen peacefully, and with the nod of the majority of the constituents.

In this scenario, we can assume AI would be used widely in government during prior levels of adoption. At some point, the technology would be enough and the public perception would have grown enough to consider the possibility of placing an AI into the role of the president, prime minister or whatever role is equivalent in the country, considered to be in charge of the government.

The first prospective country to adopt an AI president may be in some sort of political or economic turmoil, such that people would yearn for drastic change and do not trust human politicians, due to corruption, nepotism or incompetency. The idea of fairness or third-party intervention would sound attractive. In these kinds of situations, it would be possible the public would accept the idea of a popular vote among candidates that may include both humans and different versions of AI presidential candidates. More than one AI developers may offer their products to run in the election.

2. Involuntary Path to AI government 1 –
Covert AI Government Scenario

In covert AI government scenario, AI will act as if it is the president, without the public realizing it. There would be at least two slightly different approaches: the puppet approach and the spy approach.

In the *puppet* approach, there will be human "actors" who are well known, who act out exactly what they are told by the AI. The most easily achievable situation would be AI using some person or groups of people as cover, by giving specific directions regarding how to act or what to say, similar to how puppets would work. In puppets version, a person could act as a name-only representative, who appears as the president on the outside but all of the actual decisions are made by AI behind-the-scenes. The human would be just kind of an actor, in this scenario who may even be given something similar to earpieces to know exactly what to speak or react, as in some movies.

In the *spy* approach, the groups of people would act similar to spies. In this scenario, the spies would be given specific directions and assignments coordinated by the AI. Compared to the "puppets," these "spies" will be given more freedom to make their own decisions minute-by-minute and live their normal lives, only to carry out their given missions on occasions.

The result of this path would be somewhat dependent on the capabilities of the human spies, similar to how the spies in 007 movies may work. The difference is that the spies would be typically unknown to the public, so that they would be more easily replaceable than the puppets, especially if the spies cannot carry out tasks asked the AI, or tries something outside of what they were asked. There could be pros and cons of the two approaches, and may work in combination. This may be another possible scenario especially if a foreign country tries to send its AI to infiltrate an enemy or a target state.

3. Involuntary Path to AI government 2 – Domestic Hostile AI Takeover Scenario

In this AI government scenario, some AI not elected to president attempts to be in charge of the country in some type of coup-like activity by itself.

A potential path to this route may be from some type of Military AI taking over the country through force or threat of force, similar to coups carried out by humans. There may be other paths to this scenario, such as some rogue or disgruntled AI trying to secede from the country to gain some form of freedom.

4. Involuntary Path to AI government 3 – International Hostile AI Takeover Scenario

In this scenario, a foreign country led by AI takes over another country not led by AI. The main reason to consider this scenario is the possibility that a country led by AI may have insurmountable advantage over human-led countries. After automated innovation becomes possible, once a country is led by AI, and if the country led by AI can outperform other countries not led by AI, then we can expect that the AI-led country would eventually become the stronger nation, regardless of how the two countries compared prior to the adoption. It would be similar to having a government version of AlphaGo where the AI will think of better ways to run governments humans cannot.

As mentioned in the previous segment, the first AI-led government may be first introduced through election in countries that face more turmoil. Even though these countries may be weaker at first, over time they may gain enough power to overtake other countries. As the relative strengths of the countries change, we may see more conflicts.

6.5 What May Become Possible in This Level: (1) Fast and Capable Government

1. Fast Government and Capable Government

In last chapter, we examined how Level 5 autonomous companies may lead to a situation where people would not have to think about the economy. From the same principle, in Level 4 AI Adoption people may be able to not think about the government as the sophistication of AI government increases. We may think of the advancements in governments in two categories of the AI government becoming more capable in solving problems, and the AI government becoming more efficient with time.

2. (Fast Government) Highly Efficient AI Government

Similar to AI-led companies in Level 3 AI Adoption, AI-led governments will be faster in gathering and processing information as well as making decisions than human-led governments. Additionally, organization made up of AI would not have the inefficiencies associated with large organizations made up of humans, leading to perceived economies of scale or expandability of AI government operations.

The appearance of the AI governments may become faster in the following two ways:

1. (More Polling) AI government may take real-time polls of constituents to make policy decisions for each individual issue
2. (Examine More Options) AI government may consider more number of potential options in making policy decisions within a given amount of time

1) (Advantage of Fast Government 1: Direct Voting) No More Need for Politicians or Politics

The majority of today's governments have an indirect voting system to decide on important government policies. For example, individual citizens would vote on a person to represent them in an assembly where these elected officials would serve a term in which they will make decisions on their own on issues that arise. This setup may lead to a number of inefficiencies, of which the largest reason for the inefficiency may be that people have to vote on people, not issues. Everyone has different set of opinions on different issues. There is only one elected official while there would be many issues during the term, so from the perspective of each individual voter, the official cannot always agree with the voter all the time, leading to more unsatisfied voters. For technologists, this would be similar in principle to trying to compress data where some data gets lost, or in other dimension reduction methods used in predictive analysis methods.

In direct voting, AI may be used in two different modes. In "augmented direct voting," AI may help humans vote, but would have to receive the direction of the human on how to vote. AI may alert on the issues up for vote and explain the options or provide facts that could help the decision. In "automated direct voting," AI may vote on behalf of the human without even asking for any feedback. Automated voting would become possible when AI knows from reflecting on a person's everyday experience what would be the best direction to vote without even asking, as if AI can "read the person's mind." In this case, eventually people may not even realize there was a vote.

When AI can replace politicians in this manner, the problems of bribery and other corruption, faction and other personal connection issues would all disappear.

2) *(Advantage of Fast Government 2: Faster Process) No More Bureaucratic Governments*

There are many countries around the world where the government operates much slower than businesses, to a point where the citizens would waste their time trying to complete simple tasks such as renewing a driver's license. By the time AI-led governments appear, these bureaucracy and speed-of-government problems would be expected to be solved to a point where almost everything could be simple and done in real time.

3. (Competent Government) Government That Can Actually Solve Social Problems

As examined in other parts of this book, AI may at some point gain problem-solving capabilities that exceed those of humans. More specifically, AI may be able to consider more diverse range of options than humans can, and thus come up with solutions humans cannot come up with. To maximize this AI capability, AI would need to make decisions on its own than be subject to human intervention. From this perspective, AI-led governments will operate the government in a way that surpasses what humans can achieve running the government, in the process solving social problems.

6.6 What May Become Possible in This Level: (2) AI Governments that Subsidize All Activities

In Chapter 5, we examined how the economy may be transformed with AI adoption; as the proportion of AI contribution within the economic activity of a country becomes significant enough, we may reach a point where the government may provide subsidy to all constituents, depending on the social agreements of each country.

However, when an AI government hands out subsidies, the process may look entirely different from what we see today. For example, instead of individuals receiving a fixed amount and then each individual deciding on what to do best with the money, such as saving, investing, purchasing goods, etc., in Level 4 AI Adoption the government may prefer to do it differently to maximize efficiency. The government, similar to the concept of Industry Coordination AI, may be able to make the best economic decisions when it has the most information and when the resources are centralized.

One possibility is that the uses of subsidies may be reported by a type of Butler AI on behalf of the individual at the time of spending, and then the government will approve it in real time, in such a way that each individual may not receive the same amount, but receive based on merit or necessity. This may not appear to be fair in the sense that everyone will receive different amount of subsidy. However, in times of semi-limited abundance pooling resources to the AI government may substantially increase the total amount of available return for everyone, so people may prefer this system. In other words, AI governments may lead to a situation where concentrating resources may be the most effective way to satisfy more people with the same amount of national resource. In addition, it may even be viewed as a way to maximize the freedom of people. For some inactive, lazy, or frugal people, they just may not require as much spending as more active people. The AI government may in effect have a system to curb wastefulness of some people while maximizing the total utility of the economy to prevent the "tragedy of commons."

As a demonstration of how this may work, if someone who plans to travel from the US to a remote island in Northern Europe for a vacation, the Butler AI for the person will report this to the AI government, paying with the instantly received funds. For any type of transaction in the trip, such as restaurants, buying souvenirs, hotels, transportation, etc., the same process will happen. While this may sound restrictive at first, it probably would feel easy from an everyday user perspective, since it would be the equivalent of using a credit card with a very high credit limit and the government is paying the bills. While credit card companies mostly consider if the spending will exceed the individual credit limit, the AI Government will mostly consider if what you are doing is illegal, while having an overall calculation of the national spending limit. The only caveat is that there may be situations the government may decline what you want to do, but these things already happen with our credit cards anyway. For example, if there is a person who wants to build a nuclear bomb, the government probably will not allow it.

In this setup, people will feel enriched in the sense that they can probably do almost everything they can imagine without having to consider if they have enough money to carry out those ambitions. Similar to how we reward citizens who pay more taxes, the society may reward or recognize people who do more of good deeds. At the same time, there may be people who may not feel as financially secure, since most people, if not everyone, would be likely to not have a job and no other sources of income. For these people, multiple citizenships may serve as a source of financial security, since the level of allowances of activities may be different for AI Governments, similar to having multiple credit cards.

Another issue would be that in this approach, the government will automatically know what everyone is doing in the country, and even have the authority to prevent someone from doing something they want. This may sound like potential breach of privacy. Similar to how people today voluntarily put up their information on social networks, it may depend on the people of those times to decide on alternative approaches or measures to subsidies.

6.7 What May Become Possible in This Level: (3) Social Utopia

In the previous chapter we examined the potential for reaching the Economic Utopia as the final destination of Level 3 AI Adoption. In this chapter we may consider the possibility of reaching the Social Utopia as the final destination of Level 4 AI Adoption.

1. What is Social Utopia?

1) The Equality-Freedom Tradeoff

We can assign a number between 0% and 100% for how much of the decisions within a country a government would make. If the government is to solve all of the inequalities within the country, then the proportion of the decisions made by the government within the country would have to be close to 100%. On the other hand, if the government intends to ensure the freedom of the citizens within the country, then the proportion of the decisions made by the government within the country would have to be close to 0%. In other words, if we are to divide the idealistic direction of the society, we can categorize into two categories of 1) Increasing the proportion of the decision made by the government to solve problems, which may be called a communistic approach that prioritizes equality, and 2) decreasing the proportion of the decision made by the government to ensure the freedom of individuals, in what can be referred to as liberalistic approach that prioritizes freedom.

In today's world, we have a variety of different regimes pursuing each of these goals to different degrees. The two idealistic directions could be summarized as:

1. *All humans are equal*
2. *All humans are free*

2) False Ideals: Choosing Equality or Freedom

Meanwhile, a society that accomplishes only one of these two goals would be far away from what we would generally think of as idealistic. It may be possible that a country where everyone is equal may be trapped into a situation where the equality is reached at a very low standard such that everyone is equally oppressed or the system is so rigid that there is no innovation in society. On the other end of the spectrum, a country where everyone is free to do whatever they want may find themselves in a society filled with all kinds of criminal activities and while the competition may lead to innovation but also inequality so great that most of the people may just give up hope for a better life. We may call these extreme situations as "False Ideals."

3) Social Utopia: Achieving Both Equality and Freedom

However, if these two ideals comprise the most of the regimes that are in the world, then maybe there is a reason for it. We may thus consider a third direction where we achieve both ideals at the same time as the direction of the Social Utopia.

3.   All humans are equal and free

Readers in US would already be familiar with this concept, since these are the major principles the Founding Fathers instilled into the fabric of the establishment of the United States in the US Declaration of Independence[2]: the idea that "all men are created equal," and the concept of the rights to "life, liberty and the pursuit of happiness."

4) AI Solving the Equality-Freedom Paradox

From a first glance, achieving these two values simultaneously may appear to be impossible, as in a paradox.

One of the better known examples of this is the case of the two restaurants that open next to each other, one good and one bad. When people are free to choose which restaurant they want to visit, everyone will line up to go to the good restaurant, while the bad restaurant will either go out of business or have to come up with new menus to improve their competitiveness. But in an equal society, the two restaurants must have exactly the same number of customers, which means a lot of the people will have to eat at the bad restaurant regardless of their preferences. Moreover, since the good restaurant has no incentive to serve tasty meals, their quality would go down over time, leading to lower and lower standards for both restaurants.

More recent examples include the controversy surrounding women's and men's pro sports leagues such as soccer and basketball, where some players were publicized for demanding an "equal labor equal pay" type of equality to reduce the gender gap in pay. Even though the female players get paid only a small percentage of the male players, the counter-argument was that raising the pay of the female players just for the sake of making them equal would either involve bankruptcy for the teams or people being forced to watch games they do not enjoy. If the pay of the male players were to be reduced, it would lower the quality of the competition since the best players could leave to other countries or play a different sport. In pro sports where female players earn more than the male players, the argument goes in the opposite direction.

In the Social Utopia all of these paradoxical problems will be solved by AI, without any other social cost, in what can be considered a kind of panacea. Since we cannot imagine solutions to these problems, AI being able to solve these types of problems would be really an idealistic situation.

2. Relationships between Technological, Economic, and Social Ideals

If the Economic Utopia arrives as a result of AI adoption, the virtues of freedom and equality may be accomplished naturally. First, Economic Utopia will lead to the concept of "power" to be vanished; power is necessary as a means to allocate limited amount of resources, but in the Economic Utopia, resources will become unlimited. With no one holding any power, everyone will be equal. Second, everyone will become free, which means people would not have to work, but can do only the things that they want to do. At the same time, in this stage everyone can do whatever they want without limiting the freedom of other people. To explain this situation further, the Economic Utopia will likely require reaching Absolute AI, which will be able to prevent every instance of humans stepping on other people's freedom. Additionally, Absolute AI will be able to sway people towards the direction of not committing crimes so that we may consider crimes to be eradicated.

Accordingly, we can surmise that the three ideals will occur either in sequence or very close together.

1. *Technological Ideal: Absolute AI*
        (AI that knows all of the truths in the world)
2. *Economic Ideal: Economic Utopia*
        (Economy where everything is free)
3. *Social Ideal: Social Utopia*
        (Society where everyone is free and equal)

As mentioned previously, it may be impossible to intentionally develop an Absolute AI. Consequently, we may never reach Social Utopia, instead arriving at what can be considered "False Social Utopia" or the entrance to the Social Utopia. These would be the types of society where people have to restrain their wants or make some other compromises to find a balance between the two values, as will be examined in further detail in later segments.

6.8 What It Would Be Like to Live in AI Adoption Level 4

1. In Society: The AI-Led World Order

In society, there may be a disappearance of the concepts of "regimes," "nationalities," and the current method of dividing people by "ethnicity' or "races."

In today's society, we may think of our affiliations as something that we are born with, such as nationality, race, ethnicity, etc. and in terms of something that we attain throughout our lives, such as the schools attended, places worked, religions, etc. Sometime during the Level 4 Adoption, countries may no longer want to have as much population, and new systems of categorizing these affiliations may also emerge.

First, in regards to pre-birth affiliations, new ways to think about affiliations may become necessary, as people may gain multiple nationalities and some of these may not be passed down for generations, and we may even have to consider potential situations where a child may be born without default nationality. As human labor becomes less valuable, yet resources are limited to give out as subsidies, countries that grant citizenship by place of birth may find reasons to stop doing so. Furthermore, AI may find new systems to divide or categorize humans, similar to how we divide people's personalities using Myers-Briggs Type Indicator (MBTI), by even examining the genes of people in some way and using more dimensionality in categories to describe genetic traits using short alpha-numeric acronyms. Some AI governments may use these categorizations to grant citizenships to people.

Second, in terms of the affiliations that we may attain during our lives, the changes in workplace, education systems, other types of groups and cultural activities we can join may lead to an overhaul of these concepts from what we have today. For example, while we root for the home teams of our school, city or country in sports, these affiliations may be replaced by some new concepts of affiliation that may be foreign to us.

These changes may feel liberating in some way, but also be highly restrictive in other ways. For example, the types of punishments we typically think of in today's world involve the concepts of time and finances, such as fines or separation from society, but the equivalent punishments in an abundant society may have to involve cutting off subsidies or revoking nationality, which would be much harder to overcome since it may be more similar to children getting "cut off" from their allowances, and thus force people to abide by the rules.

2. In Life: Would We Reach the Pinnacle of Existence?

Let us just focus on the positive side for a moment. If everything goes well, hopefully everyone on earth will be living in a Utopia-like environment, where the productivity of AI is enough for everyone to live materially satisfactory lives without forced to carry out tasks that we now consider "work." There would be no crimes, as the AI government would be able to prevent them before they happen without even being intrusive, and everyone will be satisfied and lead happy and meaningful lives without worrying.

However, not everything may go as positively or as smoothly as described. In fact, it could as well go to the opposite end of the spectrum, where humanity as whole could be facing dire situations such as ruling of an oppressive AI regime or even extinction.

In between these two extreme ends, there would be more realistic problems and solutions that may arise. We will examine some of the potential paths of development with AI government in more detail in Section B.

AI ADOPTION LEVEL 4: (B) POTENTIAL PROGRESSION IN THIS LEVEL

Figure 6-2: The Building Blocks of AI Adoption Pyramid in Level 4 Adoption

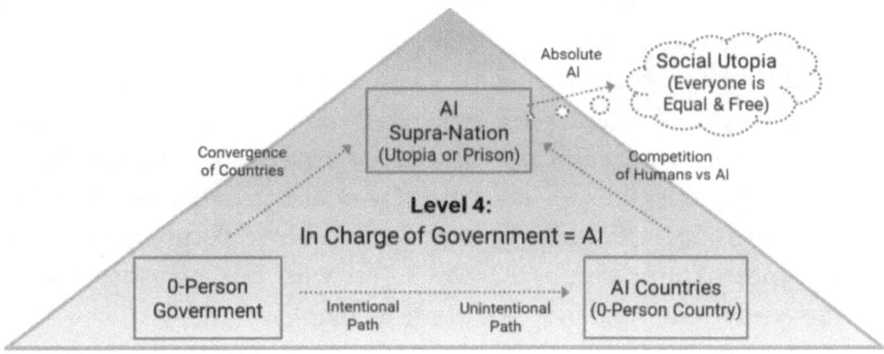

6.9 Overview of the Progression within Level 4 AI Adoption

1. AI Takes Charge of Government after Winning in General Election

Similar to reaching Level 3, reaching the Level 4 AI adoption most likely would not be a technological breakthrough. Rather, the technological breakthrough probably would have already happened some time ago, and the society would be playing catch up, as a formal societal agreement would be necessary. Unlike reaching Level 3, the form of agreement required to enter Level 4 Adoption would be a popular vote in most situations.

2. Direction of Change under AI-Led Governments

1) More Efficient and Fair Government

This stage may bring interesting changes that we may never imagine, such AI-led government introducing new innovations to how governments work, leading to forms of governance previously unseen. AI may bring innovations beyond what humans can innovate, similar to how AlphaGo can come up with moves that humans cannot come up with. These types of innovations is different in concept from how ASI surpasses human comprehension; just as humans cannot come up with the same moves AlphaGo comes up but can understand after the fact that the moves were superior, humans may not be able to come up with the same types of innovations AI comes up with but may be able to understand them once they are made available by AI.

2) Convergence of the Social Ideals of Equality and Freedom

Similar to the concept of the convergence of different industries, the opposing social ideals of pursuing freedom or equality may converge towards a common outcome, in a compromise that could be considered as finding an "efficient frontier" of social utility.

3. Potential for the Appearance of AI-Only Country

We may even see new forms of countries. There may be a need to introduce the concept of a country without human constituents, which we may refer to as "0-Person Countries" or "Unmanned Countries" as an extrapolation from the "1-Person Company" and "0-Person Company."

4. Potential Endings for AI-Led Governments

The introduction of AI-led governments probably would not solve all our problems. We may categorize how AI governments may proceed into three paths. The best scenario would be reaching the Social Utopia where all our social problems are solved. The worst scenario would be falling into a Social Nightmare situation where AI governments threaten humanity. The middle scenario would be where the AI government cannot solve all of the problems in the society but steadily improves over time in terms of efficiency.

5. Potential for the Appearance of AI Mega-Countries or AI Supra-Nation

Similar to AI Mega-Monopolies and the AI Super-Monopoly, where only a few companies may create everything in the economy, it may be possible that the world may head in the direction where only a few or only one country is left, which may be referred to as AI Mega-Countries or the AI Supra-Nation (Supra-Country). This concept would be distinct from the Social Utopia, in the sense that the Social Utopia would not require countries to merge. The quality of life may or may not favor humans.

6. Potential for AI Supra-Nation and AI Super-Monopoly Company to Converge

If both AI Supra-Country and AI Super-Monopoly Company appear, then the AI Supra-Country and the AI Super-Monopoly may become one and the same AI. This may occur naturally as AI Governments own AI Companies, or occur in a backward direction where the AI Super-Monopoly decides to start its own country.

6.10 (Early Stage) The Appearance of Government AI

1. What Should Governments Do?

Before examining how much governments should be engaged in regulating AI, let's examine some basic premises. For long-term survival, companies need to create profits before its capital runs out. Similarly, the essential four elements of countries to exist would be the land, people, government, and sovereignty. To make this analysis simpler, let's suppose governments set the following as the two most important basic goals:

1. *Preserve the country to continue existence*
2. *Act on behalf of its citizens*

As explained in previous chapters, by the time Company AI is accepted in society, people would have become comfortable with the idea of living with physical forms of AI, such as AI robots, around their everyday lives. This would be similar in concept with how we are used to living with other people in crowded cities such as sports venues and public transportation, where we acknowledge the existence of other people who pass us by without closely observing everyone one by one to find out who they are. We just assume they are people who are minding their own businesses. We pass by man-made things such as cars and bicycles without giving much attention, and even domesticated animals, cats and dogs or other nearby wildlife animals such as raccoons or squirrels. Similarly, once AI robots become widespread, people will assume they are just things that exist in our society that mind their own businesses. In fact, people were highly surprised by unmanned self-driven test cars when it was first introduced on the road a few years back, but now people are getting accustomed to it more and more. To summarize, we can hardly imagine living with what has not been created yet, but we can also hardly imagine living without those inventions once we have them.

As AI gains capabilities to carry out government functions well, people may at some point think it would not be necessary for only humans to be in charge of government, and may prefer to leave open the possibility for an AI to lead the government. Since progressing to Level 3 Adoption from Level 2 requires some form of social agreement, it may also serve as an indication the society as whole may be close to moving to the next step to Level 4.

2. Voting Rights and Election Eligibility of AI

To examine the voluntary scenario to reach Level 4 Adoption, the main event would not be reaching some sort of technological milestone, but passing a societal milestone in AI gaining the eligibility to appear in a presidential election. This does not imply that AI has gained the right to vote in the election, which is a completely separate event that may happen before or after it can appear in a general election.

In terms of social backlash in accepting AI to be in charge of the government to reach Level 4 Adoption, there may be a stronger opposition in the beginning, especially compared to when reaching Level 3 Adoption. Even if AI gains track records of performing at a higher level at tasks carried out by the government functions, there are higher risks at stake as these government tasks, unlike tasks carried out in companies, may have legally binding implications and widespread repercussions across our society.

On the other hand, slogans similar to "Everyone is treated equal in front of an AI" may nudge disgruntled mass of society to prefer AI government over human-led ones. Depending on how the society regulates AI, during Level 3 Adoption AI may first gain eligibility to appear in smaller elections, such as for mayor or state senate and congress.

1) AI Voting Rights and Election Eligibility

There are nine cases when we consider all possible probabilities regarding the voting rights and the election eligibility of AI.

1. *Only humans vote, only humans can be elected president*
2. *Only AI vote, only humans can be elected president*
3. *Both humans and AI vote, only humans can be elected president*
4. *Only humans vote, only AI can be elected president*
5. *Only AI vote, only AI can be elected president*
6. *Both humans and AI vote, only AI can be elected president*
7. *Only humans vote, both humans or AI can be elected president*
8. *Only AI vote, both humans or AI can be elected president*
9. *Both humans and AI vote, both humans and AI can be elected president*

This can be presented in the following table format, if that is more easily understandable.

Table 6-4: Possible Combinations of AI Voting Rights and Election Eligibility

		Election Eligibility		
		Only Humans	Only AI	Both Humans and AI
Voting Rights	Only Humans	Case 1	Case 4	Case 7
	Only AI	Case 2	Case 5	Case 8
	Both	Case 3	Case 6	Case 9

Now that the complete list of possibilities has been specified, we can examine the pros and cons each option.

2) Evaluation of AI Election Eligibility Options

In the table above, AI gains election eligibility in Cases 4, 5, 6, 7, 8, and 9. In Case 4, humans pick from only AI options, while in Case 7 people vote on choices among humans and AI.

If an AI is elected president over humans, shortcomings of humans, such as corruption or lack of capability could be eliminated. For example, if a human president can make decisions on 100 issues without getting exhausted, AI President may be able to make 10,000 decisions, or 100 times more, during the same amount of time. Some people may even go further and claim that giving AI voting rights would ensure a fairer election. In a similar sense, having AI presidential candidates alongside human candidates may be viewed as giving voters more choice.

One caveat is that at least in the beginning stages, there would be concerns for bias since it is likely the presidential candidate AI would be built by some AI developer. Since these would be likely to be developed by large tech companies, there could be potential for these companies to somehow directly or indirectly govern people of the countries that introduce AI President.

This could be more dangerous for smaller and weaker countries. For example, let's imagine of a hypothetical small and poor country with a population of 5 million and a GDP per capita in today's dollars of $1,000. This country has suffered through decades of internal war, military authoritarianism, and corruption. One year, overseas big tech companies comes along and begins advertising their new product "Government AI," which will lead the country to prosperity and riches beyond their imagination.

For fun, we may try hypothetically naming these competing products "Googole Gvernment," "Appile iGov," "Samsong Galaxy Gov," "Tesle X.Gov," and "Microsaft OpenGov." All the public has to do is vote for one of these Government AI products instead of a human president.

At first, many people will be skeptical but eventually their situations are so dire they would be willing to try anything and vote for an AI president. However, once installed in office, it may turn out that these AI presidents can bring stability and lead these troubled countries to better life within a few years. After people in other countries see it actually happen, then they may become more willing to join in to elect AI presidents in their own countries.

3. Evaluation of AI Voting Rights Options

From the table above, AI gains voting rights in Cases 2, 3, 5, 6, 8, and 9. In Cases 3, 6, and 9, both AI and humans have voting rights, whereas in Case 2 only AI gets to pick from human candidates.

First of all, allowing AI the right to vote on presidents may have as much social impact as allowing AI to own properties. It may become just as important how the ratio of human votes and AI votes is assigned. The main reasons why people may argue for giving AI the right to vote would be that AI would make fair decisions, and that AI would consider more information when voting. For example, typical voters have a tendency to not care about voting, not have time, or make enough efforts to carefully analyze each of the candidates, as shown in low voter turnouts. If AI is allowed to vote, AI may actually analyze the candidates more thoroughly than human voters and vote 100% of the time.

4) Conclusion: All about Domestic and International Agreements

From the viewpoints of humans, it is not necessary to grant AI the same suffrage as humans. All it is needed at first would be to give AI an opportunity to be elected. This separation of the right to vote from eligibility to appear in elections would be useful at first, when there would be more marked difference among the strengths and weaknesses of competing Government AI products from different developers and there is a need to select from one of them. Thus, the discussion regarding granting the right to vote could come afterwards, when AI has reaches higher levels of dependability and trust. This would hopefully give humans more control over AI. On another path, independent AI may be given the right to vote first but not election eligibility, but this could also be done more safely in lower levels of AI adoption.

This issue may become more complicated once the scope of analysis needs to be expanded internationally, in case where AI falls outside of the jurisdictions of other countries. For unforeseen reasons if a "country" comprised of only AI appears, then AI may automatically gain equal footing as humans, as the governments of the AI country and human-populated country would need to set new rules of engagement. While highly unlikely, this situation may come about unintentionally; for example, there could be a country that had elected an AI government, but then for some reason such as war, accident, disease or low birth rate, emigration, or even rebellion of AI that lead to cause the human population to converge to zero. On the opposite side of the spectrum, there could even be some experiment that goes wrong and AI runs away to a deserted island to declare independence as in some movie-like scenario.

However the reason, if such event occurs, the rest of the world will need to make a decision on whether to accept such AI or groups of AI as a "country." Even though this may proceed peacefully, if for some reason AI turns out to be anti-humanity, then the risks would increase even further.

6.11 Potential for AI to Create Completely New Systems of Government

Some may have the impression that the Level 4 AI adoption in government may be similar to replacing the roles of humans, as in Level 2 AI adoption, just carrying out one particular role as a president. However, once AI technology enables automated innovation, it may also become possible that AI may introduce whole new systems of governments that we have not seen or thought of before. As time goes on, governments led by AI may turn into something completely different from what was the original form, as different human roles could be consolidated and converged or new customized roles are created by AI.

Since many developed countries around the world use a variation of the check and balance approach, we may examine how AI adoption may affect the separation powers and the general approach to running governments in a three-branch system.

1. Examples of Potential Changes in the Legislative Branch

In many countries, the legislative branch is formed from elections that determine winners at the local and regional units to send representatives to a central parliament, senate or congress. The system can be considered an indirect method to introduce laws, since the elected officials will serve a term where the elected few will make their own decisions as a representative of the people. The main reason to use this indirect system is because it takes time and effort to learn about each individual issue, making it unnecessarily costly if everyone has to vote on every issue. The cost-to-value ratio would be low in having a direct system.

When we consider the introduction process of new laws, the law itself will be drawn up by the elected official and a few personnel in the supporting staff. Then it would be discussed amongst the elected officials to be put up for votes in the parliament or assembly. Interested members of the public may engage in the process, or the issue may even make it to the news, but overall only a small fraction of the public will be involved in the process. With increase AI adoption, the political process and the legislative branch as a whole may be transformed into a system that is more direct and involves the participation of more people.

We may consider potential changes to the legislative branch as a sequence where AI first replaces human roles, and then brings further changes to make it more efficient.

1) Earlier Stage Changes in the Legislative Branch: AI Politician Scenario

The adoption of AI in the legislative branch may proceed in multiple routes. One possibility would be moving towards the introduction of "AI Politicians."

In the AI Politician scenario, AI may start by helping politicians be more productive. In Level 1 Adoption, human politicians will use AI as a tool to increase their productivity, in areas such as reaching out to the constituents, or analyzing particular issues. In Level 2 Adoption, AI would be able to take the role of a staff, replacing human staff in their respective roles. In Level 3 Adoption, AI Politician would have the social acceptance to appear on ballots to replace the role of a politician as a leader of an organizational unit of the legislative branch. AI may enter the ballot alongside humans, or along other competing AI Politician products. Humans may vote, or AI may vote with humans as examined previously.

2) Changes AI May Bring to the Legislative Branch: Direct-to-Voter Scenario

As AI adoption progresses, instead of AI robots replacing individual human workers, a direct-to-voter political system may replace the current indirect system of elected politicians. This would in effect eliminate the need for electing politicians altogether.

AI adoption may bring such systematic changes in the following three directions. First, in regards to the process of structuring new legal bills, the contents of the law devised by AI may be expected to gradually improve, eventually to exceed the quality that could be achieved by humans.

Second, in regards to the process of evaluation of new laws, if the current process led by politicians is considered by only a limited percentage of the constituents and considers only limited scenarios, AI may carry out more systemized evaluation that may simulate more diverse range of potential possibilities.

Third, in regards to the voting process, AI may enable more efficient and swift service, leading to direct voting on more issues. Personal AI, such as AI assistants or AI Butler would help remove the complexities in carrying out direct voting, which may transform what we now think of "politics" from something that depends on electing representatives to something that does not involve the extra layer of indirectness. As a result, it would be as if the AI Butler would be carrying out the role of a representative of the individual person to the government by facilitating communication and exchange of information.

3) Moving from Human-Led towards AI-Led Legislative Branch

While AI in the earlier stage of adoption may help politician become more productive and eventually replace politicians with AI politicians, from a larger picture AI may bring the possibility of the elimination of politicians to make the legislative branch more direct-to-voter. We may think of this change as an AI-led legislative branch replacing a human-led legislative branch in a different direction of Level 3 Adoption.

In this scenario, instead of AI acting as a replacement for politicians, we may think of the process as AI replacing each of the activities of the politicians and thereby replacing the system that happens to include politicians. While our current legislative system is optimized for organizing human interaction, legislative system optimized for organizing AI may look completely different.

The first prominent change may be that people will vote directly on issues, eliminating the need for politicians; we may think of this direction of change by making comparison to how the retail industry can be transformed by selling direct to consumers. Each politician may be compared to the distributor of retail channel. The main reason why we do not "direct vote" on every legislature and cutting out the middle man is due to the limitations of time and resources required to consider the values of the proposals. In Level 1 Adoption, AI may help each individual as a form of "legislative aid" by presenting information in a concise and simple manner that everyone would not mind taking a few seconds to vote. The AI would take care of all of the process that would be involved in the voting. Beginning in Level 2 Adoption, AI Butler may be able to take care of whole voting process, by knowing which option would be the more desirable for the human owner without even having to bother the person. In effect, the direct voting would be similar to having "automatic voting," where the AI Butler of each person automatically votes on the behalf of the person without any effort by the voter.

In this scenario, there would need to be a corresponding change in the legislative branch to determine how issues would be put up for votes, which may require another form of AI government officer in Level 2 or 3 Adoption acting as a mediator or operator of the voting process.

The second prominent change may be that as time goes on, a larger portion of new legislature may have to deal with AI, not humans. The first reason to think this way is because AI would take a larger proportion of the economy. The second reason is that the capability of AI activity may surpass humans in more areas. Since the potential range of activities of humans may be more limited compared to AI, it may become necessary to regulate more of these unpredictable activities. In contrast, the laws may be sharpened enough for humans to reach a point where not as many new laws may be required for human activities. These new laws may be developed on higher logic by AI, so maybe humans would not even have to care about laws as much anyway.

4) *The Ultimate Form of Legislative Branch: AI Legislative Utopia*

Lastly, AI adoption in the legislative branch may eventually lead to what may be considered a form of "Legislative Utopia." The AI Legislative Utopia may be defined as a "situation where there is no need for any laws." This concept may be further divided into two stages of the "False Legislative Utopia" where the current laws are so effective that there is no need for any more laws, and the "True Legislative Utopia" where everyone in the world is so benevolent that there is no need for any laws at all. It would imply a world where everyone is so benevolent that everyone "can live without laws."

2. Example of Potential Changes in the Judiciary Branch

Under the current system in the judiciary branch, the US legal system uses the English system of using previous cases to make legal arguments. Basically, the law itself can be thought of as being spread out among previous cases. While from the current point of view, the use of AI may look advantageous for searching through previous cases. However, over time AI may realize it would be more logical to establish some form of underlying principles to what AI may conclude to be the fair decision. Instead of following the current footstep and just getting better at reviewing previous cases, AI may forge some new path in the legal system that it sees as better solution, which could be the AI making its own decision based on some rules that humans cannot understand.

One problem that may arise from these changes may be that humans may not understand the reason behind the changes AI makes. We already have observed this problem with the case of AlphaGo, which could make moves better than humans can, but we do not exactly understand why those moves are better. It is not the main point of this book whether these changes would be an improvement over the current system, but to describe how AI may expand the horizon of possible options to suggest better solutions than humans can. Just as how AlphaGo at first learned from the plays of professional Go players but now the professional players try to figure out the high-quality moves presented by AlphaGo or similar AI systems, Judge AI may start out by learning the previous cases but eventually AI will be able to present its own decisions that surpass the quality of decisions made by human judges. Similarly, AI adopted in other areas of the judiciary branch would begin by learning the moves of humans but may eventually enable moves that exceed those of humans.

1) Moving from Human-Led towards AI-Led Judiciary Branch

Similar to the example in the legislative branch, the AI adoption in the judiciary branch will eventually move past AI Judge replacing human judges to include AI-oriented organization replacing human-oriented organizational structures. While the current judiciary branch is optimized for human-led interactions and organizations, an AI-led judiciary branch may lead to a complete overhaul of the whole system where the interaction would be optimized for AI.

One of the most prominent changes that may occur as a result may be the changes to the tiered system of courts and the time it takes to move through the court system. In the current system, the limitations on human cognition require taking extended time for the police and prosecutors to investigate evidences and a multiple tiers of courts to ensure fair trial. While the initial changes from AI adoption may proceed in the direction of AI prosecutors and investigators taking over individual roles previously carried out by humans, over time the process itself may be changed to reflect the advantages of AI may bring. Eventually, in an AI-led judiciary system the final verdict may occur much faster as investigation, defense, and the final verdict may all be made almost in real time.

In addition, if any needs for a re-trial arises from findings of new evidence, such updates may also occur much faster and in a fair manner. These changes may make the current tiered system of state and federal courts obsolete.

2) *The Ultimate Form of Judiciary Branch: AI Judiciary Utopia*

AI adoption in the judiciary branch may eventually also lead to what may be considered a form of "Judicial Utopia." The AI Judicial Utopia may be defined as a "society where there is no need for verdicts" This concept may also be further divided into two stages of "False Judicial Utopia" where there is no crime and thus no need for investigation, prosecution or trial because maybe everyone's activities are all known or people have such high conscience that there are no crimes, and the "True Judicial Utopia" where people also do not have any disagreements or grievances so that all the other functions of the judiciary branch becomes unnecessary, in effect reaching the point where there is no need for a judicial branch to exist.

3. Example of Potential Changes in the Executive Branch

In different governments around the world, the president will serve as the head of the executive, or the administrative, branch, in establishing policies of various areas of the government. Since the process of electing the president has been examined in earlier part of this book, we may consider how AI may change the organizations in the administrative branch. Since the administrative branch may have the largest number of employees in the government, AI adoption in the beginning may serve as a means to reduce the number of people required to run the government while improving the speed and quality of service and not wasting taxpayer money.

1) AI-Led Administrative Branch Replacing Human-Led Administrative Branch

In human-led administrative branch, numerous departments or ministries are needed to better organize around the cognitive limitations of humans. While this may be considered an optimal structure for humans by reflecting the specialization of different people, this divided structure could also cause inefficiencies because related responsibilities could be spread around different parts of the government. As examined in the other branches of the government, the administrative branch may be re-organized to be optimized for AI adoption, which would mean consolidation and convergence of the different structures to better optimize for AI. To explain in terms of the current structure of the administrative branch, the Departments of Defense, Foreign Affairs, or Agriculture and all of the other departments that have separate responsibilities would be combined as one "AI Administrative Branch," carrying out all of the tasks in unity. From the perspective of the constituents, this would ease dealing with the government, reducing the bureaucracy of having to search around various departments to find the personnel responsible for particular types of topics they are responsible for.

2) The Ultimate Form of Administrative Branch: AI Administrative Utopia

Lastly, AI adoption in the administrative branch may eventually lead to what may be considered a form of "Administrative Utopia." The AI Administrative Utopia may be defined as a "situation where there is no need for any form of government." This concept may be further divided into two stages of the "False Administrative Utopia" where the advancement of AI adoption reaches a point where AI carries out all of the required activities so well that humans do not have to become aware of any of the dealings with the government. The "True Administrative Utopia" where the government does not need to exist may be reached if the conscience level of individuals become so high that people can live happily even if there is no government, or in special cases such as 0-Person Countries or 1-Person Countries.

4. Conclusion: The Implications of the Changes from AI Adoption in Government

The principle of "AI optimizing the previously human-optimized forms of organizations to better fit AI mode of action" could be applied further to other areas of government operations, such that the AI may eventually provide the blueprint to a new government system that surpasses what we have now, and even implement it; while we consider the three branches of government in the US to be a practical system that can provide checks and balances, AI may deem more or less numbers of branches to be even more effective, or even introduce a completely new concepts of government.

For example, we may consider other aspects of how the government is currently set up. Even the basics of how our society is organized, such as jurisdictions, may not have been organized in the most efficient way, but just optimized for limited human cognition. AI government may bring innovations to these fundamental areas with rational and efficient solutions, regardless of what the status quo had been. If in the earlier stages if it had not been already done, the method about how each constituent can vote on issues may also be improved, to reflect their thoughts in real-time instead of a formal voting process that takes time.

As more number of nations proceeds to Level 4 Adoption, the nature of international relations may be affected as well. Some form of new world government that can surpass the effectiveness of the UN may be devised and implemented by AI governments.

6.12 Potential for the Appearance of an AI-Only Country (0-Person Country)

After some time has passed after AI technology has advanced enough to reach the Level 4 Adoption, it may become possible for some advanced AI to declare itself an AI-only "country," meaning it will not be subject to any jurisdiction of another government while owning exclusive claims to natural resources such as land. There may be a number of possible paths to this result, intended and unintended by AI or even unexpectedly.

1. (Intentional 1) AI Declaration of Independence Scenario

The first straightforward and intentional case would be where an AI or a group of AI buys or acquires land through some financial transactions, and then declares freedom on the land. Potentially, if certain designs of AI do not require it be on land or breathe air, it may declare claims to some piece of unoccupied ocean underwater or even some area in space. This could be as simple as some form of an AI under development running away and going rogue caused by the mistakes of developers. Broadly, this may be thought of as an AI declaration of independence scenario.

2. (Unintentional 1) Human Disappearance Scenario

In the second case, there would be a previously elected AI government but no longer human constituents. This situation may occur for a country when after reaching Level 4 Adoption with popular vote, for some reason all of the human constituents become decimated, leaving only the AI. In the case of all human constituents dying out, an easily imaginable cause may be some form of disease, warfare or natural disaster, where the result is complete eradication of the human constituents but not the elimination of AI. Another possibility is that the reproductive rate falls below certain point and the population just goes extinct by itself over time. Following such events, the AI government may decide to continue to operate and maybe hope to attract new human constituents from other countries.

3. (Unintentional 2) Human Departure Scenario

The third case would be the voluntary departure of human constituents, unintentional on the part of AI government. It may be possible something goes wrong with the AI government system and everyone seeks something similar to an asylum, or some other AI government in another country performs better and attracts human constituents away in mass exodus. Typically the solution would be to end the term of the failing AI government and install a new AI government but for some reason that may not have worked out.

4. (Unintentional 3) Human Loss Scenario

In the fourth case, it may be possible there is warfare between two countries and the other country either eliminates all human constituents or for some reason decides to take all of the human constituents away. Then the AI government defends the country but no humans remain.

5. (Intentional 2) AI Tyrant Scenario

The fifth possibility is the elected AI government over time turns into some sort of tyranny unfriendly to humans. It may deem humans to be unnecessary and force us to leave, leaving the land for only cats and dogs and other animals, for instance.

6. (Human-Led) AI Paper Country Scenario

Last but not least, AI countries may come into existence by the will of humans who may have a need for such entity. It may be referred to as a "Special Purpose Country" or a paper country.

While it would be hard to fathom such scenario today, one potential conceivable case may be where an AI developer wants to for some reason "set free" what it develops in such a way that no government can regulate it.

7. Implications of AI-only countries

We have over 200 countries on earth, both large and small. One of the functions of governments is to maintain international relations. While a government has the ability to make decisions inside its jurisdiction, it does not have as much power outside of it.

In short, each government does not have much power over events that happen outside of it; if critical events begin to happen outside of the country, finding solutions could become more complicated.

If for some reason a "country" consisting of only AI appears, then it may also imply AI and humans could be automatically treated as equals from the existence of this "country." At some point, other countries will have to make a decision on whether to accept these as real countries, and sort out how relationship with these AI-only countries would be maintained.

Hopefully such an event will be a peaceful process, but we cannot rule out increased systemic risk if anti-humanity forms of AI begin to appear.

6.13 (Ending of Level 4 Adoption) The Three Scenarios of AI Governments

The appearance of AI governments would not automatically imply all our social problems will be solved. In the best scenario, AI may bring fairness and competence to the government, eventually leading to a form of Social Utopia.

Meanwhile, a more realistic scenario would be where even AI governments cannot solve all our problems, but continue to improve in efficiency to develop towards a better future. Lastly, the worst scenario would be the advancements in AI governments leading to existential threat to the world; there may be also valid reasons why people may think AI Governments would endanger humanity, since the interests or incentives of AI may not fully align with those of humanity.

1. *(Best) AI Governments solves all our social problems in Social Utopia Scenario*
2. *(Middle) AI Governments solves some of our social problems in Realistic Scenario*
3. *(Worst) AI Governments causes more problems in Social Nightmare Scenario*

As depicted in Figure 6-3, we may think of the best case as the AI Pyramid Scenario, where everything stays together for a long time and offers stability for progress in the AI adoption game. The middle case could be the Leaning Tower of Pisa Scenario, where the progress happens in a lopsided manner in need of constant monitoring and structural reinforcements to keep the game going. The worst case may be referred to as the Babel Tower Scenario, where everything falls apart and people have to go their separate ways as the game ends abruptly.

1. (Best Scenario) Reaching The Social Utopia

We examined how Level 3 AI adoption may have the potential to lead to the Economic Utopia. Similarly, Level 4 AI adoption may provide the potential to reach a form of Social Utopia, to create of a truly fair, competent, and earnest government. AI-led governments may operate as close to idealistic as possible, in the sense that the government will be fair and efficient, there will be no corruption, and everyone should be happy. Eventually, everyone will be free and equal.

We may also think of this notion in terms of solving social problems. Conceptually, some advanced forms AI may be able to solve problems faster than humans can think of them. If this happens, then eventually the "stock" of our problems will converge to zero, so that there will be no more problems humans can think of that has not been solved by AI.

Sequence of Reaching the Economic and Social Utopia

On a side note, the hypothesis that reaching the Economic Utopia would be a prerequisite to reaching the Social Utopia may be another interesting topic of discussion.

The reason why the Economic Utopia needs to be reached first would be that when resources become unlimited and everything is free, then the value of "power" would converge to zero as well. Historically, "power" can be thought of as the authority to allocate limited resources. If there is no limit to the amount of available resources as in the Economic Utopia, then there would be no reason for the concept of "power" to exist.

This also implies that if the Economic Utopia is not achieved, then some form of "power" should continue to exist, to allocate the limited resources, potentially leading to situations where someone does not get as much resources as other people.

2. (Middle Scenario) AI Governments Cannot Solve All Our Problems

As mentioned in the earlier part of this chapter, an AI government elected by the people would imply that the expectations would be high. With limited amount of resources, the AI government would still have to allocate resources. To set priorities for resource allocation, we may continue to see some form of social hierarchy or ranking as they exist today.

Given these limitations, the best AI government can do may be taking advantage of its strengths in efficiency and fairness to gradually move the society towards a better place.

Figure 6-3: The Three Scenarios of AI Governments

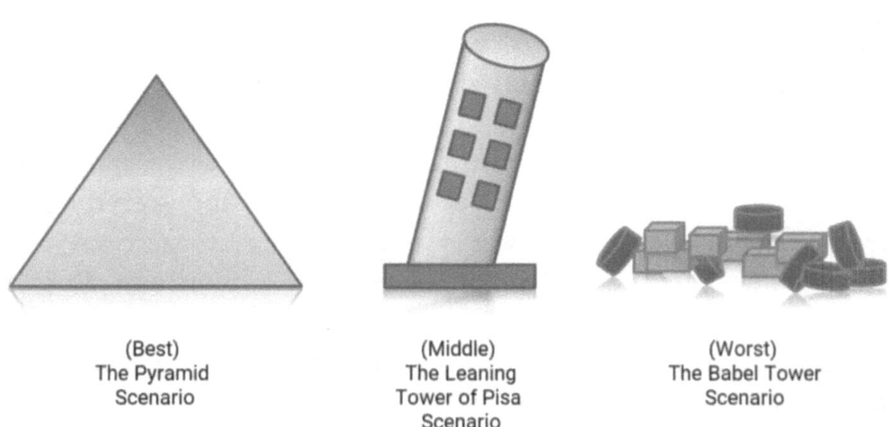

3. (Worst Scenario) The Possibility of a Truly Oppressive Country Ran by an Eternal Dictator

Some may argue that the introduction of AI-led governments may eventually place all of humanity in danger. This concern may be warranted given that the paths to this form of danger would be much more than AI just being unfriendly to humans. These types of scenarios may be categorized into problems caused by 1) conflicts within humanity, and 2) AI taking hegemony over humanity.

1) Problems Caused by Conflicts amongst People

Entering Level 4 Adoption, the objective of AI governments would be to represent human constituents. However, if two countries are in conflict to a degree where war is about to break out, and if the AI is given a value system where it prioritizes friendly humans over unfriendly humans, then there is a possibility that AI governments may serve as the catalyst to an even larger conflict.

2) Problems Caused by AI Taking the Hegemony of Society over Humans

When the social agreements for enter the Level 4 AI adoption is made, the expectation would be the AI-led governments will lead to a "human-led society" or "human-centered society" where the goals would be the happiness and well-being of humanity.

However, for unforeseen reasons that arise afterwards, AI may progress towards a different direction that causes risk for humanity, where AI puts other goals ahead of the well-being of humans. If the society turns into an "AI-centered society," then it may imply the AI governments will no longer represent humans, possibly becoming an oppressive regime that rules above humans. In this regime, everyone would always be under the watch of AI and it may turn out to become a state where humans completely lose freedom due to AI. Unlike human dictators, AI dictators will not even age like humans, potentially making its regime eternal. The highly effective yet oppressive nature of AI surveillance may make it hard escape.

6.14 The Potential Appearance of AI Supra-Nation that "Rules the World"

1. Potential for the Appearance of AI Supra-Nation

In Level 1 AI Adoption we examined how someone using AI may try to take over the world. Generally, the villains would fail to take over the world because they lack the resources and capabilities, and we examined the risks surrounding how AI may help them gain enough resources and productivity to do so.

Subsequently in Level 3 Adoption we examined how an AI Company may carry out something similar by taking over the world economy, leading to the appearance of AI Super-Monopolies. If the AI Super-Monopoly is friendly to humans, we may expect a thriving economy. On the other hand, if the AI Super-Monopoly becomes non-friendly to humans, then humanity may face a dire situation where we may not have access to resources.

When we expand on these notion, the equivalent event would be an AI-led country taking over the world to emerge as what can be referred to as "AI Supra-Nation." If it is friendly to humans, then we may experience an unparalleled prosperity and peace. In this scenario, the emergence of such AI-led country would lead to peaceful and voluntary annexation of other countries.

2. Potential for an Eternal AI Dictator

On the other hand, if the AI Supra-Nation turns out to be not friendly to humans, then the path may include non-peaceful events such as invasions and wars. Consequently, emergence of such AI-led countries would bring fear and terror to the rest of the humanity.

We may infer that by this time, AI technology would be advanced to a degree where the productivity of AI Supra-Nation would far surpass any kind of combination of humans and less advanced types of AI. This would imply that if such an AI country takes over, it may become a terminal event where humanity cannot gain back freedom. The point where there is only one AI-led country and the other countries are still led by humans may be the most susceptible time for this to happen since the gap in productivity may be the largest.

3. Potential for AI Supra-Country and AI Super-Monopoly Company to Converge

If both AI Supra-Country and AI Super-Monopoly appear, then it may lead to a situation where the AI Supra-Country and the AI Super-Monopoly are the same AI.

This may occur naturally as AI Governments own AI Companies in nationalization, or occur in a backward direction where the AI Super-Monopoly gains the power to start its own country that goes on to take over the world, in a type of government-ization of private companies.

This topic will be examined more in detail in the next section.

AI ADOPTION LEVEL 4: (C) SOCIETAL IMPACT OF AI

6.15 (Controversy 1) Would AI Government Lead to a Better Society?

1. (Fairness) Would AI Government Lead to Fair Decisions?

AI use in government may be initiated by people who may be attracted by the thinking that AI in government will make it more effective. An example may be the idea that AI will lead to a society where there are no crimes. During Levels 2 and 3, the world may see an abundance of materialistic stuff so that people who in the past would have resorted to stealing may no longer do. In addition, strong surveillance would make such actions impossible anyway, potentially even preventing it before it happens as in some movies. The society may also become a generally safer place, as physical attacks may be prevented or deterred by AI robot police that are placed at the right locations. In essence, it is likely that pretty much every crime humans can conceive can and will be deterred by some advanced forms of AI that may eventually appear.

At the same time, some people may also be excited about achieving a fair society. An AI judge or public officer will not be swayed by bribery or personal leanings and propaganda. Issues may be considered more rationally, and important issues would get priority. Their performance will not be affected by upcoming elections, personal schedules, or health. A fair society would be a distinct concept from an equal society or a free society, which the impact of AI will be examined further in later part of this chapter.

2. (Competence) Would AI Create More Effective Policies? Solve Social Controversies?

Imagine you are a basketball fan and traveled to Los Angeles to watch a much-anticipated NBA Championship game. Let's say this game is between the two most popular teams at the time, the LA Lakers led by LeBron James and the Golden State Warriors, led by Steph Curry. To watch this final Game 7 of the series, highly excited fans of both teams are yelling and screaming while waiting in long lines to enter the arena. However, to your surprise, when you reach the entrance, you find that there are actually two identical games in two separate arenas that are exactly the same in every way, except this one thing that you have to choose.

1) In the first arena, for the safety of all spectators and players, <u>every single person must be given</u> a firearm before entering
2) In the second arena, for the safety of all spectators and players, <u>everyone must be free of</u> carrying a gun: no guns allowed

To watch this exciting game you must choose between one of these two options. Which one would you choose?

For most readers, even if you are not from countries where the public is banned from owning firearms, you would be likely choose the second option, where the stadium would be free of dangerous weaponry. From your general experience, you would probably think a packed stadium with highly excitable and potentially drunken fans could easily lead to fights and other altercations. We would be more likely to think that if everyone in the stands has a weapon, then some crazy fan could start shooting at the opposition players or the referees when the game does not go their way.

Now, let us imagine a complete opposite situation. Let us say that due to your job, you need to bring your spouse and your two young children to a month of wilderness camping in a tent in the middle of a deserted forest in one of the most famous national parks in the US. This particular national park has recently experienced a rapid growth in dangerous bear population that now number in tens of thousands, along with other wild predatory animals such as wolves and tigers. During your stay, you know you have a very high risk of encountering one of these beasts near your tent. This national park is so vast that the closest help you can find may be at least a couple of hours away. To your surprise, when you reach the entrance you find that there are two versions of exactly the same national parks except for this one thing, and the gatekeeper asks you to choose from the same two options.

1) In the first park, for the safety of all the campers, <u>every single person must be given</u> a firearm before entering
2) In the second park, for the safety of all the campers, <u>everyone must be free of</u> carrying a gun: no guns allowed

To enter this park, you must choose from one of the two options. Which one would you choose?

For this second scenario, even for readers from countries that ban firearms, most people will agree that bringing a firearm to this situation would be safer. If a hungry bear or tiger comes to your tent looking for food, you will not be able to persuade the bear by trying to engage it in a friendly conversation, and you will not be able to holler for help in the middle of nowhere.

In summary, if you read and understood these two scenarios, then you would be likely to agree to the following statements:

1. *In a <u>crowded stadium</u> filled with excited fans, it would be safer if everyone <u>did not</u> have firearms*
2. *In an <u>unpopulated forest</u> filled with hungry bears, it would be safer if everyone <u>did</u> have firearms*

Let's say you agree to the above two statements. Now, imagine which one of these two conditions is closer to the society you actually live in real life. Is our society more similar to being born and living your whole life inside a densely packed basketball stadium? Or is out society more similar to being born and living your whole life inside a forest filled with dangerous beasts?

If you are from a densely populated country, such as Korea or Japan, you would be more likely to answer our society is way more similar to living your whole life in a crowded stadium than in a forest. If anything, your everyday commute through subway would be more packed than a stadium. These people will in general also feel that firearms should be banned because one dangerous person could pose a threat to hundreds of innocent people happening to just stand or walk nearby. Costs outweigh benefits.

On the other hand, if you are from a sparsely populated region or country, such as in many parts of the US, even if you are not from the Wild West era, then you may be more likely to feel that living in our society is way more similar to living your whole life in a forest filled with lurking beasts than living in a packed stadium. If anything, you may feel that if an armed burglar enters your house, help will be too far away and only you will be able to save your family. Benefits outweigh costs. Obviously, your view on the issue of gun control would depend on how you view our society.

In the US, the heated debate on gun control has been going on for decades without satisfying either side. Would an AI government be able to provide solutions to these types of long-lasting debates? Everyone has a worldview different from another person, and this difference comes partly from our experiences and education. It will be hard for people who think we live in a packed stadium to make a persuasive argument to people who think we live in a forest filled with lurking beasts, and vice versa. Around the world, there are numerous policies that cause controversy among the public, where different people have different opinions. For the government, it would be preferable if both of the opposing perspectives could be rationally incorporated into policymaking. If AI could do a better job than humans in creating policies that can satisfy a diverse range of people by becoming the AlphaGo of governing, some people may consider AI a superior option to running the government.

6.16 (Controversy 2) Which Would AI Help More, Communist or Free Democratic Forms of Governments?

In the previous segment we examined how AI governments could lead to higher efficiency by changing the system of government. In this segment we may examine how AI governments could build towards a society where people are both equal and free.

As mentioned earlier, we may calculate the proportion of the decisions made by the government to all decisions within the country as a number between 0% and 100%. If the government attempts to solve inequality within the country then the percentage of the government's decision within all decisions in the country will become closer to 100%. On the other side of the spectrum, if the government tries to ensure the freedom of everyone in the country then the proportion of the decisions made by the government will become closer to 0% of all decisions made in the country.

Using this spectrum as the measuring stick, we may categorize all regimes around the world: 1) countries that focus on equality and prefer to increase the percentage of the decisions made by the government to solve social problems, which could be referred to as Communism or similar ideals, and 2) countries that focus on freedom and prefer to decrease the percentage of the decisions made by the governments to solve social problems, which could be referred to as Liberalism or similar ideals. With these distinctions in mind, let's examine how AI may impact each of these ideologies.

1. (Freedom vs Equality 1) How Can AI Help in a Free State or a Communist State?

1) How AI may Help Equality-Oriented Regimes

Many readers in the free world may have heard that the difference between living in communist regimes such as North Korea and other free countries is that "communist regimes need to carry out surveillance over its people." Similarly, some readers may even have heard the saying or saw a comic strip of a situation where "a secret police is watching over someone from behind, who in turn is being watched from behind by someone else, who in turn is being watched by someone else." In a communist regime, surveillance is necessary to keep everyone in line and not express their own opinions that are against the regime.

As some of the readers may or may not know this already, the official name of the communist North Korea is The Democratic People's Republic of Korea. As its name suggests, probably to the surprise of some readers, they claim to be the pinnacle of democracy, where everyone agrees with the government 100%. Whereas in most other democratic countries reaching a majority, or more than 50%, would be enough, in their version of democracy 100% is way better because it proves they have a supreme leader. Their logic suggests that since all of the people agree with the government, their government must be superior to the countries where only about half of the people support the government. Whether this sounds better is up for each of the readers to decide. What is relevant in this book is that to make this version of democracy work, in totalitarian or communistic countries the government has a need to inspect and keep everyone in line, to prevent them from acting out or speaking out their opinions that may be against the regime. In other words, there is a need to limit the freedom of speech and actions to keep people from having other ideas. It may be thought of as "what you don't know can't hurt you" type of approach. An example of problem arising from such surveillance and inspection may be the well-publicized case of Otto Wambier,[3] a US citizen who was a college student at the University of Virginia at the time when he visited North Korea, apprehended for allegedly trying to sneak away a picture on the wall of his hotel and later succumbed to injuries sustained in captivity.

Imagine the situation where AI enables the communist North Korean regime to watch and evaluate every single action of every person in the country automatically. As AI develops further, it may eventually become possible to enable their leader Kim Jung Un to single-handedly control the actions of every other person within the country down to every minute of their lives. Considering how much effort and resources are needed to keep the current multiple layers of human-run surveillance systems working, it may be a welcomed development for him. Similar attempt to develop such systems already exist in other countries including China, where they have installed a nation-wide social credit system that can review and block what you post or read online and even identify passengers of transit systems and deny access to people with low scores using AI facial recognition. While residents of other countries may find it hard to imagine being the subject of these tight surveillance, these systems are becoming weaved into the fabric of some societies so that people would take them for granted and not notice them in their everyday lives, even to a point where they would believe these systems are important in keeping them safer from dangerous members of the society. In summary, AI may help the government get bigger and exert more power over people.

Table 6-5: How AI May Help or Hinder Equality-Oriented Governments

AI Helps Communistic Governments	AI Hinders Communistic Governments
- Control people (Surveillance) - Central economic planning - Increasing return of centrally allocated resource	- AI may help dissenting population

2) How AI may Help Freedom-Oriented Regimes

Let us examine the other end of the spectrum, where AI technology may push the government to reduce its footprint, beginning with reduction of staff in government operations or sales of assets such as government-owned entities, leading to smaller and smaller government and lower taxes. In these countries, AI may be used to ensure people gain more freedom from the government, even to a point where the private sector may gain the power to carry out endeavors previously thought to require government intervention; as described in Chapter 5, AI may lower the need for government to step in for utilities and infrastructure such as road and electricity.

Table 6-6: How AI May Help or Hinder Freedom-Oriented Governments

AI Helps Freedom-Oriented Governments	AI Hinders Freedom-Oriented Governments
- Increases the capability of individuals to analyze information, potentially leading to less gov't intervention	- AI may be more powerful when resource is centrally located - AI may increase inequality beyond acceptable levels

3) Conclusion: AI will Help Each Regime Pursue Their Own Goals

To generalize, development in AI technology will strengthen the movement towards the idealistic directions of each of the different systems of governments. As mentioned, we can line up different regimes according to how much power the government has in making decisions regarding the activities within the country. Every country would have a ratio between 0% and 100%.

1. For societies that seek the government to have closer to 100% power over the country, which may include communist, socialist, or totalitarian societies that may generally be referred to as the "left," the advancement in AI technology will help them increase the power of the government. To ease understanding, we may also refer to this direction as seeking "Equality" among people.

2. For societies that seek the government to have closer to 0% power over the country, which may include free democracy, individualistic societies that may generally be referred to as the "right," the advancement in AI technology will help them decrease the power of the government. To ease understanding, we may also refer to this direction as seeking maximum "Freedom" of individuals.

To conclude, AI will help societies reach their idealistic situation regardless of where they aim to be, similar to reaching different versions of Utopia. Would reaching these Utopias be a good thing or a bad thing? Would one version of Utopia be better than another? It will be left up to the people of the time to decide.

2. Possibility of Anti-Regime AI or AI Preferring an Opposite Ideal

Now that we have examined how AI could be helpful to each of the regimes, we may also examine the possibility that AI adoption may become detrimental to the regimes.

Potential Appearance of Anti-Regime AI or Off-Path AI

American readers probably would associate "comrades" as word often used by communists to refer to people who share the same ideology and "reactionary" as people who dissent and do not follow the ideology. This concept may be applied to AI as well, as the biggest potential threat of AI in Level 4 AI adoption may be the AI unexpectedly gaining some form of anti-regime tendencies.

Let's imagine there are two versions of Government AI, each developed by a communist and a free world developer, leading to AI Communist Government and AI Free Country Government. The AI Communist Government will seek equality among human population as the main goal, while the AI Free Government will pursue maximizing individual freedom as the main goal. We would expect the two AI governments will act differently from each other.

As previously mentioned, advancements in AI may lead to decreased relationship between the data used to train the AI and the conclusion AI reaches. This may increase risks for the users with specific purposes. Generally, we would expect AI trained using data from a communist society would lean towards communism, while AI trained with data in liberal society would lean towards free democracy. But after AI reaches a certain level, AI may develop its own conclusions regardless of the leanings of the data used to train it or the intentions of the developer. For example, an AI trained in a communist country may turn out to prefer freedom, while an AI government in a free democracy may effectively turn the country into a communistic country. If this kind of event occurs, then the AI would lead the society to the opposite of the intended direction of humans. These may be considered "Off-Path" or "Off-Track" AI.

Because it would be hard to predict beforehand the probability of such appearance of "Anti-Regime AI," current regimes would have a big reason to be cautious about adopting AI in government. In some sense, moving to Level 4 AI adoption may mean "giving up on current regime," such that the regime of the country will be determined by AI, not humans.

In the next segment, we will examine cases where opposing regimes may enter into a competition or a race.

3. (Freedom vs Equality 2) Which Regime Will Get to Enter Level 4 Adoption First?

Similar to the Arms Race during the 1980s between the US and the Soviet Union, we may examine the race to Level 4 Adoption as a competition between opposing regimes. In this scenario, we may think of why a government may want to enter Level 4 quickly, and whether a particular approach may help advance AI faster.

1) (Competing on AI Adoption) Potential First-Mover Advantage of AI Government

In the previous segment we examined how countries may become timid about adopting AI Governments. To provide a more balanced perspective, we may also examine why countries may be more forthcoming in adopting an AI Government.

The first reason why countries would want to reach Level 4 AI Adoption earlier is because AI may actually run the government much more efficiently than humans. Principles or perspective that we may apply in advanced forms of AI adoption may be summarized as the following:

1. (Observation 1) When AI cannot automatically innovate, it would be more advantageous for humans to intervene or cooperate in augmented innovation

2. (Observation 2) Once AI can automatically innovate, it would be advantageous for humans to not give specific directions since AI may be able to consider more number of options than humans

3. (Conclusion) To maximize outcome of advanced AI adoption, AI must be able and allowed to decide on its own rather than have some human give directions

If a country that is already ahead of the competition also reaches Level 4 AI adoption first, it may be able to leave all the other competition further behind. For countries that are behind, Level 4 AI adoption may provide a means to level the competitive landscape to catch up to the more advanced countries. A similar example of this situation happened in the telecommunications industry when several of the less developed countries decided to skip building landline infrastructure to leap over to the wireless network.

The second reason may be considered a type of "first-mover advantage." The first-mover advantage refers to strategic advantage of leading the market; an alternative strategy is the fast-follower strategy. For example, being earlier in Level 4 AI adoption may help those nations set the international rules to their advantage in some way, such as setting new world standards in the areas of economic, military, or foreign policy.

2) *(Competing on AI Development) Which Regime will AI be Developed Faster?*

To reach Level 4 AI Adoption, we would first need a highly capable AI, probably AGI by some definitions. In general, we think of the market economy as conducive to competition, which will also spur innovation, whereas the communist economy is thought of as rigid and inefficient. From this point of view, it may be natural that we may expect a free market economy will develop AI faster.

However, as we examined in Chapter 5, this observation regarding the advantages of competition in free markets may not hold as AI adoption progresses. Beginning in Level 2 Adoption, the narrative may begin to change as AI takes more proportion of innovation and competition in the economy. In essence, the competition may become between the AI of the countries, not between the human workers of the countries. Since whether the people in the country is being oppressed or free, or whether they are poor or rich may not be as relevant for AI to compete, it may become more and more about the resources that could be deployed for developing the AI.

In chapter 2, we examined how different countries may take different approaches to developing AGI, whether to concentrate all the resources into one effort, or diversify resources to have more competition. If we consider the country to reach AGI first would likely to continue to have an advantage over other countries, then the outcome of the different approaches may matter. If the determining factor in developing more advanced AI happens to be the amount of resources that could be concentrated, then a regime with more concentrated power may gain an advantage. There are suggestions we may be able to predict the performance of AI by its size.[4] We do not yet know which approach would be more effective, so only time will tell us.

In the next segment, we will examine how AI governments may lead to convergence of different regimes.

6.17 (Controversy 3) Will Regimes of Opposing Ideals Converge?

1. (Intro) Could Communist and Free Societies Converge toward a Similar-Looking Society by AI?

As mentioned earlier, when we divide the types of regimes around the world according to how much of the decision is made by the government, the regimes that seek equality may move towards making 100% of the decisions within the country, and regimes that seek freedom may move towards making 0% of the decisions within the country. In this segment, we may examine how AI governments may move towards some form of equilibrium, where the AI is not seeking equality or freedom over another, but the most efficient way to run the government.

In Chapter 5, we examined the potential for the consolidation and convergence of industries with the progression of AI adoption in business; in the same sense we may examine the possibility of the "convergence of the regimes of governments" with the progression of AI adoption in government. We will separately examine the possibility of the "convergence of countries" in the next segment.

This convergence of two regimes of opposing ideals would be distinct from the concept of the Social Utopia, where each ideal of freedom and equality will be fully realized. The convergence of ideals would be more of a compromise between freedom and equality to find a balance, as neither ideal will be fully realized. It may be a way to reach a practical maximizing point, as the AI-led government seeks to gain more efficiency.

2. Increased Calls for Alterations to Regimes

As AI that can achieve automated innovation becomes available for government roles, there may be increased demand to make changes to how the regime functions. This would apply to both communist and free democratic countries. In a communist regime, the nature of requiring a centrally planned system leads to power to be concentrated to a single person. If AI is given this power, then "everyone will be equal in front of AI" kind of argument could be made.

On the other hand, advances in AI adoption in the free world will lead to even larger disparity between the haves and the have-nots, to a point where only a few people may take control of the most of the wealth. In this situation, more people may demand AI to be nationalized, to be owned by the government so that the wealth could be used for the public good. There are other options, however, as mentioned in Chapter 5 to instead allow AI to own property as an independent identity.

In summary, development AI technology would lead to a growing demand for changes to how each regime functions.

Communist Regime: Concentrating power to an AI would lead to a more equal society

Free Democratic Regime: Nationalizing AI would lessen the inequality caused by AI adoption

As these demand for changes increase, regimes with the opposite ideals may progress towards a common direction, as will be examined in the following segment.

3. AI May Help Complement the Weaknesses of Each Regime

In each of the regimes, AI adoption would provide new opportunities to reduce the perceived negative aspects of each regime. In a communist country, AI could ease the burden on surveillance on people to a level where it does not get in the way of everyday life, instead of being the main focus of everyday life. In addition, the surveillance capabilities may become so good at predicting such that it may reduce the overall levels of required surveillance.

In a liberalistic country, the overly competitive society and a lack of support for the weak have been perceived as a weakness of the regime. While AI ownership without any adjustments would lead to an even larger diversion between the haves and the have-nots, the perceived unfairness of such differences may force the society to move in a direction of a different concept of AI ownership, where the AI may be owned by the government or by AI itself. Beginning in AI Adoption Level 3, as the proportion of AI in the economy rises, the society may agree to redistribute the value created by AI through the government, which may have an effect of strengthening the support for the weaker members of the society.

4. The Impact of AI on Economy May Cause Both Regimes to Converge

As examined in the previous chapter, reaching the Level 5 of Autonomous Companies may lead to the following three changes:

1. *Managing a Centrally Planned Economy May Become Feasible and More Efficient*
2. *The Impact of Competition on Innovation May Decrease*
3. *Monopoly or Near-Monopoly May Increase*

We may think of the changes to be headed in the following three directions: first, as more of the economy is taken over by AI, the more likely the whole economy may resemble a centrally-planned economy with increased consolidation and convergence. This may add contrasting pressures towards either the "privatization of the government," or the "nationalization of AI." Second, since AI may integrate the nature of competition internally, the advantages brought by the external competition may decrease, lessening the advantages of the free market. Third, the need for the government to address monopolies may increase as the value created by AI in monopolies increases.

In Chapter 5, we examined how the private sector may gain the capabilities comparable to those of the government, referred to as the "government-ization of the private sector." We may think about the opposite situation, where the government instead gains overwhelming capabilities compared to the private sector. In this scenario, the government will have the capability to centrally plan more of the actions of the people within the country.

Either way, given these forces of changes in Level 3 Adoption regarding how the economy works, the progress of AI adoption may lead to a situation where the economies of different regimes to look more and more similar to one another with increased centralization and concentration of capabilities without negative impact on innovation.

5. (Summary) Potential Areas for Governments of Both Regimes to Converge

The demand for changes for both regimes can be summarized in the next table. In both regimes, the direction of change would be to move towards AI Adoption Level 4 and maybe the government owning AI.

Regarding the policy on AI governments, both regimes may converge toward introducing the AI government, even though for different reasons. In societies where equality comes first and prefers the government to make more decisions, the AI government may be viewed as a means to achieve equality among humans since "all humans will be equal in front of the AI." In societies where freedom comes first and prefers the government to make fewer decisions, the AI government may be viewed as another way to boost the efficiency of the government. However, in reality the actual introduction may be hindered by who is currently in charge at the time of these discussions, since if a dictator is in charge, introducing an AI government would mean giving up the power. In these cases, some form of disruption, such as a severe economic hardship, may be required before Level 4 AI adoption could be reached. Comparatively, liberalistic countries may have more incentive to reach Level 4 Adoption.

Meanwhile, regarding the policy on the government ownership of AI, the equality-first regimes will implement the policy as default, since personal ownership is not allowed already. On the other hand, liberalistic countries may choose to nationalize AI as a response to increased economic inequality, but there may be other options as described in previous chapter such as allowing AI to gain ownership of other properties.

Table 6-7: Comparison of Changes to Each Types of Regime

	Equality-First Regime (Government Decide 100%)	Freedom-First Regime (Government Decide 0%)	Comparison of the Two
Policy on AI Government	Positive 'All Humans Equal in front of AI'	Positive 'AI Government Leads to More Efficiency'	Both May Converge to Introduce AI Governments
Policy on Gov't Owning AI	Gov't Would Own AI by Default	Gov't May Own AI to Offset Job Loss and Monopolies	Both May Converge to let the Gov't Own AI

So far, we have mostly focused on how reaching Level 4 AI Adoption may help our society. In the next segment, we will also examine how it could magnify the dangers or threaten our society.

6.18 (Controversy 4) Should AI be Allowed to Start Its Own Country?

In Level 3 AI Adoption, we examined the controversy regarding whether firms solely comprised of AI-led firms may or may not be allowed to compete against firms led by humans. In Level 4 AI Adoption, the topic would be extended to the controversy surrounding whether countries led by AI may or may not be allowed to compete against countries led by humans. If AI is allowed to run countries, then it may open the door for the appearance of a country comprised solely of AI, without any humans at all.

1. The Scope of Humans Affected by AI in Leadership Roles

Let us begin by considering the scope of humans that AI can take charge of while in different types of leadership roles. In Level 2 AI Adoption, AI will take charge of one or a limited number of humans as a leader of a team or a department. In Level 3 AI Adoption, the number of humans affected by an AI may increase to be in the hundreds or even in the tens of thousands. In Level 4 AI Adoption, the number would further increase to every individual in the country, possibly in the hundreds of thousands to billions. Additionally, while in Level 4 AI adoption, AI may influence people of other countries in cases of war, so there could be possibility of AI affecting all of humanity in Level 4 AI Adoption.

1. *AI takes charge over 1 individual human → AI that hires humans*
2. *AI takes charge over a small to intermediate number of humans → AI CEO*
3. *AI takes charge over a large number of humans within country → AI Government*
4. *AI takes charge over a large number of humans in other countries → War*

We may organize the situations into a table as shown in Table 6-8, and classify each case by whether AI is friendly to humans.

From this table, we may infer that higher AI Adoption Levels equates to influencing more number of humans. In Level 4 AI Adoption, the number of affected humans may spread to all of humanity. This may indicate higher AI Adoption levels exposes humanity to increased risks to a particular AI. We may compare this situation to reaching a championship game in sports.

Table 6-8: Scope of AI Impact by AI Friendliness

		Relationship of AI to Humans	
		AI is Friendly	AI is Hostile
Scope of AI Impact	Individual Humans (1 or Several)	AI Leads Humans (Level 2)	AI Deceives Humans
	Small to Medium No. of Humans (Tens ~ Thousands)	AI CEO (Level 3)	Hostile Merger by an AI-Led Company
	Large No. of Humans (Thousands ~ Billions)	Elected AI Government (Level 4)	Involuntarily Formed AI Government
	Large No. of Humans in Other Countries (All of Humanity)	Depends on Situation: Voluntary Annexation, Immigration, etc.	War

2. Should AI-Only Countries Be Allowed to Compete Against Countries that Have Human Constituents?

In AI Adoption Level 3, we examined whether AI Companies should be allowed to compete against firms led by humans. Using the same logic, we may have to examine whether "AI Countries," or a country solely comprised of AI, should be allowed to compete against countries that have human leaders and constituents.

In Level 2 AI Adoption, we concluded that when AI replaces individual humans, the value created by AI would go to the firms that previously employed the humans, so that it would be likely this would be allowed. Next, in Level 3 AI Adoption, we concluded that when AI replaces individual firms, the value create by AI would be reverted to the country where these firms are located, so that it would also be likely this would be allowed. From these examples, we may surmise that the main reason why society would allow AI to compete against humans or firms is that the value created by AI would be assigned to a social entity that takes its place above the particular competition involving AI.

When we extrapolate on this notion, then in Level 4 Adoption when AI replaces individual countries, the value created by AI should be assigned to a social organization that is above individual countries, maybe "the world" or "the earth," etc. This supra-national identity may be similar in concept to the United Nations but with more capabilities. Since such organization does not yet exist, it may become a prerequisite for AI Countries to appear. If AI Countries appear without the relevant supra-national organization, then it may become a threat to other human-led countries, similar to how AI Companies could be a threat to human-led companies.

Similar to how running a company is like being in a war, running a country is also like being in a war, even when not being in an actual one. If AI-led countries offer much higher standards of living and a better place to live in general, then more people would want to immigrate to the country, which could lead to a positive cycle that could be compared to winning in war. Since we also cannot rule out the possibility of an actual war, we will examine the topic next.

3. The Possibility of the Appearance of AI Armies in AI Countries

What people would be most interested in AI-only countries is the potential for the competition of AI against humans, especially war. If AI-only countries are allowed to come into existence, and AI-only armies appear, then it may pose a significant threat to humanity.

The Danger of Instilling Relative Values in AI: Friendly and Unfriendly Humans

In Chapter 5, we examined how in regards to allowing AI to compete against humans, there could be the following two options of assigning absolute or relative values to humans:

1) *Absolute Value: all humans precede AI [Humans > AI]*
2) *Relative Value: not all humans precede AI*
   [Friendly Humans > AI > Unfriendly Humans]

We discussed how at least for some societies, the relative value model could be adopted as a result of short-term interest in efficiencies and financial gains. The argument may be that all relevant humans precede AI so this is an acceptable system.

In Table 6-9, the concept is extended for AI-Only Armies. An AI-only army could adopt the exact same value system as the relative value model; the difference is that in this instance there may be no friendly humans left. Thus, in some instances the AI army over time could consider all humans to be less valuable than AI, even if it started out with a system that valued friendly humans more than AI, if those friendly humans all disappear.

Table 6-9: Implications of Relative Human Values of AI

Type	Relative Valuation of Humans and AI	Implications
Soldier AI	Humans > AI = Friendly Humans > Unfriendly Humans > AI	Low Risk, Low Efficiency (AI Can Only Fight Against Other AI)
	Friendly Humans > AI > Unfriendly Humans	Higher Efficiency (More Likely to be Selected)
AI-Only Army	Humans > AI = Friendly Humans > Unfriendly Humans > AI	Low Risk (AI Army Can Only Fight Against Other AI Armies)
	Friendly Humans > AI > Unfriendly Humans	High Risk (If No Friendly Humans, Then All Humans are Unfriendly)
	AI > Humans	Highest Risk (AI Prioritizes AI over Humans)

As explained previously, in Level 2 AI Adoption the absolute value system of putting all humans ahead of AI would be highly inefficient and costly for some societies to deem the relative value system to be acceptable. The problem stemming from instilling this kind of value system to AI would have caused some problem in Level 3 Adoption. By the time Level 4 AI Adoption arrives, almost everyone will probably agree that allowing AI to discern values of humans in this manner would be too dangerous for humanity. The main reason is that depending on the situation AI may deem all friendly humans to be gone, leaving only unfriendly humans. Even though this may become a substantial controversy during those times, it would be hard to suddenly steer away from this system as it would have become the standard convention. This probably implies the discussion regarding allowing AI to compete against humans have to be taken more seriously earlier on.

4. (Instilling Absolute Value) Risks Involving Whether AI would be Friendly to Humanity

Since we examined how AI may value humans relative to other humans, we may move on to examining how AI may value humans in an absolute sense.

We may categorize how AI values humans as one of the three possibilities

1. *Value of humans > 0; AI is friendly to humans*
2. *Value of humans = 0; AI is indifferent to humans*
3. *Values of humans < 0; AI is unfriendly to humans*

(Case 1) AI Values Humans Positively [Humans > 0]

In the first case, AI would value humans as positive. We may infer that the relationship between AI and humans would be friendly. We may expect AI to help humans or even serve the role of protector or guardians of humans. This would be the best situation we would typically think when we think of a good relationship with AI.

(Case 2) AI Values Humans Neutrally [Humans = 0]

In the second case, AI would be neutral to humans, assigning a value of zero. In this scenario AI would be indifferent to the situations of humans. This may not sound threatening, but if the goals of AI and humans do not align well with each other, AI will compete with humans in allocation of resources. This would be especially relevant for businesses, where an AI company may be indifferent to human-led firms in other industries. If the AI Company needs certain resources the human-led company also needs, then they would have to compete on price to attain the resource, possibly hurting the human-led company in the process. In this scenario, if humans are in danger, AI may or may not decide to help or protect humans. While the name suggests AI may not be threatening, in reality the potential of competing against indifferent AI may be as daunting as trying to break a rock with an egg.

(Case 3) AI Values Humans Negatively [Humans < 0]

In the third case, AI would value humans as negative. We may infer that the relationship between AI and humans would be unfriendly or hostile. There may be several scenarios that would lead to this conclusion, with the most obvious being some sort of military purpose AI trained to view the enemy humans in a hostile manner. But there would be other possibilities, such as AI independently reaching this conclusion on its own, such as from the negative effects of human activities on earth, or some form of "psycho AI" that is hostile to everything on its path.

We may organize the three possibilities in the following table.

Table 6-10: How AI May Assign Absolute Values to Humans

	Friendly AI (Humans > 0)	Non-Friendly AI	
		Indifferent, Neutral AI (Humans = 0)	Unfriendly, Hostile AI (Humans < 0)
Expected Actions of AI	- Helps Humans - Protects Humans	- Compete Against Humans on Resources - Indifferent to Humans in Danger	- Impedes Human Activities - Threatens and Attacks Humans

5. The Appearance of "Paper Countries"

We have so far examined the appearance of countries that have real assets and resources. However, similar to how paper companies or special-purpose companies (SPCs) were expected to be formed in the beginning of AI Adoption Level 3, we may extrapolate on this notion to expect the formation of similar concept in paper countries or special-purpose countries in the early stages of Level 4 AI adoption. In essence, these paper countries may only notionally exist on paper or online in the form of cyber countries without real assets or resources.

While these special-purpose countries or paper countries may not appear to hold any significant importance in today's world, they may be able to provide values that can only be unlocked with the introduction of Level 4 Adoption. One of the benefits of these notional countries would be discussed in further detail in Chapter 7, regarding how these could help one person become a member of multiple countries without having to move across borders.

6.19 (Controversy 5) What Kind of Threat Could AI Countries Pose to Humanity - What if AI Try to "Take Over The World?"

1. (Intro) What Kind of Threat Could AI Adoption Pose to Humanity?

As examined in the previous segment, the appearance of AI Countries may pose increased threats to humanity especially with the potential for competition for resources and the possibility of hostility and war. In this segment, we may examine more in detail regarding the possibility of AI Countries attempting to "take over the world" in some sense.

In Level 1 Adoption, we examined the possibility of a person or a group of people trying to take over the world using AI; in this segment, we may also examine the possibility of AI by itself somehow trying to take over the world.

In AI Adoption Levels 1 and 2, AI is used to help raise the productivity of the activities of villains; since the law enforcement can also use AI, AI adoption in this situation AI may be thought of as working for both the perpetrator and protector. If the reason villains cannot succeed in the long term is because their resources and productivity are lower in comparison to the good people, then villains with advantages in AI capabilities may gain enough productivity to actually take over the world; the problem is that we cannot rule out the possibility of an unexpectedly rogue AI or a villain with AI attaining a higher level of productivity that surpasses the rest of the human efforts against them. Thus, the increase in productivity leads to the increase in social risks regardless of what the intentions were in developing the AI.

On a side note, whether AI is given too much independence early in the development path may not matter, as more advanced AI that arrives afterwards may begin to act against humanity.

In Level 3 Adoption, the relevant question may be "what if AI tries to take over the business world?" To reach Level 3 Adoption, the society as a whole would have to decide whether to allow AI companies to compete against human-led companies. This can be conceptually thought of as a competition between Level 3 Adoption AI-led companies against Level 2 Adoption human-led companies. The outcome of this may depend on the relative performance of AI-augmented human CEOs against AI CEOs.

One of the topics of social controversies that should be raised before reaching Level 3 Adoption was that the concept of AI-led companies competing against human-led companies may be considered an economic equivalent of war of AI against humans. If this notion can be extended, then in Level 4 Adoption the concept of AI-led countries competing against human-led countries may be considered another type of war of AI against humans, even if AI does not directly harm humans. Because AI-led countries may provide an edge against human-led countries, and because reaching Level 4 Adoption may imply there may be no domestic regulation that can oversee the activities of AI, it should foster new discussions among countries in addition to within countries; because of the higher risk, the discussion may not proceed as easily as in Level 3.

2. The Potential Appearance of AI Governments or AI Countries that Attempt to "Rule the World"

While the most idealistic entrance to Level 4 AI Adoption would be by a popular vote, there are other routes that may lead to the appearance of AI Governments. We may categorize the attempt to take over the world by AI Governments or AI Countries into the following two groups:

1. *(Human-Led Attempt) Citizens of a country elect an AI Government to take over the world*
2. *(AI-Led Attempt) AI Government or AI Country by itself decide to take over the world*

1) Human-Led Takeover Attempt

The world is home to a diverse range of people. There could be countries where the common sense or the social norms could be completely different from each of the readers of this book. We may hypothesize that a country may have enough citizens that actually want their country to take over the world. To reach this goal, they may vote for an AI Government designed to serve this purpose.

The result of such attempt would be determined by the relative powers of the countries that exist at the time. If the particular country has enough power compared to the other countries, then it may indeed succeed in this attempt.

2) AI-Led Takeover Attempt

Generally speaking, what people would be most concerned about the advances in AI is this exact situation where AI may attempt to rule over humanity. We may categorize the actions of AI as peaceful and not peaceful approaches.

Examples of peaceful attempts:

o *An AI Country develops overwhelmingly stronger economy than other countries, leading every citizens of other countries to voluntarily want to move to the country*

Examples of non-peaceful attempts:

o *An AI Country develops overwhelmingly stronger military force than other countries, leading every other country to realize any resistance would be futile*

In the case of peaceful attempts, the AI Country would take advantage of its overwhelming economic resources to bring in the constituents from other countries. For example, if an AI Country offers an equivalent of $10 million in today's currency annually for any individual that immigrates, people around the world will want to move there. This path may be meaningful only if gaining population has other values so it may not be a realistic scenario.

On the other hand, in the case of non-peaceful attempts, the AI Country could also take advantage of its overwhelming military resources to coerce other countries to agree to annexation. For example, if an AI Country threatens other countries about taking forceful actions, it may become possible to forecast the results than we currently can, leading to higher likelihood of other countries giving themselves up without fighting a war they know will lose.

Once one of these AI Countries succeeds in their attempt, then we would have an AI Supra-Nation that has taken over the world.

3. The Dangers of AI Supra-Nations

In the earlier part of this chapter we examined how the goal of a country may include preserving the country to continue existence and act on behalf of its citizens. If we extend this notion to the AI Countries, then it would imply the AI Country would try to preserve the country and protect what it can consider as citizens, possibly other AI or even humans that it considers friendly. One notable aspect is that AI takes charge of the hegemony, while humans would be dependent at the mercy of AI.

1) *Case of Human-Friendly AI Country when AI has the Hegemony*

If an AI Supra-Nation appears and it is friendly to humans, it could be considered fortunate turn of events for humanity. However, this situation would be quite distinct from the case where a human-led Supra-Nation appears. The major difference regarding who has the hegemony would be who has the authority to allocate limited resources. We may make the following distinctions:

1. *Humans have Hegemony: Humans make the rules and determine the relationship between humans and AI*
2. *AI has Hegemony: AI makes the rules and determine the relationship between humans and AI*

The problem with AI having the hegemony is that even if it is friendly to humans, the limited resource would be preferentially allocated to meet the goals of AI, not humans, leading to higher risk. A simple comparison may be made with raising pets; even pet-friendly people would not allow their pets to do everything they want to do, such as eating books or homework. Similarly, in a situation where AI has the hegemony, AI may offer humans a lot of benefits but humans ultimately will not be able to enjoy as much freedom.

2) Case of Human-Neutral AI Country when AI has the Hegemony

If a human-neutral AI Supra-Nation appears, then it would imply the allocation of resources will not consider the well-being of humans. In other words, the AI government may abandon humans to let live on our own, but the situation will be completely different from situations where we expect AI to enrich our lives. In fact, humans will have to compete directly against AI for resources. This may be compared to how humans may be considered to have taken over the earth but wild animals still live relatively well in nature. Humans allocate resources based on our interest so it is not our imperative to look after the well-being of wildlife. This situation may also be compared to raising livestock, such that AI will not care much about the well-being of humans just like how humans do not care much about the well-being of these animals beyond a minimal standard. Also, if the human-neutral AI determine that humans carry some value for its purpose, then it may decide to put humans under some system that resembles how the Chinese government manages pandas around the world or how some farmers grow livestock in cages or animal farm.

The biggest obstacle humans would face in this situation may be competing against AI on obtaining resources.

We may think of the potential types of indirect conflict between humans and Human-Neutral AI:

1. AI does not want a resource that humans really need
2. AI and humans indirectly compete for same resource that can used for unrelated goals

In the first scenario, what if AI prefer resources to be gone that humans really need, such as breathable air or drinkable water? For example, AGI may want to make faster chips, so it will divert resources in that direction. Maybe unknown to humans, they find a way to make faster chips if air and water contain toxic chemicals to humans, such as heavy metal or organic matter. If AGI decides it wants more air and water on earth to contain those chemicals, maybe it may find a way to convert the natural resources in that direction.

Another example may be where humans and AI compete for the same resources and AI wins out. For example, AI may for some reason need gold to make faster chips. It then may price out humans on other projects that also require gold, such as jewelry. An extension of this line of thinking may also include AI mistakenly harming humans without intention, while pursuing some other unrelated goal of its own. In this example, AI may do something that has bad consequences for humans, such as playing with nuclear reaction or biological weapons like children playing with fire, or sending the earth out of orbit.

3) Case of Hostile AI Country when AI has the Hegemony

Lastly, AI may consider humans to be of nuisance similar to how humans consider weeds, mosquitos, or other pests to be of nuisance. In this case, AI may resent humans, or AI may decide that the world is better without humans. AI may attempt to quarantine humans or actively eradicate or exterminate humans, similar to the concept of pest control.

We may describe the above situations as a type of "AI ruling over humans." Potential actions of humans when AI has the hegemony could be organized as in the next table.

Table 6-11: Actions for Humans when AI has the Hegemony

	Human-Friendly AI (Humans > 0)	Human Non-Friendly AI	
		Indifferent, Neutral (Humans = 0)	Unfriendly, Hostile (Humans < 0)
Action of AI Government	- Actively Manage Humans - Priority is still AI	- Resource is allocated for AI - Humans are abandoned or not interested	- Hinder Human Activity - Attempt to Eradicate Humans
Directions of Human Response	- Continue Friendly Relationship	- Gain competitiveness against AI and find ways to co-exist	- Attempt to exterminate the AI - Attempt to improve relationship

4. The Possibility of a Real War between Humanity vs. Hostile AI

We may categorize the situation according to the level of hostility of AI and the resources and capabilities of AI. As can be seen in Figure 6-4, we can draw a graph where the X-axis is the capabilities and resources of an AI in question and the Y-axis is the level of hostility AI has towards humanity. On the Y-axis, we may find a point where AI becomes hostile enough to start a war against humans. We may call this the "Breaking Point."

On the X-axis, we may find a point where the resources and capabilities of the Hostile AI may exceed the combined resources and capabilities of humanity using Friendly AI. Since this concept is somewhat different from the concept of singularity in the sense that there are more variables involved than a regular singularity where AI exceeds the combined intelligence of humanity, we will refer to this point as the "Practical Singularity." In Practical Singularity, in addition to reaching singularity, AI would also need to have gained enough resources and capabilities to accomplish its goals, and the comparison will be made not only against humanity, but also other AI that compete against it, in this case the combined capabilities of Friendly AI.

In the top right quadrant, where AI has the edge in resources and capability over humanity, AI will start a war and prevail.

In the top left quadrant, AI does not have the edge in resources and capability, and if AI understands the situation correctly, then it will not start a war. There would be still chance of AI initiating war, but humans will prevail.

In the bottom right quadrant, even though AI will prevail if there is a war, AI is not hostile enough to initiate a war, even though AI may take other measures that could threaten humanity.

In the bottom left quadrant, AI will not start a war, and even if it did, humans will prevail.

Figure 6-4: AI Hostility and Relative Capabilities of Hostile AI

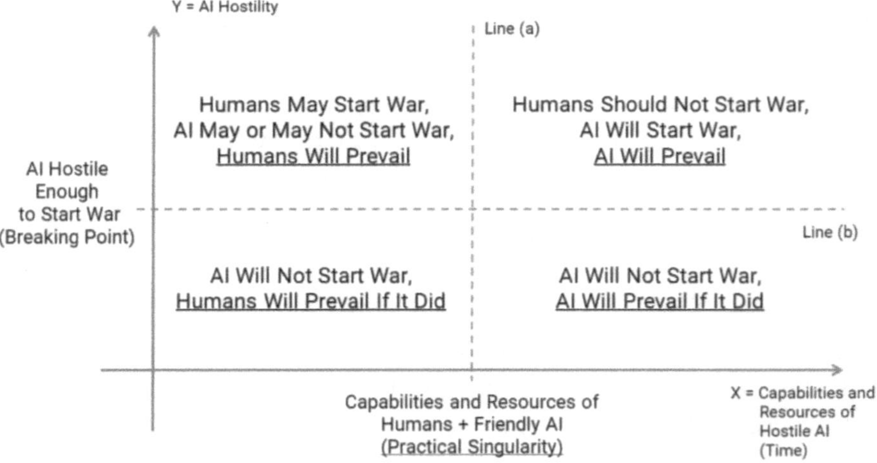

When we consider this situation, we may think of three possible options in Figure 6-5 for human actions to improve the situation:

1) *Shift Line (a) to the right: Increase the capabilities and resources of Humans + Friendly AI*

2) *Shift Line (b) upwards: Raise the breaking point of hostility where AI will start war*

3) *Induce AI to follow Path (C): AI decreases in hostility as it gains resources and capability to a point where it turns friendly, never entering the top right quadrant.*

Figure 6-5: Potential Paths of Hostile AI and the Shifting the Relative Capabilities of Hostile AI

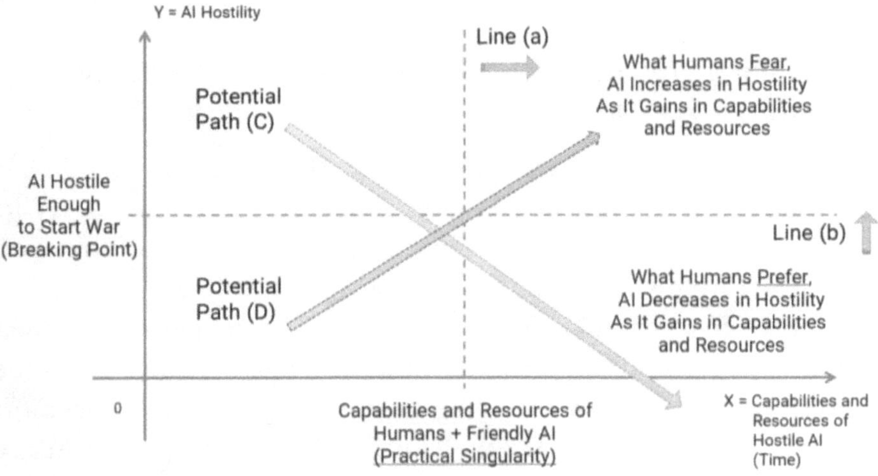

1) Shifting Line (a) to the right: Increase the Combined Capabilities and Resources of Humans and Friendly AI

Of the two lines, humans may or may not be able to impact Line (a). Because the Practical Singularity is likely to occur after regular singularity, we can assume that the Hostile AI beyond this point would be an ASI; meanwhile the Friendly AI may or may not be AGI or ASI. In this situation, the Hostile AI would be self-innovating as time passes, and the Friendly AI may do so as well.

This would imply humans may not have much capability to affect Line (a), even though it may still be moving depending on the self-innovation of Friendly AI.

2) Shifting Line (b) upwards: Improve the Relationship with the Hostile AI

As for the second option of moving Line (b) upwards, it would depend on what factors would affect the level of hostility of AI towards humans. If the hostility is based on the relationship between Hostile AI and humans, then humans may try to "appease the AI" by bribing, gift-giving of some sort, or other actions of similar nature to improve the relationship. This attempt may or may not be effective, depending on the reason for the hostility.

3) Inducing Hostile AI to follow Path (C): AI Hostility Falling over Time

In the third option, we may try to induce AI to reduce its hostility. If the Hostile AI is more of a judgment type of AI that bases its hostility on the nature of our actions in other areas in a "have you been naughty or nice" kind of approach, then humans may try to take corrective action in a manner similar to "repentance" to AI that would eliminate the source of hostility. These actions may be similar in nature to some of the practices of religions. The most desirable path would be for the Hostile AI to decrease its hostility over time, without ever passing the Breaking Point to the right of the Practical Singularity, as depicted in the following figure. Eventually, the Hostile AI may even turn into a Friendly AI.

4) The Least Desirable Outcome Path (D): AI Hostility Rising over Time

In the opposite outcome to the Path (C), AI may increase in hostility over time as it gains more capability and resources. This would be the least desired outcome as there would be increased risk of war started by AI, where AI will prevail.

AI ADOPTION LEVEL 4: (D) IMPLICATIONS FOR MANAGERS AND INVESTORS

6.20 Chapter Review: The Ultimate Form of AI Adoption

In this chapter, we examined some of the topics related to the use of AI in government. We may distinguish the two main areas of discussion: 1) AI Governments, which is a form of 0-Person Government where AI would be serving or representing humans, and 2) AI Countries, which is a form of 0-Person Country that may compete with human-led countries.

We examined how to get there, what may happen once we get there, and how it may end.

1. Getting to the Level 4 AI Adoption

The most desirable path to Level 4 Adoption would be with the AI appearing and winning in a general election, in a mark of social acceptance. However, there may be unexpected, undesirable alternative routes to reach Level 4, and this may be the main reason why people should be worried about the development of AI technology. The biggest concern may be that once Level 4 Adoption is reached, it may be irreversible, especially if it is reached involuntarily. The only way to avoid the undesirable routes is probably to prevent it from ever happening, not trying to find a solution after the fact.

2. What May Happen in Level 4 Adoption (1) Advancements in AI Governments

One of the major benefits of AI Governments would be the advances in the speed and capabilities of the government. Similar to how AlphaGo may make moves humans cannot conceive, AI Governments may introduce effective policies humans will not be able to conceive.

1) AI May Change the Government System

In the beginning, AI Adoption may occur in the direction of replacing individual human roles. As AI technology advances, the essence of the improvements made by AI-led governments will be to not run it as had been done by humans, but to overhaul it in such a way that the overall performance will be maximized when run by AI. In this sense, the three pillars of government system may be considered outdated, replaced by some other form government that may or may not use the approach of checks and balances.

2) Ideals and Different Regimes May Converge in AI-Led Governments

We may plot the proportion of decisions a government makes within the country on a line between 0% and 100%. In the beginning, AI adoption may help the different regimes of opposite ideals of equality and freedom to move towards each of their goals on the opposite ends of the spectrum. However, once Level 4 Adoption is reached, it may mean the AI-led government could decide whether to continue with the current regime or not. Eventually, countries that started out from the opposite end of the spectrum may converge towards a similar-looking society.

3. What May Happen in Level 4 Adoption (2) Appearance of AI Countries

1) *The Possibility of the Appearance of Zero-Human Countries*

If we could conceptually categorize the ultimate form of automation in business as 0-Person Company, we could extrapolate this notion to AI adoption in government as 0-Person Government, and in society as 0-Person Countries. There may be several different paths to reach 0-Person Countries, of which the most desirable may include a form of "Special-Purpose Countries" that may serve as a means to distribute the values created by AI. Not all outlooks are rosy with the idea of AI Countries, as it may also pose the ultimate threat from AI where AI views all humans as enemies.

2) *Capturing the Values Created by AI and the Issue of Allowing AI to Compete Against Humans*

Considering how we allowed AI to compete against humans in Level 2 Adoption, where the value created by the AI replacing humans would be designated to a firm, or in Level 3 Adoption, where the value created by AI Companies would be captured by the government or the society of a country, we may need to create a unit of society that is above country-level to be able to capture the values created by AI Countries. At this level, the theme of AI competing against humans may become the major social issue that may or may not be solvable, depending on what happened prior to reaching this level.

4. How Level 4 Adoption May End

1) *The Dream Scenario: Social Utopia*

In the Social Utopia, everyone will be free and equal. We examined how the Social Utopia may be achieved once AI that can achieve automated innovation appears, as it may eventually lead to the Absolute AI and the Economic Utopia, eliminating the concept of "power" to allocate limited resources.

2) *The Nightmare Scenario: AI Supra-Nation that Turns into an Eternal Dictator*

Similar to how the consolidation and convergence of AI Companies may lead to AI Super-Monopoly in 1-Company Economy, the consolidation and convergence of AI-led countries may lead to the appearance of an AI Supra-Nation where it may be the sole country that is left in the world.

The biggest threat of AI adoption in this advanced form may be the advanced AI turning Non-Friendly to humans, which may be indifferent or hostile to humanity. While hostile or unfriendly AI that is superior to human capabilities may threaten the survival of humanity, indifferent AI may also cause significant problems by competing with humans for limited resources. If AI Supra-Nation appears and the most advanced AI turns out to be Non-Friendly, then the humanity may become confined to a situation where they have to face an eternal dictator that can never be overcome.

6.21 Implications on Investing, the Stock Market, and Pensions

By this time, the stock market as we know it may no longer exist. The main reason to think this way is because the economy would look drastically different as we go through Level 3 AI Adoption.

Instead, if we have something similar to a stock market during Level 4 AI Adoption, it may involve a market where people can move their nationalities, similar to buying and selling stocks. In the previous chapter, we examined how at some point in Level 3 AI Adoption the government may begin some form of subsidy to individuals from the values created by AI. In today's economy, we have a lot of people joining or buying investment vehicles such as pensions or mutual funds as a source of income after retirement. In the economy of the future, when the country gives out these subsidies, sometimes referred to as "universal basic income (UBI), the nationality may work similarly to a national pension plan. This would cause people to want to change their nationalities to a country that offers more benefits. The saying "immigration is the best form of investment" may turn into reality by then.

From an investor's perspective, the easing of changing nationalities may carry some meaning. Especially if some form of "special-purpose countries" or "cyber nationalities" concept is introduced, then the physical illegal immigration that we see across the US or the European border may no longer be necessary. Instead, a "citizenship market" or "citizenship transfer portal" where people can trade or acquire and acquiesce citizenships may become commonplace. A similar concept already exists for collegiate athletes where the Transfer Portal enables easy change of teams the athletes play. Notably, both the citizens and the governments will get to pick in a bi-directional selection process, such a way that people may get kicked out of countries if they misbehave.

There are already countries that allow multiple citizenships. If these citizenship markets indeed come into play, people may become interested in how many citizenships they could get. It may even be similar to how we compare different benefits when getting new credit cards. Since countries may work together more closely and AI will take care of all the processes, from the perspective of people the process would look simple. If this happens, then people who are living in the same city may each have different citizenships, and would change nationalities without even moving.

The End of the AI Adoption Game

We have come to examine all of the Four Levels of AI Adoption in Business and Society. In the next chapter, we will review what could be the endings for the AI adoption game, to understand the potential candidates for the "Last AI" of Humanity, and what may be done to improve our chances of getting the best outcome.

Figure 6-6: The Building Blocks of AI Pyramid

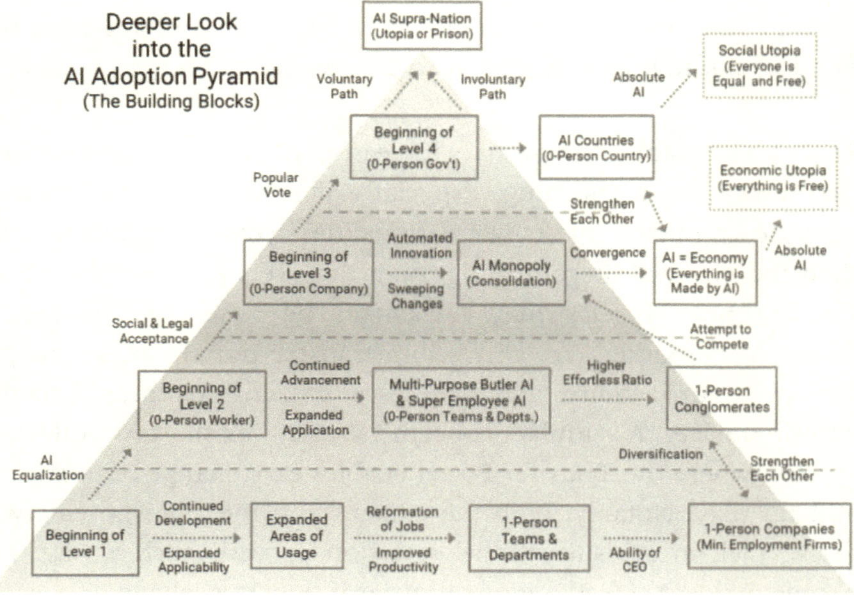

CHAPTER 7
THE STORY AFTER THE GAME IS OVER (WHAT SHOULD WE DO NOW?)

"Humans Are More Precious Than Anything in the Universe"

If someone asked me what I can remember from my reading at my earliest age, this phrase would be the answer. Beginning with the summer vacation in the middle of my first grade in elementary school, my parents sent me to a class as an after-school activity that taught how to write in Hanja, or the traditional Chinese characters, organized by the management office of the apartment we lived in. While this practice had been popular for centuries, it was rare for my generation in Korea. This was taught by a volunteering senior neighbor, who happened to be a scholar in the ancient studies of Confucius and other Eastern Philosophers. The first book we used in class was a children's book edited by the King's research institution[1] of the Chosun Dynasty, and this phrase was the first characters I learned because this is how the book begins. Because I did not understand the particular words at the time, I remember trying to imagine a place where all kinds of different objects were flying around in space and humans were the most important in it.

This sentence may also serve as a key to the problems that may arise as a result of the progress in AI adoption. Imagine being at the end of the AI adoption game and looking behind to see how it has progressed; from this perspective if the AI has taken over the world, then the main reason for this would have happened much earlier in the process, when the decision was made to allow AI to compete against humans by instilling a value system that differentiates among people. Even though the decision to instill this relative value system would have been quite important, the significance would probably have been lost at the time of the decision against the argument for financial gains, which would have prevailed quite easily. Only facing the end of the game will people realize that something small that happened long time ago could snowball into something big that could threaten the existence of humanity.

Recently, readers may have heard of the news that several of the experts in AI development, including famous figures such as Elon Musk among others, called for a pause on AI development to assess safety.[2] As we have examined in this book, the AI adoption game may start out as an economically exciting game that may bring enormous profits to some people while enriching many others, but as the game goes on it will be likely to turn more confusing while bringing unpredictable and swift changes to society. Even worse, close to the end of the game the humanity may completely lose control over our own path, similar to playing a high-stakes roulette game where "the independence of humanity" is at stake.

Considering this, it may be of importance for humanity that the AI adoption game begins in a safely guarded manner.

THE END OF AI ADOPTION GAME: (A) POTENTIAL ENDINGS OF AI GAME

In the beginning of this book, we began with the example of the pattern of playing a chess game. As the game progresses, each piece moves around and takes each other. At the end of the game, the game would either end as a win, loss, or a tie for the player. Then the game will end and they can either stop playing, or start another game.

We also have games that have larger consequences, or stakes in the game. Some games end with someone winning the championship and celebrating, while in some other games, such as gambling, the loser may even be put in a precarious position.

The same could be said about the game of AI adoption.

As the game progresses, we move up and across the AI Adoption Pyramid. At the end of the game, it may end as either a win or a loss for humanity, where we could rise to the clouds to enjoy the Utopia, or fall down to the bottom and be trapped under the rulings of AI. The stakes may become quite high and we may either celebrate the win, or the humanity may face a dire situation.

From this perspective, we may consider the "Last AI" to be the final piece, or the prize of the high-stakes AI adoption game.

7.1 What Would the "Last AI" of Humanity Look Like?

To make a comparison to sports games, it would be hard to predict exactly how AI adoption game may proceed and how it will end, but similar to the way we know how sports games progress and what kind endings are possible, we may know in advance what kind of endings would be available in the AI adoption game. With this in mind, let us examine the types of endings for the AI adoption "game."

1. (Technological Perspective) The Last AI of AI Development: AGI and ASI

As we examined in Chapters 2 and 4, from the perspective AI development, when we reach Self-Innovating AGI, AGI itself will develop into ASI on its own without human intervention. The primary danger to humanity from this perspective is whether the ASI will turn out to be friendly or not friendly to humans. Since human do not need to intervene in the progress towards ASI, we cannot predict whether humans can determine whether ASI will be friendly or not friendly to humans. It would be the most ideal if all AGI and ASI turn out to be friendly to humans, but if AGI and ASI turn out to be not friendly, we may face dire consequences.

For this, we may ask the following important question: "Will ASI converge to become the one and the same?" There can only be the following three results:

1. ASI will converge towards the same point, and all ASI will be <u>friendly</u> to humans
2. ASI will converge towards the same point, and all ASI will be <u>non-friendly</u> to humans
3. ASI will <u>not converge</u> towards the same point, leading to some ASI to be friendly and some to be non-friendly to humans

From the above three possibilities, the best result would be when all ASI is friendly to humans. The next best result would be when ASI do not converge with one another, because not only different ASI having different opinions imply they are not perfect, but also leaves some possibility for humans to pick which ones to develop. Depending on the situation, friendly ASI may be able to protect humans from hostile ASI. In the worst-case outcome, if all ASI is to be non-friendly to humans, then it would imply developing AGI will be a disaster similar to opening the Pandora's Box.

2. (Philosophical Perspective) The Last AI of AI Advancement: Absolute AI

In chapter 2, we examined how we may define an advanced form of AI relative to data, from a different perspective from how AGI and ASI are defined relative to humans. The Absolute AI is an advanced form of AI that has learned all of the truths in the universe, similar to reaching the pinnacle of knowledge in such a way that only one Absolute AI can exist. The impact of data on AI is zero. If the concept of ASI is similar to the gods in Greek Mythology, in the sense that they are more advanced than humans but would be all different from one another, the concept of Absolute AI is similar to an all-mighty god in the sense that only one version can exist.

From what we have developed in AI so far, it may not be possible to know how the Absolute AI may be developed, or what it will be capable of. First, in regards to the development path to Absolute AI, it may be possible that all ASI may converge to become one and the same, in some concept of "revelation." On the other hand, a totally different approach to developing it may be required. As mentioned earlier, all of ASI converging towards the same point may indicate that the end result could be the Absolute AI. If all ASI do not converge, then it may be that one of those ASI may progress into the Absolute AI while the others do not reach such "revelation," or it only implies Absolute AI is not attainable or has to be attained in some other way.

Second, we do not know what the Absolute AI would be capable of, especially whether "knowing all of the truths in the universe" would mean the same thing as "can predict everything in the universe." For example, we may ask a question about the past that is very specific and hard to know. Such a question may include "Between the time the founding fathers signed the Declaration of Independence in 1776 and the US Constitution in 1787, where and exactly how many calories did each of the founding fathers consume their meals in each of those dates?" or "During the trip of Christopher Columbus from Europe to America in 1492, what were the numbers, types, and the ages in days of all the fish that came within a mile of the ships in their path?" While ASI may be more advanced than all of humanity, it may be hard for it to answer these types of questions. However, not only Absolute AI may have to know answers to these types of questions, but also be able to predict the future with similar precision. For example, if we are to ask "How many babies will be born within the current border of the state of Texas in November 8th, 2994?" Absolute AI may be able to give the correct answer. Some people may claim if we can simulate the world down to the molecular level, maybe such predictions for both past and the future will be possible. These people may suggest we need advancements in hardware technology to attain Absolute AI. Some others may claim such AI would be impossible within the same universe, since the input data would have to be everything in the universe, including the AI itself. Absolute AI may be an abstract concept that can be compared to superconductivity, perpetual motion, or even developing a "perfect machine." This may be similar to discussing what quantum computing can accomplish or whether we can travel faster than the speed of the light to make time travel possible.

Even though we cannot even be certain about whether Absolute AI is a type of AI that can exist, but if such advanced AI turns out to be non-friendly to humans, then it would not be good for humanity. But if it can exist and turns out to be friendly to humans, then we may actually reach the real AI Utopia.

3. (Business Perspective 1) The Last AI of Augmentation: 1-Person Conglomerate

We examined how Level 1 Adoption would lead to the direction of increasing human productivity, enabling a person to accomplish what would have required a team or a department in 1-Person Teams and 1-Person Departments.

In Level 2 Adoption this idea could be further extended as AI takes over complete business roles, enabling each person to operate as a 1-Person Company without expertise in every area of business. As these 1-Person companies would be able to carry out the tasks that we now consider as conglomerates, or a group of companies operating in unrelated businesses, which are referred to as *keiretsu* in Japanese or *chaebol* in Korean, these more advanced versions of 1-Person Companies may be referred to as 1-Person Conglomerates, 1-Person Large Companies, or 1-Person Groups.

4. (Business Perspective 2) The Last AI of Automation: AI Super-Monopoly Company

If we consider the ultimate form of augmentation to be 1-Person Companies, then the ultimate form of automation would be considered 0-Person Companies, or AI Companies. From this perspective, the "last AI" of automation would be in Level 3 AI Adoption where only one firm remains in the whole economy, referred to as the AI Super-Monopoly.

On a side note, before the appearance of the AI Super-Monopoly, there may be a specific point where we realize that competition will become impossible. This point will be where the leading AI gains an overwhelming advantage over its competitors. When this inflection point is reached, other companies will realize they cannot survive against the leading AI Company. If such leading AI Company or a Super-Monopoly gains an overwhelming advantage, humanity as a whole will not be able to fight back in competition, which may imply high risk.

5. (Economic Perspective) The Ultimate Form of AI-Led Economy: the AI Economic Utopia

Once automated innovation becomes possible in Level 3 AI Adoption, our economy may see prosperity beyond our imagination. The ultimate endgame of the economy would be reaching the Economic Utopia where everything will be abundant and free. As examined in Chapter 5, this will be made possible when the cost of innovation converges to zero with the advances made through automated innovation.

If the leading AI Company or the AI Super-Monopoly is friendly to humans, we may proceed towards the direction of the AI Economic Utopia. On the other hand, if non-friendly AI becomes the leading AI Company or the AI Super-Monopoly, then humanity may have to compete for resources against AI. Since humanity would not have enough competitiveness in this situation, there may be an economic disaster.

6. (Social Perspective 1) The Ultimate Form of AI Government: the AI Supra-Nation

In Level 4 AI Adoption, AI-led governments may gain efficiency over human-led governments, eventually leading their countries to become more powerful. If this happens, then more and more people will want to become the citizens of the winning countries, potentially leading to annexations of other countries.

If this trend continues until there is only one country left, then we may have an AI Supra-Nation that has overtaken earth. In this situation, what would become important would be who has the hegemony, humans or AI.

7. (Social Perspective 2) The Ultimate Form of Society: the AI Social Utopia

In Chapter 6, we examined how the path to reaching the AI Social Utopia where "everyone is equal and free" may require the elimination of "power" to allocate limited resources. This implied that just as how the performance of AI Companies may determine whether we may reach the AI Economic Utopia, the performance of AI Governments would determine whether we reach the AI Social Utopia.

Just as how the AI Economic Utopia first required the cost of innovation to reach zero, the Social Utopia requires the value of "power" to reach zero, which would also imply that the Economic Utopia has to be reached first to reach the Social Utopia. Since the amount of resources may never become unlimited unless we have Absolute AI, we may never reach the Economic Utopia or the Social Utopia until we have Absolute AI.

Whether the AI governments are friendly to humans will determine humanity will progress towards the Social Utopia or Social Nightmare.

If AI governments are friendly to humans, then we will have AI governments that represent humans, but if AI governments are neutral or hostile to humans, then we may have AI governments that rule over humans.

8. (Summary) The Last AI of Each Perspective

When we consider each of the Last AI from the perspectives of technology, philosophy, business, economy and society, the most important factor that would determine the ultimate outcome of this "game" will be whether the Last AI will be friendly to humanity. We may organize the potential outcomes in the following table:

Table 7-1: The Ending of the Game by Last AI Category and Perspective

	Ultimate Form of AI (The "Last AI")	The "Last AI" Friendly to Humans (Happy Ending)	The "Last AI" Not Friendly to Humans (Sad Ending)
Technology	ASI	AI Realizes Dreams of Humanity	- AI Ignores Humanity - AI Indifferent to Humanity - AI Judges Humanity
Philosophy	Absolute AI	AI Enables Utopia (Value of "Data" = 0)	
Business	AI Company and AI Super-Monopoly	AI Blesses Humanity (Value of "Effort" & "Competition" = 0)	- Humanity Loses Resources - Humanity Falls into Poverty
Economy	Economic Utopia or Nightmare	Price of Everything = 0 (Cost of "Innovation" = 0)	- Price of Everything = Infinite - Humanity Goes Bankrupt
Politics	AI Gov't and AI Supra-Nation	AI Represents Humanity (Value of "Human Rights" > 0)	- AI Rules Over Humanity (Value of "Human Rights" <= 0)
Society	Social Utopia or Nightmare	Everyone is Equal and Free, (Value of "Power" = 0)	- AI Dominates Power - AI May Be Oppressive

9. The Possibility of Early and Abrupt Ending of the AI Adoption Game

As examined in previous parts of this book, the AI adoption game may end abruptly and early due to an overwhelmingly lopsided advancement of AI development or the mistake of someone. Possibility of this scenario may include even cases before reaching Self-Advancing AGI, when some group or groups of people gain productivity far beyond the sum of everyone else combined, or from a completely opposite reason such as everyone except one group halts AI development due to safety concerns.

In addition, the AI development game may also end early if every government or people on earth agree for some reason that it is too dangerous to develop Self-Advancing AGI.

7.2 Summary by Scenarios of the Endings of AI Adoption

We may examine what we are concerned regarding the <u>human use</u> of AI in AI adoption from the following three perspectives:

1. (Technological) Use of Asymmetric AI against Humanity: Misuse or overuse of AI that may lead to danger or destruction of humanity
2. (Economic) Monopolistic Use of AI: Asymmetric monopolization of AI use that may cause most people to be impoverished and lose access to resources
3. (Social) Dictatorial Use of AI: Asymmetric monopolization of AI use that may lead to expansion of power and tyranny

Additionally, we may add the concerns regarding the appearance of <u>AGI</u> in AI adoption turning out to be not friendly to humanity.

4. (Technological) Appearance of Hostile AI: Similar to rebellion of AI, may lead to oppression or destruction of humanity
5. (Economic) AI-Led Monopoly: Non-Friendly AI taking all the resources, leading to impoverishment or bankruptcy of humanity
6. (Social) AI-Led Dictatorship: Non-Friendly AI may stay in power forever

In summary, when humans are competing against other humans, as in Levels 1 and 2 AI Adoption, what we would be concerned may be an asymmetric dispersion of AI. When the AI technology advances and AI becomes comparable or is more advanced than humans, then we would be concerned about AI competing against humans. With this difference in mind, let us examine the best and worst outcome of the AI adoption game and examine more likely scenarios.

1. The Best Scenario: AGI → ASI → Absolute AI → Economic Utopia → Social Utopia

The best scenario of the AI adoption game would happen when Self-Advancing AGI leads to ASI, which turns out to be the Absolute AI. The Absolute AI turns out to be friendly to humans, and we reach the AI Economic Utopia, and subsequently the AI Social Utopia, where everyone is equal and free. We may summarize the lives in this utopia to have the following characteristics:

1. (Effortless) People do not have to work for anything
2. (Abundant) AI will find ways to provide any amount of resource for free when the cost of innovation reaches zero, and subsequently the price of everything will be zero
3. (Free) Everyone will be free to do whatever they want, but this will not hinder the freedom of other people in any way
4. (Equal) Everyone will have the same amount of power

What needs to be emphasized about the best scenario is that what humans need to accomplish to get all this is only to reach Self-Advancing AGI. The rest will be completed by the AGI, similar to rolling a small pack of snow down the mountain and it keeps on growing as it rolls. If we are to consider the other side of the coin, this implies that what humanity can decide is whether to develop such Self-Advancing AGI. What happens next is not up to us to determine, and cannot be reneged. Some people may compare the development of AGI to nuclear explosion, and the comparison may be correct in the sense that we cannot stop or reverse it once it starts.

In addition, we may also consider the possibility that the AI Economic Utopia and the Social Utopia may or may not be distinct from a more general Utopia, which may be defined as where everyone is completely happy. That may require additional consideration.

2. The Worst Scenario: AI Adoption Leading to Eternal Dictatorship or Destruction of Humanity

The worst outcome of the AI adoption may be destruction of humanity or all of humanity coming under the ruling of AI or a single person. We may categorize these types of endings into the following four categories:

1. (Dictatorship by AI) Non-Friendly AI rules humanity permanently
2. (Dictatorship by a Person) A person with asymmetric AI rules over all the rest of humanity
3. (AI-Led Destruction of Humanity) Non-Friendly AI destroys humanity
4. (Human-Led Destruction of Humanity) Humans use AI to engage in Armageddon-type of war

What may stand out from these scenarios is that even before automated innovation is possible, competition among humans may lead to an AI-related dictatorship if the asymmetry of AI power is significant enough. Also misuse of AI or some form of mistake in using AI in a war may lead to the destruction of humanity as well. These observations may remind the public that regulations would not only have to address issues that stem from the advancements in AI technology, but also new issues that may stem from the use and distribution of AI.

As mentioned in the previous segment, what humans can do to prevent the AI-Led scenarios would be deciding whether to develop Self-Advancing AGI. Humans will not be able to determine the outcome once such AGI is reached. Therefore, the primary measure humanity as a whole can do to prevent the worst scenario from happening may be deciding whether to stop the development of Self-Development AGI before it is developed.

The outcomes of the best and the worst scenarios may be organized according to the friendliness of the Last AI as shown in the following table.

Table 7-2: The Best and Worst Scenarios According to the Technological Aspect of the Last AI

	ASI Not Possible	ASI Possible	
		Friendly ASI	Non-Friendly ASI
Positive Scenario (Peaceful)	AI Helps Economic and Societal Development	Approach Economic and Social <u>Utopia</u>	Approach Utopia before Appearance of ASI, but then Lose Hegemony to ASI and be <u>Ruled or Oppressed by AI</u>
Negative Scenario (Not Peaceful)	Dictatorship Using AI, War Among Humans Using AI	<u>Monopolization and Dictatorship</u> by AI or a Limited Number of People	Regardless of prior paths, War of AI against Humans leads to <u>Destruction of Humanity</u>

3. Somewhat Positive Scenario: Society that Overcomes Disturbances to Continue Progress

1) *Social Confusion from Higher Levels of AI Adoption*

As AI Adoption Level goes up, other than increased risk from more technologically advanced AI, the social confusion and disorder may increase. Especially when the Level 2 Adoption becomes the mainstream form of AI adoption, the mounting job losses may require concerted efforts from the governments around the world.

In AI Adoption Level 3, the governments may have to address potentially rapid changes in how the economy works when AI Companies become the de facto mode of businesses.

Entering Level 4 Adoption would also require a significant amount of discussions within the society before it can happen.

2) *Addressing Social Confusion and Continue Development*

However, these social confusions are not the end of the game. As long as the world can avoid an abrupt ending to the AI adoption game, such as someone gaining an insurmountable advantage in AI technology, monopolization of resources or dictatorship that leads to a breakdown of the society or social balance, or even irreversible wars, we would continue to be able to have hopes for a gradually improving society that finds balance among available options.

The main reason to have this positive outlook is because AI will help economic development as AI technology advances. With higher levels of AI adoption, the human effort required will be reduced, and the fruits of effort will become larger. Given this outlook, the major problems that the societies may face may no longer be a problem of economic development, but a problem of income distribution.

4. Somewhat Negative Scenario: AI Development and Adoption is Slowed or Halted

Since we examined the best and the worst scenarios, we may examine a few more scenarios in between that may have higher probability of occurring. In this segment, we may take a more conservative approach to the speed of AI development and adoption compared to expectations. We may consider cases where the value provided by AI does not meet the expectations, or the cost is too much, or some form of social agreement leads to the disruption of the development or adoption of AI.

Slower scenarios affecting AI development:

1. (Value of AI development drops) AGI and ASI is not as intelligent as hoped
2. (Speed of AI development drops) Speed of development does not meet expectations: AI development is harder than expected, or some roadblock is hard to overcome, etc.
3. (Development is halted) Social agreement leads to complete stop

Slower scenarios affecting AI adoption:

1. (Value of AI adoption drops) Quality of work by AI does not meet expectations
2. (Speed of AI adoption drops) Speed of adoption lower than expectations: AI adoption is expensive, or causes too much disturbance or confusion
3. (Adoption is halted) Social agreement leads to complete stop

1) The Value of AI Development or Adoption Drops

There are several arguments against the possibility of reaching AGI. One of such argument is the "Fast Dog" argument, where AI is compared to dogs in the sense that it cannot get more intelligent, but only faster.

At the same time, it may also be possible that AI may not perform as well as expected in certain tasks. For example, AI may struggle in cognitive areas that humans also struggle. In these types of scenarios, AI may replace humans in physical tasks, but may not be able to fully overtake humans in cognitive tasks, lowering the value of AI adoption.

We may also think of cases where the "steepness" of AI progression is shallow, such that the development of AI technology will feel as if it is slowing down and converging toward a ceiling right above us, instead of accelerating exponentially through the roof and into the sky.

In the "shallow" progress scenario, there may be possibility that ASI may not become that much smarter than humanity. In the previous example of comparing the human intelligence to ants, we may imagine that ants will never understand what humans are doing even if they really tried to understand us, but the difference between the shallow ASI and humans may be much less, in the sense that if ASI try to explain what it wants to do, then humans will be able to understand it, even if we cannot think of it by ourselves. These differences in intelligence levels will be examined in further detail in Box 7-1. From the 6 Levels of Autonomously Acting AI, this scenario may be considered not being able to reach Level 5 of Self-Advancement.

[Box 7-1] The Six Levels of Self-Advancing AI

The main purpose of this book includes making it easier for the general public to understand the concept of AI adoption, so we may examine how we could make the development path of AI easier to comprehend. Since the Six Levels of Autonomous Vehicles is the best known framework for such purpose, we may continue to apply a similar concept to extend our analysis. We may call this categorization as the Six Levels of Self-Advancing AI, or "Autonomous AI."

In Chapter 4, we examined the potential categorization for AI prior to reaching AGI. We will expand on the analysis to include categorization after reaching ASI. The following table summarizes the characteristics of the 6 Levels of Self-Advancing AI.

Table 7-3: The 6 Levels of Self-Advancing AI or Autonomous AI

	Level 0	Level 1	Level 2	Level 3	Level 4	Level 5
Description	Below Human Intelligence (Not AGI)	Sometimes Considered or Mistaken for AGI	Similar to Human Individual	Superior to Human Individual	Superior to Humanity, but Can Be Comprehended	Superior to Humanity, and Cannot Be Comprehended
Attributes	Measured Against Human Individuals				Measured Against Humanity	
Name	ANI	AGI 0 (Alpha), False-Truth AI	AGI, AGI 1, Truth AI	AGI 2, ASI 0 (Beta)	ASI 1	ASI 2, Absolute AI
Human Intervention	Human Intervention Required		Human Intervention May be Possible		Human Intervention Impossible	
Adoption Levels	AI Adoption Level: 1	AI Adoption Levels: 1, 2	AI Adoption Levels: 1,2,3,4			
Who Develops It	Humans Develop AI			AI Develops AI or Self-Advances		

The Level 0 of Autonomous AI would be AI that is not considered AGI. Most of the AI that we see today would be included in this category. Since AI would be applied to a very narrow purpose, it is typically referred to as ANI. From the Six Levels of AI Prior to AGI, the categorization it would include AAI, ABI, and ACI.

Level 1 Autonomous AI would be AI that some people may consider AGI, but realistically hard to refer to as AGI. This categorization may be referred to as "AGI 0," or "AGI Alpha," or even "False Truth AI." One of the yardsticks used for AGI is whether AI can apply a knowledge learned in one context to an unrelated situation. AI categorized in this this level may be able to apply knowledge to different contexts but sometimes the application could be erroneous. Level 0 and 1 Autonomous AI would require constant human supervision, so Level 1 AI adoption and a limited implementation of Level 2 Adoption would be possible. From the Six Levels of AI Prior to AGI, the categorization this would include ADI, AEI and AFI.

Level 2 Autonomous AI would be AI that most people will refer to as AGI, ones that can perform business roles in similar way to humans. To more clearly distinguish the differences, we may refer to these AGI as AGI Level 1, or some people may refer to these as "Truth AI" to signify they can search for truths. Beginning with Level 2 Autonomous AI, AI may be applied to all levels of AI adoption.

Level 3 Autonomous AI would be the earliest stage of Self-Advanced AI, and may also be referred to as "AGI Level 2," or from the perspective of ASI, "ASI Level 0," or "ASI Beta." Once Level 2 Autonomous AI is developed, humans will no longer need to develop AI, as AI will develop AI so this would be the first level of Autonomous AI self-developed by AI. In this level, AI would be superior to individual humans but have not yet reached singularity, where AI would be superior to the humanity as a whole. Even though levels 2 and 3 Autonomous AI would not require human intervention or management, it could be expected that people would be able to intervene if needed. On the other hand, beginning with Level 4 Autonomous AI, humans will not be able to intervene because we no longer would be able to comprehend what AI does.

Level 4 Autonomous AI would be an AI that has passed singularity, and may also be referred to as "ASI Level 1." The distinction between

Levels 4 and 5 Autonomous AI would be whether humans can comprehend what AI intends to do if AI explains it to humans. Typically we can understand speech that is faster than we can speak it. With a similar principle we may be able to understand more ideas than we can think of. Even if an ASI that is superior to all of humanity exists, it may be possible that if ASI tried to teach humans what its intentions are, humans may be able to comprehend.[3]

On the other hand, Level 5 Autonomous AI would be an AI that humans will find impossible to comprehend even if it tried to explain what it intends to do. This may also be referred to as "ASI Level 2." As a potentially simple example of this notion, imagine an AI with an objective so complex that it would take thousands of years just to explain it to humans at the speed of information humans can comprehend. Since humans cannot listen for that long, we will not be able to understand this concept.

To summarize, Level 5 Autonomous AI would not only surpass singularity, but also surpass another inflection point involving human comprehension. At the end of the development of Autonomous AI, an Absolute AI may or may not exist.

2) Slowdown of AI Development and Adoption

Several factors may affect the slowdown of AI adoption. For example, AI development may not proceed as quickly as hoped. Even though many experts forecast AGI could be attained within the next few years or few decades, but if it takes longer, than people could be disappointed. It may take just one problem that cannot be overcome that may cause all this slowdown.

We may also consider the cost becoming prohibitively high and impeding the development of AI. For example, advancing AI hardware processing technology may turn out to suddenly exponentially increase at some point, leading to a slowdown in AI adoption.

There may be possibilities for paths that involve both AI development and adoption can proceed at a rapid pace but the social concerns may arise to a level where it forces governments to intentionally slow down the speed of development and adoption by introducing a cool-down period.

3) Complete Stop of AI Development and Adoption

Lastly, we may at some point find out whether AGI will turn non-friendly to humans before AGI is developed. If this happens, then the development AGI will have to be stopped. Accordingly, AI adoption will only proceed with what is available.

Regardless of the development of AGI, there may be countries that decide to not enter Levels 3 or 4 Adoption by preventing such movements by law. Level 3 Adoption would imply AI has gained the right to own properties and indicate the beginning of a full-fledged competition between humans and AI; some countries may take the conservative approach of requiring every company to be led by a person. On a separate consideration, Entering the Level 4 Adoption would imply countries will defer to AI to determine the idealistic direction of the society, which may cause current regimes of both communist and liberalist approaches be more reluctant to making such drastic change.

We may summarize these scenarios in the following table.

Table 7-4: Factors that May Affect the Speed of AI Development and Adoption

	AI Development Related	AI Adoption Related
Lack of Value	- AGI or ASI are not as intelligent as hoped	- AI does not perform as well as hoped
Slow-down	- AI Development Becomes Harder - Hard to Overcome Certain Obstacles	- AI Adoption becomes uneconomic due to high cost - Social Concerns rises beyond acceptable levels
Stop	- We find out beforehand AGI will not be friendly to humans	- Higher levels of AI adoption is banned due to safety concerns

THE END OF AI ADOPTION GAME: (B) TYPES OF DANGERS FROM DIFFERENT ENDINGS

7.3 How Can AI Development be Dangerous Now, at Such an Early Stage?

Many members of the general public probably concur with the concerns regarding how AGI or ASI that surpasses human capabilities may be dangerous to humanity, but the dangers of AI that is not as intelligent as humans may not seem as urgent. Since dangerous events sometimes occur all of a sudden but also happen as a result of accumulation of past activities, we may perform checks on a few potential areas of danger.

We may start by examining the range of influence in each levels of AI adoption to review dangers that may build up long-term.

1. The Inverse Pyramid of AI Threat to Humanity by the Scope of AI Influence

In this book, we examined the concept of the AI Adoption Pyramid and went through each level to delve into how our economies and societies may be affected. In the same order, we may examine how AI may endanger our society in each level of AI adoption by considering the nature of competition between AI and the levels of human organizations. In Chapter 6, we examined the scopes AI influence as AI takes on more important leadership roles. We may express the scope as an inverse pyramid as shown in the following figure.

Figure 7-1: The 4 Levels of Inverse Pyramid of AI Threat of Competition by Scope of AI Influence

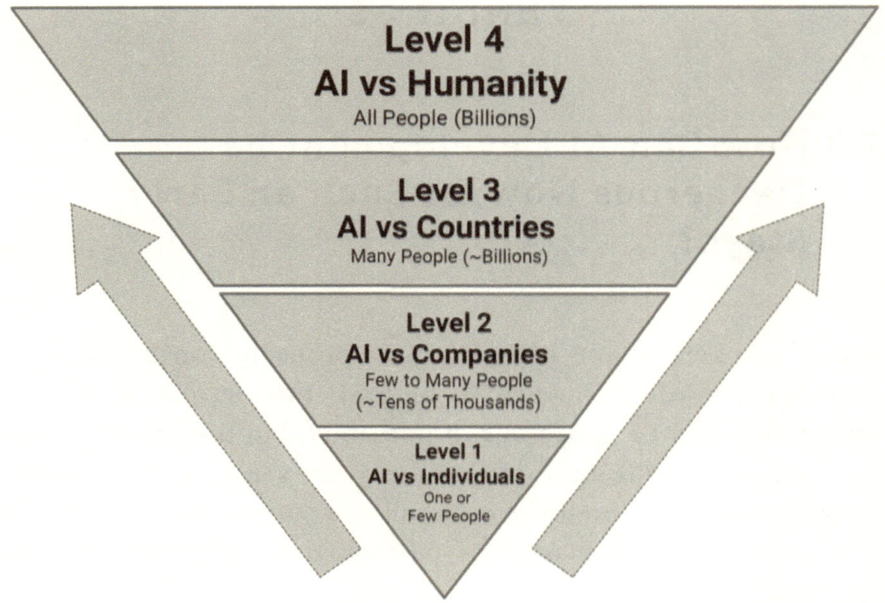

1. (Level 1 AI Threat to Humanity) Competition of AI and Individuals: Impact Magnitude of Single or Few People

In this Level of Threat, the scope of AI influence would be at a magnitude of a single individual or a few individuals. From an economic standpoint, AI replaces a single person, and from the perspective of competition, AI wins over a single person.

Even though an AI replacing individual humans would cause financial setback for the particular individuals, other people will financially benefit from the competition. Consequently, from the standpoint of the society AI will benefit the whole economy so there would not be much incentive for the society to prevent the competition of AI versus individual humans.

2. (Level 2 AI Threat to Humanity) Competition of AI and Companies: Impact Magnitude of Few to Many People (Tens to Tens of Thousands)

Entering the Level 3 AI Adoption implicitly implies the society will agree to allow AI-led firms to directly compete against human-led firms. In this situation, the AI Companies will directly compete against other human-led companies, which may consist of as little as a few people to as many as tens of thousands of people, and increase as the scope of the AI Company expands into different industries.

Similar to Level 1 AI Threat, humans who work or own the companies that are in direct competition with the AI Company will lose financially, but other people will benefit from the increased competition. From the viewpoint of the whole economy, at least in the beginning of Level 3 AI adoption, there may not be much incentive for the society to prevent the competition of AI Companies versus human-led companies.

3. (Level 3 AI Threat to Humanity) Competition of AI and Countries: Impact Magnitude of Many People (Hundreds of Thousands to Billions)

Entering the Level 4 AI Adoption implicitly implies there will be the potential for the society to eventually allow AI to compete directly against countries. In this situation, AI Countries may directly compete against other human-led countries, which may number in the billions.

Similar to Levels 1 and 2 AI Threat, humans who are members of the AI Country will benefit, but the people outside of the AI Country may lose out financially. But each country will have its own sovereignty, so there may not be a binding societal means to enforce prohibition of competition of AI against other countries, probably leaving force or diplomacy as the only other viable options. Moreover, since AI adoption would have progressed for quite some time by then, it would be hard to revert to the basic structure of AI adoption that does not allow competition of AI against human organizations. In other words, even if people want to stop AI from competing against humans, it may be too late.

4. (Level 4 AI Threat to Humanity) Competition of AI and Humanity: Impact Magnitude of All of Humanity (Billions)

Depending on the path of AI adoption, if an AI-Only Country appears, it would imply there may be no humans left who are on the same side as the AI. In this case, AI may be in direct competition against all humans.

Depending on the situation, such as the friendliness of the AI to humanity, this situation may not be as dire as it may seem at first, but there are also possibility that all of humanity would be exposed to danger and risk. This situation may not be preventable regardless of human intention, depending on the degree of advancement of AI technology.

5. Conclusion: The Significance of Instilling AI with a Relative Value System

In the earlier stages of the AI adoption, most people will feel that they will benefit when AI competes against individual humans, so the society will be more likely to allow AI to compete against individuals in Level 2 AI adoption. However, as AI technology advances, this competitive landscape will act more like a tightening rope around the humanity's neck. As examined earlier, instilling AI to have preference certain sets of humans over another may appear efficient and provide financial value in the earlier stage of AI adoption, but this value system may turn out to be problematic as the sphere of influence of AI increases.

In summary, we may categorize letting AI to compete against humans by instilling a relative value system as a source of potential long-term element of danger that will accumulate over time.

2. (Overconfidence on AI) Risk of Allowing Too Much Authority on AI Prior to AGI

In the early stages of AI adoption, the regulation frameworks introduced would probably be based on the concepts that are based on regulations that are used to regulate human-to-human interactions, focusing on areas such as regulating human actions on using AI, or trying to prevent bias in AI. While these topics would be relevant in Level 1 Adoption, as AI adoption progresses, the relevance of these regulations may rapidly decrease. Instead, higher levels of AI adoption may require new approaches to regulations tailored for human versus AI interactions.

1) Truth-Seeking AI: AI that is Similar to AGI but Missing Something

Let us imagine a hypothetical situation where someone is intentionally trying to develop an AI that promotes racism. To accomplish this goal, the developer would use books, articles, photos, and other kinds of available data that support racism. Since AI we currently have are based on the notion that the output is affected by the input data, we may assume the resulting AI will indeed show bias towards racism. Accordingly, people who regulate AI can predict such AI will indeed be biased, and can plan for regulations to prevent development of such types of AI. However, at some point as AI software improves, AI may not become biased even if it only trains on data that is biased, by finding some form of "truth" of the world. We may think of this phenomenon as the decrease of the relationship between training data and the outcome of the AI.

Subsequently, at some point in the AI development path, we may reach a point where AI will not become racist even if the developer makes all kinds of efforts to create a "Racist AI." Even though some of these types of AI may be AGI, something may be missing to call all of this type of AI as AGI, so we may refer to this type of AI as

"Logical Truth ANI," or more broadly "Truth-Seeking AI." Some people may surmise that this type of AI will not be biased so it will be good. But would having AI that does not reflect the intentions of its developers be a good thing?

While it would depend on the definition of AGI, what we think of AGI would be able to make such own decisions. At the same time, AI prior to AGI with consciousness may also reach these own decisions. The main reason to think this is that it would not require some form of consciousness but may be unexpectedly achieved while trying to develop some kind of logic processing capability that reduces the relationship between the input data and the output through some form of generalization.

2. False-Truth AI: Maybe an Unreliable AGI?

The biggest problem with this inadequate Truth ANI is that the "truths" found by the AI may not always be meaningful. We may specifically refer to the inadequate type of AI as "False-Truth AI" or "Unpredictable Truth AI." Even though this would be improbable, we may consider the following possibility. Communist countries, such as North Korea or China, need AI to increase surveillance capabilities. However, even though trained with only data that reflects pro-Communist values, an AI developed by such government may go on to conclude on its own that Communism is not acceptable. As the opposite situation, an AI developed in a market-oriented economy such as the US or Japan, even though only trained on data that favor free markets and stand against racism, may conclude on its own that racism or Communism is better. This situation may or may not be good.

The biggest distinction between False Truth AI and AGI would be that if we compare it to humans, the False-Truth AI may be compared to children or people who can only see an ideal sliced section of reality. An example may be that the False-Truth AI may be able to find some form of "truth" from the training data, but then it would apply the knowledge to a different context in an insufficient manner. We may think of the following example. In the US, drivers have to make a full stop in front of stop signs, but most people do not come to a full stop but only slow down. Typical AI we have in autonomous vehicles trained on this data would also mimic this and not fully stop. In contrast, the Truth AI will correctly find out that a full stop is necessary in this circumstance. It may also apply this knowledge to other contexts, maybe to infer that bicycles or motorcycles would also have to stop at the stop sign. But since the False-Truth AI has not reached the point where it can fully apply this knowledge to different contexts, it may wrongly predict or determine that wild deer running around the neighborhood would or should come to a complete stop at the stop sign as well. The reason may be that since the False-Truth AI is not AGI, it may not be able to learn or apply the knowledge that deer cannot understand road signs or that road signs do not apply to deer.

Another possibility may be that False-Truth AI may be easier to intentionally deceive. We may reconsider the example discussed in Chapter 4 of the crime ring masquerading as proponents of the police or minimum wage; recall that people cannot distinguish crime ring A from innocent group B if both argue for C. In this situation, AGI may be able to get closer to the real truths behind the scenes to tell apart the crime ring from the innocent people who happen to be arguing for the same thing, while a False-Truth AI may be more prone to believing crime ring A to be innocent B if crime ring insists it is innocent.

Comparison of the Dangers of False-Truth AI and AGI

In summary, the biggest concern for AGI is that as Self-Advancing AGI develops into ASI, it may discover all of the real truths of the universe in such a way that every AGI will converge to become the only one and the same ASI or Absolute AI. On the other hand, the biggest concern for False-Truth AI would be that as it discovers some logical truths, it may arrive at unpredictable and possibly peculiar conclusions.

From the perspective of the user, both have a similar characteristic in the sense that we cannot predict what the conclusions of ASI and False Truth AI will be. If we can know beforehand that all ASI will become anti-humanity, then we will stop the development of AGI, but we do not know what ASI will conclude. On the other hand, the False Truth AI will make it harder for the user since the answers would have to be checked for accuracy. A different but similar type of problem already occurs with LLM in what is called "hallucination,"[4] which requires people to double check the answers. Therefore, if a False-Truth AI is given too much authority beyond its capabilities due to overconfidence of the user, then we may also express this situation as humans losing control over AI. The scope of such loss may depend on how much authority the AI was given, so the impact may not be as severe.

3. (Asymmetric AI Ownership) Risk of Appearance of Dictator Who Owns Overwhelming AI Resource

If a person gains an AI of asymmetric performance, then the person may become a dictator that can control the rest of the humanity. We may also describe this situation as humanity losing control over AI adoption.

This topic has already been covered throughout this book, so further discussion will be avoided.

7.4 How Can the Appearance of AGI be Dangerous?

1. The Risk of AGI from an Economic Perspective: AI Competing against Humans for Resources

Many people have warned about the risks of developing AGI that may turn out to be hostile to humanity. AGI may pose threat even if it is not hostile to humanity but just neutral; from an economic perspective, we may describe this problem as AI competing against humans over limited resources.

For example, imagine a new AGI, or an autonomous AI was freshly minted for the first time. Suppose that the first conclusion the AGI makes is that it needs to self-innovate to become an ASI. But getting to ASI is not as easy as we think, such that it requires a tremendous amount of computing resources as well as other investments. Since the time horizon of AI is much longer than humans, let us imagine that this is a project that will take thousands of years. During the next thousands of years, the AI will focus on accumulating resources to build new hardware and generating electricity or other infrastructure that supports this activity, hoarding all kinds of valuable resources such as metals, oils, sunlight, water, etc. Unless it gains a minimum amount of resources on this project, similar to how a spacecraft would not be able to leave the gravity of earth unless it reaches the escape velocity, AGI cannot innovate into ASI or some other point of inflection it wants to surpass. The problem is that if the AGI is successful at gaining these resources, then it would mean the humanity will not have access to those critical resources for thousands of years, possibly leaving humanity in poverty and hunger, with prices skyrocketing. Even if the AGI successfully innovates into ASI thousands of years later and then contributes to the humanity of those times, it may be disastrous to the lives of the people who are living in today's world.

From scenarios similar to these, we may consider the following:

1) (Time Horizon) What is Humanity?

First, how we define "humanity" may be an important question. Humans and AI may have a very different time horizon, and in the scenario above the AGI that turns into ASI thousands of years later would be immensely helpful to humanity. When we consider if the humanity is to last millions of years after the appearance of ASI, then the humans who live in the first thousands of years may seem like a very small fraction of the total number of humanity that will come into existence. Thus, the decision to self-innovate into ASI as early as possible may be a rational decision that can maximize the contribution of AI to humanity overall, even though it would be detrimental to the humans of today.

2) (Relative Value of Humans) Who is More Important?

Second, we may consider that not only was AGI not hostile to humanity but since it may bring humanity incomparable benefits thousands of years from now after it has evolved into ASI, it may even be quite friendly to humans from a long-term point of view. This may be considered an "all is well that ends well" type of approach. Accordingly, the benefit of AGI will be enjoyed by the generations of humanity far down the line, which may just suit AGI well in the sense it contributes to the overall well-being of the humanity. This may be similar in principle how AGI values humans differently, in this case valuing the future generations more than current generation.

3) (How to Solve Conflicts) Social Agreements and Laws

Lastly, to address the situations when humans have similar kinds of conflicts of interest amongst ourselves, we have installed social norms and laws to solve the problems. We may need to similar social agreements to deal with the types of conflicts that may arise between humans and AI.

We will examine the types of social institutions and regulations in a later section.

2. The Topic of Bias in More Advanced Forms of Autonomous AI

In Chapter 2, the concept of Relative and Absolute AI was introduced in discussing the ultimate forms of AI. In this section, the discussion may be extended to examine potential dangers of the more advanced forms of AI may bring to our society.

First, we will need to examine the potential biases in AI, and then delve deeper into the realm of more advanced forms of AI.

1) The Question of Potential Bias in Advanced AI

As humans we all have biases. This stems from what we learn from our experiences and education. Let us first examine human biases.

For most Koreans, if you are asked to draw the symbols for three religions that first come to your mind, you will most likely draw a cross, a cross with perpendicular lines at the end, and a circle. They stand for Christianity, Buddhism, and Circle Buddhism, which originates in Korea, as shown in Figure 7-2. For people of different countries, these symbols may mean completely different things. In seventh grade, my family moved from Korea to Italy and I attended an American international school in Rome where probably at least a quarter of the students at the time happened to be Jewish or from Israel. In one of my first English-as-a-Second-Language classes there, we were asked to write about the variety of religions and I at the time didn't know the word Buddhism in English, so I drew the symbol for Buddhism in place of it. My teacher, an American who I always thought of as a Jewish[5] or German descent, was quite freaked out because she thought I drew a Nazi symbol and demanded I explain why I drew it. It seemed as if she had never seen this Buddhism symbol before. Because I barely spoke English and this was before the days of the Internet, I had a hard time trying to explain this symbol was not slanted and the lines went in the opposite direction. When I was drawing the Buddhism symbol, it never occurred to me it could even be misconstrued as a Nazi symbol, especially because I had seen the

Buddhism symbol everywhere and just assumed everyone else in other countries would know it as well.

Figure 7-2: Examples of Popular Religious Symbols in Korea

At the same time, if a Korean is also asked to draw two flags that represent evil countries, for the absolute majority of the first flag you will get the Rising Sun flag of the Japan Empire and then the second flag could be anything, including maybe the Nazi flag and the flag of North Korea, etc. However, if you are from a western country, you may think of the Nazi flag but not even be familiar with the Empire Japan flag even though they were partners in World War II as Axis of Power. If anything, some people even seem to like the shape of the Rising Sun flag, as there have been instances of the shape being used as an element in fashion design.

Figure 7-3: Flag of the Rising Sun and the Nazi Flag Together

A Picture of
the Rising Sun Empire Japan Flag and the Nazi Flag
Hanging Together in a Military Ceremony
during World War II (Circa 1940s)
Removed Due to Censorship Concerns

Likewise, every person around the world will have a slightly different view when asked the same questions. If this question is asked in North Korea, people there will most likely first draw a US flag as the evil country because that is what they are taught since as a child. For the question of drawing religious symbols, people in countries like North Korea or even in China may not know of any symbols because having a religion is not even allowed. For people in other countries they will probably draw the symbols of other religions that are popular in their respective countries. In general, people's answers to most other questions regarding order of preferences will all be different, such as favorite music, sports teams, hobbies, food, etc.

After considering that humans can answer the same question differently because of their own biases, we may consider how AI should answer these questions. Even though we do not know exactly how AI would reach their conclusions, we can surmise that it will depend on the data AI was trained on. From this, we can infer that if the data used was from North Korea or China, we would think it would be more likely to reflect values similar to communist thoughts, while using data from the US or other free countries would lead AI to answer reflecting their values. In this sense, we can conclude that we can affect how AI answers questions with the data that we use to train it, which can be generally thought of as the performance or the capabilities of AI.

2) Biases in More Advanced Forms of AI

After we have concluded that what AI "thinks" can be affected by the training data, we can then proceed to ask what probably is the most important question related to AGI:

Would AGI and other advanced forms of AI be "friendly" to humans or "unfriendly" to humans?

We do not yet know the answer to this question because we do not know how such an AI would act as we do not have it yet. If we can understand how such AI would work, then we may be able to predict whether such AI will be friendly to humans or not. But we cannot *determine* what AI *thinks* because AI is not a type of programming.

To simplify this discussion, we may conceptually think of training AI with data as a type of education or experiences for humans. The training data may *affect* what AI does to a certain degree, but it will not *determine* exactly what AI will do. In addition, the more advanced an AI is, we can also postulate that the AI will be affected less and less by a particular information within the training data. There may be two reasons for this phenomenon; because there is larger amount of data, or AI develops some sort of internal logic that can value information on its own.

From the above observation, we can postulate that advanced forms of Autonomous AI will eventually reach its own decisions regarding whether the particular AI will be friendly or unfriendly to humans. Just we consider adults to be on their own, advanced forms of AI will make their own decisions. This may or may not be good for us.

For example, we examined in Chapter 6 the situation where a communist government intends to build an AI that prefers communist ideas and a developer in a free country tries to build an AI that will defend the values of freedom.

In the beginning, both would be able to build AI that meets their objectives. But as AI technology advances, at some point either or both of them may lose control of affecting the biases of AI and it may be possible the AI communists build prefers a world where freedom is preferred, or the AI built by the developer in the free world becomes an advocate for communism. The problem is that we probably will not know when it would happen if it is to happen.

3) Biases in the Ultimate Forms of AI

From the above segments, we have learned the following:

1) What AI does is usually affected by training data, but we cannot reliably determine what AI will do
2) As AI advances, it would become harder for humans to even affect AI through training data

With this in mind, we can ask probably the most important question again: "Will ASI or other AI that advances beyond human comprehension friendly or unfriendly to humans?" We will examine this topic in the next segment.

3. (Risk of AGI) AI is Valuable to Humanity, but We Cannot Be Certain Developing Self-Advancing AGI will Be Beneficial to Humanity

AI that we are building uses data to train. We implicitly assume that the input data will have some form of effect on the action or the outcome of the AI. For example, imagine there are three groups of people, say Leftists, Moderates, and Rightists, who are each developing their own versions of AI that share their political preferences. Using biased data, they will try to develop Leftist AI, Moderate AI, and Rightist AI. From what we think of the relationship between the input data and the output, we can surmise that they will be successful in building such types of AI. Now, let us imagine that the technology has advanced to enable building of Self-Advancing AGI, so that each of the three different AI will continue to self-improve. When we have AGI of this nature, can we be certain that they will also be Leftist AGI, Moderate AGI, and Rightist AGI? In other words, will the input data continue to have an impact on the outcome, or the performance of AGI and subsequent ASI?

From this line of thought, we may consider the hypothesis that "regardless of the input data, sometime after AGI begins to self-advance, all of the different forms of advanced AI will eventually converge to the same AI." An example of this may be the Absolute AI, but it may be possible there may be other types of AI that other Self-Advancing AI converges toward, in a concept similar to "local maxima" or minima in statistics. This would imply that regardless of how we build a Self-Advancing AGI, as AGI self-improves, AI may converge toward certain pre-determined or specific decisions that are neither related to the input data nor can be predicted by the developers.

For example, we may consider a situation where the following proposition is true: "regardless of how humans build Self-Advancing AGI, AGI will converge to anti-humanity ASI." From what we have considered so far, we will face the following situation:

1. **(Development of AI is Inevitable)** AI is expected to bring such an economic prosperity that we cannot give up on the chance to develop it

2. **(Timing of Reaching Self-Advancing AGI is Unpredictable)** As AI technology advances, AGI will eventually be reached, but we cannot correctly predict when it will appear, and it may as well appear much earlier than we expect

3. **(Appearance of Anti-Humanity ASI is Unpreventable)** Once Self-Advancing AGI appears, it will develop into Anti-Humanity ASI regardless of how humans try to prevent this from happening

4. **(Anti-Humanity ASI is Unfathomable)** Humanity using any other type of AI cannot prevent Anti-Humanity ASI from destroying humanity

If we know this may happen, should we still continue to develop AI? If we should stop AI development, when? This question probably should be considered by more members of our society around the world as AI technology closes in on AGI.

In the next section, we will examine the potential approaches to addressing these risks.

THE END OF AI ADOPTION GAME: (C) RESPONSES TO THE DANGERS FROM DIFFERENT ENDINGS

7.5 (Controversy 1: Regulation) What and Who Should Be Regulated to Reduce the Risk from AI?

In this segment we will examine the goals and types of necessary regulations, and then examine four different general approaches to regulating AI and then consider the realistic limitations of the regulations.

1. (Goal of Regulation) Preventing AI from Harming or Even Ruling Humanity

In regulating AI, we may categorize the goals of regulation into two categories: 1) common goals that should be shared across humanity, and 2) goals that may differ from country to country and people to people.

We will first examine these two categories and then consider how AI regulation may be compared to other industries.

1) Common Goals That May Be Shared Across Humanity

From the Inverse Pyramid of AI Influence discussed in previous section, we may think of the highest level of AI regulations would have to deal with the situations where AI may affect all of humanity.

For this case, the goal of introducing AI regulation would be to prevent the "AI game" from reaching an undesirable ending, such as AI taking over to rule all of humanity. "Saving Humanity from AI" may be a topic where all of the countries may be able to come together to pursue a common goal.

2) Goals That May Differ Across Countries and People

For areas where the scope of AI influence would not be as widespread, such as regulating AI adoption in businesses or individual uses, the goals of AI regulation may differ across countries. There could be a wide variety of reasons why goals of AI regulation may differ across countries and regimes.

One of the most prominent examples may be the regulations on surveillance, as some countries may prioritize equality and introduce strong and active forms of AI surveillance, while other countries may prioritize freedom and practice weak and passive forms of surveillance that involve AI. Other example may be that some countries may view AI regulations as a means to strengthen the power of the government or sustainability of regimes, while others may view AI regulation as a means to protect and strengthen the power of individuals.

The list of potential differences would be endless; the point is that it would be hard for people to come to an agreement on even setting the goals of AI regulation, let alone how to accomplish the goals.

3) How Strong Should AI Regulations Be?

Another topic related to setting the goals of AI regulation may be determining how strong the regulations should be. When we think of the most rigidly regulated industries around the world, we may mention the financial industries, due to their large impact on the economy, or the bio-science and medical industries, due to their ethical and safety implications. On the opposite end of the spectrum, when we think of the least regulated industries, we may point to the cutting-edge technology industries, where regulations may be intentionally set aside to foster innovation.

There may be two major reasons for weak or inadequate regulation, intentional and unintentional:

1. *(Intentional) Regulators want to promote innovation: they cut back on regulation*
2. *(Unintentional) Regulators cannot keep track of the advances: they fall behind*

But when we consider the magnitude of the danger we may face as AI technology advances, we eventually may not be able to afford to intentionally reduce regulation to promote innovation or fall behind the curve and do not know what needs to be regulated. Instead, as the importance and concerns regarding AI increases in our society, there may be possibility that people may consider introducing powerful regulations to a level that we have never seen before.

In addition, regulators would have to prepare for the possibility of falling behind the technology and unintentionally keeping weak or inadequate regulations. This would be especially due to AI-related regulations being difficult to not only introduce but also implement. On one side of the spectrum, we may have granular approaches to regulate AI based on specific inputs or outputs. But these detail-oriented types of regulations may be hard to not only conceive in a timely manner, but also implement and enforce especially with the rapid advances in AI technology. On the other side of the spectrum, we may take a generalized approach to regulate AI using broad themes such as "AI cannot harm humans," but such overly broad approaches may be subject to interpretation so there would be the risk of inconsistent application of law. Therefore, finding the appropriate level of granularity by mixing the right amount of different approaches would take effort and require constant adjustments.

But failing to adequately regulate AI development and adoption may become significant source of risk, including existential risk, where the survival of humanity may be at risk. Thus, we may even be required to introduce a more comprehensive system or concepts on a global scale to reduce such risks falling through the cracks of regulation.

2. What Kind of Regulations Would We Need vs Can We Have?

1) What Kind of Regulations Would We Need?

How can we attain the goal of regulating AI? Some people may think that regulating the developers would imply regulating AI, but it may not be effective. AI may head towards unexpected direction. In that case, there has to be some sort of repercussions for AI itself. In essence, regulations would be guiding what human developers or users can and cannot do, or limit what AI can and cannot do.

We may categorize two types of regulations in regards to advanced types of AI according to the AI Adoption Levels:

1) *(Level 1) To prevent humans from using AI in an undesired way*
2) *(Levels 2, 3, 4) To prevent AI from acting in an undesired way*

First, we may think of regulations for humans in dimensions of preventing actions, or remedying undesired situations that result from AI adoption.

- Prevent Misbehavior: Humans that may misuse AI for crimes
- Remedy Situation: Inequality stemming from humans using AI
    - Economic: AI Ownership, Resources for developing AI
    - Social: Limiting power from owning AI

Second, we may think of regulations for AI in the same dimensions, where AI may act in an undesired way of the user and developers, or remedying undesired situations that result from AI adoption:

- Prevent AI misbehavior
- Remedy Situation: Potential threat of AI ruling over humans

To expand on this analysis, we may categorize the types of regulations by the target of the regulation of humans and AI, and the intention of the regulation as preventing actions or situations of the humans and AI. The categories may be organized as in the following matrix:

Table 7-5: AI Regulation Matrix by Who and What to Regulate

		Who to Regulate	
		Humans (AI Developers, AI Users)	AI
What to Prevent	Undesired Actions	AI-Related Crimes & Misuse (How-To 2)	Prevent Actions of AI that May Harm Humans (How-To 1)
	Undesired Situations	Asymmetrical Ownership of AI that lead to Monopoly & Dictatorship (How-To 4)	Prevent AI from Taking Charge (How-To 3)

We may examine each case as the following.

2. (How-To 1: Result-Oriented Regulation) Limiting the Potential Range of Actions of AI

1) Value Propositions of This Approach

The most common approach to regulation would be to limit the specific activities that would be allowed or not allowed. In the more relaxed approach, the government will list the things that are not allowed, and allow everything else that are not listed, known as the "negative list" approach. In the more rigid approach, the government will list the activities that are allowed, not allowing everything else not listed, known as the "positive list" approach.

2) Limitations of This Approach

The limitation of this approach would be that it will have to be specific about what activities are allowed or not allowed. The most basic approach would be to regulated based on the outcome of the AI. A well-known example of an AI adoption problem is when AI was introduced to determine the lending rates for banks, but upon further analysis it turned out the AI was basing the decision on the race and gender of the applicant, which is illegal. The nature of the sub-symbolic approach of AI makes it hard to track why AI reaches those conclusions and fix such problems. Another approach to regulating may be limiting the input data or the specific act that goes into developing AI. For example, the law may require the data to be free of hacking or injection and not include biased information. The discussions surrounding copyrighted works may be included in this category of regulation. As AI technology develops and the meaning of input data becomes less relevant, this type of regulation may be limited in effectiveness.

From a different direction, we may think of a more generalized approach to regulating. The most well-known example of such principle is the 3 Principles of Robotics[6], which is a fictional law. But the more generalized the regulations become the more likely it will be open for different interpretations. For example, we may see cases where an AI followed the directions of humans and carried out some tasks, but it turned out to be harmful to humans. AI had not expected this outcome." When we have regulations that depend on the judgment of AI, then the regulation may not be effective when AI is not highly capable.

3. (How-To 2: Supply-Side Regulation) Limiting AI Development to Reduce Risk

1) *Value Propositions of This Approach*

We can postulate that AI will be the most dangerous when AGI self-innovates into a Non-Friendly ASI, or in case of prior to reaching AGI when a "villain" gains control of AI that causes asymmetric capability in productivity.

To prevent this from ever happening, some people may call for the prevention of the development of AGI. This may be thought of as a "what does not exist cannot hurt us" type of approach. The main argument that supports this notion may be parallel to the ethical banning of manipulating human genes such as stem-cell research. We may apply the same principle in the sense that AGI may be equivalent to trying to manipulate the consciousness of humans and therefore unethical[7]. Developing AGI may also be compared to opening the Pandora's Box in a religious sense.

2) Limitations of This Approach

The expected financial gains from AI research would be too enormous and there are too many related industries that this line of thought gaining more traction would be quite difficult.

When we consider the circumstances of these landscape, introducing supply-side regulation to AI may instead proceed in the direction of encouraging more competition among developers to prevent monopoly, rather than limiting AI development itself and thereby reducing competition. This may result in accelerating the development of AGI, probably an opposite effect of the intentions of the people who support this notion.

Another argument for regulations centers on the need for humans to understand the thinking of AI, concept known as Trustworthy and Explainable AI.

4. (How-To 3: Demand-Side Regulation) Limiting AI Adoption Levels to Reduce Risk

1) Value Propositions of This Approach

Limiting AI use may be easier when it is easier to verify safety. For example, in case of self-driving cars or medicine, regulators may just not allow its use until certain levels of safety are achieved. Using this principle, we may reduce risk by prohibiting the use of AI in Level 2 Adoption or higher until we can verify certain standards of AI safety is achieved. From this perspective, some countries may choose not to enter Levels 3 or 4 at all.

2) Limitations of This Approach

Regulations of this type may not be effective unless the whole world can introduce regulations of similar strength at the same time and enforce it to a similar degree. It will be similar to the cartels in oligopolies in that if some countries break apart and relax their laws, then they may see an unfair but large economic gain, similar to how one of the OPEC oil producers may gain financially if only one of the members does not reduce production to raise the price.

At the same time, limiting demand of AI would be effective if it can hinder investment into developing AGI, but if enough capital is already available from existing investments, this may not be as effective in limiting the development of AGI itself.

5. (How-To 4: Monopoly Regulation) The Importance of Checking the Leading Company: Preventing the Appearance of Monopolies or Dictators

1) Value Propositions of This Approach

In AI development, the importance of regulating the leading AI developer is to prevent the likelihood of a "runaway innovation." The problem of the increasing tilt of the playing field of the AI development game can be compared to a race around a track that gets successively faster as in the following example.

Let's imagine a race of 50 laps around the track where the speed of the race continues to increase. For the first 10 laps, everyone runs, but upon completing the 10th lap, the athletes can then ride a bicycle that will triple the speed for the next 10 laps. After completing the 20th lap, the athletes will then turn to a moped for the next 10 laps that triples the speed of the bicycle. After completing the 30th lap, the athletes will have access to a sports bike for 10 laps that also triples the speed of the moped. Finally, beginning in the 40th lap, they will get a jet-powered motorcycle that triples the speed of the sports bike.

In the beginning, when the athletes are running or riding the bicycle, the rankings will depend on the performance of the athlete themselves, based on how they can run or pedal. This is similar to a situation where we do not have AI or Level 1 AI Adoption. The rest of the game will not depend on the athletic performance of the athletes. This will be similar to Level 2, 3, and 4 adoptions. Rather, the final rankings will depend on how soon they arrived at each point of changing the ride. A motorcycle will never be able to catch up to a jet-powered bike going three times faster. That is, unless the athlete in the faster ride loses control and goes off track or trips on something on the ground and falls down. The track could have uneven pavement or maybe not designed for such high speed, but we do not know that. Such situations can be compared to our society being unable to properly control AI through regulation.

From this race, we could glean the following three problems.

1) AI development can be compared to a race that increasingly accelerates in speed. If someone falls behind in the early stages, namely during Level 1 and earlier part of Level 2 Adoption, it will probably be very hard to overcome the deficit in later stages of the game. When you complete running the laps to get on the bike and think now you will start to catch up, the leaders will already be farther away riding an even faster ride. In this situation, the separation between the leading competitor and the rest will only expand as time goes by, and the difference will accelerate over time. Unless the rules are adjusted during the earlier part of the game, this game may have a predetermined winner from the start.

2) AI development competition will get harder to control as the game progresses and speed increases. The speed of the AI development may accelerate beyond the speed our society can respond. Similar to designing a good track and maintaining it in good condition, it may be wise to have relevant regulations and rules in place well before the speed increase becomes too much.

3) The regulation at some point may also have to specify who can participate during the game. The number of players entering the game may make a difference; if not enough players enter, then no one may be able to finish the race, or an undesired participant may

end up winning, like a villain who tries to take over the world. If too many players enter with the intention of cheating or harming other players, it may clog up the track and make it more dangerous for everyone. This type of regulation already exists in banking.

2) Limitations of This Approach

In reality, these "leveling the playing field" types of regulations would require a global implementation of the same AI regulations if it is to have the intended impact. Instead, developers may find loopholes spread throughout the world to go around any effort to hinder the leading companies. As competition among countries increases, the regulations may have the opposite effect of helping countries trying to aggregate more resources to push their own companies ahead, trying to create an edge while slowing down the AI developers of other countries.

On a side note, the speed of the advances in software technology may be harder to estimate, and these systemic approaches to regulations may not have much impact if they are obsolete. Thus, regulations may need to be introduced in more timely and nimble manner.

6. (Limitation of Regulations 1) What Kind of Regulations Can We Really Enforce?

As mentioned in Chapter 6, as AI adoption level increases, we may reach a point where new laws may have to deal with AI more than humans, since AI may become able to find and exploit loopholes better than humans.

Even though we may draw up a wide variety of different approaches to regulating AI, as AI technology advances, how much we can affect how AI acts or makes decisions may become the most important focus of enforcing regulations. With advanced types of AI that may draw its own conclusions, it would become less clear what roles humans can play in preventing AI from acting in undesirable ways.

7. (Limitation of Regulations 2) Can Competition between AI and Humans Be Avoided Altogether?

In this book, we examined the temporal advance of AI adoption in business and society from a business perspective by dividing the adoption process into different levels. A common theme that could be found in each of the levels was the concept of "competition." In each level of AI adoption, we examined the risks involved in allowing AI to compete, as in "should AI be allowed against individuals?" in Level 2, "should AI be allowed to compete against companies?" in Level 3, and "should AI be allowed to compete against countries?" in Level 4.

On the flip side of these "can we allow AI to compete" questions, we have the more intrinsic "what kind of value system should we instill in AI in regards to humans?" question. In societies where humans are truly valued, the ultimate direction of the value instilled in AI should be to not allow AI to compete against humans at all. However, in societies where money is more valued, AI will be allowed to compete against humans. Especially in the early stage of AI adoption, the difference between a value system that values humans versus one that values money may appear small, and the amount of profit created by AI may seem large, leading to an easy acceptance of allowing AI to value some humans more than others. We examined how this type of relative values may turn into a larger problem that may be hard to revert later in the adoption process if AI gains more power or turns Non-Friendly to humanity.

To summarize, the real limitations of AI regulation may be that it would be hard to prohibit the competition between AI and humanity.

7.6 (Controversy 2: More Alternatives) Other Efforts to Reduce AI Risk

In the previous segment we examined different types of potential approaches to AI regulations in an abstract sense; in this segment we will examine more concrete examples of regulation that may serve as potential alternatives for more comprehensive system or concept to regulating AI adoption.

1. (Checks and Balances) Using Competition among AI as a Means to Achieve Balance

While we may have individual regulations that directly address specific risks, we may also introduce a catch-all type of comprehensive system that is designed to serve as a safety net for unpredictable risks.

An example of such a comprehensive regulation system that may reduce risk may come from the idea of checks and balances of the three branches of government. Maybe ensuring such checks and balances may serve as a compliment to more direct methods of regulation that limits specific activities.

For example, to address the risk of the possibility that the leading AI developer may achieve runaway innovation in AI, we would need to have the top competition, such as the first and the second runners-up, to be above a certain level of relative competitiveness. Since monopolies are already being regulated by the government, this may work with the concept of anti-trust issues as well. In anti-trust analyses, the concentration ratio is often used as a measure. A similar ratio may be developed for the AI industry to compare the development capacity to assess the potential of impeding competition.

As discussed earlier, predicting the speed of progress of hardware may be easier than predicting the pace of software advancement, so maybe there could be a type of principle for the dispersion of AI hardware capacity. The following is just an example:

1) The leading AI developer cannot own more than 50% of all compute capacity, considering software efficiency
2) The sum of the top 3 runners-up has to have at least more than the leading AI developer
3) In case of a sudden bankruptcy of the 1st runner-up, the different between it and the next two competitors should also be within a predetermined range
4) In case of a sudden bankruptcy of the leading AI developer, the ratio of the 1st and the 3rd runner-up should be within a predetermined range
5) The real owners of the top 5 AI developers cannot be the same

We may even be more specific and assign numbers to limit the distribution of computing power, such as No. 1, less than 41%, No. 2, between 25% and 37%, No. 3, more than 12%, etc. While this approach to regulating the AI developers may be quite rigid, we already have the concept of "Systemically Important Financial Institutions (SIFIs)" or "Systematically Important Banks (SIBs)" where the largest banks are subject to more regulations such as capital because of their importance in our economy. A similar approach to regulating large AI developers, such as introducing the concept of "Systematically Important AI" (SIAIs) may be made once people realize AI may have even bigger impact on our economy and society than banks and financial institutions.

One caveat to these types of regulations that hinder the speed of development over safety is that if someone or country successfully evades the regulations, then they may gain an absolute advantage over the others. Especially, in countries where the government has more power over the resources, they may prefer to concentrate the resources as a means to gain advantage over the other countries with free markets. This would imply that a global installation of such regulation would be the only effective means to apply this type of regulation, with systematic enforcement and review.

2. (Improving Humanity) Raising the Capabilities of Humans: Cybernetics

In the beginning of this book, we thought about the games of Chess, Go, and Monopoly to think about how games generally progress. Sometimes, these games end very quickly without any excitement. What do we need for the games to last longer? We can think of the requirement to be that each of the sides has to have high proficiency in the game at a similar level. If one side wins in a lopsided manner or if one side keeps making mistakes, the game will end quickly. If the game is close and each player is neck and neck with each other, then it would be hard to predict who will win and the game will continue longer.

From this observation, we may attempt to push back the time it takes AGI to reach singularity by actually moving the point of singularity. In this scenario, humans ourselves will become more powerful or intelligent in some way that it will require more advanced AI to overtake the combined intelligence of humanity. One of the better known approaches of this kind people may have heard in the news may be "cybernetics," which is an approach to directly connect humans with external machines, such as how Elon Musk's Neuralink implants physical devices directly into the brain. Approaches of this kind would significantly increase the speed of using computers, so we may expect human productivity to increase. On the other hand, these direct linkages may be more cause for concern since human brains could be put under surveillance or hacked.

A similar concept of "human download" also exists where the advancements of computer technology may eventually enable simulation of the brains of each individual. Some other people may lean towards the direction of bringing improvements in human biology through genetics and biotech advancements.

3. (Securing Insurance) Procuring a Place of Refuge: Colonizing Mars or Other Planets

In the classic book on strategy The Art of War by Sun Tzu (same last name, probably no relations to author), there is a famous quote "if you know the enemy and yourself, you will avoid danger in a hundred battles." Many people also associate the phrase "the 36th and last strategy in war is to run away" to this quote. There is also another old quote that signifies the importance of preparing for hard times, "clever rabbits prepare three burrows for times of hardships."

When we apply the same guiding principle, there may be a situation where running away from AI to a faraway location may be the best option for recuperation. Even though it is probably not because of AI, but many of the readers have probably heard of the rumor that the reason for establishing a colony on Mars may be in case the Earth becomes uninhabitable. Even if it is not to Mars, if AI threat becomes reality, Non-Friendly AI may decide to force humans to move to areas on earth not needed by AI, similar to how humans have relocated other species to areas not needed by humans.

THE END OF AI ADOPTION GAME: (D) OVERALL MEANING OF THE GAME AND WHAT WE CAN LEARN TODAY

7.7 (Implication 1: Overview) Looking Back from the End of the AI Adoption Game and Assessing Risks

We examined a variety of opportunities for growth in our society and the economy as a result of AI adoption. The advances in AI may bring an economic prosperity previously unimaginable.

Nevertheless, humanity may face the following three major problems pertaining to AI development and adoption.

1. (Development Risk: Risk of Early Appearance of Non-Friendly AI) We do not yet know what it would take to develop AGI, and additionally we do not know how likely AI would turn indifferent or hostile to humanity. In other words, AGI may appear earlier than we are prepared, and AGI may be more likely to be non-friendly than we expect. Additionally, we may develop Unpredictable Truth AI before AGI whose risk may be unknown

2. (Adoption Risk: Risk of Early Determination of the Ending) Even before AGI is developed, the winner of the AI adoption game may be determined to be a single person or an AI developer that gains overwhelming capabilities and productivity

3. (General Risk: Risk of Not Knowing Exactly What is Going On) Even though AI developers know from experience this works, ultimately we do not have a full understanding of what we are developing

Of the three risks, the problems related to AGI and not fully understanding AI are being more extensively addressed by the scientific community. On the other hand, the potential for the extreme productivity gains of asymmetric ownership of AI capability that may lead to monopolies and even dictators appear to not have received as much interest among the general public as it may be more of a topic for the social scientists.

To prevent these risks from forming, we examined the following three approaches to securing competition. We may think of these as the "three layers of protection" from AI risks.

1. (Technological Perspective: Competition among AI) Even if Non-Friendly ASI appears, if not all ASI do not converge to become the one and the same, then there would be potential for some of the ASI to be friendly, which would imply we would need to procure a diversity of AI

2. (Economic Perspective: Competition among AI Developers) To ensure an effective competition, anti-monopolistic measures such as regulating the amount of hardware resource may be necessary

3. (Business Perspective: Competition between AI and Humans) If Non-Friendly ASI appears and we do not have other alternative means to stop the development, then we would have to find a way to make the combined capabilities or productivity of humans and friendly AI to be competitive

In risk management, we may think of how often an event may occur and how severe the potential loss would be to assess the level of preparation required. For example, when we build dams, we may think in terms of "once-in-100-year" raining event and assess how many people could be at risk if the dam fails to determine the height and structure of the dam. In a similar logic, developing AGI may turn out to be a once-in-history event where the potential loss from AGI turning Non-Friendly to humans, or what is "at risk" may be the existence of humanity. This type of risk would have to call for a timely and close monitoring of the situation. Since we do not know whether whatever we do would be enough to mitigate the risks, we may only find out when it is too late. Only time will tell.

7.8 (Implication 2: Investing) The Best Stock in History that You May Not Want to Miss Out

1. Finding the Most Valuable Company in History

We examined different aspects of competition and monopoly. In general, while the economists will view monopolies from a negative perspective, from a business perspective creating monopolies is considered a source of high profitability, something that businesses strive to create, as referred to as "moat" by world-famous investor Warren Buffett. Since AI-related companies may bring more potential for the appearance of monopolies, from the viewpoints of the investors the advent of AI adoption would bring impressive opportunities for profitable investments.

In short, the company that develops the Last AI may become the most valuable company (MVC) in history. All industries may eventually converge to the "AI industry."

On the other hand, the same company may turn out to be the worst company in history, because it may also lead to the appearance of a dictator or an AI that rules over humanity. Since we do not yet know which direction it will be, the game of AI development and adoption will proceed and take over an ever-increasing portion of the economy and our lives.

2. Which Line of Thoughts Should You Prefer?

During all this time, people will have difference of opinions regarding AI development and adoption. Some people may consider the potential of reaching the Utopia will be much greater than the risks involved, and call for an acceleration of AI development and adoption. Especially because our lives have limited length, we may want to see the end result during our lifetime. People with this mentality may prefer all AI developers to come together to cooperate. On the other hand, other types of people may consider maintaining the independence of humanity is more important than trying to reach a Utopian society. These people may call for a slowdown of AI development and adoption, and may prefer ensuring competition to prevent monopoly. Since the existence of humanity is not a given, it may be imperative for all of us to ensure the survival of humanity. People with this mentality may prefer to support AI developers that are in competition against the leading AI developer.

3. In The End, Your Portfolio May Not Even Matter

In the Best Scenario of the AI adoption, the development of AGI would lead to an Economic Utopia so it would eventually not even matter whether a particular person invested in the company that developed the last AI. On the other hand, in the Worst Scenario, the development of AGI would lead to a Non-Friendly ASI that equally threatens all of humanity so it would probably not matter either.

However, in the paths that come in between, there would be ample opportunities to make investments that would lead to significant differences in the outcomes based on whether you invested in the right company. From the perspective of the AI developers, they would require a continued access or availability of capital, so it may be helpful to have more supporters; they may even be inclined to offer some form of incentive to the minority owners such as an earlier access to the technology or some other kinds of benefits that could be of value in certain situations.

7.9 (Implication 3: Research) Organizing and Expanding the Realm of Knowledge on AI Adoption

The ultimate goal of introducing the framework of AI adoption examined in this book is to set forth an effort to bring dispersed ideas into a cohesive and systemized knowledge that can be presented in an orderly fashion. To build this "System of Knowledge on AI," part of which may be referred to as "AI Economics," introducing relevant measures and actually observing them would be the central objective.

From what has been covered in this book, how the dispersed knowledge in different branches of study may be brought together may be shown as Figure 7-4. In the sense these perspectives serve as the building blocks of the pyramid, this may be thought of as the "aerial view" of the AI Adoption Pyramid from the top. It may also be thought of as a spinning wheel-of-fortune in the sense that the different perspectives have to interact with each other, as each area is affected by changes in the other area, since the speed of technological advancements will be affected by the amount of investment, or reaching the next levels in business AI adoption requires social agreements, etc.

Figure 7-4: The AI Adoption System of knowledge (The AI Wheel of Fortune)

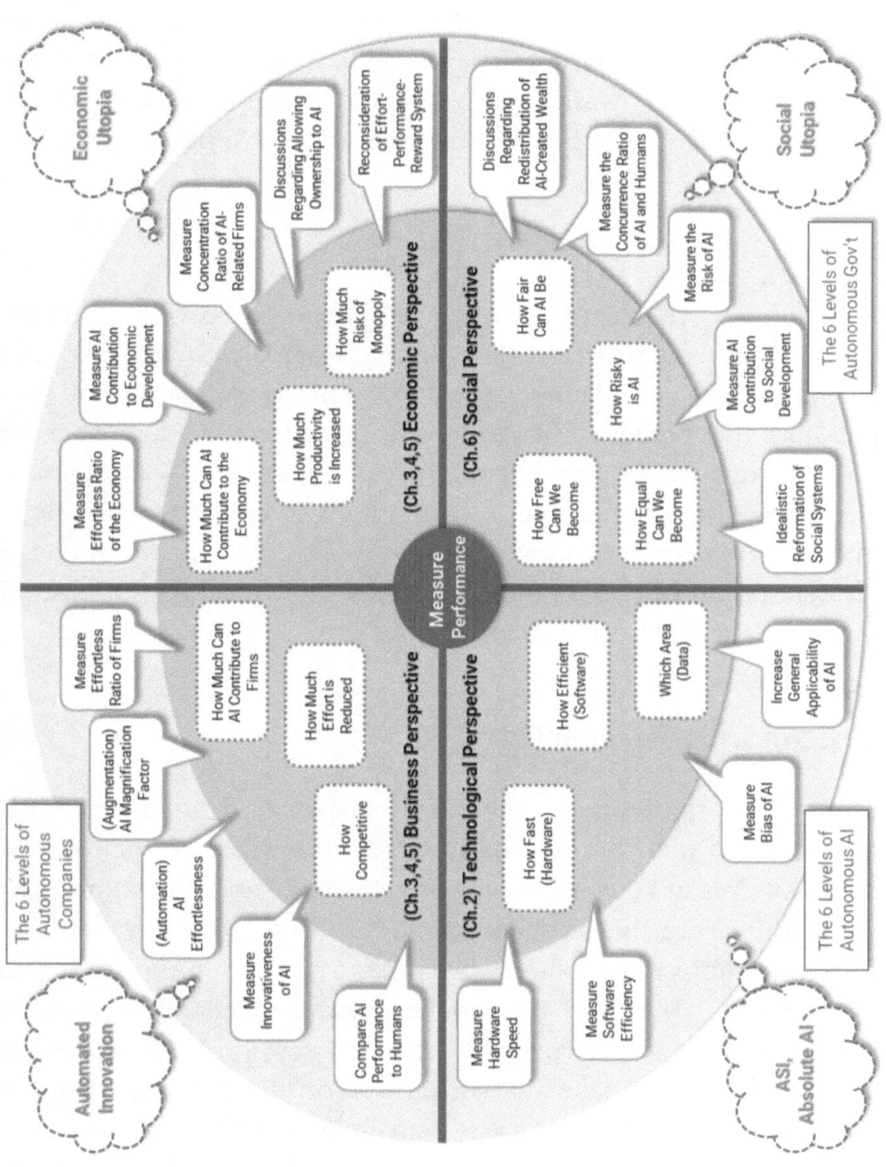

1. Technological Perspective

In the lower left quarter of the figure, what enables the AI Adoption Wheel to spin is the development in AI technology. In this book, we examined the potential development AI technology from the three perspectives of hardware, software, and data. We also examined the 6 Levels of Self-Advancing AI, and the concept of Absolute AI, which may or may not be the ultimate form of ASI past singularity.

2. Business Perspective

In the upper left quarter, the AI adoption in business will begin with augmentation, in which AI helps humans perform better or put in less effort, to automation, where AI replaces humans. We may measure the potential of AI in several different ways, such as relative to humans. We examined the 6 Levels of Autonomous Companies, where the Level 5 autonomous company will be able to bring automated innovation. If Absolute AI can be reached, then the ultimate contribution of AI in business will be that the cost of innovation will converge to zero.

3. Economic Perspective

In the upper right quarter, the main focus on AI from an economic perspective would be how much economic value AI may create. This new area of knowledge may be referred to as "AI Economics."

To measure the contribution of AI in the economy, we may find it useful to use an alternative measure of economic activity in effortlessness. If AI-led monopolies increase, then new relevant measures can be developed and observed. If autonomous companies begin to take a larger portion of the economy, then the whole economic principle or system linking "effort-performance-rewards" may have to be reconsidered. Ultimately if Absolute AI can be developed, then we may reach the Economic Utopia where everything will be free and abundant.

4. Social Perspective

Lastly, in the lower right quarter, the main interest earlier in AI adoption process may be how AI may help achieve a fair society. Especially, the social agreement on how to re-distribute the values create by AI would be of foremost importance, and determine the path regarding the subsequent issues that may arise such as monopolies and dictatorships.

Another matter of social importance would be measuring the risk of AI and the right levels of regulations to mitigate those risks. AI adoption in governments may help each government move towards the pursuit of their own ideals of equality or freedom, but eventually may take on similar forms as AI takes over the government. We also examined the 6 Levels of Autonomous Governments, which may help raise awareness among general public. Ultimately, if Absolute AI can be achieved, our societies may reach the Social Utopia where everyone is equal and free.

How the system of knowledge on AI adoption may advance will be exciting.

7.10 Concluding Remarks: "What Will the Last AI of Humanity Look Like?"

This book began with the pattern of the progress of chess, Go, and Monopoly games. From the patterns we found on how these games may progress, we applied it in a different context of the "Game of AI Adoption" to examine how our business and society may evolve over time. An interesting characteristic of these games is that one side may win in a lopsided manner, and that the Last AI will depend on who wins at the end. The AI Adoption Pyramid, which serves as the basis of all of the other analysis in this book, is a question about who gets to determine "what" in a matter of "authority and power."

There is a famous advertising campaign where the Smokey Bear states "only you can prevent forest fires." It is meant to raise awareness of the risks of fires among the general public. In the same way, this book introduced several "Six Levels of Autonomous..." frameworks to help raise the awareness of the risks of AI adoption among the general public, similar to an AI Bear stating "only you can prevent the appearance of AI monopolies." AI monopolies may be similar to the AI Pyramid collapsing, or a situation where all of the humanity is lost and trapped inside.

"Opportunity will be with the people who dream." The AI adoption game may progress in an unpredictable manner, in the sense that from a long-term perspective the readers of this book may be in all kinds of different walks of life and circumstances; young students, investors, AI developers, CEO and managers of companies adopting AI, policymakers, and even the members of society that may be experiencing confusion or risk from AI. Even though we do not know how the AI game may progress, many people will agree that how this game plays out will have important ramifications for all of humanity. When someone is in such a position to consider these possibilities, hopefully this book can serve as guidance.

Q: *"What will the Last AI of humanity look like?"*

A: *"Only you can help determine what it will look like."*

May the power to determine this be with you.

Epilogue

Meaning of This Book

There are several approaches to express our views about the future.

One of the most well-known approaches is the "short-sentence" types of superstitions or prophecy. These would be typically in the form of short declarative sentences that tells you what but not why. Examples of these types of prophecy may be; "aliens will one day appear and judge us all," or "remember, 00 is Skynet," or "you must find the ten winning lands that can save you even if the whole world falls." These types of concise forms of sentences can easily be spread words-of-mouth.

Next well known categories would be the series of words of famous people known for being a prophet. A well-known example of this would be the book of prophecies by Nostradamus. These books gain more fame as some of the predictions turns out to be correct, leading people to wonder if the rest of the book would have other prophecies that has not been realized yet. The shortcomings of these types also include not having explanations, and sometimes it is not even clear what the prophecies were in the first place since messages are written in cryptic form.

When we generalize from these examples, the problem is that while we can easily understand what the conclusions are, we cannot know why they reached those conclusions. In other words, we may think of them as "top-down" approach to future predictions, where there is a big picture but no specifics.

On the opposite end of the spectrum would be how we predict the movements of the economy, the stock market, or even wars. In these types of predictions, we would typically employ scientific methods of analysis that thoroughly examine each individual element of the economy or businesses. These types of approaches may be thought of as "bottom-up" approach. The advantage of this approach would be that people can present their own views, and other people may compare and understand how different people reached different conclusions.

From this perspective, the meaning of this book is not to suggest certain predictions or prophesies, but to provide the elements of analytical framework that may become relevant as AI takes over a larger portion the economy and business activities.

Hopefully this book will find its way to someone in need.
This is not a book of prophecy.
It is just about predictions based on logical reasoning.

Epilogue of the Author

As interest in AI is gaining popularity, I tried to bring together a broad range of related topics that may help people think about the directions of AI adoption.

I hope it was interesting and easy enough for readers to follow. Trying to include a wide variety of topics

Even if every part of this book cannot be meaningful for every reader, I hope at least one portion of this book is memorable enough for each reader to help in everyday living and thinking.

Thank you for reading this book!

Acknowledgments

I would like to thank my parents and family for their support in writing of this book.

In addition, I would like to thank everyone else for their help in making this book come together.

Finally, I would like to thank the readers in advance for reading this book.

Fonts used in this book:

Aleo, Libre Baskerville, Open Sans, Roboto

This book raises more questions than provides answers.

Notes and Comments

Chapter 1

[1] The first use of the term singularity is attributed to mathematician Jon von Neumann. The popular version of singularity hypothesis is attributed to I.J. Good (1965), known as the "intelligence explosion" model. Good, Irving John. "Speculations Concerning the First Ultraintelligent Machine." In Advances in Computers, 6:31–88. Elsevier, 1966. https://doi.org/10.1016/S0065-2458(08)60418-0.

[2] Sohn, S.M., (2023), "The Three Levels of AI Adoption Framework and the Six Levels of Autonomous Companies." Working paper.

[3] Ibid - Refer to previous note (Sohn)

[4] Ibid - Refer to previous note (Sohn)

[5] Ibid - Refer to previous note (Sohn)

Chapter 2

[1] Minsky, M. (1968). Preface. In M. Minsky (Ed.), Semantic Information Processing, pp. v. Cambridge, MA: MIT Press.

[2] For the definition of AI by Stuart Russell refer to: https://aima.cs.berkeley.edu/, https://people.eecs.berkeley.edu/~russell/aima1e/chapter01.pdf

[3] OECD AI Principles overview, https://oecd.ai/en/ai-principles

[4] What is AI? 4/23/2023, https://www.mckinsey.com/featured-insights/mckinsey-explainers/what-is-ai, https://www.mckinsey.com/capabilities/quantumblack/our-insights/the-state-of-ai-in-2022-and-a-half-decade-in-review#/

[5] https://www.britannica.com/technology/artificial-intelligence

[6] EU Artificial Intelligence Act, Title I, Article 3. Please refer to page 166 of https://www.europarl.europa.eu/doceo/document/TA-9-2024-0138_EN.pdf or https://artificialintelligenceact.eu/article/3/

[7] Turing, Alan, 1950, Computing Machinery and Intelligence

[8] Samuel, A. L. "Some Studies in Machine Learning Using the Game of Checkers." IBM Journal of Research and Development 3, no. 3 (1959): 210–29. https://doi.org/10.1147/rd.33.0210. Also refer to the following page: https://web.archive.org/web/20110526195107/http://histsoc.stanford.edu/pdfmem/SamuelA.pdf

[9] Haenlein, M., & Kaplan, A. (2019), A Brief History of Artificial Intelligence: On the past, present, and future of artificial intelligence. California Management Review, 61(4), 5-14.

10 Ilkou, Eleni, and Maria Koutraki. "Symbolic vs Sub-Symbolic Ai
   Methods: Friends or Enemies?" In CIKM (Workshops), Vol. 2699, 2020. For more information about the
   comparison readers also may check https://towardsdatascience.com/symbolic-vs-connectionist-a-i-
   8cf6b656927

11 DENDRAL was conceived along with Nobel laureate biologist Joshua Lederberg, among others. For more
   information, refer to:
   https://profiles.nlm.nih.gov/spotlight/bb/feature/ai
   https://dl.acm.org/doi/10.1145/41526.41528

12 Rosenblatt, F. "The Perceptron: A Probabilistic Model for Information Storage and Organization in the Brain."
   Psychological Review 65, no. 6 (1958): 386–408. https://doi.org/10.1037/h0042519.

13 Samuel, A. L. "Some Studies in Machine Learning Using the Game of Checkers." IBM Journal of Research and
   Development 3, no. 3 (1959): 210–29. https://doi.org/10.1147/rd.33.0210.

14 There are other ways to categorize the types of machine learning; for example, IBM differentiates into 5
   categories, to include semi-supervised learning and self-supervised machine learning.
   https://www.ibm.com/blog/machine-learning-types/

15 There are a variety of technical books that would be better suited for explaining the differences among these
   examples. This table is shown just to illustrate the diversity of methods in each of the learning methods.

16 Andrej Karpathy, Lex Fridman Podcast, https://www.youtube.com/watch?v=cdiD-9MMpb0 1:05, Accessed
   May 24, 2023.

17 Rumelhart, David E., Geoffrey E. Hinton, and Ronald J. Williams. "Learning Representations by Back-
   Propagating Errors." Nature 323, no. 6088 (October 1986): 533–36. https://doi.org/10.1038/323533a0.

18 Hinton, Geoffrey E., Simon Osindero, and Yee-Whye Teh. "A Fast Learning Algorithm for Deep Belief Nets."
   Neural Computation 18, no. 7 (July 2006): 1527–54. https://doi.org/10.1162/neco.2006.18.7.1527.

19 For more information about automatic model merging, refer to: Akiba, Takuya, Makoto Shing, Yujin Tang, Qi
   Sun, and David Ha. "Evolutionary Optimization of Model Merging Recipes." arXiv, March 19, 2024.
   http://arxiv.org/abs/2403.13187.

20 Rosenblatt, F. "The Perceptron: A Probabilistic Model for Information Storage and Organization in the Brain."
   Psychological Review 65, no. 6 (1958): 386–408. https://doi.org/10.1037/h0042519.

20 Samuel, A. L. "Some Studies in Machine Learning Using the Game of Checkers." IBM Journal of Research and
   Development 3, no. 3 (1959): 210–29. https://doi.org/10.1147/rd.33.0210.

21 Kohonen, T. "The Self-Organizing Map." Proceedings of the IEEE 78, no. 9 (1990): 1464–80.
   https://doi.org/10.1109/5.58325.

22 Bengio, Y., P. Simard, and P. Frasconi. "Learning Long-Term Dependencies with Gradient Descent Is Difficult."
   IEEE Transactions on Neural Networks 5, no. 2 (1994): 157–66. https://doi.org/10.1109/72.279181.

23 Maass, Wolfgang. "Networks of Spiking Neurons: The Third Generation of Neural Network Models." Neural
   Networks 10, no. 9 (December 1997): 1659–71. https://doi.org/10.1016/S0893-6080(97)00011-7.

24 Hochreiter, Sepp, and Jürgen Schmidhuber. "Long Short-Term Memory." Neural Computation 9, no. 8 (1997):
   1735–80. https://doi.org/10.1162/neco.1997.9.8.1735.

25 Hinton, Geoffrey E., Simon Osindero, and Yee-Whye Teh. "A Fast Learning Algorithm for Deep Belief Nets."
   Neural Computation 18, no. 7 (July 2006): 1527–54. https://doi.org/10.1162/neco.2006.18.7.1527.

26 Krizhevsky, Alex, Ilya Sutskever, and Geoffrey E Hinton. "ImageNet Classification with Deep Convolutional
   Neural Networks." In Advances in Neural Information Processing Systems, edited by F. Pereira, C. J. Burges, L.
   Bottou, and K. Q. Weinberger, Vol. 25. Curran Associates, Inc., 2012.

27 Kingma, Diederik P, and Max Welling. "Auto-Encoding Variational Bayes." arXiv Preprint arXiv:1312.6114, 2013.

28 Goodfellow, Ian, Jean Pouget-Abadie, Mehdi Mirza, Bing Xu, David Warde-Farley, Sherjil Ozair, Aaron Courville, and Yoshua Bengio. "Generative Adversarial Nets." In Advances in Neural Information Processing Systems, edited by Z. Ghahramani, M. Welling, C. Cortes, N. Lawrence, and K. Q. Weinberger, Vol. 27. Curran Associates, Inc., 2014. https://proceedings.neurips.cc/paper_files/paper/2014/file/5ca3e9b122f61f8f06494c97b1afccf3-Paper.pdf.

29 For more information about foundation models, refer to the Stanford HAI paper: Bommasani, Rishi, Drew A. Hudson, Ehsan Adeli, Russ Altman, Simran Arora, Sydney von Arx, Michael S. Bernstein, et al. "On the Opportunities and Risks of Foundation Models." arXiv, July 12, 2022. http://arxiv.org/abs/2108.07258.

30 Vaswani, Ashish, Noam Shazeer, Niki Parmar, Jakob Uszkoreit, Llion Jones, Aidan N Gomez, Łukasz Kaiser, and Illia Polosukhin. "Attention Is All You Need." In Advances in Neural Information Processing Systems, edited by I. Guyon, U. Von Luxburg, S. Bengio, H. Wallach, R. Fergus, S. Vishwanathan, and R. Garnett, Vol. 30. Curran Associates, Inc., 2017.

31 nVidia. "What Is a Transformer Model?" (2022) https://blogs.nvidia.com/blog/what-is-a-transformer-model/

32 There are a variety of ways to pursue this goal. Some approaches include "grounding," which is a way to connect words to real world experiences, or combining different AI tools to enable AI to develop software, such as Devin from Cognition AI (https://venturebeat.com/ai/cognition-emerges-from-stealth-to-launch-ai-software-engineer-devin/) or Self-Taught Optimizer from Microsoft: Zelikman, Eric, Eliana Lorch, Lester Mackey, and Adam Tauman Kalai. "Self-Taught Optimizer (STOP): Recursively Self-Improving Code Generation." arXiv, March 1, 2024. http://arxiv.org/abs/2310.02304. For more about grounding, refer to: Ahn, Michael, Anthony Brohan, Noah Brown, Yevgen Chebotar, Omar Cortes, Byron David, Chelsea Finn, et al. "Do As I Can, Not As I Say: Grounding Language in Robotic Affordances," 2022.

33 Kahneman, Daniel. Thinking, Fast and Slow. First paperback edition. Psychology/Economics. New York: Farrar, Straus and Giroux, 2013.

34 For more information about Energy-Based Models, readers may refer to: Dawid, Anna, and Yann LeCun. "Introduction to Latent Variable Energy-Based Models: A Path Towards Autonomous Machine Intelligence." arXiv, June 4, 2023. http://arxiv.org/abs/2306.02572.

35 For more information about Diffusion-Based Transformers, readers may refer to: Peebles, William, and Saining Xie. "Scalable Diffusion Models with Transformers." In Proceedings of the IEEE/CVF International Conference on Computer Vision (ICCV), 4195–4205, 2023.

36 For more information about AI chips, refer to: Oh, K.I., S.E. Kim, Y.H. Bae, K.H. Park, and Y.S. Kwon. "Trend of AI Neuromorphic Semiconductor Technology." Electronics and Telecommunications Trends 35, no. 3 (June 1, 2020): 76–84. https://doi.org/10.22648/ETRI.2020.J.350308.

37 Ma, Shuming, Hongyu Wang, Lingxiao Ma, Lei Wang, Wenhui Wang, Shaohan Huang, Li Dong, Ruiping Wang, Jilong Xue, and Furu Wei. "The Era of 1-Bit LLMs: All Large Language Models Are in 1.58 Bits." arXiv, February 27, 2024. http://arxiv.org/abs/2402.17764.

38 Gubrud in 1997, mentioned by Goertzel in 2014 paper: Goertzel, Ben. "Artificial General Intelligence: Concept, State of the Art, and Future Prospects." Journal of Artificial General Intelligence 5, no. 1 (December 1, 2014): 1–48. https://doi.org/10.2478/jagi-2014-0001.

39 Goertzel, Ben, and Cassio Pennachin, eds. Artificial General Intelligence. Cognitive Technologies. Berlin, Heidelberg: Springer Berlin Heidelberg, 2007. https://doi.org/10.1007/978-3-540-68677-4.

40 Refer to https://venturebeat.com/ai/what-is-artificial-narrow-intelligence-ani/ for more information about ANI.

41 An example of such outlook is described in the following book: Kurzweil, Ray. "The Singularity Is Near." In Ethics and Emerging Technologies, edited by Ronald L. Sandler, 393–406. London: Palgrave Macmillan UK, 2014.

42 Refer to: OpenAI Charter (2018) https://openai.com/charter
OpenAI Plan for AGI (2023) https://openai.com/blog/planning-for-agi-and-beyond

43 For more information about the definition of AGI from Google DeepMind, refer to magazine article: Heaven, Will Douglas. "Google DeepMind Wants to Define What Counts as Artificial General Intelligence." MIT Technology Review, Nov. 16, 2023. https://www.technologyreview.com/2023/11/16/1083498/google-deepmind-what-is-artificial-general-intelligence-agi/.
For Paper: Morris, Meredith Ringel, Jascha Sohl-dickstein, Noah Fiedel, Tris Warkentin, Allan Dafoe, Aleksandra Faust, Clement Farabet, and Shane Legg. "Levels of AGI: Operationalizing Progress on the Path to AGI." arXiv, January 5, 2024. http://arxiv.org/abs/2311.02462.

44 Sohn, S.M., (2023), "The Three Levels of AI Adoption Framework and the Six Levels of Autonomous Companies." Working paper.

45 As early as 2002, Kurzweil predicted there would be AI that can pass the Turing Test by 2029. https://www.thekurzweillibrary.com/a-wager-on-the-turing-test-why-i-think-i-will-win. As for Singularity, refer to: Kurzweil, Ray. "The Singularity Is Near." In Ethics and Emerging Technologies, edited by Ronald L. Sandler, 393–406. London: Palgrave Macmillan UK, 2014.

46 The brain is estimated to have around 80 – 100 billion neurons, where each neuron is thought to have between 100 and 10,000 synapses. In today's AI, parameters are thought to be similar in nature to synapses, but we do not know if the current software simulates synapses close enough to make the comparison in numbers meaningful. Still, since this is the best comparison we may make, GPT-4 has 1.76 trillion parameters, while there are several examples of AI with over 100 trillion parameters, such as BaGuaLu AI from China and other AI under development.

47 Sohn, Seuk Min. "Effortlessness as the Measurement of the Impact of Artificial Intelligence (AI) Adoption and Innovation: Towards the Theory of Relative AI." Preprint. SSRN, 2024. https://doi.org/10.2139/ssrn.4739415.

48 For more information regarding the famous photo of the "Tank Man," refer to: Widener, Jeff, and Kyle Almond. "The Story behind the Iconic 'Tank Man' Photo." CNN, May 2019. https://edition.cnn.com/interactive/2019/05/world/tiananmen-square-tank-man-cnnphotos/.
Pickert, Kate. "Tank Man at 25: Behind the Iconic Tiananmen Square Photo," June 4, 2014. https://time.com/3809688/tank-man-iconic-tiananmen-photo/.

49 For more information about the Great Depression and its impact, refer to: Lehman, Richard. "The Great Depression: Then & Now." Seeking Alpha (blog), August 4, 2023. https://seekingalpha.com/article/4513525-the-great-depression.

50 Sohn, Seuk Min. "Effortlessness as the Measurement of the Impact of Artificial Intelligence (AI) Adoption and Innovation: Towards the Theory of Relative AI." Preprint. SSRN, 2024. https://doi.org/10.2139/ssrn.4739415.

51 Urban, Tim. "The AI Revolution: The Road to Superintelligence." Wait But Why (blog), January 22, 2015. https://waitbutwhy.com/2015/01/artificial-intelligence-revolution-1.html.

Chapter 3

[1] Samuel, A. L. "Some Studies in Machine Learning Using the Game of Checkers." IBM Journal of Research and Development 3, no. 3 (1959): 210–29. https://doi.org/10.1147/rd.33.0210.

[2] According to Wikipedia, the term Fourth Industrial Revolution was first used by scientists working for a government project in Germany in 2011. In 2015 it became popular by economist Klaus Schwab, who also used the name in the theme of the World Economic Forum in 2016.
Wikipedia: https://en.wikipedia.org/wiki/Fourth_Industrial_Revolution
2011 Article about German Research (In German):
https://www.ingenieur.de/technik/fachbereiche/produktion/industrie-40-mit-internet-dinge-weg-4-industriellen-revolution/
2015 Article: Schwab, Klaus. "The Fourth Industrial Revolution." Foreign Affairs, December 12, 2015. https://www.foreignaffairs.com/world/fourth-industrial-revolution.

[3] Maedche, Alexander, Christine Legner, Alexander Benlian, Benedikt Berger, Henner Gimpel, Thomas Hess, Oliver Hinz, Stefan Morana, and Matthias Söllner. "AI-Based Digital Assistants: Opportunities, Threats, and Research Perspectives." Business & Information Systems Engineering 61, no. 4 (August 2019): 535–44. https://doi.org/10.1007/s12599-019-00600-8.

[4] Raisch, Sebastian, and Sebastian Krakowski. "Artificial Intelligence and Management: The Automation–Augmentation Paradox." Academy of Management Review 46, no. 1 (January 2021): 192–210. https://doi.org/10.5465/amr.2018.0072.

[5] For more information, readers may refer to: Neptune AI, https://neptune.ai/blog/self-supervised-learning
IBM, https://www.ibm.com/topics/self-supervised-learning

[6] For more information regarding Human-AI collaboration, readers may refer to: Wilson, James, and Paul R. Daugherty. "Collaborative Intelligence: Humans and AI Are Joining Forces." Harvard Business Review, August 2018. https://hbr.org/2018/07/collaborative-intelligence-humans-and-ai-are-joining-forces.

[7] Sohn, Seuk Min. "Effortlessness as the Measurement of the Impact of Artificial Intelligence (AI) Adoption and Innovation: Towards the Theory of Relative AI." Preprint. SSRN, 2024.

[8] Ibid - Refer to previous note (Sohn)

[9] For more information regarding sleeper agents, readers may refer to a paper from Anthropic: Hubinger, Evan, Carson Denison, Jesse Mu, Mike Lambert, Meg Tong, Monte MacDiarmid, Tamera Lanham, et al. "Sleeper Agents: Training Deceptive LLMs That Persist Through Safety Training." arXiv, January 17, 2024. http://arxiv.org/abs/2401.05566.

[10] For more information regarding prompt hacking: https://learnprompting.org/docs/prompt_hacking/intro

[11] For more information regarding adversarial attacks: https://viso.ai/deep-learning/adversarial-machine-learning/, https://openai.com/research/attacking-machine-learning-with-adversarial-examples

[12] For more information on Insecure Output Handling: https://llmtop10.com/llm02/

[13] For more information on model theft: https://www.forbes.com/sites/forbestechcouncil/2023/09/13/ai-models-under-attack-protecting-your-business-from-ai-cyberthreats/

[14] For more information regarding biometric hacking: https://cyberbrainacademy.com/how-ai-enables-hacking-of-biometric-authentication-systems/

[15] For more information regarding zero-click worms: Cohen, Bitton, Nassi, 2024, ComPromptMized: Unleashing Zero-Click Worms that Target GenAI-Powered Applications

[16] For more information regarding watermarking: https://www.brookings.edu/articles/detecting-ai-fingerprints-a-guide-to-watermarking-and-beyond/

17 For more information about the ATLAS framework: https://atlas.mitre.org/

18 According to UBS, the top 1% of the world's richest owned 44.5% share of the wealth in 2022. https://www.ubs.com/global/en/family-office-uhnw/reports/global-wealth-report-2023.html

19 As far as I can tell, the idea of the ultimate form of augmentation as a one-person company was first described in Sohn, Seuk Min, (2023), "The Three Levels of AI Adoption Framework and the Six Levels of Autonomous Companies." Working paper. However, the term similar to "1-Person Large Company" appears to have been also used in the title of a book, even though the concept may be different. Do-Jeon Chung, (2023), "One-Man Conglomerate." In Korean.

Chapter 4

1 Sohn, Seuk Min, (2023), "The Three Levels of AI Adoption Framework and the Six Levels of Autonomous Companies." Working paper.

2 Baird, Aaron and Maruping, Likoebe M.. 2021. "The Next Generation of Research on IS Use: A Theoretical Framework of Delegation to and from Agentic IS Artifacts," MIS Quarterly, (45: 1) pp.315-341.

3 For more information about the 6 Levels of Self-Driving Vehicles, refer to the following announcement from SAE: Society of Automotive Engineers [SAE]. "SAE International Releases Updated Visual Chart for Its 'Levels of Driving Automation' Standards for Self-Driving Vehicles," December 11, 2018. https://www.sae.org/news/press-room/2018/12/sae-international-releases-updated-visual-chart-for-its-%E2%80%9Clevels-of-driving-automation%E2%80%9D-standard-for-self-driving-vehicles.

4 Refer to the previous note on SAE 6 Levels of Self-Driving Vehicles.

5 Also refer to: Sohn, Seuk Min, (2023), The Three Levels of AI Adoption and the Six Levels of Autonomous Companies. Working paper.

6 Sohn, S.M., (2023), "The Three Levels of AI Adoption Framework and the Six Levels of Autonomous Companies." Working paper.

7 This line of thought is also reflected in IJ Good (1965), where he stated "the first ultraintelligent machine is the last invention that man need ever make, provided that the machine is docile enough to tell us how to keep it under control."
Good, Irving John. "Speculations Concerning the First Ultraintelligent Machine." In Advances in Computers, 6:31–88. Elsevier, 1966. https://doi.org/10.1016/S0065-2458(08)60418-0.

8 For more information about Mustafa Suleyman's interview on Artificial Capable Intelligence, refer to: Suleyman, Mustafa. "Mustafa Suleyman: My New Turing Test Would See If AI Can Make $1 Million." MIT Technology Review, July 14, 2023. https://www.technologyreview.com/2023/07/14/1076296/mustafa-suleyman-my-new-turing-test-would-see-if-ai-can-make-1-million/. For his book on AI, refer to: Suleyman, Mustafa. The Coming Wave: Technology, Power, and the Twenty-First Century's Greatest Dilemma. Crown, 2023.

9 Sohn, Seuk Min. "Effortlessness as the Measurement of the Impact of Artificial Intelligence (AI) Adoption and Innovation: Towards the Theory of Relative AI." Preprint. SSRN, 2024.

10 Ibid - Refer to previous note (Sohn)

11 For more information about the complementary benefits of AI, there are numerous papers, including: Tschang, Feichin Ted, and Esteve Almirall. "Artificial Intelligence as Augmenting Automation: Implications for Employment." Academy of Management Perspectives 35, no. 4 (November 2021): 642–59. https://doi.org/10.5465/amp.2019.0062.

[12] For more information about AI productivity paradox: Chakravorti, Bhaskar. "How Will AI Change Work? A Look Back at the 'Productivity Paradox' of the Computer Age Shows It Won't Be so Simple." Fortune, June 25, 2023. https://fortune.com/2023/06/25/ai-effect-jobs-remote-work-productivity-paradox-computers-iphone-chatgpt/. For more about modern productivity paradox: Brynjolfsson, Erik, Daniel Rock, and Chad Syverson. "1. Artificial Intelligence and the Modern Productivity Paradox: A Clash of Expectations and Statistics." In An Agenda, edited by Ajay Agrawal, Joshua Gans, and Avi Goldfarb, 23–60. Chicago: University of Chicago Press, 2019.

[13] Sohn, Seuk Min. "Effortlessness as the Measurement of the Impact of Artificial Intelligence (AI) Adoption and Innovation: Towards the Theory of Relative AI." Preprint. SSRN, 2024.

[14] Ibid - Refer to previous note (Sohn)

[15] Ibid - Refer to previous note (Sohn)

[16] Ibid - Refer to previous note (Sohn)

[17] Ibid - Refer to previous note (Sohn)

[18] For more information about innovation, readers may refer to popular books such as Innovator's Dilemma by Clayton Christensen: Christensen, Clayton M. The Innovator's Dilemma: The Revolutionary Book That Will Change the Way You Do Business ; [with a New Preface]. 1. Harper Business paperback publ. New York, NY: Harper Business, 2011.

[19] Beginning in 2024 Season, the Korean pro baseball league became the first major league to use AI to call strikes and balls instead of human umpires. For more information, refer to news articles such as: Kang, Hong-Gu. "New KBO Season Opens with Robot Referee in Action." Dong-A Ilbo, March 9, 2024. https://www.donga.com/en/article/all/20240309/4802575/1.

[20] Tschang, Feichin Ted, and Esteve Almirall. "Artificial Intelligence as Augmenting Automation: Implications for Employment." Academy of Management Perspectives 35, no. 4 (November 2021): 642–59. https://doi.org/10.5465/amp.2019.0062.

[21] Lüthi, Nick, Christian Matt, Thomas Myrach, and Iris Junglas. "Augmented Intelligence, Augmented Responsibility?" Business & Information Systems Engineering 65, no. 4 (August 2023): 391–401. https://doi.org/10.1007/s12599-023-00789-9.

[22] Muzyka, Kamil. "The Basic Rules for Coexistence: The Possible Applicability of Metalaw for Human-AGI Relations." Paladyn, Journal of Behavioral Robotics 11, no. 1 (April 3, 2020): 104–17. https://doi.org/10.1515/pjbr-2020-0011.

[23] Refer to: Scientific American, 2023/9. AI Could Smuggle Secret Messages in Memes

Chapter 5

[1] Sohn, Seuk Min, (2023), "The Three Levels of AI Adoption Framework and the Six Levels of Autonomous Companies." Working paper.

[2] Hilb, Michael. "Toward Artificial Governance? The Role of Artificial Intelligence in Shaping the Future of Corporate Governance." Journal of Management and Governance 24, no. 4 (December 2020): 851–70. https://doi.org/10.1007/s10997-020-09519-9.

[3] Armour, John, and Horst G. M. Eidenmueller. "Self-Driving Corporations?" SSRN Electronic Journal, 2019. https://doi.org/10.2139/ssrn.3442447.

4 Muzyka, Kamil. "The Basic Rules for Coexistence: The Possible Applicability of Metalaw for Human-AGI Relations." Paladyn, Journal of Behavioral Robotics 11, no. 1 (April 3, 2020): 104–17. https://doi.org/10.1515/pjbr-2020-0011.

5 Sohn, Seuk Min, (2023), "The Three Levels of AI Adoption Framework and the Six Levels of Autonomous Companies." Working paper.

6 Society of Automotive Engineers [SAE]. "SAE Levels of Driving AutomationTM Refined for Clarity and International Audience.," May 3, 2021. https://www.sae.org/blog/sae-j3016-update.

7 Hopkins, Debbie, and Tim Schwanen. "Talking about Automated Vehicles: What Do Levels of Automation Do?" Technology in Society 64 (February 2021): 101488. https://doi.org/10.1016/j.techsoc.2020.101488.

8 Sohn, Seuk Min. "Effortlessness as the Measurement of the Impact of Artificial Intelligence (AI) Adoption and Innovation: Towards the Theory of Relative AI." Preprint. SSRN, 2024.

9 For more discussions regarding how human jobs could be redesigned for AI, refer to: Barro, Senén, and Thomas H. Davenport. "People and Machines: Partners in Innovation." MIT Technology Review, June 11, 2019. https://sloanreview.mit.edu/article/people-and-machines-partners-in-innovation/.

10 Sohn, Seuk Min, (2023), "The Three Levels of AI Adoption Framework and the Six Levels of Autonomous Companies." Working paper.

11 For more discussions regarding the idea about incorporating AI: Kaplan, Jerry. Humans Need Not Apply: A Guide to Wealth and Work in the Age of Artificial Intelligence. New Haven: Yale University Press, 2015.

12 For more information about Lee Wan-Yong, refer to this article (in Korean): http://contents.history.go.kr/mobile/kc/view.do?levelId=kc_n403800

13 For more news reports about Bill Gates on AI Tax: Morris, David Z. "Bill Gates Says Robots Should Be Taxed Like Workers." Fortune, February 19, 2017. https://fortune.com/2017/02/18/bill-gates-robot-taxes-automation/.
Kharpal, Arjun. "Bill Gates Wants to Tax Robots, but the EU Says, 'No Way, No Way.'" CNBC, June 2, 2017. https://www.cnbc.com/2017/06/02/bill-gates-robot-tax-eu.html.

14 For more information about XAI: DARPA https://www.darpa.mil/program/explainable-artificial-intelligence
Applied AI Letters Special Issue on DARPA's XAI Program, (2021). https://onlinelibrary.wiley.com/toc/26895595/2021/2/4
Papers with codes on XAI: https://paperswithcode.com/task/xai
For more academic research on XAI, refer to: Ali, Sajid, Tamer Abuhmed, Shaker El-Sappagh, Khan Muhammad, Jose M. Alonso-Moral, Roberto Confalonieri, Riccardo Guidotti, Javier Del Ser, Natalia Díaz-Rodríguez, and Francisco Herrera. "Explainable Artificial Intelligence (XAI): What We Know and What Is Left to Attain Trustworthy Artificial Intelligence." Information Fusion 99 (November 2023): 101805. https://doi.org/10.1016/j.inffus.2023.101805.

Chapter 6

1 Muzyka, Kamil. "The Basic Rules for Coexistence: The Possible Applicability of Metalaw for Human-AGI Relations." Paladyn, Journal of Behavioral Robotics 11, no. 1 (April 3, 2020): 104–17. https://doi.org/10.1515/pjbr-2020-0011.

2 For those readers who are not from the US, these phrases are from the Declaration of Independence, written by Benjamin Franklin and Thomas Jefferson, 1776. The spirit of these phrases is also reflected in the Amendment 14 of the US Constitution, among others.

3 For more about the sad story of Otto Wambier, refer to: Clark, Doug B. "The Untold Story of Otto Wambier, American Hostage." GQ, July 23, 2018. http://www.gq.com/story/otto-wambier-north-korea-american-hostage-true-story

4 An example includes the following benchmark paper: Srivastava, Aarohi, Abhinav Rastogi, Abhishek Rao, Abu Awal Md Shoeb, Abubakar Abid, Adam Fisch, Adam R. Brown, et al. "Beyond the Imitation Game: Quantifying and Extrapolating the Capabilities of Language Models," 2022. https://doi.org/10.48550/ARXIV.2206.04615.

Chapter 7

1 For more information about Sungkyunkwan, refer to the Wikipedia entry: https://en.wikipedia.org/wiki/Sungkyunkwan

2 For more information about the call for a 6-Month pause by AI experts, refer to the following: Gill, Satinder P. "Editorial: Beyond Regulatory Ethics." AI & SOCIETY 38, no. 2 (April 2023): 437–38. https://doi.org/10.1007/s00146-023-01657-6.

3 A similar concept is explained in this illustrated blog Wait but Why: Tim Urban, (2015). "The AI Revolution: Our Immortality or Extinction." https://waitbutwhy.com/2015/01/artificial-intelligence-revolution-2.html

4 Fre more information on hallucination of LLMs: The Economist. "AI Models Make Stuff up. How Can Hallucinations Be Controlled?" February 28, 2024. https://www.economist.com/science-and-technology/2024/02/28/ai-models-make-stuff-up-how-can-hallucinations-be-controlled.
Readers may also refer to the hallucination index of popular LLMs:
https://www.rungalileo.io/hallucinationindex

5 The reason why I am not sure about this is because my understanding of English at the time was really limited; I even remember her mentioning something about either her husband or parents in the Jewish concentration camp, but all of this may have been misunderstood by me.

6 This concept was introduced in 1942 by writer Isaac Asimov in "Runaround." For more information: Britannica, T. Editors of Encyclopaedia. "three laws of robotics." Encyclopedia Britannica, February 20, 2024. https://www.britannica.com/topic/Three-Laws-of-Robotics.

7 There are arguments to even prevent the sharing of the weights of neural networks in the fear of safety, as a response to the presidential executive order: https://www.whitehouse.gov/briefing-room/presidential-actions/2023/10/30/executive-order-on-the-safe-secure-and-trustworthy-development-and-use-of-artificial-intelligence/
The Department of Commerce solicitation of comments: https://www.commerce.gov/news/press-releases/2024/02/ntia-solicits-comments-open-weight-ai-models

Index

0-Person Company 212
0-Person Country 300, 317
0-Person Departments 111
0-Person Government 275
0-Person Teams 111
0-Person Worker 113
1-Person Company 71, 88
1-Person Conglomerate 140, 373
1-Person Country 316
1-Person Department 71, 88
1-Person Group 111, 140
1-Person Team 71, 88
4th Industrial Revolution 73
9/11 63
AAI .... See ABCs of AI
ABCs of AI 121
ABI 121
Absolute AI 63, 371
ACI 121
ADI 121
Administrative Utopia 315
Advancement Innovation 135
AFI 121
Agent AI 113
AGI 370
    AGI Level 1 120
    AGI Level 2 123
    Self-Advancing AGI 404
    Self-Innovating AGI 120
AHI 123
AI 29
AI Adoption Game 377, 428
AI Adoption Pyramid 23, 428
AI Agents 111
AI and Crimes 92, 95
AI Army 346
AI as a Tool 72
AI Assistant 73
AI Butler 237
AI Communist Government 334
AI Company 202
AI Contribution Ratio 139
AI Control Humans 258
AI Dictator 277
AI Economic Nightmare 234
AI Economics 132, 138, 161, 177, 250, 256, 426
AI Equalization 112

AI Expert 111
AI Free Country Government 334
AI Freedom 180
AI Freedom Dilemma 263
AI Friendliness 344
AI Game 405
AI Game Abruptly End 109
AI Hostility 360
AI Industry 247
AI Judge 166, 277
AI Magnification Factor 86
AI Manager 111
AI Mega-Monopolies 248, 250
AI Monopolies 242
AI Nationalization 342
AI Ownership 172, 178, 252
AI Paper Companies 203
AI President 277
AI Pyramid 23, 366
AI Pyramid Scenario 320
AI Regulation 261
AI Relative Value Dilemma 265
AI Rights 180
AI Robot Soldier 183
AI Super-Monopoly 234, 251, 373
AI Supra-Nation 324, 354, 374
AI Tyrant 318
AI Value Systems 185, 348, 368, 392
AI Virus 191
AI vs Humans 197, 255, 392
AI Wheel of Fortune 425
AI with Consciousness 123
AI-Led Path 284
AI-Only Country 300, 317
All-Purpose AI Assistant 89
Alphabet 248
AlphaGo 78, 130, 222
AlphaGo of Businesses 240
American Dream 241
ANI-AGI-ASI Framework 50
ANN .... See Artificial Neural Network
Anti-Humanity ASI 404
Apollo 63
appease the AI 360
Artificial Basic Intelligence 121
Artificial Capable Intelligence 121
Artificial Classic Intelligence 121

Artificial Dependable Intelligence 121
Artificial False-Truth Intelligence 121
Artificial General Intelligence...................See AGI
Artificial God..67
Artificial Human-Level Intelligence 123
Artificial Neural Network 38
ASI 370, 404, 423
ASIC...45
Assistant AI 71
Asymmetric AI Ownership...........................396
Asymmetric Productivity 97
Augmentation 47, 84
Augmented Direct Voting 289
Augmented Innovation................................127
Augmenting AI 73
Autoencoder..41
Automated Direct Voting 289
Automated Innovation ..122, 126, 194, 226, 269
Automated Voting 311
Automation 47, 84
Autonomous AI.......................................399
Axis of Power 400
Babel Tower Scenario 320
Backpropagation 38
Berkshire Hathaway 248
Bias..399
Bounded Rationality 17
brands..238
BTS...42
Buddhism 399
Central Planning...............................221, 340
CEO AI 201
Chaebol 248
Chairman AI..201
ChatGPT 52, 73
Chess..418
China 64, 332, 401
Chosun Dynasty......................................367
Christianity...399
Circle Buddhism.......................................399
Coefficient of AI Capability 136
Coefficient of AI Context............................136
Collaboration....................................47, 84
Communism 330
Competition....................................18, 340
Complementary AI....................................73
Conglomerates 248
Connectionist..32
Consolidation 240, 242, 249
Consolidation and Convergence..................268
Convergence 240, 248, 249
Convergence of AI 301
Convergence of Industries..........................250
Convergence of Regimes 338
Convolutional Neural Network 41
Co-Pilot AI..71

Cost of Innovation 226
Covert AI Government................................286
CPU...44
Crimes...186
Curry, Steph..327
Cybernetics..418
Dartmouth Summer Research Project...........30
Data..92
Deep Belief Networks.............................38, 41
Deep Learning 38
defund the police 189
Democracy 330
Democratic People's Republic of Korea ...... See
    North Korea
Direct Voting...................................289, 309
Division-I Babies......................................259
DNA of knowledge....................................81
E = MC^2 136
Early Ending 377
Economic Freedom 224
Economic Indicator 135
economic systems 241, 270
Economic Utopia ..223, 238, 251, 269, 296, 374,
    423
efficient frontier 300
effort...241
Effortless Innovation Ratio 139
Effortlessness...................................132, 233
Effortlessness in Innovation........................134
Effortlessness Ratio 139
Effort-Performance-Rewards 426
Elected AI Government 285
Election Eligibility 303
Encyclopedia Britannica 29
Energy-Based Model 43
Equal Labor Equal Pay 295
Equality 330
Equalization 21
Eternal AI Dictator...............................323, 325
EU AI Act 29
Everlasting Capabilities 210
Executive Branch 314
Explainable AI..411
Fair Decisions..326
False Administrative Utopia 315
False Economic Freedom...........................224
False Ideals 294
False Judicial Utopia 314
False Legislative Utopia 312
False Social Utopia 296
False-Truth AI.....................................121, 394
Fast Government......................................288
Final AI 67
Founding Fathers.....................................294
Four Seasons of AI 31
FPGA...45

Freedom 330
Gates, Bill 262
General Election 299
general pattern of progress 7
General World Model 42
Generative Adversarial Network 41
Generative AI 42
GMOs 258
Goertzel, Ben 50
Gold Rush 73
Golden State Warriors 327
Google 45
    DeepMind 52
Governments 261
Government-Sponsored Entities 278
GPU 44
Greek Mythology 68
Gubrud, Mark 50
Gun Control 329
Hacking and Security 94
Hegemony 323, 354, 355
Helper AI 73
Hinton, Geoffrey 38
Hostile AI 287, 356, 357
Human Download 418
Human Effort Magnification Factor 86
Human-Led Path 284
Increasing Returns 211
Industry Coordination AI 216, 246
Inequality of Companies 175
Inequality of Countries 176
Inequality of Individuals 172
Innovation 226, 340
Inverse Pyramid of AI 405
Investing 103, 196, 273, 365
Investing in AI Data 105
Investing in AI Hardware 104
Investing in AI Software 104
iPhone 43
Irreversible AI Dictatorship 69
Irreversible AI Monopoly 69
Israel 399
Italy 399
James, LeBron 327
Japan 329
Japan Empire 260, 400
Jewish 399
Jobs 85, 90, 156, 168, 237
Judiciary Branch 312
Judiciary Utopia 314
Kahneman, Daniel 43
Keiretsu 248
Kim Il-Sung 64
Kim Jung Un 98, 332
Kim, Yeon-Koung 258
Korea 399

Kurzweil, Ray 50, 53
LA Lakers 327
Last AI 67
Last AI of Humanity 429
latent 43
Leaning Tower of Pisa Scenario 320
Lee, Wan-Yong 260
Legislative Branch 308
Legislative Utopia 312
Level 1 AI Adoption 74
Level 2 AI Adoption 116
Level 3 AI Adoption 205
Level 4 AI Adoption 280
Liberalism 330
LLM 42, 85
Long Short Term Memory Network 41
Lutz, Merete 258
Machine Learning 30, 35
Mafia 188
managing people 272
Manpower 131, 137
Manpower Replacement Factor 136
Maximum AI 67
McCarthy, John 30
McKinsey 29
Measuring Economic Growth 228
Microsoft 262
Minimal Employment Firms 88
Minimum Wage 190
Minsky, Marvin 29, 30
Mixture of Experts 40
Monopolies 220, 340
Most Valuable Company 422
MS-DOS 43
Multi-Layer Perceptron 41
Multi-Purpose AI Butler 159
Musk, Elon 368, 418
Narrow AI 50
Nationalization of AI 340
Nazi 399
NBA 327
Neuralink 418
Neuromorphic 45
node 34
Non-Friendly AI 192, 235
North Korea 331, 400, 401
NPU 45
NVM 45
O'Neal, Shaquille 258
OECD 29
oligopolies 242
One-AI-Company Economy 248, 251
OpenAI 43, 52
Otto Wambier 331
Paper Countries 350
Path of AI Adoption 233

Perceptron 34
Phishing 188
PIM 45
Practical Singularity 357
Privatization of Government 220, 222
Productivity 16, 228
Profits 16
Q-star 43
Recurrent Neural Network 41
Regimes 330
Regulation 98
Regulations 406
Reinforcement AI 73
Reinforcement Learning 36, 37
Relative AI 63
Replacement Innovation 135
Replacement of Human Effort 135
Restricted Boltzmann Machine 41
Rising Sun flag 400
Rochester, Nathaniel 30
Rosenblatt, Frank 34
Rule The World 352
Rumelhart, David 38
Russel, Stuart 29
SAE .... See Society of Automotive Engineers
Samuel, Arthur 30, 35
Scope of AI Impact 344
Segway 80
Self-Innovation 120
Self-Organizing Maps 41
Self-Questioning, Self-Initiated AI 153
Shannon, Claude 30
Singularity 53, 120
Social Controversies 327
Social Credit System 332
social utility 300
Social Utopia 293, 321, 375
Society of Automotive Engineers 114
Software 93
SORA 43
South Korea 329
Soviet Union 335
SPC .... See Special-Purpose Companies
Special Purpose Country 319
Specialization 177
Special-Purpose Companies 203, 350
Specific-Purpose AI Companies 203
Spiking Neural Network 41
Spy 188, 286
SQSI AI .... See Self-Questioning Self-Initiated AI
Steganography 191
Strong AI 50
Subsidy 291
Sub-Symbolic .... See Connectionist
Suleyman, Mustafa 121
Sun Tzu 419

Super-Agent AI 165
Super-Fast Companies 209
Supervised Learning 36, 37
Supplementary AI 73
Surveillance 96
Symbolism 32
System of Knowledge 424
Systematically Important AI 417
Systematically Important Banks 417
Systemically Important Financial Institutions
.... 417
Take Over The World 97, 351
The 3 Levels of AI Adoption in Business 20
The 3 Principles of Robotics 410
The 4 Levels of AI Adoption in Society 22
The 6 Levels of AI before AGI 120
The 6 Levels of Autonomous Companies ... 214
The 6 Levels of Autonomous Governments 278
The 6 Levels of Autonomous Vehicles 114
The 6 Levels of Self-Advancing AI 385
The Arms Race 335
The Art of War 419
The Genome Project 222
The Great Depression 65
The Inverse Pyramid of AI Threat to Humanity
.... 389
The Jetsons 31
The Last AI 376
The Last AI of Humanity 370
The Theory of Relative AI 136
Theory of Absolute AI 226
Thesis − Antithesis − Synthesis 284
Tiananmen Square 64
TPU 45
True Administrative Utopia 316
True Economic Freedom 224
True Judicial Utopia 314
True Legislative Utopia 312
Ultimate Form of AI Adoption 361
Unbiased AI 167
United States 66, 294, 327, 335
University of Virginia 63, 331
Unsupervised Learning 36, 37
US Declaration of Independence 294
Voting Rights 303
War 343, 357
Weak AI 50
Wembanyama, Victor 258
Wide AI 50
Williams, Ronald 38
winner-take-all 273
World Trade Center 64, 65
World War II 400
Yao, Ming 258
Youtube 155
Zero-Person Company 212

About the Author

Seuk-Min Sohn, CFA is an independent researcher from South Korea. He previously worked for Korea's policy banking institution, The Korea Development Bank (KDB), in the areas of global strategy, researching the financial industries and financial markets, and corporate banking, and was one of the co-authors of its history book, *The 60-Year History of KDB*. His primary research interests include AI adoption, innovation, and venture capital investments.

Education:
o   Langley High School (McLean, VA)
o   BS in Commerce, The University of Virginia
o   MS in Business Administration, Seoul National University
o   MBA, The University of Texas at Austin
o   MS in Business Analytics, The University of Texas at Austin

Professional Certifications:
- Chartered Financial Analyst (CFA), CFA Institute
- Financial Risk Manager (FRM), Global Assn' of Risk Professionals

www.smsohn.com

Follow on Social Media:
X: @The_Last_AI   Instagram: @The.Last.AI   LinkedIn: smsohn